ARMS & EQUIPMENT OF THE BRITISH ARMY, 1866

ARMS & EQUIPMENT OF THE BRITISH ARMY, 1866

Victorian Military Equipment from the Enfield to the Snider

●

EDITED BY JOHN WALTER

GREENHILL BOOKS

This edition of *Arms & Equipment of the British Army, 1866*
first published in 1986 by Greenhill Books,
Lionel Leventhal Limited,
2–6 Hampstead High Street, London NW3 1QQ.

This edition © Lionel Leventhal Limited, 1986.

All rights reserved. No part of this publication may be reproduced, stored in a retrieval system or transmitted in any form by any means electrical, mechanical or otherwise, without first seeking the written permission of the copyright owner and the publisher.

ISBN 0-947898-43-3

Publishing history
Arms & Equipment of the British Army, 1866 combines a substantial part of *Equipment of Infantry* ('forming Part V. of the Series of Army Equipments'), published by HMSO in 1865, with the drill section of *Field Exercises and Evolutions of Infantry*, published by HMSO in 1867.

Where appropriate, minor cross-references to other parts of the original books have been deleted.

Owing to the age of the original books, imperfections in the Victorian typesetting have – of necessity – been reproduced.

Greenhill Books
welcome readers' suggestions for books that might be added to this Series. Please write to us if there are titles which you would like to recommend.

Printed by Antony Rowe Limited,
Chippenham, Wiltshire

Contents

PART ONE: ARMS & EQUIPMENT

Organization

Present Organization of the Infantry of the British Army 12
Composition and Strength of Battalions and Regiments............13

Equipment

Colours 16
Personal Equipment of Officers...22
Personal Equipment of Non-commissioned Officers and Men
    Arms and Drummers' Appointments 28
    Musical Instruments..45
    Accoutrements and Appointments (Pioneers' Tools).........46
    Ammunition..57
    Clothing..58
    Necessaries...77
    Armourer's Forge 83
    Musketry Instructions, article for 89
    Books, Blank Forms and Stationery 91
    Hospital Equipment 95
    Camp Equipment 97

Detail of Equipment for the several Classes of Infantry

List of Equipment for a Battalion of Guards 103
List of Equipment for a Battalion of Highlanders....................117
List of Equipment for a Battalion of Rifles 128
List of Equipment for a Battalion of Line.................................137
Comparative Annual Cost of Personal Equipment 148

Transport

System of marking Packages and Stores..................................150

List of plates 151
The Plates..152

PART TWO: RIFLE EXERCISES

GENERAL DIRECTIONS

I. Names of Parts of the Rifle 199
II. Formation of Squad 199
III. Instructor to have Rifle 199
IV. The Rifle to be used with care 199
V. How to carry the rifle 199

MANUAL EXERCISES

1. The Manual Exercise with the Long Rifle 201
2. The Manual Exercise with the Short Rifle 217
3. The Manual Exercise for the Long and Short Rifles 231

PLATOON EXERCISES

4. The Platoon Exercise for the Long and Short Snider Rifle 233
5. Preparing for Cavalry 247

FIRING

6. To fire a *Feu-de-Joie* 249
7. Street Firing 250
8. Application of the Modes of Firing 251

EXERCISES FOR SERJEANTS

9. Rifle Exercises for Serjeants 252

REVIEW

10. Review Exercise 253

INSPECTING

11. Manner of Inspecting a Company on Parade 255

BAYONET EXERCISE

12. Bayonet or Sword Bayonet Exercise 256

The Plates 264

Introduction

Arms & Equipment of the British Army, 1866 is a compilation of important British official textbooks. Originally produced for purely limited circulation, these have not only been unavailable for many years but also unseen outside select official circles.

During the period 1860–1900, few books were written on the day-to-day existence of the British army; even fewer spared more than an occasional, often critical thought for its firearms and equipment. Despite the efforts of Hans Busk and, particularly, William Greener (whose *Modern Breech-Loaders* of 1871 has recently been reprinted by Greenhill), virtually all the reliable information is found in the 'official' government-inspired textbooks. *Arms & Equipment of the British Army, 1866* simply combines two classic, invaluable works from that important post-Crimean period when the army was exchanging its muzzle-loading rifles for breech-loaders.

Equipment of Infantry was compiled by Captain Martin Petrie of the 14th (Buckinghamshire) Regiment of Foot and originally appeared "under the Superintendence of Her Majesty's Stationery Office" in 1865. After a brief and somewhat selective historical note – interesting, and typical of nearly all such works – the book describes the weapons, equipment and accoutrements in detail, together with costs and scales of issue. Its highlights include a series of 22 delicate, steel-engraved plates showing everything from the officers' swords, through the P/53 and P/60 ('Enfield') rifle-muskets to belts and straps, drums, pioneers' equipment and armourers' tools. As the British authorities took great pride in draftsmanship, the delineation of the plates is surprisingly accurate.

Equipment of Infantry was produced at a time when the muzzle-loading rifle-musket was still in vogue in the British Army. The relevant plates (IV–VII) all show the 'Enfield' pattern. However, the book was published contemporaneously with the end of the four-year American Civil War, when the muzzle-loader's reputation had been seriously damaged by efficient metallic-cartridge breech-loaders such as the Maynard, the Henry and the Spencer. Additional lessons learned from the Seven Weeks' War of 1866, when Prussian armies armed with their somewhat rudimentary breech-loading Dreyse needle-guns shot the more-conventionally armed Austrians to ribands, forced the hasty approval of a breech-loading conversion system for the Enfield. The winner of the trials had been submitted on behalf of a New Yorker, Jacob Snider. The closed breech was simply replaced with a side-hinged block, through which the firing pin ran, facilitating the transformation of existing guns while a better design (destined to be the Martini-Henry) was sought. The remainder of the gun was virtually unchanged, and the infantry tactics, too, continued to demonstrate the same rigid subservience to 'drill-by-numbers' that had characterized most European armies since the seventeenth century.

To complement *Equipment of Infantry*, therefore, the smallarms drill prescribed by *Field Exercises and Evolutions of Infantry*, printed in 1867, has been added. This reveals each of the standard drill movements in words and pictures, an ideal animated foil for the staid lists of priced stores. *Field Exercises and Evolutions for Infantry* was produced at the very time the Army began to change to the Snider (the rifle was adopted on 18th September 1866) and, though the drill diagrams all show Enfields, Plate X actually depicts Snider conversions of the standard P/53 and P/60 short rifle muskets – the forefront of contemporary technology, and helping to provide a most up-to-date book in 1867!

Select bibliography

Anon.: *List of Changes in Artillery Matériel, Small Arms, Accoutrements and Other Military Stores*. HMSO, London, 1860–72.

De Witt Bailey II: *British Military Longarms, 1715–1865.* Arms & Armour Press, London. Combined volume, 1986.

Howard L. Blackmore: *British Military Firearms, 1650–1850.* Herbert Jenkins, London, 1961.

Captain Vivian D. Majendie and Charles O. Browne: *Military Breech-Loading Rifles.* Royal Artillery Institution, London, 1870.

Christopher H. Roads: *The British Soldier's Firearm, 1850–1864.* Herbert Jenkins, London, 1964.

Brian Robson: *Swords of the British Army* ('The Regulation Patterns, 1718–1914'). Arms & Armour Press, London, 1975.

Ian D. Skennerton: *A Treatise on the Snider* ("The British Soldier's Firearm, 1866–*c.* 1880"). Margate, Queensland, Australia, 1978.

B. A. Temple: *The Boxer Cartridge in the British Service.* Brisbane, Australia, 1977.

EQUIPMENT

OF

INFANTRY.

COMPILED BY

CAPTAIN MARTIN PETRIE, TOPOGRAPHICAL STAFF.

FORMING PART V. OF THE SERIES OF ARMY EQUIPMENTS

PREPARED AT THE TOPOGRAPHICAL AND STATISTICAL DEPARTMENT, WAR OFFICE.

COLONEL SIR HENRY JAMES, R.E., F.R.S., &c., DIRECTOR.

PRINTED BY ORDER OF THE SECRETARY OF STATE FOR WAR.

LONDON:
Printed under the Superintendence of Her Majesty's Stationery Office,
AND SOLD BY
W. CLOWES AND SONS, 14, Charing Cross; HARRISON AND SONS, 59, Pall Mall;
W. H. ALLEN & Co., 13, Waterloo Place; W. MITCHELL, 39, Charing Cross;
and LONGMAN & Co., Paternoster Row;
ALSO BY
A. AND C. BLACK, Edinburgh;
ALEX. THOM, Abbey Street, and E. PONSONBY, Grafton Street, Dublin.

ON THE PRESENT ORGANIZATION OF BRITISH INFANTRY.

The infantry of the regular army may be considered as composed of two classes, viz., the Guards and the Line. There are besides a few colonial regiments and corps, and a force of local and native infantry in the East Indies.

Men enlisting in the Guards are required to have a minimum height of 5 feet $8\frac{1}{2}$ inches; for the whole of the line the minimum height is 5 feet 5 inches.

As regards equipment, the principal difference consists in the pattern and superior quality of the clothing supplied to the Guards, as detailed at page 59. The arms and ammunition are identical with those issued to the rest of the infantry. The accoutrements are also similar.

The Line, which now has a strength of 141 battalions, includes 109 regiments and the Rifle Brigade; nine of these are Highland regiments, nine are distinguished as "Light Infantry," and five as Fusiliers. The total number of battalions of rifles is eight, the 60th Rifles and Rifle Brigade having four each. The Rifles are all dressed in dark green, and their accoutrements are of black leather, while the rest of the infantry have the scarlet or red tunic, with black* trousers and white accoutrements. The short Enfield rifle musket is issued to all ranks of rifles. This weapon is also carried by the serjeants of other regiments, the rank and file being furnished with the long Enfield rifle musket.

The 9 Highland regiments are distinguished by their peculiar Highland costume. Five of them, viz., the 42nd, 78th, 79th, 92nd, and 93rd wear the kilt, and four, viz., the 71st, 72nd, 74th, and 91st, the trews. The 71st, 74th, and 91st have a cap of special pattern, the remaining six regiments wear the highland bonnet feathered with black ostrich feathers.†

All differences in arms and equipment, and most of the distinctive characteristics in uniform of light infantry and fusilier regiments, have been gradually abolished, and the appellations may now be regarded only as honorary titles, which have been in some instances conferred upon regiments for gallant deeds of arms. The principal distinctions in equipment consist in light infantry using bugles instead of drums, and wearing a green plume on the shako instead of a ball tuft. The Fusiliers have a white plume. Serjeants of light infantry and rifles have a whistle and chain attached to the pouch belt, intended to convey signals to the men in their vicinity when acting in open order in woody localities. Light infantry bear the bugle on the forage cap and knapsack. Rifles have no device or number on their forage caps.

The uniforms of regiments are distinguished by their "facings," the colours of which comprise various shades of blue, red, yellow, white, green, black, &c. They are shown upon the collars, cuffs, and shoulder straps of all ranks, besides round the edges of the badges and chevrons of non-commissioned officers. The regimental colour also corresponds

---

* Dark blue in summer, and white in stations between the tropics.
† The 25th, 26th, 73rd, and 75th regiments wear a forage cap with diced border, similar to that worn by the non-kilted corps, as a mark of their national origin.

in hue with the facings. Regiments bearing the title "Royal" have blue facings, and scarlet bands round the forage caps of officers and staff serjeants.

The Ceylon Rifles and Royal Canadian Rifles are dressed and equipped similarly to other rifle battalions.

The Cape Mounted Rifles, though enlisted and classed as infantry, are armed, accoutred, and clothed similarly to light cavalry.

The five West India regiments are armed and accoutred similarly to the line, but they have the Zouave dress.

COMPOSITION AND STRENGTH OF BATTALIONS AND REGIMENTS.

The tactical unit in the infantry service is invariably the *battalion*, two, three, four, or occasionally six battalions being united in the field to form a brigade. The *regiment*, on the contrary, we may regard as in some measure the administrative unit.

In the armies of the continental powers a regiment of infantry consists of two, three, and sometimes four battalions. The full colonel usually exercises the actual command of the whole, each battalion having its own *chef de bataillon* or officer of corresponding rank.

The conscription, which has taken root as a permanent institution in almost every European country, brings an annual influx of recruits into the ranks, while a corresponding number of trained soldiers are permitted to return to their homes on " congé limité," and can be called in again when required until their term of service expires.

The term during which conscripts remain liable for service varies considerably, seven to ten years may perhaps be taken as an average, but the period actually passed in the ranks during peace is regulated entirely by circumstances. Thus there is always a large reserve of men available, who are not only trained but have also been accustomed to serve in company. This is the means of giving great elasticity to the strength, and regiments can pass from a "peace" to a "war" establishment at a few days' notice. Although the numerical total present with the colours is thus very variable during peace, there is always a "cadre," consisting of officers and non-commissioned officers, whose number remains unaltered.

The subjoined table shows the numerical strength of battalions and regiments belonging to some of the principal European powers:—

	Peace Establishment.			War Establishment.	
	Service Battalion.	Regiment.		Service Battalion.	Regiment.
France -	425	3 service battalions - 1,356 1 depôt „ - 496		719	3 service battalions - 2,239 1 depôt „ - 802
Austria -	627	2 service „ - 1,312 2 depôt „ - 528		760	3 service „ - 2,350 1 depôt , - 386
Prussia -	545	3 battalions - - 1,635		1,048	3 service „ - 3,186 1 depôt „ - 1,048
Italy -	380	4 service battalions - 1,599 1 depôt „ - 92		740	4 service „ - 3,019 1 depôt „ - 250
Spain -	565	2 service „ - 1,153 2 reserve „ - 120		1,177	2 service „ - 2,377 2 reserve „ - 2,350
Russia	898	3 service „ - 2,700 1 reserve „ - 667		1,092	3 service „ - 3,317 3 reserve „ - 3,276 2 depôt „ - 2,184

The military institutions of Great Britain cause the system pursued to differ considerably from the foregoing. Colonels of regiments are never effective as regimental officers, though they often hold other military appointments. The actual command is exercised by the lieutenant-colonel. For a series of years preceding 1858 it was exceptional for a regiment to consist of more than a single battalion, so that the two words were almost synonymous.

The terms "peace" and "war establishment" are not generally applicable in the British service, but the numerical strength is regulated by the authority of the Secretary of State for War, according to the requirement of different stations, the nature of the duties to be performed, and the general exigencies of the service.

In fixing the establishment of a battalion the following principles are generally observed :—

Officers.— The field officers comprise one, or sometimes two lieutenant-colonels, and two majors ; the regimental staff consists of an adjutant, an instructor of musketry, a paymaster, quartermaster, surgeon, and one or two assistant surgeons. A captain and two subaltern officers are allowed to each company ; one of the latter, however, holds the appointment of instructor of musketry on the battalion staff.

Non-commissioned officers and men.—The regimental staff-serjeants are nine in number, exclusive of the drum or bugle major. The proportion of serjeants is one for every 20 rank and file, a corporal being included in the latter number. To every company there is allowed in addition, one drummer and one bugler, or in the case of light infantry and rifle battalions, two buglers. The colour-serjeants, of which there is one to each company, are included in the establishment of serjeants.

A battalion as thus constituted, comprises the serjeant-master tailor authorized to be borne upon the strength by circular memorandum, dated Horse Guards, 11th March 1862, and the regulated strength of the band, consisting of one serjeant, one corporal, and 19 privates, in addition to the bandmaster-serjeant, besides a corporal of pioneers, and a pioneer per company.*

The serjeant-major takes precedence of all other non-commissioned officers. War Office Circular, No. 821, 25th May 1863, specifies that the schoolmaster is to rank after him ; the quartermaster-serjeant, serjeant instructor of musketry, and bandmaster-serjeant rank next in sequence. All the foregoing are styled 1st class staff-serjeants (*see* War Office Circular, No. 698, 27th July 1861). All regiments have not as yet been provided with band-master-serjeants, for these non-commissioned officers require to be trained at the recently instituted military school of music at Kneller Hall, and are posted to regiments as they are qualified.

The drum or bugle-major is mustered and borne upon the returns as a "drummer" or "bugler," he, however, as also the pipe-major of Highland battalions, ranks with the 1st class staff-serjeants. The paymaster-serjeant, armourer-serjeant, hospital-serjeant, and orderly-room clerk, are termed 2nd class staff-serjeants, and take precedence relatively to one another according to the dates of their appointments. Armourer-serjeants are posted to regiments from the corps of armourers, and if reduced by sentence of court-martial they revert to the position of privates in that corps.

---

* By General Order, dated Horse Guards, 13th July 1863, a serjeant cook is authorized to be borne upon the strength of regiments, but the numerical establishment remains the same, as there is to be one private less.

The band-serjeant and serjeant-master tailor rank with platoon-serjeants. Circular memorandum, dated Horse Guards, 11th April 1862, authorizes the special enlistment of civilian tradesmen as serjeant-master tailors, but they are to be subject to the Mutiny Act, &c., and may be reduced by court-martial. A subsequent memorandum, dated 11th April 1863, provides that men already serving may volunteer to go through a course of instruction in the Royal Army Clothing Factory, Pimlico, and when qualified receive the appointment of master tailor. Drummers, buglers, and pipers rank as privates.

In regulating the interior economy of a battalion the officer commanding is empowered to appoint a proportion of corporals and privates to be acting or "lance" serjeants or corporals to assist in the general duties.

The pioneers are to be as far as practicable able-bodied artificers and mechanics, and selected for their superior intelligence; there should, if possible, be at least two carpenters and a smith among them.

The organization of the Guards differs in some respects from the foregoing. Each of the three regiments has a regimental staff, consisting of a colonel, a lieutenant-colonel, and a solicitor. The colonel is not effective as a regimental officer. There is one major only to each battalion; and they have no paymaster, his duties being performed by the quartermaster.

There are no hospital-serjeants or paymaster-serjeants borne upon the strength, but one of the platoon-serjeants is attached to the hospital, one per regiment is appointed drill-serjeant, and is charged with the training of recruits, and one in each battalion is called battalion drill-serjeant, his office being to aid the serjeant-major and take his place in his absence.

The Scots Fusilier Guards and Highland regiments have a pipe-major and five pipers in addition to their drummers and musicians.*

Battalions of the line are generally divided into ten service and two depôt companies.

It was formerly the practice in regiments of the line that were not light infantry, fusiliers, or rifles, to have two of the companies composed of men selected for height, appearance, activity, and soldierlike demeanour. These companies were styled "grenadiers" and "light infantry" respectively, and formed the right and left companies when the regiment was drawn up in line. The system of having "flank companies," as they are termed, now, however, no longer exists, his Royal Highness the Field Marshal Commanding-in-Chief, having been pleased to order by a circular memorandum (No. 38, Horse Guards, 30th May 1860), that no selection of men is to be made for any particular companies, and that officers commanding are to place such companies on the flanks as they may from time to time deem most expedient. A further circular memorandum on the same subject (No. 183, 12th February 1862) lays down that the several companies are to stand on parade habitually according to the seniority of their captains, the senior captain being on the right, and the next senior on the left, and so on from flanks to centre.

The depôt battalions, of which there are 22, were organized in 1854; each of them is constituted similarly to a battalion of an infantry regiment. The field officers include a lieutenant-colonel and one or two majors; the staff is composed of a paymaster, an adjutant, a quarter-

---

* The 25th and 26th are permitted to have three pipers per battalion, but their establishments are the same as other battalions of the line.

master, a surgeon and two assistant surgeons, besides an establishment of non-commissioned officers.

Each depôt battalion consists of from four to seven regimental depôts. In addition to the staff enumerated above, there are an instructor and an assistant instructor of musketry, but these are selected from the regimental officers of the depôts and are included in their establishments.

The Guards have no depôts. In the event of any of the battalions proceeding on foreign service, those stationed at home act as depôts for them, enlisting and training recruits, and furnishing such reinforcements as are required.

Horses.

The field officers and adjutants of regiments of infantry are required to be mounted upon suitable chargers when on duty. Brevet field officers, when doing duty as field officers in camp or garrison, are also to be mounted.

Officers are in all cases required to provide their own horses and bât animals.

The following table shows the maximum number of horses for which forage is allowed to be drawn, as authorized by Warrant contained in Circular No. 847, and dated 8th January 1864.

Rank of the Officers.	At Home.	Abroad.		
		Not with an Army in the Field.	With an Army in the Field.	
	Horses.	Horses.	Riding Horses.	Baggage Mules or Horses.*
				Bât. / Pack.
Field officer commanding a regiment or body of troops, of not less than 400 men	2	2	2	2 —
Field officer not commanding	1	1	2	1 —
Captain	—	—	—	1 / 1
Captain instructor of musketry, depôt battalions	1	—	—	— / —
Officer instructor of musketry	1	1	1	1 / —
Subaltern	—	—	—	1 / —
Adjutant	1	1	2	1 / 1
Surgeon-major or surgeon	1	1	1	1 / 1
Assistant surgeon	—	—	1	1 / —
Paymaster	—	—	1	1 / 1
Quartermaster	—	1	1	1 / 3

* Baggage animals that are the private property of officers and used for the conveyance of their tents and baggage are denominated "bât" animals, and are to be distinguished from "pack" animals, these latter being public property. The second baggage or "pack" horse allowed to captains for the conveyance of shoemakers' tools and materials, company books, and other stores is given free at first, but in case of loss must be replaced at the officer's own expense.

COMPOSITION AND STRENGTH.

COMPOSITION and DISTRIBUTION of a REGIMENT of GUARDS, consisting of Two or Three Battalions, with an Establishment of 1,000 Rank and File each.

Rank.	Battalion of 10 Companies.	Regiment of 2 Battalions.	Regiment of 3 Battalions.	Remarks.
OFFICERS.				
Lieutenant-colonel	—	1	1	
Majors	1	2	3	
Captains and lieutenant-colonels.	10	20	30	
Lieutenants and captains	11	22	33	
Ensigns and lieutenants	8	16	24	
Adjutants	1	2	3	
Instructors of musketry	1	2	3	
Quartermasters	1	2	3	
Surgeons	1	2	3	
Assistant surgeons	2	4	6	
Total officers	36	73	109	
NON-COMMISSIONED OFFICERS AND MEN.				
Serjeant-majors	1	2	3	
Schoolmasters	1	2	3	
Quartermaster-serjeants	1	2	3	
Serjeant instructors of musketry.	1	2	3	
Bandmaster	—	1	1	
Drum-major	1	2	3	
Pipe-major	—	—	—	In Scots Fusiliers only.
Armourer serjeants	1	2	3	
Hospital-serjeant	—	1	1	
Regimental clerk	—	1	1	
Orderly-room serjeants	1	2	3	
Regimental drill-serjeant	—	1	1	
Battalion drill-serjeants	2	4	6	
Serjeant-master tailors	—	1	1	
Colour-serjeants	10	20	30	
Band-serjeant	—	1	1	
Serjeants	38	74	111	
Corporal of band	—	1	1	
Corporals of pioneers	1	2	3	
Corporals	49	97	146	
Musicians	—	19	19	In the Scots Fusiliers 3 of these are styled timebeaters, and wear a distinctive uniform.
Pioneers	10	20	30	
Hospital orderlies	—	—	—	
Privates	940	1,861	2,801	
Drummers and buglers	20	40	60	
Pipers	—	—	—	5 in Scots Fusiliers only.
Total non-commissioned officers and men.	1,077	2,158	3,234	
Total of all ranks	1,113	2,231	3,343	

COMPOSITION AND STRENGTH.

COMPOSITION and DISTRIBUTION of a REGIMENT of the LINE, consisting of a single Battalion, with an Establishment of Ten Service Companies with 1,000 Rank and File, and Two Depôt Companies of 100 Rank and File each.

Rank.	Ten Service Companies.	Two Depôt Companies.	Total.	Remarks.
OFFICERS.				
Colonel	—	—	—	Not regimentally effective.
Lieutenant-colonel	1	—	1	
Majors	2	—	2	
Captains	10	2	12	
Lieutenants	11	3	14	
Ensigns	9	1	10	
Adjutant	1	—	1	
Instructor of musketry	—	—	—	Included in subalterns.
Paymaster	1	—	1	
Quartermaster	1	—	1	
Surgeon	1	—	1	
Assistant surgeon	2	—	2	In India generally 3.
Total officers	39	6	45	
NON-COMMISSIONED OFFICERS AND MEN.				
Serjeant-major	1	—	1	
Schoolmaster	1	—	1	
Quartermaster-serjeant	1	—	1	
Serjeant instructor of musketry.	1	—	1	
Bandmaster-serjeant	1	—	1	
Drum-major	1	—	1	"Bugle-major" in light infantry and rifles.
Pipe-major	—	—	—	In Highland regiments only.
Paymaster-serjeant	1	—	1	
Armourer-serjeant	1	—	1	
Hospital-serjeant	1	—	1	
Orderly-room clerk	1	—	1	
Serjeant-master tailor	1	—	} 61	
Serjeant cook	1	—		
Colour-serjeants	10	2		
Band-serjeant	1	—		
Serjeants	38	8		
Corporal of band	1	—	} 60	
Corporal of pioneers	1	—		
Corporals	48	10		
Musicians	19	—	} 1,139	
Pioneers	10	2		
Hospital orderlies	5	—		
Privates	915	188		
Drummers and buglers	20	4	24	Buglers only in light infantry and rifles.
Pipers	—	—	—	5 in Highland regiments.
Total non-commissioned officers and men.	1,080	214	1,294	
Grand total of all ranks	1,119	220	1,339	

The staff of a depôt battalion includes 2 or 3 field officers, 1 adjutant, 1 captain instructor of musketry, 1 assistant instructor of musketry, 1 paymaster, 1 quartermaster, 1 surgeon, 2 assistant surgeons, and 8 non-commissioned officers.

EQUIPMENT.

The munitions of war, matériel and other stores required for troops of all arms are classified according to the military departments which are charged with their administration, and responsible for taking due measures to maintain the necessary supplies of them in a state of readiness and efficiency.

Under the Adjutant-General's department are included all articles of equipment which would be paraded with troops when in heavy marching order, and which move in their possession, together with reserves, and materials for the repair of the same. Also clothing, and extra clothing for the regular forces, armaments, and articles for siege purposes, besides engineer professional equipments.

The Quartermaster-General's department is charged with the issue and efficiency of all stores required for camping and quartering troops, as well as such as are needed in addition to the regular equipment supplied; and generally with all stores not appertaining to the department of the Adjutant-General, and which do not move in the possession of the troops.

Food, forage, fuel, and light are provided by the Commissariat department.

The Army Medical department is responsible for the supply of medicines, medical appliances, and surgical instruments.

The Purveyor's department is charged with the provision of medical comforts, subsistence for the sick, and the furniture and equipment of hospitals.

The principal veterinary surgeon has the care of providing horse medicines and veterinary surgical instruments.

Munitions of war, military matériel, and stores of all kinds, with the exception of those appertaining to the commissariat department, are kept in charge of the Military Store department both at home and abroad. When an army is on foreign or active service this department is to receive, take charge of, and issue all stores with the exception of those of the commissariat, medical, purveyors, and veterinary departments. See War Office Circular, No. 824.

All demands for Military Stores, as before described, are to be made on the Chief Military Store officer through the proper channel, and upon no account are requisitions to be sent home from any office or department on service, except through the Military Store Department, upon which the responsibility of supply must then rest.

In order that the wants of the army may be anticipated, the heads of civil and military departments are responsible for furnishing periodical estimates of their probable requirements to the Adjutant-General and Quartermaster-General, by whom they will be made known to the military store officer in charge. He is then responsible under the authority of the Commander of the Forces for making timely provision to meet all the store requirements of the service by the transmission of demands to the Director of Stores; the final approval and order for the supply rests with the Secretary of State for War.

Officers demanding stores are to take care that all requisitions contain full and exact details as to the number and particular description of every article required, because the military store officers are responsible only for providing and issuing them in accordance with the lists thus furnished.

In the case of stores authorized by a *General Order* to be issued to troops at certain seasons or under particular circumstances, the requisition may be sent *direct* to the military store officer by the commanding officer, the general order itself constituting sufficient authority for their issue; this must, however, be quoted in the demand.

COLOURS.

Colours are classed as part of the personal equipment of an army.

Applications for new colours are to be addressed to the Secretary of State for War, through the adjutant-general, accompanied by the proceedings of a board of survey on those in possession, and should they not have lasted the prescribed period, a report must be made of the circumstances under which they have become unserviceable.

The period of duration assigned for colours and standards on home service and under ordinary circumstances is five years in the Guards, and 20 years in other services. On foreign stations the duration of these articles will vary according to the climate and the nature of the service, but the above period must be kept in view as far as practicable.

Repairs to colours are to be executed in the regiment, and the expense thereof charged in the pay list, supported by vouchers and the usual certificates.

A pair of colours is supplied to each battalion of infantry with the exception of Rifle corps. They are made of silk, their dimensions being 3 feet 9 inches flying, and 3 feet deep at the pike. The poles are of ash, 9 feet 10 inches in length, $1\frac{1}{8}$ inch in diameter; the heads are surmounted by a Royal Crown and Lion " passant gardant," and they are shod with a brass ferrule.

The Royal or first colour of every regiment is to be the Great Union, being the Imperial colour of the United Kingdom of Great Britain and Ireland, in which the cross of St. George is conjoined with the crosses of St. Andrew and St. Patrick on a blue field,—the Imperial Crown with the number of the regiment underneath it in gold characters, are embroidered in the centre.

Those regiments which bear a royal, county, or other title, are to have such designation on a red ground round a circle within the Union wreath of roses, thistles, and shamrocks. The number of the regiment in gold characters to be in the centre.

In such regiments as bear any distinguishing badge, the badge is to be on a red ground in the centre, and the number of the regiment in gold characters underneath; the royal or other title to be inscribed on a circle within the Union wreath of roses, thistles, and shamrocks.

The regimental or second colour bears the Union 12 inches square in the upper canton; the colour of the flag is the same as the facings of the regiments, except for regiments whose facings are red, white, buff, or black. For regiments with red, white, or buff facings, the second colour is to be the red cross of St. George on a white field; for those with black facings, it is to be the St. George's cross in red on a black field. The number of the regiment is to be embroidered in gold Roman characters in the centre.

This colour is also to bear the devices, distinctions, and mottoes which have been conferred by Royal authority, the whole to be ensigned with the Imperial Crown.

The fringe round the borders of the colours is 2 inches wide; for the Royal colour it is of gold and crimson, the regimental colour has its fringe made of gold combined with the same colour as the flag itself.

The cords and tassels are crimson and gold mixed; their length is 3 feet.

COLOURS.

No addition or alteration is to be made in the colours of any regiment without Her Majesty's special permission and authority, signified through the Commander-in-Chief of the Army.

Covers for colours are made of black varnished leather and have pointed brass caps.

The cost of colours is about 32*l*. 15*s*. per pair, the weight of each is 5 lbs. 14 oz. with cover complete.

The custom of the service assigns old colours to the full colonel of the regiment. It has, however, been usual to deposit them as trophies in the cathedral or principal church of the town or place whose name the regiment bears, or in some public building or institution.

Colour carriages are made of buff leather $2\frac{1}{2}$ inches wide. Their cost is 1*l*. 15*s*., and weight 2 lbs. 8 oz. per pair; they are renewable after being 12 years in wear.

Camp Colours, Saluting Colours, Adjutant's Aides, and Pace Sticks.

These articles are to be provided for every battalion of infantry, Rifles included, in the following proportions :—

—	Cost.	Weight.	Number.
	s. d.	lbs. oz.	
Camp colours, with varnished leather cases -	5 0	2 15	8
Saluting do. do. -	5 0	2 15	1
Adjutant's aides, with staff and socket -	3 $5\frac{1}{2}$	0 11	4
Pace sticks - - - - -	7 6	1 7	5, in addition to 1 per company.

The Camp colours to be 18 inches square, and of the colour of the facings of the regiment, with the number of the regiment upon them. The poles to be 7 feet 6 inches long.

The Saluting colour to be an ordinary camp colour, distinguished only from the other camp colours by a transverse red cross; when the facings are red, by a transverse blue cross.

The aides to be 33 inches in the pole, and the bunting of the same size as that of the camp colour. They are to be carried in the hand, and when elevated, placed on the muzzle of the firelock. Steel sockets for fixing to the poles will be supplied without charge on application to the Secretary of State for War.

Pace sticks are to last 10 years, and the other articles five, the bunting being renewed when required. Captains of companies are to provide one pace stick per company. The expense of the colours and other pace sticks is to be defrayed out of the Postage and Stationery Fund.

For regulations respecting colours, with particulars respecting the colours of the facings of regiments and their mottoes and devices, *see* Queen's Regulations, p. 14, *also* Regulations for the Provision of Appointments, &c., 24th August 1857, p. 52.

PERSONAL EQUIPMENT OF OFFICERS.
PLATE I. to III.

Officers are required to provide themselves with everything necessary for their personal equipment at their own expense. Any non-commissioned officer, however, who receives a commission without purchase, is allowed the sum of 100*l.* by the public, in aid of the expense of his first outfit.

Mounted officers are to purchase their own chargers and other horses.

All articles of accoutrements, appointments, and uniforms, are required to be in exact accordance with the regulated sealed patterns which are deposited at the office of Her Majesty's Adjutant-General.

Swords and *appointmeuts* for officers of infantry are of the following patterns:—

DESCRIPTION.	SERVICE.
Sword, steel mounted, half basket hilt, with distinctive badge of each regiment pierced and chased in the guard. Length of blade $32\frac{1}{2}$ inches, width at the shoulder $1\frac{1}{8}$ inch, and at 12 inches from the shoulder 1 inch; thickness of back $\frac{3}{8}$ inch, and at 18 inches from the hilt $\frac{1}{4}$ inch; solid flat shoulder $1\frac{1}{2}$ inch deep, and blade hollowed from the flat to within 9 inches of the point, which is spear-shaped. Weight not less than 1 lb. 15 oz. without the scabbard - Scabbard, steel, lined with wood; German silver mouth-piece - - -	Guards.
Sword, gilt half basket hilt, with the Queen's cypher inserted in the outward bars, and lined with black patent leather; the gripe of black fish skin, bound with a spiral of three gilt wires. Dimensions of blade same as above. Weight not less than 1 lb. 15 oz. - - - - Scabbard—for regimental field officers, brass; for adjutants, steel; for other officers, black leather with gilt mountings - - - -	Line, except Highlanders and Rifles: Medical staff officers under rank of Inspector General: Commissariat: Unattached officers and Civil staff of Royal Engineers.
Sword,—same as above, except that the hilt and mountings are steel, and the device a crown and bugle - - Scabbard for do., steel - - -	Rifle corps.
Claymore, with steel hilt lined with scarlet cloth, straight cut-and-thrust blade, $1\frac{1}{2}$ inch wide at the shoulder, and 32 inches long - - - Scabbard, black leather with steel mountings; steel in the field for regimental field officers - - -	Highland regiments.
Dirk - Skeen Dhu } regimental pattern - -	Highland regiments only.

OFFICERS.

Description.	Service.
Knot, sword, gold acorn and twisted gold cord, for dress occasions	For Guards only.
Knot, sword, gold acorn and twisted white cord, for other occasions	
Knot, sword, gold acorn and crimson and gold strap	Line, Highlanders and Rifles excepted, besides all other officers wearing the line pattern sword.
Knot, sword, black leather, acorn and strap	Rifle corps.
Belt, waist, of 1½ inch gold lace, sword carriage of inch gold lace and gilt hook, for dress occasions	All officers of Guards, except quartermaster and medical officers.
Belt, waist, white enamelled leather, 1½ inch wide, with sword carriage and gilt hook	All officers of infantry, excepting paymasters, quartermasters, medical officers, and those of Rifle corps.
Plate or union locket for both the belts above; a round clasp, gilt, having in the centre the regimental number surmounted by a crown, both in silver, and on the circle round it the title of the regiment in silver letters.	
Belt, waist, black leather, 1½ inch wide, with sword carriages, silver snake clasp and mountings	All officers of Rifle corps.
Belt, waist, same as above, but furniture gilt	All paymasters, quartermasters, medical officers, commissariat, &c.
Belt, dirk, and plate, regimental pattern.* Belt, dirk; undress, with plate or hook	Highland regiments.
Belt, shoulder, white enamelled leather, with sword carriages and breast plate, of regimental pattern	All officers of Highland regiments below rank of field officer.
Pouch, black patent leather, with silver bugle on the flap	Rifle corps.
Belt, pouch, black patent leather, 3 in. wide, with silver regimental plate, whistle and chain	
Belt, shoulder, black patent leather, with case of surgical instruments, and gilt ornaments	All medical officers.
Sash, crimson and gold, for dress occasions, with fringe ends and runner	Guards only.
Sash, crimson silk patent net, with fringe ends and runner	All officers, excepting those of Rifle corps, paymasters, quartermasters, and medical officers.
Spurs, yellow metal, with crane necks 2 in. long	Field officers and mounted officers ranking with them.
Spurs, steel, with crane necks 2 in. long	Adjutants and musketry instructors.

---

* To be worn with slings by field officers on full-dress occasions.

Horse Appointments.

Description.	Service.
Saddle, hunting	All mounted officers.
Holsters, covered with bearskin	For all field officers and adjutants, except when serving in tropical climates where they are to be covered with black patent leather. Medical and non-combatant officers have them also covered with the latter.
Saddlecloth, cloth same colour as the facing of the regiment, trimmed with gold lace or gold cord, according to regulation	Field officers and adjutants, except those of Rifle corps.
Saddlecloth, same as above, but trimmed with black silk lace	All medical officers.
Shabraque, black lambskin	Field officers and adjutants of Rifle corps.
Bridle, brown leather, cavalry pattern, bent branch bit, with bronze bosses	Field officers and adjutants of Rifle corps.
Bridle, do., but bosses gilt	Field officers and adjutants of all other regiments.
Bridle, do., without bosses	Medical and other non-combatant officers.
Breastplate, according to pattern	Mounted officers.
Steel chain reins	All combatant mounted officers.

Uniforms.

Exact and detailed descriptions of the several articles of uniform, and also the lace, embroidery, and distinguishing devices and badges permitted to be worn, by the various regiments and corps, are contained in the "Regulations for the Dress of the Army."

The various grades and duties of officers of infantry are shown on their uniforms and appointments according to the following system:—

In the Guards.—The field officers and captains are distinguished by gold embroidery round the top and bottom of the collar of the tunic, also on the edge of the skirt flaps and edge of sleeve flaps, and two rows of embroidery round the top of the cuffs. The other officers of the Guards have embroidery on the top only of the collar, and one row round the cuffs. The embroidery is half an inch wide.

In Rifle Corps.—The field officers have the collar of the jacket laced all round with black lace and figured braiding within the lace, sleeve ornament of lace and figured braiding eleven inches deep. Captains have the collar laced round the top with black lace and figured braiding below it, sleeve ornament, knot of square cord with figured braiding eight inches deep. Subalterns the same, but plain braid takes the place of the figured braiding.

In all other regiments field officers wear gold lace round the top and bottom of the collars of their tunics and coats, down the edge of the skirts behind, also on the edge of the skirt flaps and edge of the sleeve flaps; two rows of gold lace round the top of the cuffs. Other officers have gold lace on the top only of the collar, one row round the top of the cuff, none on the edge of the skirts, and gold lace loops on the skirt flaps and sleeve flaps.

The different ranks of officers have the following badges at each end of the collar, embroidered in silk for rifle corps, and in silver for all other regiments :—

    Colonel - - - A crown and star.
    Lieutenant-colonel - - A crown.
    Major - - - A star.
    Captain - - - A crown and star.
    Lieutenant - - - A crown.
    Ensign - - - A star.

Officers in the Guards wear the badges corresponding to their rank in the army.

Field officers have the crown or star, or both, according to rank, embroidered on their saddlecloths, except in rifle corps, in which latter shabraques of black lambskin take the place of saddlecloths, and are without any devices.

The *adjutant* is to wear the uniform of his rank, and in the field a steel scabbard and steel spurs with crane neck two inches long.

Paymasters, quartermasters, surgeons and assistant-surgeons wear the uniforms of their respective regiments, with the distinctions of their corresponding ranks, excepting that they are to have cocked hats, black waist-belts with slings, and no sash. The paymaster wears no feather, the quartermaster has a hackle feather, 5 inches long, of regimental colour in the Guards; in fusilier regiments all white; in regiments of the line three inches white and two inches red at the bottom; in light infantry regiments green. The surgeon and assistant-surgeon wear a feather of black cock's tail, drooping from a feathered stem 5 inches in length.

The surgeon and assistant-surgeon also wear a black shoulder-belt with a small case of instruments, as before described. The regimental staff of Highland regiments are not required to wear the kilt. In rifle corps the paymasters and quartermasters wear a plain shako with no tuft.

Officers are required to have the following articles of personal equipment :—

    Sword and scabbard.
    Sword knot (one of each kind for Guards).
    Sword belt, with union locket complete.
    Sword belt, full-dress, for Guards only.
    Pouch belt, for rifles only.
    Shoulder belt, for medical officers only.
    Sash, if required by regulation.
    Brooch -⎫
    Dirk and belt - ⎬ for Highland regiments only.
    Skeen Dhu -⎭
    Head dress for full-dress occasions, with cover.

Forage cap and cover.
Stock.
Tunic or full-dress coat or jacket.
Shell jacket.
Blue frock coat or undress jacket.
Gloves.
Trousers, winter.
   „ summer.
   „ full-dress with gold stripe, for Guards only.
Boots.
Cloak or great coat.
Belted plaid, ⎫
Kilt, |
Purse, |
Hose,   ⎬ for Highland regiments only.
Garters, |
Shoes and buckles, |
Scarf,   ⎭
Spurs,   ⎫
Horse appointments, ⎬ for mounted officers.

Officers serving in North America are permitted to wear the following articles of winter uniform for all ordinary parades and duties, viz. :—

Busby of black Astrakhan or other fur, with covers for the ears.
Frock coat of grey cloth, double breasted, with horn buttons, and trimmed with grey Astrakhan fur.
Fur gloves.
Canadian boots.

The number of the various articles of uniform, appointments, &c., and the quantity and description of equipment of other kinds required by officers, must depend upon the peculiarities of the station and climate, the facilities for transport, and the general nature of the service that they are employed upon.

Every officer must possess a copy of the Queen's regulations, and also one of the regulations for Field Exercise.

Conveyance of Baggage.

Officers are entitled to have a certain amount of baggage conveyed at the public expense when travelling with troops or otherwise on duty. On home service a commuted allowance is granted for the purpose. (*See* Royal Warrant and Regulations, § 36).

Every package is to have the owner's rank and name distinctly written upon it, and the weight of any one package is on no account to exceed 400 lbs.

Equipment of Officers on active Service.

The means of transport and the nature of the country in which the military operations are carried on must in a great degree regulate the equipment of an officer on active service. Field officers commanding, are allowed forage for two bât horses each, other officers for one each, for the conveyance of their personal effects. This proportion is considered to be sufficient to carry clothing, bedding, means of cooking, and other articles required for the preservation of health and the performance of duties. Captains, surgeons, and paymasters are allowed a second pack animal for the conveyance of public stores.

Writing materials and a telescope may both be considered as indispensable on service in the field.*

Indemnification for Loss of Equipment.

The circumstances under which indemnification is authorized to be given in case of unavoidable loss of horses or effects are detailed in Royal Warrant, pp. 89 to 112.

The following table exhibits the maximum rates of indemnification allowed, according to the rank of officers and the nature of the service they are employed upon.

Rank or Employment of Officers.	Uniforms.	Linen, &c.	Boots, &c.	Sword and Appointments.	Writing Case, Telescope, and Portmanteau.	Total Baggage.	Horse Equipments.	Canteen Bedding and Tent Furniture.	Marquee, when not provided at the Public Expense.
LIGHT EQUIPMENT ON SERVICE IN THE FIELD.	£ s.	£ s.	£ s.	£ s.	£ s.	£ s.	£ s.	£ s.	£ s.
Field officer	33 10	9 10	5 0	9 10	6 0	63 10	18 0	24 0	18 0
Captain and brevet field officer.	33 10	6 10	5 0	9 10	3 0	57 10	18 0	20 0	12 0
Captain	31 10	6 10	4 7	9 10	3 0	54 17	—	20 0	12 0
Subaltern	31 0	6 10	4 7	9 10	2 0	53 7	—	16 0	12 0†
Adjutant	31 0	6 10	5 0	9 10	3 0	55 0	18 0	16 0	12 0
Paymaster, surgeon	29 0	6 10	4 7	5 5	3 0	48 2	—	20 0	12 0
Quartermaster	29 0	6 10	4 7	5 5	3 0	48 2	—	16 0	12 0
Assistant surgeon	29 0	6 10	4 7	5 5	3 0	48 2	—	The same as a subaltern.	
FULL EQUIPMENT AT A STATIONARY COMMAND.									
Field officer	54 10	16 0	7 0	9 10	8 10	95 10	18 0	24 0	18 0
Captain and brevet field officer.	54 10	11 0	7 0	9 10	5 0	87 0	18 0	20 0	12 0
Captain	50 0	11 0	6 7	9 10	5 0	81 17	—	20 0	12 0
Subaltern	49 0	11 0	6 7	9 10	4 0	79 17	—	16 0	12 0†
Adjutant	49 0	11 0	7 0	9 10	5 0	81 10	18 0	16 0	—
Paymaster, surgeon	47 10	11 0	6 7	5 5	5 0	75 2	—	20 0	12 0
Quartermaster	47 10	11 0	6 7	5 5	5 0	75 2	—	16 0	12 0
Assistant surgeon	47 10	11 0	6 7	5 5	5 0	75 2	—	The same as a subaltern.	

* Suggestions for the equipment of officers in the field are contained in the "Theory of War," by Colonel Macdougall, p. 294.

† For the subalterns of each company.

ARMS.

PLATES IV. TO X.

The following articles appertaining to the infantry service are classed under the general head of "arms." Military store officers are only to issue them upon receiving the order of the Secretary of State for War, or that of the officer commanding the troops on foreign stations or on active service :—

    Muskets with their appurtenances.
    Swords and claymores with their scabbards.
    Drums, bugles, and flutes, with cases, &c.
    Armourers' forges and tools.

Application for arms. Regiments in Great Britain are to direct their applications to the Adjutant-General to the forces, Horse Guards, London; regiments in Ireland to the Deputy Adjutant-General, Dublin; and regiments abroad to the general officer commanding, by whom they will be transmitted to the Adjutant-General to the forces, with the view of their being forwarded to the War Office.

All applications for arms are to be made in duplicate, according to the prescribed forms.

Issues from stores on the spot, under the authority of general officers in command of stations abroad, are to be restricted as much as possible to cases of unforeseen emergency, in which the delay attending a reference to the authorities at home would cause inconvenience to the public service. All such cases are to be specially reported to the adjutant-general.

The War Department undertakes the payment of the carriage of arms, only on their first direct issue from the War Department stores, either to the head-quarters of a regiment or to a detachment, as may be stated in the requisition; and when arms have once been despatched in conformity with such requisition, no subsequent charge can be admitted on account of any further distribution.

Duration of arms. All arms are to be kept in a state fit for service for 12 years, with the exception of bayonet scabbards and bugles, trumpets and bugles for dismounted services, which are only required to last six years. The armourer's forge is to be kept in a serviceable state for 20 years, with the exceptions stated at page 83.

If arms have become unserviceable after being these periods in use, they will be exchanged on a report being made to the adjutant-general as to their condition and the time they have been in wear.

When new arms are issued, the old ones with the exception of drums, are to be carefully returned to the nearest military store.

Should any articles become unserviceable in less than the prescribed periods, the causes to which their unserviceable state is to be attributed are to be *specially* reported to the adjutant-general, accompanied by an inspection report of three or more officers.

Drum-heads and strings for bugles are to be renewed by the drummers or buglers who have them in charge, the rate of pay they receive being calculated to enable them to meet these expenses.

Receipt of arms. When arms or any other stores supplied by the War Department are issued to troops, they are immediately to be examined by a regimental board of survey; the contents of the several packages should be counted and carefully examined in presence of the board, and any deficiencies or damages are at once to be reported to the military store officer who issued the stores, in order that he may determine whether the damages or deficiencies were caused by the fault of the carriers.

The date of the year is punched upon the stock, on the lock side of the flat part of the butt, before the arms are issued from the stores. Marking of arms.

Arms are not to be taken into use without being properly marked. The heel plates of the muskets, the hilts of the swords and their scabbards, are to be marked with the number of the battalion and regiment, and to be numbered consecutively from 1 to 1000, or whatever the establishment may be, thus:—

1 Bⁿ. 24th. Reg^t.
297.

The bayonets, scabbards, rammers, nipple wrenches, and muzzle stoppers are to be marked with consecutive numbers only.

The letters and numbers are to be invariably *engraved*, and in no case punched or stamped upon the arms (*see* W.O Cir. 582, 21st April 1860). The figures on the bayonet scabbard should be engraved on the button and not on the brass mouth-piece. No marks of any kind are to be put upon the barrels of muskets.

Armourer-serjeants are required to mark all the arms, including those of serjeants, without extra remuneration.

Arms will be marked by the War Office before being issued, provided a proper description of the marks to be engraved thereon be forwarded by the officers commanding with their applications for arms.

Arms which are from time to time supplied for *temporary purposes* are *not to be marked;* and when no longer required, the application for leave to return them is to be made through the adjutant-general,—accompanied by a report of the number and condition of the arms, and the period during which they have been in use.

An annual inspection of the whole of the arms in possession of regiments and depôts is to be made as soon as possible after the termination of the prescribed course of musketry instruction, the board consisting of not less than three officers, one of whom is to be a field officer. Officers who have been trained at Hythe are to be selected for this duty, when any such are available; and, when practicable, the assistance of one of the viewers of the War Department is to be obtained. The arms are to be minutely examined, and if the means are at hand, any barrels suspected of being dented or damaged in the bore or rifling-grooves are to be accurately gauged. Inspection of arms.

In stating the condition of the arms due allowance is to be made for the period they have been in use, and for fair wear and tear, such as dents in the stocks, &c., which do not impair the efficiency of the weapon. It should then be shown what rifle muskets can be repaired by the armourer at the expense of the regiment, and if it is considered that any repairs executed by him are fairly chargeable to the public, the usual evidence, showing the circumstances under which the injury was effected, should be taken, and appended to the proceedings.

The usual special report by the board should be made on all such rifles, or parts of rifles, as are considered unserviceable, and which are required to be exchanged for new ones, stating the date of issue, the reason of the damage, and on whom the cost incurred is to fall, and whether, provided the parts are supplied by Government, the repair can be executed by the armourer of the regiment.

A mean deviation of over three feet, at 500 yards, is to be considered a sufficient inaccuracy to condemn a rifle suspected of being inferior, and is to be tested by shooting as prescribed by the circular memorandum, dated Horse Guards, 25th of February, 1861, No. 109.

Requisitions in duplicate, for whatever is required, should accompany the proceedings.

The report of the board is to be made on form, page 181,[*] and sent to the general or other officer commanding the division, district, or station, for transmission to the Adjutant-General, and submission to the General Commanding-in-Chief.

Delivery of arms into store. When regiments at home, by reduction of establishment, or from any other cause, have a considerable number of spare arms at their quarters, the commanding officers are to make application through the Adjutant-General, to return them into store; and upon sanction being obtained, they are to cause such arms to be delivered into the nearest military store, accompanied by a statement of their description, number, and condition. In cases of regiments abroad, application is to be made to the general officer in command, who will communicate with the storekeeper on the station. A receipt, specifying their number, description, and condition, is to be taken from the storekeeper. Commanding officers of regiments are not, however, to return into store any surplus arms which are likely to be again required within a short period.

Whenever arms are delivered into store by regiments, a statement is to accompany them, showing the period they have been in use, together with their condition, and should they require repairs or be unserviceable, the causes of their having become so must be stated. When arms that have not been in use the regulated period are sent into store by regiments abroad, a board consisting of the senior military store officer, (assisted by the civil armourer where there is one), the inspector of warlike stores, and the instructor of musketry of the regiments or corps, will assemble, and examine all the arms, with the view of assessing any damages that may exist, and these will be charged to the regiment in accordance with the scale laid down in the Queen's Regulations (see page 40), and in the case of interchangeable rifle muskets according to the cost specified at page 37. The sums to be levied upon the regiment should, however, only be the cost of such repairs as ought to have been executed by the regimental armourer-serjeant. Any further expense to make the arms fit for reissue for service will be borne by the department.

Classification of arms. All fire-arms used in the service are divided into three classes:—

Class I. consists of *new* arms of such patterns as are issued to the various services entitled to be furnished with first-class arms.

Class II. consists of new second-class arms of existing patterns, and all thoroughly repaired arms, whether originally first or second class.

These two classes include only such arms as are of the bore ·577, as distinguished from those patterns that are considered obsolete for existing services.

"Reserve" arms include such as are of obsolete patterns, whether new or otherwise, likewise those of existing patterns that are considered to be too much worn to justify a complete repair.

1st class are distinguished by the figure I., about a quarter of an inch in length, on the lock side of the *butt*; this is stamped upon them previously to being sent into store from the manufactories.

2nd class are marked similarly with the figure II., an additional I. being added each succeeding time that the arm is repaired, until from sufficient wear they fall into the reserve division.

[*] Not reproduced in this edition

ARMS. 31

Reserve are marked with the letter R. in addition to the number of their class, thus :—

53 I. C. R.	42 III. C. R.
53 II. C. R.	Flint I. C. R.
53 III. C. R.	Flint II. C. R.
42 I. C. R.	Flint III. C. R.
42 II. C. R.	&c. &c. &c.

It is understood that all arms so marked have been properly cleaned and are in sufficient repair to be used.

Arms classed as "*reserve*" are only intended for issue to levies and irregular forces, or to meet any contingencies that may arise until the stock of 1st and 2nd class new pattern arms shall attain such an amount as to render the issue of these reserve arms no longer necessary under any circumstances.

The fire-arms issued to the infantry of the regular army are of four patterns; these are—

The Enfield Rifle Musket, pattern 1853 (interchangeable).
The Short Enfield Rifle Musket, pattern 1856 (non-interchangeable).
The Short Enfield Rifle Musket, pattern 1860 (interchangeable).
The Whitworth Rifle, pattern 1863 (experimental).

All ranks of Rifle battalions have hitherto been armed with the short rifle musket, pattern 1860. The rank and file of all other classes of infantry are armed exclusively with the Enfield rifle musket, pattern 1853, and the serjeants with the short rifle musket, pattern 1856; but it is intended to issue those of the pattern of 1860 as the arms at present in use become unserviceable, and are exchanged for new, and non-interchangeable arms are to be kept for Militia, Volunteers, and other forces.

The Enfield rifle musket, pattern 1853, was adopted for service in the year 1853, after experiments carried on at the Royal Manufactory, Enfield Lock, in 1852. It is sighted up to 1,000 yards, but its practice is good at a longer range. Length, 54 inches; weight, 8 lbs. $14\frac{1}{2}$ oz. Bayonet, length beyond muzzle, 1 foot $5\frac{1}{4}$ inches; weight, $13\frac{1}{2}$ oz. Arm complete, with bayonet: length, $71\frac{1}{2}$ inches; weight, 9 lbs. 12 oz. Barrel: length, 39 inches; diameter of bore, 0·577 inches. or 24 bore; three rifled progressive grooves making one spiral turn in 78 inches. *Enfield rifle muskets, patterns 1853 and 1860.*

The short rifle musket, pattern 1860, is sighted up to 1,250 yards. It is $48\frac{3}{4}$ inches long, and weighs 8 lbs. $8\frac{1}{2}$ oz. Sword bayonet, length beyond muzzle, 1 foot $10\frac{3}{4}$ inches; weight, 1 lb. $11\frac{1}{2}$ oz. Arm complete, with sword bayonet: length, $71\frac{1}{4}$ inches; weight, 10 lbs. $4\frac{1}{2}$ oz. Barrel: length, 33 inches; diameter of bore, ·577 inches; five rifled progressive grooves. The pattern of 1856 has a thinner barrel, with three grooves, and is $5\frac{1}{2}$ oz. lighter.

Rifle muskets are made with two different lengths of butts, the variation being one inch; they are usually issued in the proportion of one-third long to two-thirds short butts, unless specially demanded otherwise.

A pattern Whitworth rifle was approved on the 18th December 1863 to govern the supplies. Length, $48\frac{3}{4}$ inches; weight, 9 lbs. 14 oz. Sword bayonet: length beyond muzzle, $22\frac{3}{4}$ inches; weight, 1 lb. $11\frac{3}{4}$ oz. Arm, complete, with bayonet: length, $71\frac{1}{2}$ inches; weight, 11 lbs. $9\frac{3}{4}$ oz. Barrel: length, 33 inches; weight, 5 lbs. $\frac{3}{4}$ oz.; calibre, 0·4895 inches across angles, 0·4495 across sides; diameter of cylinder 0·451; one uniform spiral turn in 20 inches. *Whitworth rifle, pattern 1863. Experimental.*

A new pattern for the lower and middle bands of rifles was approved on the 3rd June 1861. These are now made without projections for the screw, by which economy of manufacture is attained, and liability to injury of the soldiers' accoutrements is diminished. The new pattern bands are called "Baddeley's" bands, having been invented by Col. Baddeley, R.A.

Rifle muskets made at the Royal Small Arms Factory are distinguished by the word *Enfield* engraved on the lock-plate, and have their corresponding parts exactly identical in size and interchangeable. Those made on the same principle by the London Armoury Company have L.A.C. on the lock-plate.

Rifle muskets manufactured by contract have the word TOWER on the lock-plate.

All rifles belonging to government are marked with a crown and the letters V.R., besides a small crown and broad arrow on the lock-plate and barrel.

The barrels and breech pins of Enfield rifles are not interchangeable articles; to prevent their being mismatched when taken asunder, the breech pins and breech end of the barrels are marked with corresponding letters and numbers.

The following table shows the parts of all the portions of arms manufactured at Enfield that are interchangeable one with another.

Those parts which will not interchange have the word "Special" written opposite them.

The lock for the short rifle musket, pattern 1860, is identical with that of the /53 pattern, but it is what is termed "double freed" in the tumbler and sear; being more highly finished in all parts, its cost is $8\frac{1}{2}d.$ more.

Description of Part of Arm, &c.	Interchangeable Rifle Musket, Pattern 1853.	Interchangeable Short Rifle Musket, Pattern 1860.	Artillery Carbine, Pattern 1861.	Cavalry Carbine, Pattern 1861.
STOCK.				
Machine stock, complete	Special	Special	Special	Special.
Nose cap { brass, without screw	Special	—	Special	Special.
Nose cap { iron, „	—	Special	—	—
Nose cap { screw	Special	Interch.	Interch.	Special.
Ramrod	Special	Special	Special	Special.
Rod, spring (spoon pattern)	Interch.	Interch.	Interch.	Interch.
Rod, pin spring	Interch.	Interch.	Interch.	Interch.
Rod, stop { iron	Interch.	Interch.	Interch.	—
Rod, stop { brass	—	—	—	Interch.*
Band, old pattern { upper	Special	Interch.	Interch.	Special.
Band, old pattern { middle	Special	—	—	—
Band, old pattern { lower	Interch.	Interch.	Interch.	Special.
Screws for O.P. bands { upper	Interch.	Special	Interch.	Special.
Screws for O.P. bands { middle	Special	—	—	—
Screws for O.P. bands { lowe	Interch.	Interch.	Interch.	Special.
Band screw nuts	Interch.	Interch.	Interch.	Interch.
Bands, new pattern { middle	Special	—	—	—
Bands, new pattern { lower	Interch.	Interch.	Interch.	Special.
Screws for N.P. bands { middle	Special	—	—	—
Screws for N.P. bands { lower	Interch.	Interch.	Interch.	Special.
Band swivel	Interch.	Interch.	Interch.	—
Trigger guard, brass	Special	—	Interch.	Interch.
Trigger guard, iron	—	Special	—	—
Trigger guard, pin	Interch.	Interch.	Interch.	Interch.
Trigger guard, screw	Interch.	Interch.	Interch.	Interch.
Trigger plate, brass	Special	—	Interch.	Interch.
Trigger plate, iron	—	Interch.*	—	—

* Interchangeable, but of a different metal.

ARMS.

Description of Part of Arm, &c.	Interchangeable Rifle Musket, Pattern 1853.	Interchangeable Short Rifle Musket, Pattern 1860.	Artillery Carbine, Pattern 1861.	Cavalry Carbine, Pattern 1861.
Trigger	Interch. -	Interch. -	Interch. -	Interch.
Trigger screw	Interch. -	Interch. -	Interch. -	Interch.
Breech screw	Interch. -	Interch. -	Interch. -	Interch.
Side screw	Interch. -	Interch. -	Interch. -	Interch.
Side screw cup { brass	Interch. -	—	Interch. -	—
{ iron	—	Interch.*-	—	—
Guard { swivel	Special -	—	—	—
{ screw for do.	Special -	—	—	—
Butt swivel	—	Interch. -	Interch. -	—
Screw, snap cap	Interch. -	Interch. -	Interch. -	Interch.
Brass heel plate	Interch.†	—	Interch. -	Interch.
Iron ,,	—	Special -	—	—
Heel plate screw	Interch. -	Interch. -	Interch. -	Interch.
Lock (assembled).				
Main spring	Interch. -	Interch. -	Interch. -	Interch.
Sear spring	Interch. -	Interch. -	Interch. -	Interch.
Steel sear	Interch. -	Interch.‡	Interch. -	Interch.
Bridle	Interch. -	Interch. -	Interch. -	Interch.
Hammer	Interch. -	Interch. -	Interch. -	Interch.
Tumbler { steel	Interch. -	Interch.‡	Interch. -	Interch.
{ swivel	Interch. -	Interch. -	Interch. -	Interch.
{ screw (iron)	Interch. -	Interch. -	Interch. -	Interch.
Lock plate	Interch. -	Interch. -	Interch. -	Interch,
Sear spring screw	Interch. -	Interch. -	Interch. -	Interch.
Bridle screw	Interch. -	Interch. -	Interch. -	Interch.
Sear screw	Interch. -	Interch. -	Interch. -	Interch.
Barrel.				
Nipple	Interch. -	Interch. -	Interch. -	Interch.
Breech	Special -	Special -	Special -	Special.
Front sight	Fixture -	Fixture -	Fixture -	Fixture.
Elevating back sight	Special -	Special -	Special -	Special.
Sight leaf, with cap and slide	Special -	Special -	Interch. -	Interch.
Slide	Interch. -	Interch. -	*Interch. -*	*Interch.*
Sight { spring screw	Interch. -	Interch. -	*Interch. -*	*Interch.*
{ spring	Special -	Special -	*Interch. -*	*Interch.*
{ axis pin	Interch. -	Interch. -	*Interch. -*	*Interch.*

A bayonet and scabbard, nipple, rammer, snap cap and chain, and a muzzle stopper are issued with each rifle musket. A proportion of 30 per cent. of spare nipples are issued with arms. — *Appurtenances of rifle muskets.*

Every man armed with a rifle musket is provided with a nipple-wrench. This is made of two patterns, one with a cramp and the other without. They are served out in the proportion of 10 per cent. of the former to 90 per cent. of the latter.

The nipple-wrench for serjeants includes the following implements, nipple-wrench, cramp, pricker, drift, worm, ball drawer, large and small screw-drivers. The pattern for privates has nipple-wrench, pricker, worm, large and small turnscrew, and oil bottle.

The barrels of rifle muskets, those of serjeants included, as well as the hilts of the bayonets, are to be browned every second year or oftener. — *Browning of rifle muskets.*

---

    * Interchangeable, but of a different metal.
    † Interchangeables for short butts.
    ‡ Will interchange, but are not identical in figure.

if necessary, by the armourer-serjeant. He is not entitled to any extra pay or remuneration for this service, but he may be granted the assistance necessary for the purpose from the regiment, the men employed nder his direction being allowed the usual working pay.

Browning recipe,—

Tincture of steel	4 oz.
Sweet spirits of nitre	3 ,,
Spirits of wine	3 ,,
Nitric acid (concentrated sp. gr. 1·42)	2 ,,
Blue vitriol (sulphate of copper)	1 ,,
Rain water	2 quarts.

In mixing the ingredients the blue vitriol should be dissolved in cold rain water, and the other ingredients subsequently added.

The mixture must be kept in a cool place, in glass bottles well stoppered, as it will soon lose its virtue if kept in earthenware jars, or if the stoppers do not fit well.

Directions for browning.

Before the mixture is applied to the barrel the nipple hole should be carefully stopped up, to prevent any water or browning mixture getting inside, and the muzzle should also be stopped with a peg, made of pine or deal, about 12 inches long, 4 inches of which are to be inserted in the barrel ; the remainder will serve as a handle to the workmen.

1st. Coat the barrels with wet lime, clean with dry lime, and brush and wipe them with coarse linen cloth ; coat them with the mixture with sponge, and then let them stand in the drying-room 12 hours in 90 degrees heat.

2nd. Scratch them with wire-card, after which let them stand one hour to get thoroughly cold, coat them as before and let them stand in the drying-room six hours.

3rd. Scratch them with wire-card, let them stand one hour, coat them and stand them in the drying-room six hours.

4th. Scratch them with wire-card, let them stand one hour, coat them and stand them in the drying-room six hours, after which immerse them in boiling water, every one being in the copper five minutes ; then let them stand one hour, coat them and stand them in the drying-room six hours.

5th. Scratch them with wire-card, let them stand one hour, coat them and stand them in the drying-room six hours.

6th. Scratch them with wire-card, let them stand one hour, coat them and stand them in the drying-room six hours.

7th. Immerse them in boiling water, after which scratch them with wire-card.

8th. Immerse them in boiling water, finish them with wire-card, and then oil them.

It will be observed that the time allowed for drying is in the first instance 12 hours, and the subsequent stages six hours. The barrels will generally be dry in this time, but as the atmosphere has a great effect upon the acids of which the browning mixture is composed this will not be *invariably* the case. It can be easily ascertained whether the barrels are dry or not by applying the steel scratch card, when, if dry, the rust will fly off quickly, but if not dry the rust will adhere firmly, and the barrel will have a streaky appearance.

Fine and dry weather should invariably be chosen for the operation of browning, as far as the exigencies of the service will permit.

ARMS.

In consequence of the mixture for browning arms supplied from England having been found liable to deteriorate by fermentation on its voyage to distant colonies, the ingredients for making the browning liquid are to be furnished to foreign stations in an unmixed state. No corrosive sublimate or other materials but those specified in the instructions will be supplied or are to be used in browning arms.

The *bands* of rifle muskets are to be *blued* and not browned.

The lock-plates are on no account to have the hardening colour renewed upon them, as the process has a very injurious tendency in destroying the texture of the case-hardened iron of which they are made.

The following materials are allowed to be issued out of the ordnance stores free of charge whenever the periodical browning of arms is ordered to take place :—

Bone dust - - - lbs.	5	
Borax, for soldering - oz.	8	
Brass spelter - - „	½	
Browning mixture - quarts	6	
Brushes, hard - - -	3	
Charcoal (supplied by barrack-master, *see* page 42).		
Emery flour (size, 80 holes),lb.	1	
„ cloth, No. 1. quires	2	
Glass paper, fine, No. 1½ „	2	
„ „ coarse, No. 2 „	2	
Glue - - - - lbs.	4	
Oil, Rangoon - - gallons	2	
Plugs, wood, for holding barrels - - - - -	6	
Rosin - - - - lb.	½	
Sal ammoniac - - oz.	2	
Scalding trough, pattern at Pimlico - - -	1	
Scratch card - - yards	3	
Sheeting, old - - lbs.	24	
Sponges - - - -	2	
Tin, bar, for soldering - lbs.	1	
Tow - - - - „	6	

This quantity is considered sufficient for all purposes, including the occasional oiling of the spare arms belonging to a battalion of ordinary strength.

All ordinary repairs of arms are to be executed by the armourer-serjeant, assisted when necessary, by men carefully selected from the ranks. In the case of a depôt or detachment out of the reach of the head-quarters of the regiment, the officer commanding is to apply to the nearest storekeeper, stating the number of arms which require to be repaired, and the nature of the repairs, when the War Department will, on the storekeeper's report, direct the repairs to be effected by an armourer of the department, if it should appear that it can be done without inconvenience, and on condition that the actual expenses shall be repaid. *Repairs of rifle muskets.*

When arms in the possession of troops serving at home are directed to be returned into store for repair and re-issue to the same regiment or corps, they shall be forwarded direct to the repairing factory at Pimlico. Commanding officers, when forwarding arms for repair, will send with them vouchers, showing the actual number and description of each article returned, to enable the superintendent of the Royal Small Arm Factories to keep a proper account with regiments of the articles sent in. Forms for this purpose may be obtained on application to the War Office.

All materials for the repairs of interchangeable arms, as well as the implements and ingredients for browning them, are supplied on the requisition of the officer commanding the battalion, and are to be kept in charge of the quartermaster under the direction of the commanding officer. The cost of these articles, as well as the expense of transit to the regiments, is borne by the public.

Allowances to armourer-serjeants.

Armourer-serjeants receive pay at the rate of 5s. a day for seven days in the week exclusive of beer money. They are also entitled to receive the following allowance of fuel and light for the armourer-shops of regiments having the interchangeable rifle musket:—

    Coal, $1\frac{1}{2}$ bushel per week, throughout the year.
    Wood, 3 lbs. per week, throughout the year.
    Candles, 1 lb. per week, for the winter months only.
    Charcoal, as required for blueing, to a maximum of 4 lbs. for the year.

When, however, the arms of an entire regiment shall require to be browned, &c. at one time, which will only be requisite once every two years, barrack masters are authorised, on receiving a certificate from the officer commanding, that a period of two years has elapsed since the date of the commencement of the previous similar issue, to furnish the following increased allowances *in lieu* of the above, viz. :—

    For a regiment 850 strong,—
    Coals, 3 bushels per week, for 20 weeks.
    Coke, $4\frac{1}{2}$,, ,, ,,
    Wood, 3 lbs. ,, ,,
    Candles, $1\frac{1}{2}$ lbs. ,, for the winter months only.
    Charcoal, 42 lbs., for the operation of blueing.

Barrack masters will attach the certificate of the officer commanding to the first weekly fuel return wherein, after each biennial interval, these issues are included.

At Foreign Stations, similar or corresponding issues may be made by the Commissariat Department, under the same conditions.

In consideration of the foregoing allowances armourer-serjeants are required to perform all repairs to *interchangeable* arms belonging to their respective regiments without remuneration, and also to examine and clean them periodically.

They are required besides to keep up the set of tools belonging to the Field Forge at their own expense.

The sum of 1s. a year for each interchangeable rifle musket is to be deducted from the captain's contingent, and credited to the public as a reimbursement for the repair of arms.

All repairs to arms injured either intentionally or by carelessness are to be paid for by the men at the regulated rate specified in the annexed statement. The captains of companies will be responsible for receiving the charges for these damages, and for crediting the amount to the public, less the amount which is to be paid to the armourer-serjeants (*see* list, on next page).

The armourer-serjeant will be held strictly responsible that all such interchangeable arms as are delivered into store before they have been the regulated period in use are actually in a serviceable state.

All casualties, therefore, whether of an accidental or wilful description, which may be discovered in such arms, when inspected by any viewers of the Small Arms Department, and which ought properly to have been made good previous to the return of such arm or arms into store, will be charged to the regiment and recovered from the armourer-serjeant. This charge will include all the expense of repairs, exclusive of the value of the materials which are supplied gratuitously.

When arms have been directed to be returned into store, immediate notice is to be given by the captains of companies to the serjeant-armourer, in order that the repairs required by the regulations may be executed, and, generally, they will afford the serjeant-armourers every facility and proper opportunity for examining and repairing them. In the event of any captain neglecting or refusing to do so when required, he will render himself responsible for any charge that may be made on account of repairs deemed necessary by the Small Arms Department; any such special case to be decided by a board of officers.

As these amended regulations do not exonerate captains of companies from their responsibility for the perfect efficiency of the arms belonging to their companies, they must satisfy themselves, by frequent and careful inspection, that all repairs are promptly and properly performed by the armourer-serjeant.

An account is to be rendered annually to the War Office by officers commanding regiments, of the receipts and expenditure of the materials supplied for the repair of the *interchangeable* arms, and of the number of the several articles remaining in the possession of the quartermaster. The account should also show what portion of the materials has been expended to replace or repair damages occasioned wilfully or by negligence; the sums recovered for such materials, and in what pay list they are credited to the public.

ARTICLES required for the REPAIR of the INTERCHANGEABLE RIFLE MUSKET, pattern 1853, and the prices to be paid for each.

Description of Parts of Arms, &c.	Value of each Article.	Amount to be paid to Serjeant Armourer by Soldiers for repairs required through carelessness.	Estimated Per-centage for repair for one Year.
STOCK.	s. d.	s. d.	
Machine stock complete, including cost of stock and rammer stopper.	7 2	0 4	—
New rough stock	4 0	—	—
Re-stocking with rough stock complete	—	6 0	—
Splices	0 6	—	—
Splicing { with long splice	—	2 6	—
{ „ short „	—	1 6	—
New brass nose cap, without screw	0 6	0 1	$\frac{1}{4}$
New nose cap screw	0 0$\frac{1}{2}$	—	3
New rammer spring (spoon pattern)	0 3	—	1
New wire pin for rammer spring	0 0$\frac{1}{10}$	—	1
New stopper for rammer	0 0$\frac{1}{4}$	—	$\frac{1}{2}$
New upper band, with swivel complete	1 0$\frac{1}{4}$	0 1	1
New band screws, upper	0 0$\frac{3}{4}$	—	1
A new band swivel	0 4$\frac{1}{2}$	0 0$\frac{1}{2}$	1
A new middle band, with swivel complete	0 7$\frac{3}{4}$	0 1	1
New band screws, middle	0 0$\frac{3}{4}$	—	1
A new lower band, with swivel complete	0 7$\frac{3}{4}$	0 1	1
New band screws, lower	0 0$\frac{3}{4}$	—	1
A new brass trigger guard	1 0$\frac{1}{2}$	0 1	$\frac{1}{2}$
A new wire pin for guard	0 0$\frac{1}{10}$	—	1
A new guard screw	0 0$\frac{3}{4}$	—	1, in sets of 5
A new brass trigger plate and re-fitting the trigger.	0 5$\frac{1}{2}$	0 1	$\frac{1}{2}$
A new trigger	0 5$\frac{1}{4}$	—	1
„ „ screw	0 0$\frac{1}{2}$	—	1
A new breech screw	0 1$\frac{1}{4}$	—	1
A new side screw	0 1$\frac{1}{4}$	—	1
A new brass side screw cap	0 1	—	1
A new guard swivel	0 3$\frac{3}{4}$	0 0$\frac{1}{2}$	1
A new screw for guard swivel	0 0$\frac{3}{4}$	—	1
A new brass heel plate	1 0	0 1	$\frac{1}{4}$
A new heel-plate screw	0 1$\frac{1}{4}$	—	1, in sets of 5

Description of Parts of Arms, &c.	Value of each Ariicle.	Amount to be paid to Serjeant Armourer by Soldiers for repairs required through carelessness.	Estimated Per-centage for repair for one Year.
Lock.	*s. d.*	*s. d.*	
New main spring	1 6	—	5
New sear spring	0 6¾	—	2½
New steel sear	0 7¾	—	2½
New bridle	0 7	—	1
New hammer	1 4	—	2½
New tumbler { steel	1 3	—	2½
New tumbler { swivel	0 1¾	—	5
New tumbler { screw, iron	0 1	—	1
New sear spring screw	0 1	—	1
New bridle screw	0 1	—	1
New sear screw	0 1	—	1
Barrel.			
New nipple	0 2½	—	5
New breech, threaded	0 6	—	½
Clipping the breech	—	0 3	—
New front sight	—	0 3	—
New elevating back sight	3 5	0 8	1
New sight leaf, with cap and slide	1 8	0 1	1
New slide	0 3½	—	3
New sight spring screw	0 0¼	—	2
" " "	0 2¾	—	1
New axis pin	0 0¼	—	1
Browning a barrel, including smoothing	—	0 8	—
Bayonet.			
New bayonet, with locking ring complete	4 4¼	0 1	2½
New locking ring, with screw	0 5½	—	2½
" " screw	0 0¾	—	2½
Rammer.			
New steel rammer	1 5½	0 1	1
Clipping rammer	—	0 4	—
Threading "	—	0 1	—

Note.—In case of repairs being executed by the armourer-serjeant which have to be charged to the soldier on account of carelessness or wilful damage, the expense of fitting, &c. in the second column, is allowed to be charged by the armourer-serjeant. This sum, together with the cost of the material in the first column, will be the total charge against the soldier. But as the materials are originally supplied without charge, their value when thus used to make good loss and damage, must be credited to the public.

If the armourer replaces a spoilt stock with a machine stock, for which the soldier is to be charged, he will receive 4*d.* for his labour, and 7*s.* 2*d.* will be credited to the public, making a total charge against the soldier of 7*s.* 6*d.*

If a rough stock be supplied to the armourer, he will receive 6*s.* for stocking, screwing, and finishing complete, and 4*s.* will be credited to the public on account of the rough stock, making a total charge of 10*s.* against the soldier. But if the armourer be called upon to furnish the rough stock he will receive 4*s*. for the same in addition to 6*s*. for his labour.

The third column shows the per-centage *estimated* to be required for rèpairs in a year, and which should be kept in store in garrisons. In the field this proportion should be doubled.

All the materials, with the exception of the breech pin, will be supplied in the finished state.

Repairs of short rifled musket, pattern, 1856, and other non-interchangeable arms.

Repairs to short rifle muskets and other non-interchangeable arms are to be paid for by captains of companies, the armourer-serjeant furnishing the materials; if damaged by carelessness or inattention the amount is chargeable to the individual causing it.

The following materials for repairs are supplied exclusively by the War Office upon demands from serjeant-amourers through the commanding officers of their respective regiments, the cost price and expense of transit being paid for by the armourers through the medium of the regimental agents, viz.:—

Description of parts of Arms, &c.	Cost of each.	Weight of each.	
	d.	lbs.	ozs.
Stocks	68·80	2	2
Nose cap, in the cast state	1·39	0	$1\frac{3}{4}$
Rivets for nose cap (brass), in the finished state	1*s*. 2*d*. per lb.	0	$0\frac{1}{28}$
Spring, rammer, in the finished state	2·43	0	$0\frac{1}{4}$
Band and spring each	4·23	0	$2\frac{1}{4}$
Swivel { shaft, in the finished state	3·63	0	$0\frac{1}{4}$
Swivel { butt, " "	4·25	0	$0\frac{3}{4}$
Screws, handle, sets in the finished state	0·58	0	$0\frac{1}{4}$
Handle, in the cast state	4·26	0	3
Trigger-plate, in the cast state	1·32	0	$1\frac{1}{2}$
" in the forged state	0·74	0	1
Screw { breech, in the forged state	2·01	0	$4\frac{1}{2}$
Screw { side, " "	0·47	0	$0\frac{1}{2}$
Heel-plate, in the cast state	5·90	0	$4\frac{1}{4}$
Screws, heel-plate, set, in the finished state	0·98	0	$0\frac{3}{4}$
Lock-plate, in the forged state	2·49	0	$6\frac{1}{4}$
Spring { main, in the forged state	2·33	0	$1\frac{1}{4}$
Spring { sear, " "	0·62	0	$0\frac{1}{4}$
Sear, in the forged state	0·27	0	$0\frac{1}{2}$
Bridle, " "	0·84	0	$1\frac{1}{4}$
Cocks, " "	2·99	0	$6\frac{1}{4}$
Tumbler " "	3·00	0	$1\frac{3}{4}$
Screw, tumbler, in the forged state	0·20	0	$0\frac{1}{4}$
Screw { sear { spring, in the forged state	0·11	0	$0\frac{1}{4}$
Screw { sear { in the forged state	0·14	0	$0\frac{1}{4}$
Screw { bridle, " "	0·14	0	$0\frac{1}{4}$
Nipple, in the finished state	2·26	0	$0\frac{1}{4}$
Sight { front	0·06	0	$0\frac{1}{4}$
Sight { back	39·24	0	2
Bayonet	50·61	0	$13\frac{1}{2}$
Rammer	13·89	0	11
Wire, iron, lbs. { No. 10 per lb.	3·00	1	0
Wire, iron, lbs. { No. 13 "	3·00	1	0
Pin clippings "	12·00	1	0
Borax "	7·00	1	0

In executing repairs every article is to be fitted to its place with the utmost accuracy and finished in the best style of workmanship.

Repair of non-interchangeable arms.

LIST of PRICES to be allowed to ARMOURER-SERJEANTS of REGIMENTS for the REPAIR of NON-INTERCHANGEABLE ARMS.

(Queen's Regulations, p. 106, &c.)

Description of Repair.	Rifle Muskets fitted with solid Bands and Springs.		Rifle Muskets fitted with Screw Bands and Rammer Springs.		Short Rifle Musket, Pattern 1856.		Artillery Carbine.		Lancaster Carbine.	
	s.	d.	s.	d.	s.	d.	s.	d.	s.	d.
STOCK.										
New stock and re-stocking complete	12	0	12	0	12	0	12	0	12	0
Splicing stock, including long splice	5	0	4	0	4	0	3	0	4	0
short	2	6	2	0						
New brass nose cap and fitting	0	9	0	9	1	0	0	9	0	9
New brass handle or guard and fitting	1	2	1	2	1	6	1	2	1	2
New brass heel plate and fitting	1	3	1	3	1	6	1	3	1	3
New brass trigger plate, and re-fitting the trigger	1	3	1	3	1	6	1	3	1	3
New brass side nail-cup, and fitting	0	2	0	2	0	3	0	2	0	2
New fore, or shaft swivel, with nail and fitting	0	5	0	5	0	5	0	5	0	5
New handle, swivel, and fitting	0	4	0	4	0	6	0	6	0	6
New trigger filed up, fitted, and hardened	0	6	0	6	0	6	0	6	0	6
New stopper for rammer and fitting	0	2	0	2	0	2	0	2	0	2
New side or breech nail, filed, tapped, and hardened	0	6	0	6	—		—		—	
New wood screw, fitted and hardened	0	1	0	1	0	1	0	1	0	1
New wire pin, and fitting	0	0½	0	0½	0	0½	0	0½	0	0½
New rammer spring, and ditto	—		0	9	0	6	0	6	0	6
New bands, fitted and hardened, or blued — front with swivel	1	5	1	5	—		—		—	
middle	0	10	0	10	—		—		—	
back	0	10	0	10	—		—		—	
New front band with sword bar, and swivel and fitting	—		—		2	3	—		—	
Ditto with swivel only and fitting	—		—		1	5	1	5	1	5
New back band and fitting	—		—		0	10	0	10	0	10
New band, spring, and fitting	0	4	—		—		—		—	
New band screw, with nut and fitting	—		0	3	0	3	0	3	0	3
LOCK.										
New lock plate, filed, hardened, and fitted	2	6	2	6	2	6	2	6	2	6
New cock, filed, fitted, and hardened	2	3	2	3	2	3	2	3	2	3
New steel sear, filed, fitted, and tempered	1	5	1	5	1	6	1	5	1	5
New bridle, fitted and hardened	1	0	1	0	1	3	1	0	1	0
New steel tumbler, fitted, hardened, and tempered	—		—		2	9	2	6	2	6
New mainspring, to weigh from 13 lbs. to 14 lbs. at half bent, including fitting	2	0	2	0	2	3	2	0	2	3
New sear spring and fitting	1	0	1	0	1	0	1	0	1	0
New swivel, fitted and tempered	0	8	0	8	0	8	0	8	0	8

ARMS.

Description of Repair.	Rifle Muskets fitted with solid Bands and Springs.		Rifle Muskets fitted with Screw Bands and Rammer Springs.		Short Rifle Musket, Pattern 1856.		Artillery Carbine.		Lancaster Carbine.	
	s.	d.	s.	d.	s.	d.	s.	d.	s.	d.
New steel nail, filed, tapped, and tempered — tumbler	0	4	0	4	—		—		—	
— lock of sorts	0	3	0	3	—		—		—	
Oiling and cleaning lock, including correcting the "pull off"*	—		—		0	2	0	2	0	2
BARREL.										
New nipple and fitting	0	6	0	6	0	6	0	6	0	6
Clipping the breech-pin	0	9	0	9	0	9	0	9	0	9
New front sight, filed up and fitted†	0	8	0	8	0	8	0	8	0	8
New elevating sight-bed and fittings	2	0	2	0	1	9	—		1	9
New elevating sight-flap or leaf and ditto	2	0	2	0	1	9	1	6	1	9
New slider for sight and ditto	0	9	0	9	0	9	—		0	9
New cap or top piece for sight and fitting	0	8	0	8	0	8	—		0	8
New sight-spring and ditto	0	8	0	8	0	8	—		0	8
New sight-screw and ditto	0	2	0	2	0	2	—		0	2
New centre-pin for joint of sight, and fitting	0	2	0	2	0	2	0	3	0	2
New elevating sight, including soldering on, adjusting, cleaning off, and browning bed of sight	7	4	7	4	5	0	5	0	5	0
Graduating and marking bed of sight	0	1	0	1	0	1	0	1	0	1
Ditto, flap or leaf	0	2	0	2	0	2	0	1	0	2
BAYONET.										
New bayonet with locking ring complete, including fitting and adjusting, &c.	6	6	6	6	—		—		—	
New locking ring and fitting	1	3	1	3	—		—		—	
New screw or stud for locking ring	0	2	0	2	—		—		—	
Setting bayonet when bent	—		0	3	—		—		—	
SWORD BAYONET.										
New grip or scale and fitting	—		—		0	9	0	9	0	9
New rivet and fastening	—		—		0	2	0	2	0	2
New grip, spring, and fastening	—		—		0	9	0	9	0	9
New bolt and fastening	—		—		0	9	0	9	0	9
New pommel, fitting, and remounting complete	—		—		2	6	2	6	2	6
Fitting a new sword bayonet (supplied from store)‡	—		—		0	9	0	9	0	9
RAMMER.										
New steel rammer, complete	2	0	2	0	1	6	1	4	1	6
Clipping rammer when broken	—		—		0	6	0	6	0	6
Tapping thread for worm	0	1	0	1	0	1	0	1	0	1

Repair of non-interchangeable arms.

* This service is inserted in lieu of a special allowance for adjusting the "pull off," which should be discontinued.

† The front sights of arms with sword bayonets should be *soft* soldered to the barrel, and not brazed.

‡ No prices for repair of sword scabbards are inserted, as these articles when damaged should be returned into store and replaced by serviceable scabbards.

PERSONAL EQUIPMENT.

Chests sufficient in size to contain materials for the repair of 1,000 interchangeable rifle muskets for two years are issued to regiments.

The expenses incidental to the repair of arms and accoutrements are to be rendered upon W.O. Form 1011, D. and E., discontinuing the practice hitherto in force of including receipts and payments for this service in the quarterly account of "expenses incidental to clothing."

Stores of arms. Arms and materials for their repair are kept in store and issued from the following stations at home and abroad:—

HOME.

London (Tower).	Pembroke Dock.	Dublin.
Chatham.	Chester.	Athlone.
Dover.	Edinburgh.	Cork.
Portsmouth.	Stirling Castle, N.B.	Guernsey.
Devonport.		Jersey.

ABROAD.

Barbadoes.	St. Helena.	Newfoundland (St. John's).
Bermuda.	Hong Kong.	New South Wales (Sydney).
Cape Coast Castle.	Hobart Town.	
Cape of Good Hope:—	Jamaica.	New Zealand (Auckland).
Cape Town.	Malta.	
Grahamstown.	Mauritius.	Nova Scotia (Halifax).
Ceylon (Colombo).	Melbourne.	
Demerara.	Montreal.	Quebec.
Gambia.	New Brunswick (St. John's).	Sierra Leone.
Gibraltar.		

Unserviceable arms are received at the above stations and also at all other military stores.

Packing arms. When rifle muskets are forwarded from the government stores, they are packed in cases containing 20 each. Those for the 1853 pattern musket are 5 feet long by 19 inches wide by 15 inches deep; cubical measurement, 10 cubic feet; weight, 292 lbs. The cases for the short rifle musket are 55 inches in length by 22 wide by 17 deep; cubical measurement, $11\frac{11}{12}$ cubic feet; weight, 324 lbs.

If muskets in the possession of troops have to be packed for transport they are to be put in chests properly fitted with cleats by the armourer-serjeant and the arms packed in the same manner as at the government factory, so as to secure them from injury. In the case of non-interchangeable arms the proper bayonet belonging to each musket is to be attached to the guard swivel by a piece of string, and it must not be separated without precautions being taken for its re-appropriation to the right musket. This is not necessary for interchangeable muskets as their bayonets fit universally. *See* G.O. No. 787, Horse Guards, 2nd May 1861.

When arms are packed in chests for transport or for store the following composition is to be rubbed over all the parts made of metal, in order to preserve them from rust:—

    Beeswax, 1 lb.
    Mutton suet, 1 lb.
    Price's Rangoon oil, 1 pint.

This last-mentioned article is to be used in the ordinary cleansing and preservation of muskets, as it is considered preferable to any other description of oil.

Alkanet root is not to be used for the stocks.

Officers commanding regiments and others are responsible that all chests or cases conveying arms or stores of any kind, empty zinc percussion cap cases, or powder barrels, &c., are carefully made over, as soon as they can be dispensed with, to the officer in charge of the nearest military store station.

General List of Arms, &c.

Description.	Cost.			Weight.		To what Ranks issued.
	£	s.	d.	lbs.	oz.	
Muskets.						
Rifle musket, pattern 1853, with rammer and bayonet, but without leather scabbard; interchangeable.*	3	0	0	9	12	Rank and file of all infantry excepting rifle corps.
Bayonet for do. separately -	0	5	0	0	13½	} One issued with each rifle musket, pattern 1853.
Scabbard, leather, for do. -	0	1	3	0	5½	
Short rifle musket, pattern 1856 (bar on barrel), with rammer and sword bayonet, but without scabbard.	4	15	9	9	13½	Serjeants of all infantry excepting rifle corps, but will be replaced by the 1860 pattern as soon as those in store are expended.
Do. with bar on band - -	5	1	6	9	13½	
Short rifle musket, pattern 1860 (with bar on barrel), with rammer and sword bayonet, but without scabbard.	5	1	6	10	4	Serjeants and rank and file of rifle corps.
Sword bayonet for short rifle musket.	0	10	6	1	11½	} One issued with each short rifle musket.
Scabbard, leather, for do. -	0	3	0	0	7½	
Whitworth short rifle musket, pattern 1863 (bar on barrel), with rammer and sword bayonet, but without scabbard.	-	-	-	11	9¾	Issued experimentally to rifle battalions.
Appurtenances.						
Caps, snap, with chain -	0	0	1½	0	0½	One issued with each rifle musket.
Nipples - - -	0	0	1¾	-	-	Spare nipples issued in the proportion of 30 per cent. of the arms.
Stopper, muzzle - -	0	0	2¼	0	0½	One issued with each rifle musket.
Wrench, nipple, with cramp -	0	1	11½	0	6½	One issued with each rifle musket, 10 per cent. with cramp, 90 per cent. without.
Do. do. without do. -	0	0	11½	0	4½	
Swords.						
Line pattern, staff-serjeant's, with leather scabbard, hilt and mountings gilt.	1	12	6	2	10¾	Schoolmasters of all infantry. Staff-serjeants, drum and bugle majors and band-serjeants of all excepting rifle corps and Highland regiments.
For rifle regiments, staff-serjeant's, with leather scabbard, hilt and mountings steel.	1	12	0	2	10	Staff-serjeants, bugle-major, and band-serjeants of rifle corps.
Line pattern, drummers, with leather scabbard, hilt and mounting brass - -	0 0	12 11	6 6	2	9	Drummers, buglers and band of all excepting rifle corps; all hospital orderlies.
For rifle regiments, buglers', with leather scabbard, hilt and mountings steel and iron.	0	9	3	2	9	Buglers and band of rifle corps.
Pioneer's, pattern 1856, with saw-back, leather scabbard, hilt and mountings brass.	0	11	10	3	0	Pioneers of all infantry.

* The cost of non-interchangeable rifle muskets, pattern 1853, is 3*l.* 2*s.* 6*d.*

PERSONAL EQUIPMENT.

Description.	Cost.	Weight.	To what Ranks issued.
Swords—cont.	£ s. d.	lbs. oz.	
Claymore, staff serjeant's, with leather scabbard, hilt and mountings steel.	1 18 6	3 6½	Staff-serjeants, drum-major, pipe-major, and band-serjeant of Highland regiments.
Claymore, piper's, with leather scabbard, hilt and mountings steel.	1 14 9	3 3½	Drummers, pipers, and band of Highland regiments, and pipers of Scots Fusiliers.

BUGLES, DRUMS, AND FLUTES.

Description.	Cost.	Weight.	Set for a Service Battalion.		Set for a Depôt Battalion.				
			12 Companies.	10 Companies.	7 Depôts.	6 Depôts.	5 Depôts.	4 Depôts.	3 Depôts.
	£ s. d.	lbs. oz.							
Bugle	0 11 0	1 6½							
String for bugles, green	0 2 0	0 4¾							
String for bugles, variegated or "Royal" *	0 2 0	0 4¾	12	10	14	12	10	8	6
Drum, bass	4 15 0	22 12							
Sticks for bass drum, pair	0 1 9	0 6½	—	—	1	1	1	1	1
Case, ticken, for do.	0 3 0	3 8							
Drum, side, brass	2 2 0	7 12							
Sticks for brass side drum pair	0 1 3	0 6	12	10	14	12	10	8	6
Case, ticken, for do.	0 2 6	1 0							
Drum, silent, for practice	0 15 0	—	—	—	—	—	—	—	—
Flute in B♭	0 9 3	0 3¾							
Case for flute in B♭	0 5 0	0 4½	8	6	10	8	6	4	3
Flute in F	0 10 9	0 7							
Case for flute in F	0 4 3	0 5½	2	2	2	2	2	2	1
Piccolo in E♭	0 7 9	0 2							
Case for piccolo in E♭	0 4 6	0 5	1	1	1	1	1	1	1
Piccolo in F	0 8 0	0 2							
Case for piccolo in F	0 4 6	0 5	1	1	1	1	1	1	1

* Issued to regiments bearing the title of "Royal," the green are issued to all others.

Light infantry and rifles are supplied with 2 bugles for each company, but are not furnished with drums, flutes, or piccolos.

Highland pipes are provided at the expense of the band fund of regiments using them.

MUSICAL INSTRUMENTS.

Musical instruments, including bass drums with carriages and aprons for bass drummers, music, and all other articles required for regimental bands, as also the drum-major's staff, are to be provided at the discretion of the officer commanding, the expenses being defrayed out of the band fund of regiments. (*See* Queen's Regulations, 1859, p. 135.)

The band of an infantry battalion is ordered to consist of 1 bandmaster-serjeant, 1 serjeant, 1 corporal, and 19 privates, making the total strength 22. The exact pattern, character, or proportion of musical instruments is not fixed by regulation, but the following may be considered a suitable selection.

The prices are the average of those charged by London tradesmen, but if application is made to the Adjutant-General of the Forces for instruments when they are required, they will be obtained of uniform pitch for the whole army, and the prices will be 28¾ per cent. cheaper than the prices given below.

The expense of Highland bagpipes for Highland and other regiments having pipers in their establishment is defrayed out of the band fund.

Description.	Cost of each.			Weight of each.		Number.
	£	s.	d.	lbs.	oz.	
Flutes	8	8	0	1	10	3
Oboe	8	8	0	0	14	—
Clarionets, E♭, Alberts	8	8	0	1	12	1
Clarionets, B♭, Alberts	8	8	0	2	0	6
Bassoon	15	15	0	8	0	—
Horns (with valves)	12	12	0	6	0	2
Pistons (with valves)	8	8	0	3	0	2
Alt horn, B♭ (with valves)	10	10	0	4	0	1
Trumpet, with valves	9	9	0	5	0	1
Drum, bass	4	15	0	22	12	1
Trombones, tenor (with slides)	7	7	0	2	5	2
Trombone, bass (with slides)	8	8	0	3	5	1
Euphonium (valves)	14	14	0	6	0	1
Bass horn E♭ (with valves)	16	16	0	8	0	1
Bass ,, F (with valves)	16	16	0	8	0	1
Sticks for drum pairs	0	1	9	0	9½	1
Ticken for do.	0	3	0	3	8	1
Apron, buff, bass drummer's	0	8	0	2	14	1
Carriage, buff, bass drum	0	3	9	0	12½	1
Bagpipes, Highland	8	8	0	4	11	6

ACCOUTREMENTS AND APPOINTMENTS.

PLATES XI. to XVI.

Under the general head of accoutrements and appointments for infantry are included all belts, drum carriages, sword knots, musket slings, pouches, pioneers' tools with their leather cases, havresacks, canteens, and squad bags.

All accoutrements and appointments supplied by the War Department are in accordance with the standard sealed patterns approved for the respective services.

The accoutrements of rifle regiments are invariably of black leather; those for all other classes of infantry are of white buff leather, excepting the pouches, the belts for schoolmasters, and those for the pipers of Scottish regiments, all of which are black.

The pattern of the pioneers' tools are such that in the event of any of them becoming broken or damaged on service, no difficulty will be experienced in replacing them at any government store or depôt. For details as to the manner in which the tools are carried, *see* Queen's Regulations, page 136; *see* also Circular Memorandum, dated Horse Guards, 18th November 1856, Pioneers $\frac{231}{B.81}$.

Applications for accoutrements. Applications for accoutrements are to be forwarded by commanding officers, through the Adjutant-General to the Forces, to the Secretary of State for War. These are invariably to be sent in duplicate, and upon the prescribed form (*see* page 189),[*] showing the condition of the articles in possession, and also the number lost by neglect, desertion, or deficient through any other cause.

Accoutrements and appointments supplied by the War Office are, as soon as they are received, to be examined by a regimental Board of Survey. The report of their condition is to be forwarded to the Adjutant-General.

Duration of accoutrements. Accoutrements and appointments are required under ordinary circumstances to last twelve years, with the exception of havresacks, for which the regulated duration is five years in rifle corps, and three in other infantry regiments. Squad bags are to last ten years under ordinary circumstances, and to be kept in repair during that period by the troops.

On foreign stations, however, the duration will vary according to the climate and nature of the service, but they must be kept serviceable for that time if practicable. In the case of any articles becoming unfit for service in less than the prescribed period, a full explanation of the cause of such unfitness is to be given in the inspection reports.

Inspections of accoutrements. The commanding officer of every corps, together with the two officers next in rank, is to make an inspection of accoutrements and appointments between the 1st November and 1st January in each year, and oftener if necessary. The condition of all the articles is to be specified, dividing them into "serviceable," "repairable," and "unserviceable." The report is to be made on W. O. Form No. Π100, and is to accompany the requisition referred to above. When a new supply of accoutrements are received, the old ones that have been condemned as unserviceable are to be delivered to the military storekeeper at such stations as

---

[*] Not reproduced in this edition

ACCOUTREMENTS AND APPOINTMENTS.

may be ordered by the Secretary of State for War, except in India, in which case the articles should be sold to the best advantage, and the proceeds credited to the public in the contingent accounts, supported by a certificate of the officer commanding.

Accoutrements when issued are marked thus $\underset{\text{W.D.}}{\wedge}$. Before being taken into wear, they are marked consecutively to correspond with the arms, also with the number or appellation of the regiment, battalion, or corps, and with the date of issue; the marks being carefully and legibly placed on the inside or back part of the belts, pouches, slings, &c. *Marking of accoutrements.*

Types and stamping irons will be supplied at the public expense, but no charge will be admitted for marking.

Canteens and squad bags should be marked with paint, cutting, punching, or branding the heads of the former being forbidden.

Accoutrements and appointments are to be repaired in regiments of infantry by the regimental shoemaker or other competent person, and the actual cost of the same (if chargeable to the public) is to be included in the pay list, supported by vouchers showing the repairs done to each article, with its regimental number. This account is to be signed by the captain of the company, and certified by the officer commanding. *Repair of accoutrements.*

The sum to be charged to the soldier who loses or damages by neglect any article of accoutrements or appointments, is to be based on the value of the article according to the cost prices circulated by the War Office (*see* next page), and taking also into consideration the time the articles have been in wear.

The amount to be charged for articles lost or damaged by neglect which have been in wear the prescribed periods is to be the proportionate value for one year.

Should any spare parts of accoutrements be required to replace others lost or worn out, the cost of which is chargeable to the public, application may be made for the same to the Secretary of State for War.

If these spare parts are required to replace others lost or damaged by neglect, or worn out before the prescribed time, and the cost of making them good is chargeable to the regiment or soldier, the Secretary of State will consider the propriety of acceding to the application; the commanding officer is however to accompany it by a certificate that the articles needed, cannot be procured on the spot of the required quality and pattern, and at a reasonable cost. The several things are to be paid for according to the approved lists of cost prices issued from time to time by the War Department; and the cost of carriage is also to be made good.

When accoutrements are issued from military stores they are usually packed in quarter casks. An ordinary quarter cask is 32 inches high and 28 inches in diameter, and will contain 62 pouches, or 370 pouch belts, or 340 waist belts with lockets, or 800 frogs, or 600 slings, or 950 cap pockets, or 200 ball bags with oil bottles. When full, the weight varies from 168 lbs. to 282 lbs., according to the contents. *Packing of accoutrements.*

If accoutrements have to be sent by the overland route to India, they are usually put up in boxes; these are of two sizes, one holding 50 complete sets each, and the other 25 sets. The dimensions and weights when packed are as follows:—

Box holding 50 sets, 35 ins. × 28 ins. × 26 ins.; weight, 296 lbs.; measurement, $14\frac{9}{12}$ cubic feet.

Box holding 25 sets, 35 ins. × 14 ins. × 26 ins.; weight, 156 lbs.; measurement, $7\frac{4}{12}$ cubic feet.

All cases or casks in which accoutrements, &c., are forwarded to regiments, should be returned when empty to the nearest military store station, and the store officer will give a receipt for them.

Casks or barrels should be taken to pieces, and the staves tied up in bundles, so as to economise the cost of carriage or freight as much as possible.

General List of Accoutrements and Appointments.

—	Price. s.	d.	Weight. lbs.	oz.	To what ranks issued.
Apron, buff, for bass drum	10	6	2	14	One to each depôt battalion; provided out of the band fund of other battalions.
Apron, leg, buff, for side drum	4	0	0	10	Drummers of all classes of infantry.
Bag, ball, black leather, with zinc oil bottle.	2	3	0	8	Issued to all men carrying rifle musket, rifle corps.
Bag, ball, buff do. do.	2	6	0	7	Issued to all men carrying rifle musket, Guards, Line, and Highland regiments.
Bag, squad	—		—		One issued to every 25 non-commissioned officers and men.
Belt, pouch, black leather [1]	1	6	0	9	Issued to all men carrying rifle musket, rifle corps.
Belt, pouch, buff [2]	2	6	0	8	Issued to all men carrying rifle musket, Guards, Line, and Highland regiments.
Belt, shoulder, black japanned leather	5	6	0	14½	Pipe-major and pipers of Scots Fusiliers, Highland regiments, and 25th and 26th regiments.
Belt, shoulder, buff, with fixed frog	6	6	0	14½	Staff-serjeants, drum-major, and band-serjeants of Highland regiments wearing the kilt.
Belt, shoulder, buff, with fixed frog	5	0	1	0	Drummers, buglers, and band of all Highland regiments.
Belt, waist, black japanned leather, with sword carriages and snake hook, gilt furniture.	4	9	0	12½	Schoolmasters.
Belt, waist, do. do. silver plated furniture.	6	0	0	12½	Staff-serjeants, bugle-major, and band-serjeants of rifle corps.
Belt, waist, black leather, with snake hook.	2	0	0	5½	Serjeants, rank and file, band, buglers, and pioneers of rifle corps.
Belt, waist, buff, with sword carriages, gilt furniture, and slide.	4	6	0	9	Staff-serjeants, drum-major, and band-serjeants of Guards, Line, and Highland regiments wearing the trews.
Belt, waist, buff, with gilt slide	1	9	0	5½	Band of Guards.
Belt, waist, buff [3]	1	9	0	5½	Serjeants, rank and file, and pioneers of Guards; Line and Highland regiments; drummers and buglers of Guards and Line; band of Line.
Canteen, wooden, with strap	2	6	1	12	All ranks, but only when on active service.
Carriages, buff, for bass drum, with swivel.	3	6	0	12½	One to each depôt battalion; provided out of the band fund for other battalions.
Carriages, buff, for side drum, O.P.	4	6	1	2½	Drummers of all classes of infantry.
Carriages, buff, for side drum, N.P.	2	6	1	2½	Drummers of all classes of infantry.
Frog, black leather	1	0	0	3¼	Serjeants, rank and file, buglers, and band of rifles.
Frog, black leather, with shifting loop	1	3	0	3½	Pioneers of rifles.
Frog, buff	1	6	0	2½	Band of Guards.
Frog, buff	1	3	0	2½	Serjeants and rank and file of Guards, Line and Highland regiments, drummers and buglers of Guards and Line, and band of Line.
Frog, buff, with shifting loop	1	6	0	3½	Pioneers of Guards, Line, and Highland regiments.
Havresacks, white	1	0	0	10	All ranks of Guards, Line, &c.
Havresacks, black, waterproof	2	6	0	3	All ranks of Rifles.
Knot, sword, black japanned leather	1	6	0	3¾	Schoolmasters and staff-serjeants, bugle-major, and band-serjeants of rifles.
Knot, sword, buff	1	3	0	1½	Staff-serjeants, drum-major, and band-serjeants of Guards and Line.

[1] Made in three lengths, viz., 50, 52, and 53 inches. Usual proportion issued, 20 per cent. short, 50 per cent. medium, and 30 per cent. long.

[2] Made in three lengths, viz., 50, 53, and 54 inches. Proportion issued, 20 per cent. short, 30 per cent. medium, and 50 per cent. long.

[3] Made in three lengths, viz., 42, 43, and 44 inches. Proportion issued, 20 per cent. short, 30 per cent. medium, and 50 per cent. long.

ACCOUTREMENTS AND APPOINTMENTS.

		Price.	Weight.	To what ranks issued.
		s. d.	lbs. oz.	
Locket, union, reg^l pattern — gilt	Grenadier Guards	5 0	0 4¾	Serjeant-major, quartermaster-serjeant, drum-major, regimental clerk, and band-master of Guards.
	Scots Fusiliers	8 0	0 4¾	
	Coldstream Guards	12 0	0 4¾	
	Line regiments	1 4	0 4¾	Other staff-serjeants and band-serjeant of Guards, and staff-serjeants, drum or bugle-major, and band-serjeant of Guards, Line, and Highland regiments wearing the trews.
	Guards (for band only)	2 0	0 4¾	Band of Guards.
gilding metal, serjeant's		0 8	0 4¾	Serjeants of Guards, Line, and Highland regiments (numeral or device, according to regiments).
brass, other ranks		0 5	0 4¾	Rank and file, drummers, buglers, and pioneers of Guards, Line, Highland regiments, and band of Line and Highland regiments.
Plate for pouch belt, bronzed		2 0	—	Serjeants of rifle brigade.
Pouch — black leather	20 round, with tin magazine.	—	—	These pouches are still issued to the Guards, but will be superseded by the new pattern.
	60 do. do.	—	—	
	20 round, with fur cap pocket.	4 3	1 4	Serjeants of Guards, Line, and Highland regiments.
	50 do. do.	5 0	2 1	Rank and file of Guards, Line, and Highland regiments, and all ranks of rifles.
	for percussion caps	0 9	0 2	Serjeants and rank and file of rifles.
buff	do. do.	1 0	0 2	Serjeants and rank and file of Guards, Line, and Highland regiments.
Slings, musket	black leather	1 0	0 4½	One issued for each musket, Rifle Corps.
	buff	1 0	0 3½	One issued for each musket, Guards and Line.
Whistles and chains	bronzed { 60th rifles	2 6	0 3½	Serjeants of 60th rifles.
	{ rifle brigade	2 9	0 3½	Serjeants of rifle brigade.
	plated, light infantry	2 6	0 3½	Serjeants of light infantry regiments.

LIST OF PIONEERS' TOOLS.

Description.	Cost.			Weight.		Set for 10 Service Companies.	Set for 2 Depôt Companies.
PIONEERS' TOOLS AND CASES.	£	s.	d.	lbs.	oz.		
Auger, screw	0	1	9	1	5	1	—
Axes { broad	0	2	3	3	9	1	—
felling	0	3	0	5	12	5	1
hand	0	2	0	2	0	2	—
pick	0	2	3	6	0	5	1
Bar, crow	0	2	3	7	0	1	—
Bill, hooks	0	2	0	1	12	10	2
Chisels { cold	0	1	0	0	14½	1	—
socket	0	1	3	1	3½	1	—
File, saw	0	0	3	0	2½	1	—
Hammer, claw, large	0	2	0	1	15	1	—
Saw, hand	0	2	9	1	14	1	—
Shovels	0	2	9	5	7	5	1
Spades	0	2	9	4	6½	3	1
Spikes, gun, common	0	0	4	0	1¼	22	2
Cases, black leather, for—							
Axes, felling, tipped with brass	0	2	2	0	8	5	—
Axe, broad, and axe hand, with shoulder belts	0	7	0	1	5	1	—
Axes, pick	0	3	0	0	8	5	1
Bar, crow (set of caps with strap)	0	3	3	0	6½	1	—
Bill hooks (with loop for belt)	0	2	9	0	8	10	2
Saw, hand, and axe hand, case and cap, with shoulder belt and straps	0	11	6	2	14	1	—
Shovel, with shoulder belt and straps	0	6	9	1	11	5	1
Spades, with shoulder belts and straps	0	6	9	1	11	3	1
Small tools, with shoulder belt	0	8	6	1	13	1	—

List of Spare Parts of Accoutrements for Infantry.

Description.	Cost.
	£ s. d.
Billets, black, for pouch belt	0 0 1
" buff, "	0 0 2
" " for flaps of pouches	0 0 3
Bottles, oil, zinc, for ball bags	0 0 4
Buckles, brass, for musket slings	0 0 1
" " "	0 0 1½
" " shoulder belts	0 0 2
" " waist belts	0 0 1½
" iron tinned, with chapes, for 50-round pouches, per pair	0 0 6
Buttons, black leather, for musket slings	0 0 0½
Cap, with brass tip and buckle for crowbar	0 1 0
Chains for whistles, bronze	0 0 6
" " white metal	0 0 6
Flaps or leaves for pouches	0 3 0
Hooks, snake, for waist belts, with catches	0 0 8
Loops for pouch belts, buff	0 0 1
Ornaments for pouches, Guards, Grenadier	0 0 4
Ornaments for pouches, Guards, Scots Fusilier	0 0 3
Ornaments for pouches, Guards, Coldstream	0 0 3
Ornaments for pouches, 29th regiment	0 0 3
Plate, bronze, for whistle and chain, 60th regiment and militia	0 0 3
Plate, bronze, for whistles and chain, rifle brigade	0 0 3
Runners for musket slings, buff	0 0 1
Runners for musket slings, black leather	0 0 1
Safes for waist belts, buff	0 0 2
Slide, brass, for shoulder belts	0 0 2
Straps, back, for pouches	0 0 8
Studs, brass, for waist belts	0 0 0½
Swivel iron for bass drum carriages	0 0 6
Tab, buff, for waist belts	0 0 1½
Thongs for musket slings	0 0 1
Tip, brass, for shoulder belts of pioneers	0 0 4
Tip, brass, for pickaxe cases of pioneers	0 0 4
Whistle and sheath, with back plate, nuts and screws, bronze	0 1 9
Do. do. do. do. white metal	0 1 9

AMMUNITION.

The small-arm ammunition at present issued for the several branches of the service is of the following kinds:— *Various descriptions of ammunition.*

1st. Ball cartridge for Enfield rifle musket, pattern 1853; short rifle musket, patterns 1856 and 1860; sea service rifle musket, pattern 1858; and Lancaster carbine; elongated bullet with plug of baked clay; weight 530 grains; length, 1·095 inch; diameter, 0·55 inch; charge, $2\frac{1}{2}$ drams E. R., or Enfield rifle powder. (This powder is an improvement on the F. G., or fine grain, being larger and more even in grain; the charcoal used is made of dogwood, and the materials are more perfectly incorporated.) Penetration at 50 yards, $11\frac{1}{2}$ elm boards 1 inch thick, placed 1 inch apart. Price of cartridges, 2*l.* per 1,000.

2nd. Ball cartridge for artillery and cavalry carbines, same as foregoing, but the quantity of powder is only 2 drams.

3rd. Ball cartridge for rifle pistol, elongated bullet without plug; weight, 388 grains; diameter, ·568 inch; charge, 1 dram.

4th. Ball cartridge for Whitworth small bore rifle musket, pattern 1864; weight of bullet, 480 grains; charge, 75 grains.

5th. Ball cartridge for Westley Richards' carbine; weight of bullet, 400 grains; diameter of rim, ·467 inch; diameter of body, ·447 inch; charge, 2 drams.

6th. Ball cartridge for Terry's carbine; weight of bullet, 530 grains; diameter, ·568 inch; charge, 2 drams.

7th. Blank cartridge for all arms of ·577 bore except breech-loaders; charge, $3\frac{1}{2}$ drams.

8th. Blank cartridge for Westley Richards' breech-loading carbine; charge, 3 drams.

9th. Blank cartridge for Terry's carbine; charge, 3 drams.

Ball ammunition is made up in white or whited-brown paper, excepting the cartridges for Westley Richards' carbine, which are made with yellow paper.

Blank ammunition is made up in purple paper, except that for Westley Richards' and Terry's carbines, the former of which is put up in blue, and the latter in white paper with purple band round it.

There are other kinds of ammunition for arms of older patterns, but these are never used by the regular forces.

All the foregoing kinds of ammunition are made into packets containing 10 each.

The special cartridges for Dean and Adams's and Colt's revolvers are put up in packets of 20 and 18 respectively.

Copper Percussion Caps.—One kind of these is used throughout the service.

Ball ammunition is packed in quarter barrels and in boxes. For all stations within the tropics or for service in the field, as well as for China, small-arm ammunition is packed in boxes; those for tropical countries are made of teak, with mahogany ends.

Quarter barrels of service ammunition for the Enfield rifle musket are $14\frac{1}{4}$ inches long and $11\frac{5}{8}$ inches in diameter. The gross weight is $75\frac{1}{2}$ lbs. The caps are contained in a zinc cylinder. They bear the following label in black letters upon white paper, the head of the barrel being black:—

FOR
RIFLE MUSKET /53
BULLET ·55 DIAMETER.
WAX—
Powder 2½ Drs.
WOOD PLUG.
CARTRIDGES 700.
CAPS 1,050.
WATERPROOF BAGS.

Boxes of service ammunition for the Enfield rifle musket are $16\frac{1}{2}$ inches long, $7\frac{1}{4}$ broad, and $8\frac{1}{2}$ deep, external dimensions over all. The caps are contained in a zinc box. The label is similar to that for the quarter barrels. The number of rounds in each box was formerly 560 with 700 caps, but as the cartridges are now made up with a new description of powder and are put up in waterproof bags with an increased proportion of caps, the number is 440 rounds with 660 caps, as the bags occupy more room than the former wrappers. Each box weighs about 48 lbs.

Quarter barrels of ammunition for the Whitworth rifle contain 500 cartridges in each, and weigh 56 lbs. They are labelled thus in black letters upon white paper :—

PATTERN 1864.
For
WHITWORTH RIFLE.
BULLET 480 GRAINS.
Powder 75 Grains.
CARTRIDGES 500.
CAPS H.P. 750.
WATERPROOF BAGS.

Ammunition used formerly to be issued specially for practice packed in quarter barrels containing 700 cartridges, and 770 caps in a zinc cylinder. The label was printed in black letters upon blue paper. According to the existing regulations ammunition is not *packed* for the purpose of practice, but when issued from store the surplus caps are removed from each package, so as to reduce the proportion to 11 for every 10 cartridges, or to the actual number required.

Ammunition for the cavalry and artillery carbine is packed in quarter barrels and boxes, similarly to that for the /53 pattern rifle musket. The label specifying the nature of the arm, quantity of powder, and number of rounds, &c.

Ammunition for rifle pistols is packed in quarter barrels, weighing about 63 lbs. each. They are labelled thus :—

FOR
RIFLE PISTOL
BULLET ·568 DIAMETER.
WAX—
Powder 1 Dram.
CARTRIDGES 900.
CAPS H.P. 1350.
WATERPROOF BAGS.

For smooth-bore pistols the packages of cartridges contain 1 dram each, and are usually packed in quarter barrels.

Blank ammunition is packed in half barrels 17 inches long and $13\frac{1}{2}$ in diameter. The caps are contained in a zinc cylinder. The number of common blank cartridges in a half barrel is 1,800, with 1,980 caps, and the weight 45 lbs. But a half barrel holds 2,500 rounds for Terry's or Westley Richards' breech-loading carbines. The labels descriptive of the contents are stencilled on the heads of the barrels in blue letters.

AMMUNITION. 53

Officers commanding regiments or depôts in the United Kingdom are to address their applications for ammunition to the Adjutant-General of the Forces. Abroad and in the field they are to be forwarded to the Adjutant-General's department of the district or division. The demands are in both cases to be in duplicate. *(Applications for ammunition.)*

Ammunition for practice and exercise, and that for *service*, are to be applied for separately.

The proportion of ammunition allowed to Royal Engineers and regiments of infantry for practice is as follows :— *(Ammunition for practice.)*

For each trained soldier an annual allowance of 90 rounds of ball cartridge, 60 rounds blank, and 165 percussion caps. This quantity is due on the 15th March in Great Britain, North America, &c., and on the 15th September in the Mediterranean and other stations, where on account of the heat the annual course of training is required by the " Instructions of Musketry " to commence on that date.

For the training of each recruit, 110 rounds of ball cartridge, 20 blank ditto, 143 percussion caps, besides 20 ditto for snapping practice. This latter allowance is applied for as wanted, in such quantities as may be justified by the number of recruits actually present, or expected to join soon.

The ammunition for recruits will generally be issued to the depôt, and the regulated supply of blank cartridges will also be issued to depôts, for field days, battalion and light infantry drill, &c.

The annual allowance of practice and exercise ammunition for a regiment of infantry of 40 serjeants and 800 rank and file is estimated to require magazine accommodation for 27 half and 108 quarter barrels, and if that quantity cannot be stowed in the magazine of the station at which a regiment may happen to be quartered, the commanding officer is in the first instance to apply for such portion only as can be accommodated, taking care to indent for the residue in ample time to prevent the possibility of interruption to the practice.

When a regiment, battalion, or depôt is quartered where the target practice range does not extend 300 yards, no ammunition is to be demanded for practice at that station.

When there is a probability of the quarters of a regiment or depôt being changed at an early period, the commanding officer is to delay the application for the *whole annual allowance* required for practice and exercise, until the corps shall arrive at its destined quarters, in order that the inconvenience of returning the ammunition into store, or the expense of removing it, may be avoided ; he is only to apply for *such portion* as may be sufficient for carrying on the prescribed course of rifle instruction until the regiment moves.

The service ammunition in the men's pouches is to be expended annually in practice, and is to be replaced by a similar quantity of ammunition supplied for the annual practice of the corps. A return of *service* ammunition received, expended, and remaining in possession, is to be sent with every application for ammunition for *practice and exercise*.

All regiments are to have, in the constant possession of each man, 20 rounds of service ammunition, which is to be carefully packed, and to be under the daily inspection of officers of companies. Application for this proportion of service ammunition is to be addressed to the adjutant-general according to the prescribed form. *(Ammunition for service.)*

When any emergency shall arise to call for a further supply, it will be issued to the full extent of *sixty* rounds per man, so as to fill the pouches. Application for this extra supply of service ammunition is to be made to the general or other officer commanding the station where the regiment is employed.

This portion of service ammunition is to be carried by the soldier, and should the emergency require a still further supply, such excess is to be kept in the barrack store or magazine, and on the march is to be carried with other regimental stores under the special charge of the quartermaster.

Military store officers are authorized to issue, on the application of the senior officer on the station, such *service ammunition* as may be required *on any urgent occasion*, in addition to the quantity kept in the constant possession of the men. Whenever circumstances may render it expedient for the troops to be supplied with an extra quantity of *service* ammunition, officers commanding regiments or detachments are to make application accordingly, and they are to use their best exertions to prevent it from being injured or wasted.

When the emergency shall cease, the excess in possession of the men, as well as that in charge of the quartermaster, is to be delivered into store as soon as the regiment shall come within the immediate vicinity of any of the stations at home or abroad from which ammunition is supplied.

Ammunition on embarkation.

When troops are ordered to embark in steam vessels, to proceed by railways, or send their baggage by that mode of conveyance, they are to return into the nearest military store the whole of their ammunition (both service and practice), with the exception of that which is carried in the men's pouches. A receipt is to be taken from the superintendent of stores for the ammunition thus returned, which receipt is to be appended to the first requisition made by the corps on the military store officer at the station to which the regiment proceeds.

When regiments or armed detachments are warned for foreign service, application is to be made to the adjutant-general for a supply of service ball cartridges at the rate of 20 rounds per man for serjeants and 60 rounds per man for rank and file, to be put on board the vessel in which they are to proceed to their destination, and which will be provided with a proper magazine for its security. Previously to embarkation the whole of the ammunition *in possession* is to be given into the most convenient military store, care being taken to ascertain that the requisite supply has been put on board the ship.

When a regiment quits a station, all service ammunition in possession except the portion carried in the men's pouches may be re-delivered into a military store, if there should be one in the immediate vicinity. The receipt taken for the quantity so returned into store, is to be transmitted with the next application for a fresh supply.

If a battalion or detachment has returned its ammunition into store on proceeding from one station to another by railway or steamboat, and has to fire a feu de joie on Her Majesty's birthday or on any other public occasion, before it has been replaced, on arriving at the new destination, application may be made to the military store officer in charge for the quantity necessary for this purpose.

Loss of ammunition.

When *ammunition* is lost or destroyed through neglect of the soldiers, it is to be charged for, at the rate of 1*d.* a *round*, and *copper caps* at the rate of 5*s.* a thousand.

Conveyance of ammunition.

All ammunition not carried in the men's pouches is to be kept and conveyed under charge of the quartermaster, who is to preserve a correct distinction in his accounts between ammunition issued for *practice* and *exercise* and that issued for *service ;* he is strictly to avoid the use of

AMMUNITION.

iron hoops or iron nails in the heading up of cartridge barrels, or the presence of iron or grit among the percussion caps, cartridges, or loose powder. The use of iron nails in fastening on cards of address is also prohibited.

Commanding officers are held responsible for the exact observance of these orders, and no ammunition is ever under any circumstances to be left in barracks or quarters, or transferred from one regiment to another.

Metal cylinders are to be used for the conveyance of small quantities of small-arm ammunition by railways, in order to expedite the issues to regiments, and also to reduce the expense incurred by the employment of powder vans, these metal cylinders having been found upon trial to be a convenient substitute and equally safe.

They are to be conspicuously marked with the name of the station to which they belong, and with the letters W. ⋀ D.

Commanding officers of regiments, volunteer corps, &c., are immediately upon their receipt, to empty and return them with the spanners and bags to the military store officer at the station from which they were sent, by the same mode of conveyance which brought them.

In order to save the expense of escorts in the transmission of ammunition, small quantities, not exceeding five quarter barrels, protected by a proper covering and labelled "*ammunition*," may be sent by careful carriers, who should be informed of the contents of the packages; the consignee is to be informed of the quantity he is to receive, by what conveyance it is forwarded, and the rate of carriage agreed upon.

No more than five quarter barrels of ammunition should be removed by the same land conveyance without an escort, except by railway. Should there be more than that number, and an escort cannot be conveniently obtained, or to save the expense of one, under ordinary circumstances, the quantity may be divided and sent by different opportunities. Officers commanding troops are not to draw quantities exceeding the above without furnishing a proper escort.

When ammunition is sent by railway, notice is to be given to the railway company of the nature of the contents of the packages. Similar notice is to be given to carriers or others employed to take it to the station.

Every barrel or package is to be covered with a wadmiltilt or other sufficient protection, and a layer of similar material is to be placed between each tier.

The following are the stations in Great Britain and Ireland from which ammunition is supplied :— *Ammunition stores.*

Great Britain.

Bristol.	Hull.	Woolwich.
Bull Point, near Devonport.	Hyde Park.	Brecon.
	Manchester.	Newport.
Chatham.	Preston.	Pembroke.
Chester.	Priddy's Hard, near Portsmouth.	Edinburgh.
Dover.		Fort George, N. B.
Harwich.	Tynemouth.	Stirling Castle.

Channel Islands.

Alderney.	Guernsey.	Jersey.

Ireland.

| Athlone. | Cork Harbour. | Enniskillen. |
| Charlemont. | Dublin. | Limerick. |

Ammunition Reserves in the Field.

The Commander of the Forces is responsible for the supply of the ammunition of the army.

From the officers commanding the artillery reserves, officers commanding corps in the field will obtain their ammunition on requisitions approved by the Assistant Adjutant-Generals of divisions (on the relevant form). When, however, the army or part of it is actually engaged, the officers commanding the artillery reserves may issue ammunition, on the requisition of the officer in immediate command of any corps or detachment that may be in want of it.

Small-arm ammunition for service in the field is packed in boxes containing 440 rounds each and weighing about 48 lbs. (*see* page 52).

First Reserve. The first reserve of about 40 rounds per man is carried in the small-arm ammunition wagons attached to the artillery. Each of these is drawn by six horses and can carry 39 boxes or 17,160 rounds. The wagons are also ordered to be provided with "ladders;" these enable the boxes of ammunition to be carried by the leading horses of the team to such positions as could not be reached by the wagons themselves. Each horse or mule can carry four boxes by this means. Should the state of the country in which the army is acting render it necessary to adopt any other method of transporting this reserve, the means by which it is to be accomplished are to be determined by the Commander of the Forces, and carried out by the Royal Artillery. This first reserve is always to be at hand, and the wagons containing it are to be in some spot easily accessible to the troops, so that no delay may occur in renewing the supply to any corps which has exhausted the contents of the men's pouches.

Second Reserve. The second reserve (40 rounds per man) is also to be conveyed by the Royal Artillery in wagons of the service, or by such other means as circumstances may require. It is always to be kept up with the army, and as far as practicable out of reach of the enemy's fire.

Third Reserve. The third reserve of 50 rounds per man is carried in charge of the Military Store Department, and should not exceed an ordinary two days' march in rear of the army; it is to be advanced to the front at the discretion of the Commander of the Forces, who will direct its transport to be provided in such manner as may be most convenient.

Should the base of operations where the grand depôt of reserve is placed, be further distant than an ordinary two days' march from the place where the third reserve is stationed, intermediate reserves will be required: the officer commanding the artillery and the chief military store officer should report upon the organization and disposition of these to the Commander of the Forces, who will determine the course to be followed, so as to ensure a regular and sufficient supply of ammunition from the grand depôt of reserve for the use of the army.

The 1st and 2nd reserves are to be completed from the third and other reserves in charge for the Military Store Department, upon requisitions from the officer commanding the Royal Artillery supported by receipts for the issues which have been made to the troops.

On emergency however, the military store officers are to make issues on requisitions from officers commanding the Royal Artillery reserves,

AMMUNITION.

but such issues will require the covering authority of the Adjutant General.

Before issuing the boxes containing ammunition to the *second* reserve, the screws securing the lids are to be removed in the presence of the officer or non-commissioned officer to whom the boxes are to be delivered.

As a general rule the proportion of small-arm ammunition sent with an army will be about 1,000 rounds per man, in the case of an expeditionary force about 10,000 strong, but for a larger army the number of rounds would be specially considered ; the whole of this quantity is to be sent ready packed in boxes adapted to the ammunition wagons, and suited in weight and construction for being conveyed on pack saddles. After the troops are supplied and the reserves completed as mentioned, the main quantity will be kept in store at the grand depôt or base of operations. General Reserve.

Empty boxes are to be taken care of and returned by the troops to the officer commanding the artillery reserves, who will return them to the store department by the artillery wagons sent to be replenished from the third reserve. In order that they may be refilled the chief military store officer is always to keep a sufficient quantity packed in boxes to complete the three field reserve proportions.

For regulations respecting ammunition, *see* Queen's Regulations, page 96, § 18, and pages 105 to 109 ; also War Office Circulars, 413, 12th April 1859 ; 416, 25th April 1859 ; 417, 25th April 1859 ; 590, 16th May 1860 ; 620, 17th August 1860 ; 626, 30th August 1860 ; 657, 20th December 1860 ; 677, 20th April 1861.

Regulations respecting reserves of ammunition in the field and in garrison are contained in Circular Memorandum, Horse Guards, No. 120, 21st March 1861.

CLOTHING AND NECESSARIES.

Standard patterns of clothing and necessaries have been approved by Her Majesty, and a set of the various articles sealed by the authority of the inspecting officer acting under orders of the Field Marshal Commanding in Chief, will be sent for the information and guidance of officers commanding battalions or corps. When fresh supplies are received they are to be compared with these patterns.

No officer is to allow any articles of appointments, clothing, or necessaries differing from the sealed patterns, to be adopted without the authority of the Field Marshal Commanding in Chief. Should any case of urgent or unavoidable necessity arise, so as to require a deviation to be made, the same is to be reported to the Field Marshal Commanding in Chief, for Her Majesty's consideration. No deviation from the regulation respecting clothing or necessaries is to be permitted without special sanction communicated through the Secretary of State for War. Letters respecting clothing and necessaries addressed to the Secretary of State for War by officers commanding regiments and corps are to be in duplicate and on half margin.

The latest regulations respecting clothing and necessaries are contained in the Royal Warrant, dated 2nd January 1865, and published in W.O. Circular No. 891, 2nd January 1865, the appendix of which contains fac-similes of all the printed W.O. forms connected with the several articles; these will be supplied upon demands addressed to the Secretary of State for War, describing accurately the form required.

Incidental expenses connected with clothing and necessaries are to be charged in the regimental pay list, supported by a voucher on W.O. Form No. 616.

Special application must be made for authority to make any charge not authorized by regulation.

All sums received on account of clothing and necessaries will in like manner be credited in the pay list under their respective heads, supported by W.O. Form, No. 617, and vouchers detailing the source from which the credit has been received.

The paymaster will make such advances to the quartermaster from time to time as may be considered necessary, upon requisitions from the latter officer, approved and signed by the officer commanding. But no advances should be charged in the paymaster's accounts unless supported by details of the expenditure upon a bill receipted by the tradesman or person who performs the work.

In depôt battalions the demands for advances of money for each depôt will be made by the quartermaster to the paymaster of the battalion.

A separate account will be kept for each depôt, as well as one for the staff of the depôt battalion.

Conveyance. Upon the removal of a regiment or depôt from one station to another, the expense of conveying such surplus clothing and necessaries as are unavoidably in store will be defrayed by the public; the sum actually expended may be charged in the pay list, properly supported by vouchers.

Store chests for the carriage of surplus clothing and necessaries will be provided, when actually required, at the public expense, upon application to the Secretary of State for War. The number allowed is not to exceed two for the service companies of each infantry regiment, and one for each depôt. When application for a renewal of these articles is made, a statement must be forwarded by the officer commanding, showing how long they have been in use, and the circumstances under which they have become unserviceable.

CLOTHING AND NECESSARIES.

Clothing.

Requisitions. All requisitions for the clothing of infantry corps are to be made out in duplicate on the prescribed forms, and in time of peace forwarded to the Secretary of State for War : they are to be signed by the quartermaster and officer commanding the regiment or corps, who will be held responsible that the forms of requisition are strictly adhered to in every instance, and that the columns showing the effective strength of the regiment in non-commissioned officers and men, and those showing the quantities of clothing in store and required for the year, are properly filled up ; a size roll is to be correctly and carefully filled in with all the information requisite for making the garments of the proper size.

The periods at which the requisitions are to be forwarded from the several stations are as follow :—

Great Britain, Ireland, and Channel Islands	9 months before the clothing is due.
Mediterranean	10 months before the clothing is due.
St. Helena, and West Coast of Africa	12 months before the clothing is due.
North America, West Indies, and Bermuda	
Ceylon	
Australian Colonies	
China	14 months before the clothing is due.
Mauritius	
Cape of Good Hope	
British Columbia	

The times for sending in the yearly requisitions must be strictly adhered to ; and in cases where uncontrollable circumstances may occasion any delay in forwarding them, a special report of the same must be made by the officer commanding the regiment or corps to the Secretary of State for War.

Soldiers under instruction at Kneller Hall will receive their clothing at that establishment. The Commandant will forward to the War Office the usual requisitions and size rolls, intimating to the officers commanding the several corps to which the men belong that he has done so.

Clothing when in the field. Demands for *regular* clothing for an army in the field are to be passed through the Adjutant-General at the regulated periods to the Chief Military Store Officer, who will forward them to the Director of Stores, by whom the requisite supplies will be obtained from the Clothing Department.

The articles included under the head of clothing that are issued to the several classes of infantry are as follows :—

Guards.

Pipe-major and Pipers of Scots Fusilier Guards not included.

Article	Frequency	Ranks
Chaco	Biennially	Time beater.
Bear skin cap and bag	Every six years	Other ranks.
Tunic	Annually	All ranks.
Tunic, undress	—	1st class staff-serjeants, band-serjeants, regimental clerk, regimental drill-serjeant.
,, ,,	Biennially	Battalion drill-serjeant, hospital-serjeant.
Shell jacket, white	Annually	Other ranks.
Shell jacket, scarlet	,,	Time beater, besides tunic and white jacket.
Trousers, cloth	Annually	All ranks.
,, serge	Biennially	,,
Boots, two pairs	Annually	All ranks.

E

PERSONAL EQUIPMENT.

Gloves, white leather	Annually	Staff-serjeants and serjeants.
Sashes, silk	Every two years	Staff-serjeants, 1st class, band-serjeants, drum-major, and pipe-major.
Sashes, worsted	,, ,,	Staff-serjeants, 2nd class, and serjeants.
Sword knots, gold	Annually	Staff-serjeants, 1st class, drum-major, regimental drill-serjeant, regimental clerk.
Tassels, gold lace, for drum-major's staff.	,,	Drum-major.
Drum carriage, gold lace, bass drum.	,,	One per regiment.
Drum carriage, gold lace, side drum.	,,	Two ,,
Instrument slings, gold lace	,,	Eleven ,,

Pipe-major and Pipers of Scots Fusilier Guards.

Glengarry cap	Annually	Pipe-major and pipers.
Tunic	,,	,, ,,
Shell jacket	,,	,, ,,
Plaid	Every three years	,, ,,
Kilt	Annually	,, ,,
Shoes, two pairs	,,	,, ,,

Regiments of the Line, including Rifle Corps but not Highlanders, except those serving at Cape of Good Hope, Ceylon, Mauritius, St. Helena, Hong Kong, and the West Indies exclusive of Bermuda.

Chaco and cover	Triennially*	All ranks.
Tunic	Annually	,,
Trousers, cloth	,,	,,
,, serge†	Biennially	,,
Boots, two pairs	Annually	,,
Sash, silk	Every two years, but not issued to rifles.	1st class staff-serjeants, drum or bugle major, and band-serjeant.
,, worsted	,, ,,	2nd class staff-serjeants and serjeants.

Regiments of the Line and Rifle Corps serving in the West Indies, exclusive of Bermuda.

Chaco and cover	Triennially	All ranks.
Tunic	Annually	,,
Trousers, serge	,,	,,
,, ,,	Biennially	,,
Boots, two pairs	Annually	,,
Socks, cotton, three pairs	,,	Staff-serjeants and serjeants.
,, ,, two pairs	,,	Other ranks.
Sash, silk	Every four years, but not issued to rifles.	1st class staff-serjeants, drum or bugle major, and band-serjeant.
,, worsted	,, ,,	2nd class staff-serjeants and serjeants.

Should the second pair of serge trousers due biennially not be required, compensation at the rate laid down in page 72 will be credited to the soldier, and the sum is to be expended, on the 1st April of the following year, in such articles as the soldier may require.

Should the second pair of boots, due on 1st October, not be required, compensation at the rate laid down will be credited to the soldier, and the sum is to be expended, on the 1st January following, in such articles as the soldier may require. These sums are to be charged in the pay list, supported by certificate on W.O. Form No. 947.

---

* If of cork, quadrennially.   † In rifle corps tartan.

CLOTHING.

Regiments of the Line, including Rifle Corps but not Highlanders, serving in Cape of Good Hope, St. Helena, China, and Mediterranean.

Wicker helmet and puggaree in China.	Biennially	All ranks.
Chaco and white cover at St. Helena, Cape, and Mediterranean.	Triennially	,,
Tunic	Biennially	,,
Serge frock in the year in which tunics are not supplied.	,,	,,
Trousers, cloth	Annually	,,
,, serge or tartan	Biennially	,,
Boots, two pairs	Annually	,,
Sash, silk	Every two years, but not issued to rifles.	1st class staff-serjeants, drum-major, and band-serjeant.
,, worsted	,, ,,	2nd class staff-serjeants and serjeants.

In the year in which the tunic is not issued, compensation at the rate of 1*l.* 10*s.* 3*d.* for staff-serjeants, drum-major and band-serjeant; 10*s.* 0*d.* second class staff-serjeants and serjeants; and 8*s.* 6*d.* for rank and file, will be credited annually to each man. One-fourth of the amount may be expended at the end of each quarter in such articles as the soldier may require, and is to be charged in the pay list, supported by certificate on W.O. Form 946.

Should the second pair of boots, due on 1st October, not be required, a further compensation at the rate laid down in par. 72 will be granted, to be expended on the 1st January following in such articles as the soldier may require. These sums are to be charged in the pay list, supported by certificate on W.O. Form No. 947.

Regiments of the Line, including Rifle Corps but not Highlanders, serving at Ceylon and Mauritius.

Wicker helmet and puggaree	Biennially	All ranks.
Tunic	,,	,,
Serge frock in the year in which tunics are not supplied.	,,	,,
Trousers, serge or tartan	Annually	,,
,,	Biennially	,,
Boots, two pairs	Annually	,,
Socks, cotton, three pairs	,,	Staff serjeants, serjeants, and drum-major.
,, ,, two ,,	,,	Other ranks.
Sash, silk	Every two years, but not issued to rifles.	1st class staff-serjeants, drum-major, and band-serjeant.
,, worsted	,, ,,	2nd class staff-serjeants and serjeants.

In the year in which the tunic is not issued, compensation at the rate of 1*l.* 10*s.* 3*d.* for 1st class staff-serjeants, drum-major, and band-serjeant; 10*s.* 0*d.* for 2nd class staff-serjeants and serjeants, and 8*s.* 6*d.* for rank and file, will be credited annually to each man. One-fourth of the amount may be expended at the end of each quarter in such articles as the soldier may require, and charged in the pay list, supported by certificate on W.O. Form No. 946.

Should the second pair of boots, due on 1st October, not be required, a further compensation at the rate laid down at page 72 will be credited, the amount to be expended on the 1st January following, in such articles as the soldier may require, and to be charged in the pay list, supported by certificate on W.O. Form No. 947.

Highland Regiments wearing the Kilt.

Item		Frequency	Ranks
Bonnet every eight years (unless otherwise ordered at tropical stations).	-	-	All ranks.
Bonnet, cover, oilskin	-	Biennially	,,
Hackle feather	-	,,	,,
Coat	-	Annually	,,
White shell jacket	-	,,	,,
Kilt, to be made into trews at the expense of the soldier at the expiration of the period of duration.		,,	,,
Plaid	-	Every three years	Staff serjeants and band piper.
Plaid scarf	-	,, ,,	,,
Gaiters, pair	-	Annually	All ranks.
Shoes, two pairs	-	,,	,,
Sash, silk	-	Every two years	1st class staff-serjeants, drum-major, pipe-major, and band-serjeant.
,, worsted	-	,, ,,	2nd class staff serjeants and serjeants.

Highland Regiments wearing the Trews.

Item		Frequency	Ranks
Bonnet	Regiments wearing the bonnet.	Every eight years	All ranks.
Bonnet cover, oilskin.	,, ,,	Biennially	,,
Hackle feather, with oilskin cover.	,, ,,	,,	,,
Chaco and cover	For regiments wearing the chaco.	Every four years	,,
Coat	-	Annually	,,
White shell jacket (except 91st Regt.)		,,	,,
Trews	-	,,	,,
,,	-	Biennially	,,
Shoes, two pairs	-	Annually	,,
Sash, silk	-	Every two years	1st class staff-serjeants, drum-major, pipe-major, and band-serjeant.
,, worsted	-	,, ,,	2nd class staff-serjeants and serjeants.

Highland corps, when serving in the Cape of Good Hope, Ceylon, Mauritius, St. Helena, and China, shall receive the same clothing as at other stations, with the exception of the coat, and the second pair of boots and shoes, which may be supplied biennially; and, in the alternate years, the soldier shall be credited with the regulated compensation for the same, according to the rates herein-after provided at page 72, one-fourth to be expended quarterly in such articles as the soldier may require, and charged in the pay list, supported by certificate on W.O. Form No. 946.

Ceylon Rifle Regiment.

Item	Frequency	Ranks
Wicker helmet and puggaree	Biennially	All ranks.
Tunic, dress	Annually	For the European non-commissioned officers.
Jacket, undress	,,	,, ,,
Trousers	,,	,, ,,
,,	Biennially	,, ,,
Jacket, dress	,,	For native non-commissioned officers and men.
,, undress	,,	,, ,,
Trousers	Annually	,, ,,

Sixteen shillings in money to each serjeant, and 12s. to each soldier of other ranks, annually, in lieu of boots; to be paid half on 1st April and half on 1st October, and charged in the pay list, supported by certificate on W.O. Form, No. 947.

Cape Mounted Riflemen.

Head dress and holland bag	-	Quadrennially -	All ranks.
Tunic - - - -	-	Biennially	,,
Jacket, stable - -	-	,,	,,
Waistcoat, flannel	-	,,	,,
Boots, Wellington, pair -	-	,,	,,
Gloves, pair of -	-	Annually -	,,
Boots, ancle, pair	-	,,	,,
Overalls, strapped and cuffed with cloth.		,,	,,
Drawers, cotton -	-	,,	,,
Trousers, cloth -	-	Biennially	,,

West India Regiments.

Fez and two turban cloths	-	Biennially	- All ranks.
Jacket - - -	-	,,	,,
Waistcoat -	-	Annually -	,,
Breeches, dress -	-	,,	,,
,, undress	-	Biennially	,,
Leggings, one pair	-	,,	,,
Gaiters, pair	-	Annually -	,,
Stockings, two pairs	-	,,	,,
Shoes, two pairs	-	,,	,,

The Royal Canadian Rifle regiment is entitled to the same clothing as other rifle corps.

Infantry serving in the North American Colonies.

The following articles of winter equipment are to be provided for all ranks, viz.:—

    One fur cap.
    One pair Canadian boots.
    Two flannel waistcoats.
    Two pair of flannel or worsted drawers.

An allowance of 40s. may be charged for each non-commissioned officer and soldier, present and effective at the commencement of his first winter, in aid of the expense of these articles in the event of their not being supplied from the public stores.

This allowance is only to be drawn once for each soldier, and is to be charged in the pay list, supported by a certificate signed by the commanding officer, stating that the sum has been expended in the supply of the articles above named, and that no men have been included, except those who to the best of his belief had not received the allowance previously, since their arrival in the country. Volunteers, or men transferred from other regiments who have already received the allowance, will not be entitled to it again, but must bring their winter equipment with them. Men re-enlisting will, however, be entitled to the allowance on the 1st October following their re-enlistment.

Each soldier present and effective in the North American colonies on the 1st October of each subsequent year will be allowed 7s. 6d. to defray the expense of renewals or repairs to the above equipment.

Whenever the regimental cap in the infantry serving on the North American station can be made to last an additional year, the soldier shall receive the regulated compensation in lieu of a cap for one year, the amount of which shall be credited to the soldier's account, in aid of the expense of renewing or repairing his winter clothing.

PERSONAL EQUIPMENT.

Schoolmasters.

Cap	Biennially.
Frock coat, with collar badges of his rank	Annually.
Shoulder-knots, pair	Biennially.
Trousers, one pair	Annually.
,, ,,	Biennially.
Boots, 1*l*. in lieu of, annually	one half on 1st April. one half on 1st October.

Cloak every ten years.
Silk sash every four years.
Great coat, in North America only.

The coat and trousers will be supplied in materials, and the following sums will be allowed for making up, viz. :—

Frock coat	10*s*.
Trousers, per pair	3*s*.

which sum, and the compensation in lieu of boots, is to be charged in the pay list, supported by receipts of tradesmen and the schoolmaster.

Requisitions, according to W.O. Form, No. 76, for the articles required, are to be sent to the Secretary of State for War, through the officer commanding the regiment or garrison to which the schoolmaster may be attached, with the demands for other regimental or garrison clothing, and at the dates laid down at page 65, for troops serving at the various stations. If attached to Royal Artillery or Royal Engineers the requisitions to be sent through their respective deputy adjutants-general.

Head dresses. The *bear-skin caps* of the Guards are very nearly identical in pattern for the three regiments, and are of one quality for all ranks. The Grenadiers have a white plume on the right side, and the Coldstreams a red plume on the left side. The Scots Fusiliers have no plume.

The *bonnets* with black ostrich plumes for Highland regiments are of two qualities, one for staff-serjeants and the other for all other non-commissioned officers and men.

The new pattern cloth *chacos* of the Line are of two qualities, one for 1st class staff-serjeants, drum and bugle majors, and band-serjeant, and one for all other ranks. All are provided with oilskin covers.

Qualities of cloth. The cloth used for the tunics and coats of infantry is of four qualities, viz. *staff cloth* (scarlet) for 1st class staff-serjeants, drum and bugle-majors, pipe-major, and band-serjeant, and band of Guards.

Scarlet cloth for 2nd class staff-serjeants, serjeants, and band of Guards, and also for serjeants of Royal Engineers.

Scarlet cloth for 2nd class staff-serjeants and serjeants of Line, and rank and file of Guards and Royal Engineers.

Red cloth for rank and file and drummers of Line.

Red serge for serge frocks is of one quality for all ranks.

White cloth is of three qualities, viz., one for tunics and jackets of bandmaster-serjeants and band-serjeants, one for tunics and jackets of musicians, and a white kersey for the jackets of Guards and Highlanders.

Green cloth for Rifles is of six kinds, one for tunics and jackets of 1st class staff-serjeants, bugle-major, and band-serjeant ; one (doeskin) for trousers of the same ranks ; one for tunics and jackets of 2nd class staff-serjeants, serjeants, buglers, and musicians ; one (kersey) for trousers of the same ranks ; one for tunics and jackets of rank and file, **and a** kersey for trousers of rank and file.

CLOTHING.

The *black cloth* for trousers is of four qualities, viz., doeskin, for 1st class staff-serjeants, drum and bugle-majors, and band-serjeants of Royal Engineers; Oxford mixed, for 2nd class staff-serjeants, serjeants, and band of Guards; Oxford mixed, for 2nd class staff-serjeants, serjeants, and musicians of Line; Oxford mixed for rank and file.

The *tartan cloth* for summer trousers, which is black for Guards, green for Rifles, as well as the *blue serge* for summer trousers of the Line, is of two qualities, viz., one for staff, and one for other ranks.

The *tartan* for the kilts and trews of Highland regiments is of special pattern for each regiment. The qualities are three in number, issued to the same ranks as receive the several qualities of coats. The plaids are of the same quality and pattern as the kilts.

Sashes are of two qualities, one made of crimson silk, and the other of worsted; they are made in two sizes, one 56 inches and the other 53 inches between the tassels; the length of the latter is 10 inches. Sashes.

Boots are of one quality for all ranks. They are made in 13 different sizes, the smallest marked No. 3, and the largest No. 15. The proportion generally required for each 100 men is as follows:— Boots and shoes.

No. 5 size	3 pairs.
„ 6 „	12 „
„ 7 „	31 „
„ 8 „	35 „
„ 9 „	11 „
„ 10 „	6 „
„ 11 „	2 „
	100

Officers commanding may, however, demand any proportion of the several sizes that they require.

Shoes for Highland regiments wearing the kilt, and pipers of other regiments, are also of one quality, and made in sizes similar to the boots.

Forage caps are of three qualities, one for 1st class staff-serjeants, one for serjeants, and one for rank and file.

Drum-majors of the Guards have a *state dress*, consisting of a tunic of velvet richly laced and embroidered, with a velvet cap of jockey pattern.

The *band of the Guards* have their tunics laced with gold. The undress tunics for staff-serjeants of the Guards differs from the dress tunic in having no chevrons on it.

Badges and Distinctions of Rank.—The several ranks of the non-commissioned officers are shown by chevrons worn on the right arm between the shoulder and the elbow, as follows:— Distinctions of rank.

Serjeant-major, quartermaster-serjeant, serjeant instructor of musketry, drum or bugle-major, and band-serjeant, chevron on tunic composed of four bars of double half-inch gold lace. The chevron of the serjeant-major is surmounted by a crown, that of the serjeant-instructor of musketry by a pair of muskets crossed, and that of the drum or bugle-major by a drum or bugle respectively. The bandmaster-serjeant has no chevrons, but shoulder knots of gold cord; paymaster-serjeants and orderly-room clerks who have attained the rank and privileges of colour-serjeants, have three bar chevrons of double gold lace.

Colour-serjeants,—colour badge on tunic consisting of one bar of double gold lace surmounted by a device representing a union flag, embroidered in silk, and cross-swords in silver. On serge frocks and shell jackets three bars of single gold lace surmounted by a gold crown are worn.

Second-class staff-serjeants or serjeants and lance-serjeants have three bars half-inch white worsted lace.

Distinctions of rank.

Corporals have a chevron of two bars of the same; lance-corporals have one bar. All these are of double lace for tunics, serge frocks, and jackets.

Non-commissioned officers of *Guards, light infantry, Fusiliers, and Highlanders* wear the chevrons and badges on both arms, but colour-serjeants of Light Infantry, Fusiliers, and Highlanders have three bars of half-inch double gold lace on the left arm of the tunic instead of a second colour badge.

The badges of the Guards differ somewhat from those of the Line, the serjeant-major's chevrons having the royal arms embroidered upon them, and the colour-serjeant's a colour badge of special pattern for each regiment worked in silk over the bars.

Full serjeants and musicians of Guards have the chevrons of gold lace instead of worsted. Acting serjeants, corporals, and acting corporals wear similar chevrons to the corresponding ranks in the line.

Pioneers of Grenadier Guards are distinguished by a badge on the left arm consisting of a grenade and two axes crossed worked in worsted.

Non-commissioned officers of 60th *Rifles* and Rifle Brigade have chevrons on both arms. The Ceylon and Royal Canadian Rifles wear them on one arm only. They are similar badges to those of the same rank in other regiments of the line, but they are all made in black worsted lace. The badge for colour-serjeants consists of one bar on the right arm surmounted by a wreath containing a crown, cross swords, and a bugle, embroidered in silk, and three bars on the left arm.

Shooting badges.

Shooting badges are worn above the cuff of the right arm. They are of three kinds, viz. :—

1st Prize, crossed muskets, embroidered in gold lace, surmounted by a crown.
2nd Prize, cross muskets, embroidered in gold lace.
3rd Prize, cross muskets, embroidered in white worsted, except in regiments having white, yellow or buff facings, in which cases they are worked in red worsted.

In the 60th (Royal) Rifles the 1st and 2d prizes are worked in scarlet silk, and the 3rd prize in scarlet worsted. For other Rifle corps the 1st and 2nd prizes are worked in green silk, and the 3rd prize in green worsted.

Good-conduct badges.

Good-conduct badges are made of single worsted lace, black for Rifles and white for other regiments, and are worn over the cuff of the right arm. Musicians of Guards have them of gold lace.

The lace with which the tunics of *drummers and buglers* are trimmed is of a special pattern for each regiment, and represents the livery lace of the landed proprietor or other person of distinction who first raised the regiment, and was commissioned as its colonel.

Board of Survey.

When the clothing of a regiment or corps arrives at the place where the troops are stationed, it is to be immediately inspected by a Board of Survey, composed of the three senior officers present with the regiment (the commanding officer excepted), and in the case of the supply of the annual clothing of the whole force, where practicable, of an officer of another corps, and an officer of the Military Store or Barrack Department, and the proceedings are to be forwarded in duplicate by the officer commanding to the Secretary of State for War through the Adjutant-General on W.O. Form No. 620. To enable the board to arrive at a correct decision, a sealed pattern of each article will accompany the supply, and after serving the purposes of comparison, until the next sealed patterns are received with the next annual supply of clothing, will be taken into wear.

In the event of any deficiencies in or damage to the articles received, or their not being equal to sealed pattern in materials or workmanship, or not corresponding in measurement to the size tickets affixed to the garments, (a number of which, not under 10 per cent. on the whole, will be fitted to men of corresponding measurements in presence of the board,) a statement of the same is to be made in the report of the board, and an estimate furnished of the cost at which they can be rendered fit for issue.

Whenever regimental boards find it necessary to condemn any articles issued from the Government stores on account of damage received in transit, or inferiority to pattern, such articles are not to be considered as finally rejected.

The officer convening the board will make a representation on the subject to the senior officer at the station, who after making such inquiry or personal inspection as he may think fit, will, in the case of regiments at home, refer the report with his opinion to the Adjutant-General; and in the case of regiments abroad, will decide whether the articles condemned by the board shall be taken into use or not. In either case the proceedings of the board, with a special report, are invariably to be forwarded in duplicate to the Secretary of State for War through the Adjutant-General.

The report of the proceedings of the board of officers must in all cases be entered in the regimental books, in order that there may be a proper record of it.

The officer commanding is to make a report and forward the same in duplicate to the Secretary of State for War through the Adjutant-General at the end of the military year, stating his opinion as to the quality of the clothing supplied, and whether it has worn well; he will specify any defects either in quality or make, to which he may think it advisable to call attention.

When clothing is received at the head-quarters of a regiment or corps, the officer commanding will take the best measures for forwarding it to the detachments, wherever they may be stationed. The expense incurred for carriage must be charged in the clothing account and included in the pay list, supported by vouchers of receipt for the money expended. In the colonies, the clothing for men at out-stations is to be forwarded through the Commissariat Department. *Detachments.*

The clothing supplied to a regiment or corps will be accounted for yearly in a clothing return, according to W.O. Form No. 602, blank forms of which will be sent to officers commanding depôt and regiments at home and abroad. This return is to be forwarded to the Secretary of State for War, direct, as soon as possible after the 31st March of each year. The object of this return is to show how the new and part-worn clothing has been disposed of. *Account of clothing.*

Officers commanding troops or companies will furnish at the end of each quarter a quittance roll, bearing the receipt of every non-commissioned officer and man of the troop or company, for all articles of clothing or compensation in lieu thereof received during the quarter; these returns are to be made out upon W.O. Form No. 629, and to be kept as records in the Quartermaster's office. Any compensation in money is to be charged in the pay list, supported by a certificate of the commanding officer upon W.O. Form No. 604, showing the articles the men have received and the compensation paid in lieu of those not issued.

The clothing for infantry corps will be supplied, made up and complete, with the exception of that for the serjeant-major, quartermaster-serjeant, serjeant instructor of musketry, bandmaster-serjeant, band-serjeant, drum-major, and band, and ten suits per company, which may be demanded in materials. *Altering and fitting.*

Altering and fitting.

All good-conduct badges are to be demanded with the clothing, but no charge will be admitted for sewing them on.

Such suits as are supplied in materials will be made up in the regiment under the direction of the master tailor, at the following rates:—

		s.	d.
Tunics	1st class staff-serjeants, drum-major, and band-serjeant*	8	0
	2nd class staff-serjeants, serjeants, drummers, and band†	5	0
	Rank and file‡	3	4
Jacket	1st class staff-serjeants, drum-major, and band-serjeant	4	0
Kilt	All ranks wearing it	0	9½
Trousers	Cloth or serge — 1st class staff-serjeants, drum-major, and band-serjeant	3	0
,,	Cloth — 2nd class staff-serjeants, serjeants, and band	1	5
	Serge — 2nd class staff-serjeants, serjeants, and band	1	2
,,	Cloth or serge. Rank and file, and drummers	1	2

The sums expended for making up the clothing sent in materials are to be charged in the pay list, supported by voucher, according to W.O. Form No. 949.

Should any alteration be required in made-up garments, new or part worn, the actual and unavoidable expense of the same will be allowed as a charge against the public where there is no regularly enlisted master tailor. The amount is not to exceed :—

8d. for each tunic.
3d. for each pair of overalls or cloth trousers.
2d. for each pair of serge trousers.

In Highland regiments :—

8d. for each tunic. | 2d. for each pair of trews.
3d. for each waistcoat. | 2d. for each kilt.

In regiments or corps provided with a specially enlisted serjeant-master tailor, the expense of the necessary alterations to the annual clothing will be defrayed by him out of the allowance of 44l. a year granted him for that purpose.

In the Ceylon Rifles 8d. per suit will be allowed every second year for the alteration of the clothing.

All clothing remaining in store must be fitted and issued before any portion of a new supply is begun upon, and all garments of every supply that can be made available by alteration must be appropriated and issued.

Commanding officers will see that all such alterations are carried out to the full extent before any report of inability to fit the corps is made.

Tunics may be reduced to almost any extent in the size of the body, and most of them may be reduced to fit a shorter man.

There is only a quarter of an inch of cloth in the length of the back for every inch in the height of the man, and a reduction of one inch of cloth or four sizes of height, may be easily made in the length of any tunic.

Trousers may be similarly treated.

Issue.

Soldiers of all ranks shall be provided if possible by the 1st of April in each year with such articles as are required to complete their clothing for the ensuing year. Boots and shoes however, are furnished twice in each year, one pair being issued on the 1st of October.

Marking.

All articles of clothing are to be marked with the number and battalion of the regiment, and also the name and regimental number of the wearer.

Tunics are marked with white paint, inside across the middle of the back ; trousers with black paint on the waistband.

---

* Highlanders, 12s. ; Rifles, 18s.   † Highlanders, 6s. 3d. ; Rifles, 5s. 3d
‡ Highlanders, 6s. ; Rifles, 3s. 4d.

CLOTHING.

Chacos, boots, and shoes are marked by means of branding irons with the number of the regiment and regimental number of the wearers; the former are marked on the under side of the peak and the latter inside the upper leather.

Recruits finally approved between 1st April and 30th September shall receive— **Clothing of Recruits.**

    One new tunic.
    One new pair cloth trousers.
    One new pair serge trousers.
    One pair of new boots.
    One new white jacket.*

One pair of new boots, to last till 1st October in ensuing year.

Men joining in this period will not be entitled to boots on 1st October in the year in which they join.

Recruits joining between 1st October and 31st December :—

  One new pair of boots, and part-worn clothing equal to that in wear at time, or such part-worn articles as may be in the store and the remainder new.

Should there be no part-worn clothing in store, new clothing as above. In this case the recruit will receive on the 1st April following :—

    One new tunic.
    One new pair cloth trousers.
    One new pair serge trousers.

  And on the 1st October a new pair of boots.

Recruits joining between 1st January and 31st March :—

    One new tunic.
    One new white jacket.*
    One new pair cloth trousers.
    One new pair serge trousers.
    Two new pair boots.

To last to 31st March of the following year, and a pair of new cloth trousers and a new pair of boots on the 1st October after final approval.

Recruits joining Highland regiments wearing the kilt, if finally approved between 1st April and 30th September :—

One new coat.	One new pair gaiters.
One new kilt.	One new waistcoat with sleeves.
One new pair shoes.	One new plaid.

Those joining in this period will not be entitled to shoes on the 1st October.

Recruits joining between 1st October and 31st December :—

  One new pair of shoes and part-worn clothing equal to that in wear by the rest of the corps, or such part-worn articles as may be in store and the remainder new.

Should there be no part-worn clothing in store, complete new clothing. In this case the recruit will receive on 1st April following :—

    One new coat.
    One new pair gaiters.
    One new kilt.

  And on the 1st October, one pair of shoes.

Recruits joining between 1st January and 31st March :—

One new coat.	Two new pairs of shoes.
One new waistcoat with sleeves.	One new pair gaiters.
One new kilt.	One new plaid.

To last till the 31st March of the following year, and a waistcoat with sleeves and a pair of shoes on the 1st October after final approval.

---

* For the Guards only.

PERSONAL EQUIPMENT.

Highland Regiments wearing trews. If finally approved between 1st April and 30th September :—

| One new coat. | Two new pairs of boots. |
| One new waistcoat with sleeves. | Two new pairs trews. |

Those joining in this period will not be entitled to boots on 1st October.

Recruits joining between 1st October and 31st December, one new pair of boots, and part-worn clothing equal to that in wear by the rest of the corps, or such part-worn articles as may be in store, and the remainder new.

Should there be no part-worn clothing in store, complete new clothing. In this case the recruit will receive on the 1st April following :—

One new coat.
Two new pairs trews.
And on 1st October one pair new boots.

Recruits joining between 1st January and 31st March :—

| One new coat. | Two new pair trews. |
| One new waistcoat with sleeves. | Two new pair boots. |

To last to 31st March of the following year, and a new pair of trews and a new pair of boots on 1st October after final approval.

Part-worn helmets, caps, or busbies (should there be any in store), shall in all cases be issued to recruits in the cavalry and infantry, to last till the first or second issue, according to the condition they may be in at the time the recruits receive them.

Part-worn plaids and bonnets (should there be any in store) must in all cases be issued to recruits.

Recruits of all corps or regiments entitled to the biennial issue of trousers, who may be finally approved between 1st April and 31st December, will receive the biennial trousers on the 1st April following.

If finally approved after 31st December this issue will not be made until the commencement of the second military year after enlistment.

Recruits of all mounted corps entitled to the biennial issue of boots who may be finally approved between the 1st of April and 30th of September, will receive the biennial boots on the 1st April following. Those finally approved after the 30th September will not receive the biennial boots until the commencement of the second military year after enlistment.

Transfers. Transfers to other corps will take with them their great coats, and such articles of clothing (except head dress) as can be worn in the new regiment. The expense actually and necessarily incurred for changing the facings, buttons, &c. will be allowed as a charge in the pay list if supported by a certificate from the commanding officer.

Transfers to corps where the clothing of the former regiment cannot be made available will be allowed to take with them one pair of cloth trousers or trews and one pair of boots or shoes, and will be dealt with for clothing in the new corps as recruits.

Deserters rejoining. Men who may rejoin from desertion, or who may return to their duty from confinement, if they require clothing, shall, whatever may be the date of their rejoining, be supplied with part-worn clothing when practicable; should there be none in store, they will be dealt with for clothing as recruits.

Promotions. A corporal or private who is promoted to be serjeant after the yearly issue of clothing, will when practicable, exchange clothing with his predecessor; if not practicable and the promotion takes place before 1st October, he will receive new clothing of his rank and return the old into store; if promoted on or after 1st October, he will retain his clothing, and receive the difference in money between serjeant's and rank and file clothing at the regulated rates, from the date of his promotion to the 31st March following.

When the appointment of a drummer takes place, the same rule will be observed, but no compensation granted.

When a serjeant is reduced to the ranks, an exchange of clothing should be effected with his successor if possible, or part-worn clothing will be issued to him; should there be none in store, he will be treated as a recruit, returning his former clothing into store. *Non-commissioned officers reduced.*

The clothing so returned must be in a serviceable state, after allowing for fair wear and tear, otherwise the soldier will be charged for the unnecessary damage.

Soldiers brought forward for discharge between 1st April and 31st December, will be allowed to take with them from their regiment or depôt, in addition to boots or shoes that have been six months in wear, and the biennial trousers after 12 months' wear,— *Discharged soldiers.*

    One part-worn tunic.
    One pair part-worn cloth trousers or trews.
    One pair part-worn boots or shoes (Royal Engineers excepted, if after 30th September).

These men will not be entitled to any compensation for that year's clothing.

If discharged after 31st December they will be allowed to take with them such clothing as would have become their property on the following 1st of April, except the regimental head dress, which must be returned into store, and for which no compensation will be allowed. Care is to be taken that soldiers brought up for discharge during the first quarter of the year, namely from 1st April to 30th June, receive no new clothing, but compensation up to the period of discharge.

All clothing that has been in wear the prescribed period becomes the property of the soldier when replaced by the next issue; but may be continued in wear, at the discretion of the general officer commanding, for an additional period.

The boots and shoes of soldiers becoming non-effective in corps receiving two pairs per annum will not be required to be returned into store after six months' wear, nor the biennial trousers after 12 months' wear.

All compensation when sanctioned shall be paid to non-commissioned officers and men at the rates detailed at page 72, (which show the value per month of each article detailed), the amount may, however, be expended in articles for their benefit, at the discretion of the commanding officer; the said compensation shall be paid in the currency of the country in which the regiment may be serving, at the rate at which the soldier receives his pay and other allowances. *Compensation.*

Applications for compensation in lieu of clothing, to regiments or portions of the same detached from head-quarters, must be made to the Secretary of State for War through the adjutant-general.

Applications for individuals may, however, be sent direct to the Secretary of State for War.

Claims for compensation for part of a month will be dealt with upon the following principle:—

Should the soldier have a claim for 15 or more days of a month, he will be entitled to compensation for that month.

No claim will be admitted for less than 15 days of one month.

When soldiers are sent from any regiment, corps or depôt, to another regiment, corps or depôt, or an invalid depôt for discharge or otherwise, the officer commanding is to take care that any compensation that may be due to them is paid up to the end of the month preceding that in which they leave the regiment or depôt, and that a return according to W. O. Form (No. 607, for soldiers sent to an invalid depôt, and No. 32, for those sent to other corps) is forwarded, sealed up, to the officer commanding the regiment, corps, or depôt to which the soldiers are going.

This document will be the authority upon which all further claims for compensation will be settled previous to the final discharge of the men.

All sums so paid are to be charged in the pay list, supported by the respective returns as vouchers.

When the date on which an invalid will be discharged is known, the officer commanding the division to which the soldier is attached will enter in the return received with him, and also in his pocket ledger, the amount of compensation (if any) in lieu of clothing which may have accrued to him since the date up to which he was settled with on leaving his regiment. The invalid will sign the above-mentioned return for the amount of compensation entered therein, he will also sign the entry of the same in his pocket ledger. The officer commanding his division will then hand the return to the paymaster, who will either pay the amount to the soldier or credit it in his accounts. The total amount so paid for each corps to be charged in the pay list, accompanied by an account made out according to W. O. Form, No. 612.

In the case of men being forwarded from the invalid depôt to their regiments or depôts a certified extract from the above return will be sent by the superintendent of the invalid depôt to the commanding officer, in order that the men's final claims may be settled at their regiments or depôts.

The following table shows the regulated rates of compensation for various articles of clothing.

Corps.	Articles.	Staff Serjeants.			Serjeants.			Other Ranks.		
		£	s.	d.	£	s.	d.	£	s.	d.
Foot Guards	Cap	0	1	1	0	1	1	0	1	1
	Dress tunic	0	12	6	0	5	3	0	1	11
	Undress tunic	0	5	0	0	2	8		—	
	Jacket, white	-		-	0	1	3½	0	0	6½
	Trousers, cloth, per pair	0	1	9	0	1	4	0	0	11
	Boots, per pair	0	1	5	0	1	5	0	1	5
	Gloves for serjeants, per pair	0	0	2	0	0	2		—	
	Trousers, tartan, per pair	0	0	9½	0	0	4	0	0	4
Infantry, Battalion, Fusileer, and Rifle Regiments, Garrison Staff, Recruiting Districts, and Invalid Depôts	Cap	0	0	2¾	0	0	1¼	0	0	1¼
	Tunic	0	3	10	0	1	6¼	0	1	4½
	Trousers, cloth, per pair	0	1	6¼	0	0	11	0	0	8¾
	Boots, per pair	0	1	5	0	1	5	0	1	5
	Socks, per pair	0	0	0¾	0	0	0¾	0	0	0¾
	Trousers, serge, per pair	0	0	7¾	0	0	3½	0	0	3½
	Serge frock	0	1	3¾	0	0	8¼	0	0	8
Highland Regiments wearing the kilt or trews	Coat	0	5	0	0	1	10¼	0	1	6
	White jacket	0	2	1	0	1	0½	0	0	6¼
	Shoes, per pair	0	1	3	0	1	3	0	1	3
	Bonnet	0	0	8	0	0	6	0	0	6
	Kilt	0	3	0	0	1	5	0	1	1
	Plaid	0	0	4¼	0	0	1¼	0	0	1¼
	*Trews, per pair	0	2	0	0	1	4½	0	1	1½
	Cloth chaco	0	0	3¾	0	0	1½	0	0	1½
	Gaiters, per pair	0	0	1½	0	0	1½	0	0	1½

* Compensation for the biennial trews to be calculated at one half these rates.

CLOTHING.

Corps.	Articles.	Staff Serjeants.			Serjeants.			Other Ranks.		
		£	s.	d.	£	s.	d.	£	s.	d.
West India Regiments	Fez - - - -	0	0	1¼	0	0	1¼	0	0	1¼
	Turban cloth - -	0	0	1½	0	0	1½	0	0	1½
	Jacket, red, without sleeves - - -	0	0	11	0	0	3	0	0	2¾
	Waistcoat, white, with sleeves - - -	0	2	1¾	0	0	6¼	0	0	5¾
	*Trousers, per pair -	0	1	10¼	0	0	9¼	0	0	9¼
	Gaiters, per pair -	0	0	1¼	0	0	1¼	0	0	1¼
	Stockings, per pair -	0	0	1¼	0	0	1¼	0	0	1¼
	Shoes, per pair -	0	1	3	0	1	3	0	1	3
	Leggings, per pair -	0	0	1¼	0	0	1¼	0	0	1¼
	Breeches, Dungaree, per pair - -	-	-	-	0	0	3¾	0	0	3¾
Ceylon Rifles - -	Tunic - - -	0	4	2	0	1	7¾	—		
	Jacket, dress -	0	1	1½	0	0	6	0	0	6
	†Jackets, undress -	0	2	3	0	1	0	0	1	0
	Trousers, cloth, per pair	0	1	8	0	1	1	0	0	9
	Trousers, serge, per pair	0	0	7¾	0	0	3½	—		

Disposal of surplus.

Surplus clothing remaining in store until the next general issue must be carefully preserved from injury by moth, damp, or any other cause ; and any loss arising from negligence in this respect must be defrayed by the person in whose charge the articles were placed, and whose duty it was to have them frequently examined and preserved from harm.

Any new articles of clothing which may be surplus in store, and not likely to be wanted by the corps for the current year, may be sold to such soldiers as may require them at the prices fixed for compensation ; the amount to be credited in the pay list, supported by certificate according to W. O. Form, No. 605.

Part-worn clothing.

Part-worn clothing in other arms of the service at home, which has not been in wear the prescribed period, or such a time as to make it the property of the soldier, is to be taken into store by the quartermaster, and issued to recruits (or others dealt with as such) or sold by auction; in the latter case the proceeds must be credited in the pay list, supported by certificate according to W. O. Form, No. 605.

When a regiment is divided into depôts and service companies or troops, the part-worn clothing at the depôt is to be dealt with as above stated. The part-worn clothing that may remain in the service companies serving in Great Britain, Ireland, and the Channel Islands, is to be sent to the depôt by the cheapest conveyance, *if fit and suitable for issue to recruits.* If pronounced unfit for issue by a board of officers, it is to be sold by auction, and the proceeds credited in the pay list of the service companies, supported by a certificate according to W. O. Form, No. 605.

When the service companies or troops of a regiment are stationed abroad, the part-worn clothing is not to be sent to the depôt, but taken into the regimental store, under the charge of the quartermaster, and sold by auction at the end of each quarter, and the proceeds credited in the pay list as directed above.

---

* Compensation for the biennial serge breeches of staff serjeants to be calculated at one half these rates.

† Compensation for the biennial undress jacket to be calculated at one half these rates.

GREAT COATS.

The new pattern great coat for the infantry, sealed March 1863, is made in two qualities of grey kersey; one for first class staff-serjeants, drum and bugle majors, and band-serjeants, and the other for all other ranks.

They are made in four different sizes, which may be demanded by regiments in such proportions as may be requisite.

The weights are from 6 lbs. to 6 lbs. 4 oz.

The staff-serjeant's great coat is to last five years; its price is 2*l*. 1*s*. 11*d*.

The other is to last four years, and its price is 1*l*. 2*s*. 9*d*.

Regiments having blue, green, black, red, purple, or sky-blue facings are to have the chevrons on the great coats of golden yellow worsted laid on cloth of the colour of the facings.

Regiments having white, yellow, or buff facings are to have the chevrons blue.

All second battalions are to have them red.

The 60th Rifles scarlet, and other rifle corps Lincoln green.

Requisition and supply. — New great coats may in general be supplied, if reported necessary by a board of survey, at the expiration of the periods of duration specified in New Clothing Warrant.* For troops employed in North America, or in active or continued operations in the field, these articles may if necessary, be supplied one year earlier; in these cases the necessity of supplying them must be specially certified by the general or other officer commanding at the station; and it is in all cases to be understood distinctly, that new great coats are not to be supplied to a regiment or corps as a matter of course immediately on the termination of the respective periods above stipulated, but only when the commanding officer shall certify that such supply is required.

The officer commanding the regiment is to forward to the Secretary of State for War a duplicate of the requisition, also a statement of the numbers of old great coats returned into store.

* The periods of duration laid down are as follows:—

		Value when new. £ s. d.	Duration in Years.	Value when worn out. £ s. d.
Infantry staff serjeants	- great coat	2 1 11	5	0 5 0
Infantry, other ranks West India regiments Army Hospital corps Garrison staff Recruiting districts Invalid depôts	great coat	1 2 9	4	0 3 0
School of Musketry Librarians	great coat	1 2 9	5	0 3 0
60th Rifles Rifle Brigade Ceylon Rifles Canadian Rifles	great coat	1 2 9	4	0 3 0
Schooolmasters	- cloak	1 17 8	10	0 3 0
Barrack serjeants	- great coat	2 7 8	5	0 5 0

GREAT COATS.

A sealed pattern great coat to be sent to the head-quarters of each regiment, with every supply of not less than 100 great coats, in order that those received may be compared with the same, and reported upon in a similar manner to the regimental clothing.

Great coats will be accounted for by regiments and depôts in the annual clothing return.

At the following stations, namely, Cape Town, Halifax, N.S., Montreal, Hobart Town, Sydney, and Auckland New Zealand, a supply of great coats will be always kept in charge of the superintendent of stores, and when an issue of the same is required by the troops quartered in those localities, it will be made upon requisitions from the officer commanding the regiment or corps, approved by the general or other officer commanding at the station.

All cloaks, capes, or great coats which may be reported unserviceable, are at the time of the delivery of the new articles to be transferred as condemned stores to the nearest barrack-master; ten per cent. of the quantity condemned may be retained at the regiment for issue to invalids or time expired men under orders for discharge, and such numbers as may be certified by the commanding officer to be actually necessary for the repair of others in wear by the regiment or corps, the expense of which repairs is to be borne by the soldier.

The barrack master will immediately report the receipt of the unserviceable cloaks, capes, or coats to the Director of Clothing, with suggestions for their disposal.

Every great coat, new or part-worn, is to be marked inside upon the middle of the back, with the number or designation of the regiment, and also the regimental number and name of the wearer; the mark is to be made with white paint, and an allowance of 2d. will be granted for this service, the same to be charged in the pay list, accompanied by a certificate according to W.O. Form, No. 857. *Marking.*

Chevrons may be added to the sleeves of great coats of non-commissioned officers (including lance-serjeants and lance-corporals), for this an allowance of 2d. for each bar of a chevron will be granted. *For N. C. Officers.*

When great coats of the old pattern are issued, those for serjeants are to have cuffs and collars added to them at the head-quarters or depôt of each corps; these shall be made of army coat cloth of the same quality and colour as the facings of the corps. The actual and necessary expense of such addition, not exceeding 1s. 7d. per coat, will be allowed.

These expenses may be charged in the pay list, supported by the usual vouchers.

In case of the loss or damage of a great coat by neglect, the amount to be charged to the soldier is to be based on the value of the article and the time it has been in wear, keeping in view the regulated value of the article when worn out, as previously laid down. *Loss or damage.*

When a soldier becomes non-effective in the service companies of a regiment or corps, his great coat should be retained and issued to the next man whose great coat is worn out.

Should the number of non-effectives in the service companies be so great as to cause an inconvenient accumulation of part-worn great coats, and should the regiment be ordered to move, the commanding officer will send the part-worn great coats, if on home service, to the depôt of the regiment for issue to recruits, accompanied by a transfer return of the same; if on foreign service, to the nearest superintendent of stores or barrack-master, who is to report the receipt of them to the Secretary of State for War. *Disposal of surplus.*

3976. F

All soldiers discharged as invalids or time-expired men will be allowed to take with them from their regiment or depôt an old cloak or great coat.

Leather Leggings.

Leather leggings are made of one pattern and quality for all ranks. They are issued to dismounted men only, at home and on certain foreign stations.

They may be replaced, if above three years in use, on the report of a board of officers that they have become unserviceable from fair wear and tear.

One penny per pair will be allowed for marking leggings. The amount to be charged in the pay list, supported by a voucher in Form 27, appended.

Should leggings become unserviceable in less than three years from the date of the first issue, they must be made good at the expense of the soldier, unless under such special circumstances as shall be satisfactory to the Secretary of State for War.

Leather leggings will be accounted for in the annual clothing return.

The price of a pair of new leggings is 3s. 4d., and the sum to be paid by the soldier in making good deficiencies will be regulated by the time the damaged or lost articles had been in wear.

The old leggings to be returned to the charge of the nearest superintendent of stores or barrack-master, when new supplies have been issued.

Should a regiment in possession of leggings be ordered to a station where they are not worn, the leggings will be sent to the nearest superintendent of stores or barrack-master, who will report the receipt of the same to the Secretary of State for War.

Transfers to other corps will not take their leather leggings with them unless specially ordered.

NECESSARIES.

Every battalion will be provided on requisition to the Secretary of State for War, with patterns of necessaries sealed by authority of the Inspecting Officer acting under the orders of the Field Marshal Commanding in Chief. *Requisitions.*

All necessaries will be provided by the Secretary of State for War instead of by commanding officers of regiments as hitherto.

They are supplied to the troops according to priced lists, which will be revised if necessary and published in General Orders, not oftener than once in three months. The depôts from which the articles are to be obtained will also be notified in General Orders.

Each requisition from a depôt battalion should be accompanied by a separate requisition for fatigue jackets and numerals for each depôt in the battalion.

Officers commanding will be careful to demand only such quantities as will be sufficient for the requirements of the soldiers under their command, and to avoid accumulating an unnecessary stock.

All necessaries should be inspected by a regimental board as soon as they are received and a report thereon forwarded to the Secretary of State for War. Should there however be any complaint, a duplicate should be transmitted to the adjutant general for the information of the Field Marshal Commanding in Chief.

The necessaries will be kept by the quartermaster, who will issue them upon the requisitions of officers commanding troops and companies at prices which will be notified by the War Office. The commanding officer will be responsible for the care and preservation of these public stores; and in the event of the troops being employed upon active service in the field, the necessaries in store of each regiment should be given over to the store officer accompanying the army, to whom all requisitions should be addressed, and who will obtain such further supplies from England as may be requisite.

The paymaster is to keep the accounts of the necessaries, observing such directions as may be given him by the Secretary of State for War. And the quartermaster is to furnish him with a periodical statement of the articles to be charged to each troop or company.

The amount realized by the sale of regimental necessaries to depôts in a depôt battalion will be credited quarterly in the pay-list of the depôt battalion, supported by voucher, on W.O. Form No. 606.

In regiments and corps not connected with a depôt battalion, the Quartermaster will in like manner render an account to the Paymaster of the regimental necessaries to be charged to each troop or company, and the amount will be credited quarterly in the pay list supported by a voucher on W.O. Form No. 606.

The necessaries will be accounted for yearly in the kit account, which is to be sent to the War Office on the 31st March in each year, on W.O. Forms 608, 609 and 910, (according to services,) showing the receipts and issues during the year. Four of W.O. Form 611 should accompany each account, so as to show the necessaries issued on repayment during each quarter, and the sum credited in the pay list of each quarter for the same. *Yearly accounts.*

Every recruit joining the army is to receive a complete kit of necessaries free of all charge as a single issue, but the articles are to be kept up at his own expense. Any soldier re-engaging after the *Issue to recruits.*

PERSONAL EQUIPMENT.

expiration of his first period of service is also entitled to a complete kit or commutation in lieu, at the rates laid down below.* The amount is to be charged on the pay list, supported by a voucher on W.O. Form 1057.

Transfers. In all cases of transfers from one service to another, the officer commanding the corps to which the man is transferred should provide him gratis from the quartermaster's store, with such articles of regimental necessaries as are requisite in consequence of any difference of pattern existing between the two regiments or corps.

Supply when in the field. When an army is engaged in the field a reserve store of necessaries will be placed in charge of the military store department. The number and description of these will be proposed by the Adjutant-General, and after the approval of the Commander-in-Chief has been given will be decided by the Secretary of State for War.

Commanding officers requiring necessaries will make their demands *direct* upon the military store officer, by whom a consolidated return will be sent at the close of each quarter to each officer in command, detailing the articles supplied, so that their value may be credited to the public in the regimental accounts according to the published prices.

These consolidated returns will be attached to the quarterly pay list and credit given to the public accordingly; and in order to check the same a duplicate will be sent by the chief military store officer direct to the accountant-general.

In order that the reserve store of necessaries may be adequately maintained, the commanding officer of each regiment, corps, or detachment will transmit to the chief military store officer, at least quarterly, through the adjutant-general, an estimate of the quantity of each article he is likely to want, and the chief military store officer will then take measures, under the authority of the commander of the forces, for the provision of such further supplies as may be necessary.

These estimates must be at least three months in advance of the time when the stores will be required; thus, for stores to be demanded in July the estimates must be with the military store officer on the 1st April, or sooner if necessary because of the distance from the source of supply.

No delivery of stores to any regiment, &c. is to be made "on account." A receipt, to be considered as a final voucher, must be obtained at every issue. All temporary receipts are strictly forbidden.

Stoppages. No soldier shall be put under stoppages to pay for any articles of clothing or necessaries not ordered by these Regulations to be provided at his expense, except in cases where the absolute necessity of replacing articles of clothing supplied by the public shall have been occasioned by his own neglect or misconduct, or by the articles being worn out before the period for the next delivery of clothing.

The pay of the soldier on every station shall be liable to a stoppage of 1s. 1d. per week in the foot guards; and of 1s. 6d. per week in other corps, for keeping up his clothing and necessaries; which rates

---

	£	s.	d.
* Infantry of the line, rifle and colonial regiments, excepting West India regiments	2	0	0
Highland regiments wearing trews	1	12	0
Highland regiments wearing kilts	2	9	0
Commissariat staff corps	2	18	0
West India regiments	2	0	0

of stoppage shall not be exceeded unless by sentence of a court-martial. But the stoppages are not to be made in advance before the necessaries are required, except either by the desire of the soldier or when any expensive article is likely to be soon wanted, in which case the regulated stoppages may be resorted to during the month prior to the delivery of such article.

Men losing their necessaries on becoming prisoners of war shall have no claim against the public on account thereof, but on rejoining their corps they shall, if requisite, and if recommended under the provisions of the Mutiny Act, be supplied with fresh necessaries at the public expense. Prisoners.

When a soldier is sentenced to imprisonment by the civil power for a term not exceeding one year, his kit is to be retained by the corps, and re-issued to him on his release.

Should the term of imprisonment exceed one year, and the man be still retained on the strength of the corps, his kit will be sold, and the balance, if any, after paying his debts, will be credited to the public; on rejoining he will be supplied from the quartermaster's store at the public expense with such articles as were sold.

When a soldier serving in a regiment is handed over to another corps from which he had deserted previous to the receipt of a free kit, those articles of his kit which can be made use of in the corps he is to join are to be sent with him, the remainder to be sold, and the proceeds remitted to the regiment he is to join, in aid of any expense which may be incurred by him in the provision of articles to complete his kit.

When a soldier becomes non-effective from any cause, within two years from the date of his receiving or providing himself with a new knapsack, a board of officers is to be assembled to inspect it, and if found fit for issue to a recruit, the board will fix its value, and the quartermaster will then take possession of it. The sum declared to be the value of the knapsack is to be charged to the public through the pay list, supported by W.O. Form No. 618; this will be credited to the captain of the company, and accounted for with the man's effects. Knapsacks of non-effectives.

The knapsack is to be issued to the first recruit who may join, and the difference between the value of the article so issued and that of a new knapsack, is to be paid to the recruit as compensation for not being supplied with a new knapsack.

The sum thus paid to the recruit is to be charged in the pay list, supported by the proper voucher.

Should the board of officers find the knapsack unfit for issue, it will be sold with the rest of the man's effects.

A soldier receiving his discharge will have the option of taking his knapsack with him.

The above rule is only to apply to depôts or to the head-quarters of corps where recruits join. In all other cases the knapsack is to be sold with the rest of the man's effects, the intention being that no expense should be incurred for the carriage of the articles from one place to another.

When an officer is called upon to certify an account or bill of any kind for payment, he is to take every precaution that his signature is not given twice for the same articles, and it is to be clearly understood that should any double payment be made in consequence of his having certified twice over, he will be held responsible for the amount so overpaid. Certificates.

PERSONAL EQUIPMENT.

Marking.

Every article is to be marked with the number or appellation of the regiment, the owner's name and number, and the date of delivery, before it is issued from the quartermaster's store.

The knapsacks are to have the regimental number in arabic numerals painted in white in the centre of the back. Fusiliers are to have the grenade, and light infantry and rifle regiments are to have the bugle painted over the number. Number plates for the knapsacks of every regiment are furnished on application, by the director of army clothing.

Linen and woollen articles are to have the marks written on them in indelible ink; and knives, forks, spoons, razors, and such other articles as cannot be written upon, are to have the necessary marks engraved or cut upon them.

The following sums are allowed to be charged to the public for the marking of kits issued to recruits:

	s.	d.
Infantry and Highland regiments wearing trews	1	8
Regiments wearing the kilt	2	0
Rifle corps	1	7

When small numbers of articles are issued, one halfpenny per article will be allowed for marking.

The following sums may be charged for painting the regimental number and device on the knapsacks of recruits, or men transferred:—

Foot Guards	4d.
Line	1
Fusiliers, light infantry, and rifles	2

Soldiers are to defray the expense of marking their necessaries, with the exception of the first kit.

GENERAL LIST OF NECESSARIES.

For articles of necessaries issued as sea kit only, *see* page 146.

Description.		For what Rank.	Cost of each.			Weight of each.		Pattern.
			£	s.	d.	lbs.	oz.	
Blacking tin		⎫	0	0	2	0	8	All arms.
Braces, pair		⎪	0	0	10½	0	4	,,
Brass, button		⎪	0	0	1½	0	2	,,
Brush { brass		⎬ All ranks	0	0	7¼	0	3	,,
clothes		⎪	0	0	11½	0	3½	,,
shaving		⎪	0	0	3¾	0	1	,,
shoe, set of two		⎭	0	1	2¾	0	6½	,,
Cap, forage { with gold band and peak.		Staff serjeants	0	18	6	0	7½	Guards.
with gold band		Serjeants	0	16	4	0	6½	,,
		Privates	0	2	6¼	0	7	Grenadier and Coldstream Gds.
		,,	0	2	10½	0	7	Fusilier Guards.
blue cloth		1st class staff serjeants.	0	10	6	0	6½	Line.
blue Kilmarnock		2nd class staff serjeants and serjeants.	0	3	6	0	5	,,
,, ,,		Privates	0	1	6	0	5	,,
green cloth		Staff serjeants	0	17	6	0	6½	Rifles.
green Kilmarnock		{ Serjeants	0	3	0	0	5½	,,
		{ Privates	0	1	6	0	5½	,,

Description.	For what rank.	Cost of each. £	s.	d.	Weight of each. lbs.	oz.	Pattern.
Cap, forage—blue cloth, with diced band.	Staff serjeants	1	0	0	0	6½	Highland.
Cap, forage—blue Glengarry, with diced band	Serjeants	0	3	6	0	5	
	Privates	0	2	4	0	5	
Cap, forage—badges for forage caps—							
numeral, brass	All except 1st class staff serjeants	0	0	0½	0	0½	Line.
bugles, brass		0	0	0¾	0	0½	Light Infantry.
grenades, brass		0	0	0½	0	0½	Fusilier regiments.
Cap, forage—tuft for forage caps		0	0	2¼	0	0½	Line, rifles.
Comb	All ranks	0	0	2½	0	0½	All arms.
Fez		0	5	0¾	0	1½	West India regiments.
Tassel for ditto		0	1	0	0	0½	
Fork		0	0	2	0	2	All arms.
Gaiters, white duck, pair		0	2	2	-	-	West India regiments.
" " "		0	1	3	0	5	Highland, wearing kilt.
Garters, pair		0	1	2	0	1½	" "
Holdall		0	0	5	0	2½	All arms.
Hose tops, tartan, pairs		0	2	3	0	4½	Highland, wearing kilt.
Jacket, fatigue—scarlet cloth	Staff serjeants	1	11	0	1	7	Line.
Jacket, fatigue—scarlet cloth	Serjeants	0	14	6	1	8	"
Jacket, fatigue—red cloth	Privates	0	9	10	1	10	"
Jacket, fatigue—materials for privates.	"	0	8	10¼	1	10	"
Jacket, fatigue—green cloth	Staff serjeants	2	4	0	1	7	Rifles.
Jacket, fatigue—green cloth	Serjeants	0	13	6	1	8	"
Jacket, fatigue—green cloth	Privates	0	11	0	1	10	"
Materials for privates, West India pattern.							
Knapsack	All ranks	0	4	10¾	3	13	Infantry.
Slings for ditto, buff		0	1	3¾			Guards, line.
Knapsack		0	4	8½	3	13	Rifles.
Slings for ditto, black leather		0	1	4¾			
Knife, table		0	0	2¾	0	3	All arms.
Mitts—white		0	0	11½	0	3¾	Guards and line.
Mitts—black		0	0	11½			Rifles.
Purse and belt	All ranks	0	10	6	0	14½	Highland, wearing kilt.
Pipeclay, pieces, per doz.		0	0	5	-	-	All arms.
Razor and case		0	0	4¾	0	2¾	"
Shirt—cotton		0	4	3¼	0	15	"
Shirt—flannel		0	4	8¾	0	14	"
Shirt—cotton, West India pattern.		0	1	10	-	-	West India regiments.
Soap, yellow		0	0	2½	1	0	
Socks, worsted		0	1	0¼	0	4	All arms.
Sponge		0	0	9	0	0¾	"
Spoon		0	0	2½	0	2¼	"
Stock and clasp		0	0	5¾	0	2	"
Stockings, brown cotton		0	0	10¾	0	7	West India regiments.
Strap for forage cap	All, except 1st class staff serjeants.	0	0	1	0	0½	All arms.

PERSONAL EQUIPMENT.

Description.	For what Rank.	Cost of each.			Weight of each.		Pattern.
		£	s.	d.	lbs.	oz.	
Straps for folded great coat - - pair	All ranks	0	2	1¼	0	5	Guards.
Straps, great coat { black leather	All ranks	0	0	10	0	5	Rifles.
Straps, great coat { buff	All ranks	0	1	0½	0	5	Line.
Tin, mess - - -	All ranks	0	1	2½	1	9	Infantry.
Cover for mess tin -	All ranks	0	0	5½	1	9	,,
Straps for ditto { buff	All ranks	0	0	3¼	1	9	Line.
Straps for ditto { black	All ranks	0	0	2¾	-	-	Rifles.
Towel - - -	All ranks	0	0	9¼	0	8	All arms.
Trews - - -	1st class staff serjeants.	1	3	8½	1	7	Highland.
	Other ranks	0	13	7½	1	7	,,

Two cotton frocks are to be added to the kit in warm climates, they are to be provided and kept up by the men.

All soldiers will be supplied with peaks and covers for forage caps previous to embarkation for St. Helena, West Indies, Mediterranean, Cape of Good Hope, Mauritius, Ceylon, India, and China; also white chaco covers for any of the above stations where chacos are worn.

When jackets are furnished in materials, 1s. 4d. will be allowed for making up each jacket.

When jackets are issued made up, the necessary and unavoidable expense of fitting the same, not exceeding 4d., will be allowed.

These sums to be charged in the pay list, supported by the usual vouchers.

ARMOURER'S FORGE.
PLATES XVII. TO XX.
New Pattern.
(Approved 29th September 1859.)

Dimensions—length, 40 inches ; width, 20 inches ; depth, 36 inches ; cubical measurement, 16 cubic feet 8 inches.

The field forge and set of tools hitherto in use was arranged so as to pack into two boxes, and was intended to be carried on a pack-saddle. It has now been superseded by the new pattern forge, which is contained in a single chest.

The anvil, bellows, and other apparatus are larger and more substantial, and the set of tools generally more complete than in the old pack-saddle forge.

As this chest requires wheeled transport for its conveyance, it is only suited for troops in stationary quarters. For active service a pair of boxes to be carried on a pack saddle have been approved ; these are to contain a selection of tools and materials, and an assortment of parts of interchangeable rifle muskets, so that any repairs of a slight nature can be executed.

The duration assigned to the armourer's forge is 20 years, after which period it will be exchanged if it is unserviceable. All the tools and materials are to be kept up in the mean time, and renewed as they become worn out, at the expense of the armourer serjeant. The screw plates and taps, however, will be renewed at the public expense after they have been five years in wear. These, as well as the countersinks or plugs, grinders, drills, and ovals for fitting parts of the locks of interchangeable muskets, will be supplied exclusively by the War Office, upon demands of the armourer serjeant, through the officer commanding the regiment or battalion, the cost price and expense of transit being paid for through the medium of the regimental agents.

By a recent order all battalions of infantry proceeding on foreign service are to be supplied with the new pattern forge. Those on home service are to retain the old ones until they are renewable on account of having been the regulated period in wear.

Lists of Tools and Materials in New Pattern Forge.

Description.	Cost of each.			Weight of each.		Number.
Tools and Implements.	£	s.	d.	lbs.	oz.	
Anvil - - - - - - -	0	8	0	28	11	1
Bags for earth to balance bellows - -	0	0	4	0	4	2
Bellows, armourer's - - - -	0	18	6	20	0	1
Bit, boring, for rod, pattern 1853 - -	0	1	6	0	8	1
Bit, copper, for soldering - - - -	0	3	6	1	9	1
Bits { Centre { $\frac{3}{8}$ inch - - - -	0	0	8	0	1	1
$\frac{1}{4}$,, - - - -	0	0	8	0	$0\frac{3}{4}$	1
Rimer { Half round - - -	0	0	4	0	$1\frac{1}{2}$	1
Square - - -	0	0	4	0	1·	2
Rosehead - - - - -	0	0	4	0	1·	1
Screw driver - - - - -	0	0	4	0	$1·\frac{1}{2}$	1
Spoon - - - - - -	0	0	4	0	1	1

PERSONAL EQUIPMENT.

Description.	Cost of each.			Weight of each.		Number.
	£	s.	d.	lbs.	oz.	
Blades, Awl - - - - - -	0	0	1	0	0¼	1
Block for Anvil - - - - -	0	2	6	14	9	1
Brace, iron - - - - - -	0	3	0	1	2	1
Chisels. Armourer's, 2½ in., splatter -	0	1	9	0	9	1
Firmer 1 in., ,, - -	0	0	8	0	5·	1
¾ ,, ,, - -	0	0	7	0	4	1
½ ,, ,, - -	0	0	6	0	3·	1
¼ ,, ,, - -	0	0	5	0	2	1
⅛ ,, ,, - -	0	0	4	0	1·½	1
Clams, breech, gun metal, for barrels, prs. -	0	1	9	1	1	2
Drift, wire - - - - - - -	0	0	9	0	0¾	1
Drilling apparatus Bow, drill, cane - - -	0	1	6	0	6	1
Boxes, drill, wood - - -	0	0	3	0	1	2
Breastplate, wood - - -	0	0	9	0	4	1
Drills, set of 5 - - -	0	0	1	0	1	1
Stock, drill - - - -	0	1	3	0	2·5	1
Strings, drill, catgut, knots -	0	0	4	0	2	2
Driver, screw. *See* Screw driver.						
Feeder, tin, oil, with screw top - - -	0	1	0	0	2	1
Files Bastard Safe edge, flat 10 inch	0	0	6	0	11¼	2
8 ,,	0	0	4	0	7	2
Taper, 8 inch	0	0	5	0	5	2
flat 6 ,, -	0	0	3	0	2	2
Half round 10 inch -	0	0	6	0	8	2
8 ,, -	0	0	5	0	4	2
6 ,, -	0	0	4	0	1½	3
Knife - 5 ,, -	0	0	3	0	0¾	4
Round 8 inch -	0	0	4	0	2⅓	2
4 ,, -	0	0	2	0	0¼	2
Three square 6 inch -	0	0	3	0	2¼	2
Warding - 5 ,, -	0	0	3	0	0½	2
Rough Half round 10 ,, -	0	0	7	0	8	2
Three square 9 ,,	0	0	5	0	7	2
6 ,,	0	0	3	0	2¼	2
Smooth Bent - 4 ,, -	0	0	4	0	0½	3
Flat Safe edge 8 inch -	0	0	6	0	6½	2
Taper 8 ,, -	0	0	6	0	5	2
6 ,, -	0	0	5	0	2¼	2
Half round 8 inch	0	0	7	0	4	3
6 ,,	0	0	5	0	1¾	2
Halfround, flat back, 5 inch	0	0	4	0	0¾	2
Pillar, safe edge, 5 inch -	0	0	4	0	1¼	2
Plain back, 4 inch -	0	0	3	0	0½	2
Three square, 4 inch -	0	0	3	0	0½	2
Floats Barrel (pattern 1853) - - -	0	6	6	0	8	1
Rod - - - - -	0	2	9	0	3	1
Flute tools - - - - - -	0	0	8	0	2¾	1
Gauges, metal, for stocking set of 5 -	2	7	10½	5	0	1
Gimlets of sizes - - - -	0	0	2	0	5	6
Glue pot, copper, half pint, double - -	0	1	6	0	11	1
Gouges Armourers' Barrel - -	0	1	0	0	9	1
Pipe - -	0	0	9	0	3½	1
Firmer ¾ inch - -	0	0	7	0	3½	1
⅝ ,, - -	0	0	7	0	3¼	1
½ ,, - -	0	0	6	0	2	1
¼ ,, - -	0	0	5	0	1¾	1
⅛ ,, - -	0	0	5	0	1½	1
Flat 1 ,, - -	0	0	8	0	5	1
½ ,, - -	0	0	6	0	2¾	1

ARMOURER'S FORGE.

Description.			Cost of each.			Weight of each.		Number.
			£	s.	d.	lbs.	oz.	
Grinders, set of 5	Side screw	head						1
		shank						1
	Lock pin	head						1
		shank						1
	Breech screw head							1
Counter sinks or plugs, set of 3	Breech screw		0	16	6	1	3¾	1
	Side screw							1
	Lock pin							1
Drill, for pivot oval								1
Oval, for pivot								1
Drill, for sear oval								1
Sear oval								1
Hammers, rivetting, handled	1½ lbs.		0	1	6	1	12	1
	¼ ,,		0	0	6	0	8	1
Handles	Brad awl		0	0	1	0	1	7
	File	large	0	0	2	0	2½	2
		small	0	0	2	0	1½	2
Horses, wood			0	0	2	2	3	2
Knife, drawing			0	1	3	1	4	1
Mallet, wood			0	1	1	1	14	1
Pan, with back and tewel			-			40	8	1
Pincers, pair			0	1	6	0	11	1
Planes.	Groving	¾ inch	0	1	6	0	10½	1
		⅝ ,,	0	1	6	0	8½	1
		¼ ,,	0	1	6	0	10¾	1
	jack, single iron		0	1	9	3	2	1
	smoothing, double iron		0	2	0	1	10	1
Plyers, pair			0	0	7	0	4	1
Poker			0	0	9	0	7	1
Pot, glue. *See* Glue pot.								
Punch, 6½ inch			0	0	4	0	6½	1
Plates, screw, (pattern 1853)	large, with 3 taps		0	6	6	0	8	1
	small, with 4 taps		0	2	6	0	6	1
Rasps, half round	11 in.		0	1	6	0	14	2
	9 ,,		0	1	3	0	8¼	2
Saws	hand 24-inch		0	2	9	1	4	1
	slitting		0	1	6	0	9	1
Screw driver, 4 inch			0	0	5	0	3½	1
Screw plate. *See* Plate screw.								
Shovels, stocker's			0	0	6	0	2½	2
Slice, 9 ounce			0	0	6	0	11	1
Spindle and rock staff, 4 lb.			-			3	13	1
Spoke shave, 3 inch			0	0	8	0	4¼	1
Stone, oil, Turkey, in box			0	4	0	0	8	1
Sticks, buff			0	0	10	0	7	3
Tongs		pair	0	0	10	1	0	1
Vices	bench, field forge, 40 lbs.		0	14	3	40	0	1
	hand, 16 ounce		0	2	3	1	5	1
Wrenches	breech		0	3	2	1	13½	1
	nipple		0	1	9	0	2½	1
Materials.								
Borax			0	0	2	0	2	—
Bottle, gutta percha, for sal ammoniac			0	1	0	0	2	1
Emery	fine		0	0	1	0	8	—
	superfine		0	0	1	0	8	—
Glue, common			0	0	4	1	0	—
Paper, glass	coarse, No. 2, quire		0	0	2½	1	0	½
	fine, No. 1½, ,,		0	0	2½	0	11	½
Resin			0	0	0½	0	4	—

Description.	Cost of each.			Weight of each.		Number.
	£	s.	d.	lbs.	oz.	
Sal ammoniac - - - - - -	0	0	1	0	2	—
Spelter, brass - - - - - -	0	0	2	0	2	—
Tin, grain - - - - - -	0	0	4	0	4	—
Wire, iron { hard, No. 13 - - -	0	0	2	1	0	—
{ soft, No. 20 - - - -	0	0	1½	0	8	—
Wire, steel, soft, No. 10 - - - -	0	0	7	1	0	—
Tumblers, swivelled, ground but soft, bents not cut.	-		-	-		⎫
Sears, filed but soft - - - - -	-		-	-		⎪ To be de-
Springs { main, finished and tempered, but not ground.	-		-	-		⎬ manded as re-
{ sear, finished and tempered, but left large.	-		-	-		⎪ quired.
Bench and woodwork - - - -	-		-	176	0	—
Total forge, complete, packed -	25	16	8	394	0	—

System of Packing the Forge

In the space under the false bottom the following articles are stowed:—Set of five metal gauges, hand and slitting saws, jack, smoothing and three grooving planes, glue pot, tin oil feeder, cane drill-bow, two hammers, drawing knife, four file handles and seven bradawl handles, breech wrench, poker, tongs, slice, copper soldering bit, bags for earth, two packets of emery, borax, tin, brass spelter, resin, glue.

When the false bottom is put in its place the body of the forge is packed thus:—The rock staff and spindle are placed at the back, with the boring bit next them; then the vice, and afterwards the anvil; the block for anvil is placed with its larger end next the tail of the bellows. The tewel, brace, wire, glass paper, and buff sticks follow in succession; and lastly, the fire pan with its bottom to the anvil, after which the door is put in.

The drawer is divided into compartments thus:—

		No. 1.	
	No. 4.	No. 2.	
		No. 3.	
	No. 5.	No. 6.	No. 7.

No. 1 compartment contains the smooth files, 22 in number.

No. 2 compartment contains 15 bastard files, viz., two safe-edge 8-inch, two taper flat 8-inch, two taper flat 6-inch, two half-round 8-inch, three half-round 6-inch, two round 8-inch, and two round 4-inch.

No. 3 compartment contains 14 files, viz., two three-square 6-inch bastard, four knife 5-inch, two warding 5-inch, two three-square 9-inch rough, two three-square 6-inch rough, and three half-round 9-inch rasps.

No. 4 compartment contains two half-round 11-inch rasps, two 10-inch safe-edge bastard files, two half-round 10-inch bastard files, two half-round 10-inch rough bastard files, two flat gouges, five firmer gouges, barrel and pipe gouges, catgut strings, breastplate, and spokeshave.

No. 5 compartment contains five firmer chisels, one armourer's chisel, barrel and rod floats; one flute tool, one stocker's shovel, six gimlets, screw-driver, drill stock, and drills, eight bits for brace, nipple wrench, wire drift, awl blade.

No. 6 compartment contains one pair of pincers, one pair of plyers, two screw-plates with taps, hand vice, set of grinders counter-sinks drills and ovals, punch, and gutta-percha bottle of sal ammoniac.

No. 7 compartment contains oil stone, two pair clams, screws for horses, and wedges for vice.

The wooden horses and mallet are put inside the anvil block.

To set up the forge for use—take out the drawer and the door; take out the fire pan and tewel, and fix them in the three holes on the side of the bench, pressing them well home; fix the vice in its place, and set up the spindle and rock staff. The holes for these latter are in the top of the case, and are plugged with cork.

Supplementary List of Tools required for permanent Armourers' Shop in garrison or elsewhere at home and abroad, in addition to those included in the New Pattern Forge.

Description of Article.	No.	Description of Article.	No.
Anvils, large, weight 1 cwt. 1 qr. 12 lbs.	1	Grinders { wrench, nail - set	1
Bayonet setter	1	{ side nail - ,,	1
Bellows, 24″	1	{ lock- - ,,	1
Bits, centre, $\frac{3}{16}''$	1	Letters, steel, $\frac{1}{16}''$ - ,,	1
Brace, large	1	Ladle, iron, large -	1
Brushes { hard	1	Lathe { turning, and tools	1
{ soft	1	{ polishing	1
Chisels { upright	1	Maundrils { bayonet	1
{ $\frac{3}{16}''$	1	{ band	1
{ $\frac{1}{16}''$	1	{ scabbard	1
Cutters { cup for wood	1	Machine for testing sights	1
{ ,, brass	1	Nipple leveller	1
{ stud, trigger plate	1	Parallels, iron	1
{ trigger plate bottomer	1	Pans, iron, large (blueing)	1
{ ,, for brass	1	Pans, oil, tin	1
{ nose for barrel	1	Plugs for testing barrels, pattern /53 - set	1
{ swivel	1	Rods { for leading barrels	6
{ tool for cutting out top of sight	1	{ wiping	6
Clamps, wood - pairs	4	{ for soldering sights	6
Cork, slips	4	Saws { tenon	1
Files { bastard, safe edge, 10″	2	{ butt	1
{ rough flat, 12″	2	{ slit, trigger plate	1
{ smooth { flat, 12″	2	Spring balance, small	1
{ { safe edge, 10″	2	Stakes, bench	1
{ { 3 square, 5″	2	Sears { oval and drill	1
Figures, steel, $\frac{1}{16}''$ set	1	{ axle and drill	1
Gauges { metal, for short butts set for sighting, pattern /53, to 1,000 yards - set	1	Stock and die, tumbler	1
		Turkey slips	1
		Tools, flute, small	1
{ for sighting to 1,250 yards - set	1	Taps and clamps for breeching barrels	1
Gouges { ½ round, $\frac{3}{16}''$	1	Trough for browning barrels	1
{ barrel	1	Vice, standing, 40 lbs.	1

SPECIAL LIST of TOOLS issued for the use of ARMOURERS who have been instructed at the Royal Small Arms Factory, Enfield, to enable them to repair the barrels of Rifle Muskets.

No. of Tool.	Description.
1, 2, 3, 4, 5	Set of plugs tapered at both ends, diameters increasing by successive gradations, used to raise dents in the "lands" of barrels.
6	Copper rod, used for forcing the plugs down the barrel.
7	Wooden mallet for striking the rod.
8	Float, long and narrow, for filing off lumps in the grooves near the muzzle.
9	Float, similar to No. 8, but finer cut.
10	Steel plug with two moveable wings, one rough and the other smooth, for filing off dents or "lumps" in the grooves of barrels with 6' 6" pitch of rifling.
11	Steel plug with wings, same as No. 10, but adapted for barrels with 4 foot pitch of rifling.
12	Long scraper for detaching rust in barrels.
13	Block of wood for using with vice to hold the barrel.
14	Clam, made of copper.

ARTICLES FOR MUSKETRY INSTRUCTION.
PLATES XXI. AND XXII.

A complete set of articles authorized for musketry instruction is issued to each battalion, regiment, or depôt battalion on application to the barrack-master at the station; if any articles are lost or destroyed through neglect the cost price will be charged against the troops; when worn out by fair wear and tear they will be renewed free of charge.

On a regiment or battalion leaving a station, the whole of the musketry articles are to be handed over by the officer instructor of musketry to the quartermaster, who will deliver them into the barrack store again.

The cord or gunters' chain, 900 yards long, which used to be issued, was superseded in 1861 by the stadia with tripod stand, staff and reel with 40 yards of measuring tape, all of which are contained in a box 7 feet 4 inches long, 8 inches wide, and $4\frac{1}{2}$ inches deep. A new pattern of stadiometer has since been approved. In this latter the single tripod stand is replaced by a support at either end. And there are two 20 yards length of chain instead of the measuring tape.

Chalk, whiting, lamp black, and glue are to be demanded from the barrack master in small quantities as they are required. The following annual allowances of paper and fine sand for practising the manufacture of cartridges are granted:—

For each depôt battalion, where recruits are trained,—

    Cartridge paper - - 6 quires.
    White   ,, - - 20 ,,
    Sand   ,, - - $\frac{1}{2}$ bushel.

For all other corps and battalions, per company,—

    Cartridge paper - - 3 sheets.
    White   ,, - - $\frac{1}{2}$ quire.
    Sand   ,, - - $\frac{1}{2}$ pint.

LIST of ARTICLES for MUSKETRY INSTRUCTION.

		Cost.			Weight.		Number.
		£	s.	d.	lbs.	oz.	
Bags, sand, bushel - - - -	each	0	0	5	0	10	12
Board, black, 6 feet by 4 feet - -	,,	1	0	0	56	0	1
Easel for do. - - - - -	,,	1	0	0	27	0	1
Brushes, for colouring { paint, ground	,,	0	2	0	0	$7\frac{1}{4}$	2
targets { sash tool, No. 8	,,	0	0	8	0	$3\frac{1}{4}$	2
Cap, with cross wires - - - -	,,	0	0	5	0	$0\frac{1}{4}$	1
{ Bullets for rifle musket, pattern 1853 - - -	per 1,000	0	17	8	75	12	50
	Formers, hard wood -	each	0	0	2	0	$0\frac{1}{2}$	12
Cartridges,	Funnels, tin, with spouts - -		0	1	0	0	10	1
implements	Knife, large - - - -	each	0	1	4	0	$7\frac{1}{2}$	1
for making,	Forming plugs, wood - -	,,	0	0	2	0	$0\frac{3}{4}$	12
viz.:	Measures, tin, $2\frac{1}{2}$ drams	set of 5	0	0	11	0	$0\frac{1}{2}$	5
	Patterns, tin, showing shape of paper for cartridges - -	set	0	0	2	0	$3\frac{1}{2}$	1
	Straight-edge, wood, with brass edge - - - -	each	0	2	1	0	14	1
Compasses, with holder to contain chalk -	pair	0	3	2	0	11	1

ARTICLES FOR MUSKETRY INSTRUCTION.

	Cost.			Weight.		Number.
	£	s.	d.	lbs.	oz.	
Files, for documents - - - - - doz.	0	1	1	0	1¼	12
Flags { bunting, red, 6 feet square - each	0	6	3	1	5½	1
shalloon, 2½ feet square { dark blue - - ,,	0	1	10	0	4¼	2
red - - - ,,	0	1	10	0	4¼	4
upper half red, lower white - each	0	1	10	0	4¼	2
white - - ,,	0	1	9	0	4¼	2
Locks, with cocks, hardened, swivel pattern, complete - - - - - - each	0	9	0	0	9¼	6
Model, wooden, with suspended wires - ,,	0	9	0	1	4	1
Box for ditto - - - - - ,,	0	3	2	2	0	1
Mantlets - - - - - - - ,,	19	18	0	2,254	0	—*
Poles, lance, 10 feet long, shod with iron - ,,	0	2	1	5	10	11
Plug, cylindrical wooden, with hole through centre - - - - - - each	0	0	2	0	0⅛	1
Rifle musket barrel, pattern 1853 - ,,	1	0	0	4	4	1
Ruler, flat, hard wood, 3 feet long - ,,	0	0	7	0	8	1
Sponge, pieces of 2 oz. - - - each piece	0	2	4	0	2	1
Stadia, pattern 1863, complete with box - each	2	10	0	40	0	2
Tripod rests, with rings - - - ,,	0	6	3	16	0	12
Wrenches, nipple, with cramp - - ,,	0	1	11½	0	6½	6
Targets, iron, complete with staves, bolts, &c., each	3	3	4	430	0	10
,, new pattern, with stays, &c. - ,,	8	0	0	505	0	—
MATERIALS.						
Chalk - - - - - - per cwt.	0	1	7	—		—
Lamp black - - - - per lb.	0	0	2	—		—
Glue to make size - - - ,,	0	0	6	—		—
Plugs† for bullets { boxwood - - -	—			—		—
baked clay - - -	—			—		—
Whiting - - - - - per cwt.	0	1	7	—		—
Sand, fine - - - - per bush.	0	1	7	—		—
Paper { cartridge - - - - per ream	0	1	8	45	0	—
white, for envelopes of cartridges ,,	0	1	6	13	0	—

* Issued only when required by circumstances, on special demand and approval.

† In consequence of the difficulty experienced in obtaining the necessary supplies of boxwood, plugs of baked clay for the bases of elongated rifle bullets were approved on the 15th December 1863 (W. O. Circular 855, 17th March 1864).

BOOKS, WAR OFFICE FORMS, AND STATIONERY.

Books of Regulations, &c.

The following works are published by authority. The discipline and instruction of the troops, and the various duties to be performed by officers, non-commissioned officers, &c., are to be regulated in strict accordance with the rules and principles laid down upon the several subjects:—

Description.	Price.	Remarks.
	s. d.	
Artillery Manual, 1860, 304 pp. demy 8vo.	2 4	For Artillery service.
Pocket edition of do. - -	1 0	,, ,,
Artillery Exercises (Field), with diagrams, 1861, 246 pp. demy 8vo.	5 0	,, ,,
Pocket edition do. - -	1 6	,, ,,
Artillery, Standing Orders, Dress Regulations, and Trumpet and Bugle Sounds, 286 pp., demy 8vo.	5 0	,, ,,
*Bugle Sounds, Infantry, by Edward Potter.	4 6	
Cavalry, Formations and Movements of, demy 12mo., 1864.	3 0	For Cavalry service.
Cavalry, Formations of a Brigade or Division, 1863, demy 12mo., cloth boards.	3 0	,, ,,
Dress Regulations of the Army, royal 8vo., 156 pp., 1864.	2 6	One copy furnished to the commanding officer at the public expense.
*Drum, Method of Beating, by Edward Potter.	4 6	
*Fife, Method of Playing, by Edward Potter.	3 0	
Gymnastic Exercises, Military System of, Maclaren's, 194 pp. crown 8vo., cloth boards.	1 6	One copy furnished to the commanding officer at the public expense.
Infantry, Field Exercises, and Evolutions, 1862, 560 pp. demy 8vo., with numerous diagrams.	4 0	One copy furnished to the commanding officer at the public expense; copies furnished to regiments at the public expense in the proportion of one for each serjeant; one copy to be provided by each officer at his own expense.
Pocket edition do. - -	1 0	
Medical Regulations, 250 pp. demy 8vo.	1 8	Every medical officer is required to provide himself with a copy at his own expense.
Military Train Manual, 72 pp. demy 8vo.	1 0	For military train.
Musketry Instruction, Regulations for 1864, 174 pp., crown 8vo.	1 0	One copy furnished to the commanding officer at the public expense.
Mutiny Act and Articles of War, royal 12mo., published annually.	4 0	One copy to the commanding officer, one to the adjutant, one to the paymaster, and one to each officer in command of a troop, battery, or company, furnished annually at the public expense.

* These works are not published by Her Majesty's Stationery Office, but they contain the system authorized to be followed under existing regulations.

3976.

BOOKS, STATIONERY, ETC.

Description.	Price.	Remarks.
	s. d.	
Paymasters, Instructions for, 96 pp., imperial 8vo.	1 0	One copy furnished to the commanding officer and one to the paymaster at the public expense.
Purveyor's Regulations, 236 pp., demy 8vo.	3 0	For hospital service only.
Queen's Regulations and Orders for the Army, 1859, demy 8vo., 462 pp.	3 6	One copy furnished at the public expense to the commanding officers, one to be provided by each officer at his own expense.
Pocket edition do. - -	1 0	
Sword Exercise, Infantry - -	0 6	One copy furnished at the public expense to the commanding officer.
War Office Circulars and Warrants.	- -	One copy furnished to the commanding officer as they are published from time to time.
Horse Guards' General Orders and Circular Memoranda.	- -	

Books for Administrative and Statistical Entry.

The authorized books that are required for duties of the orderly room and for the paymaster and quartermaster are furnished to regiments and battalions at the public expense. Requisitions for the same, as well as for all W.O. Forms are to be made on W.O. Forms 406 and 407.

The cost of all company books, settlement sheets, and soldiers' small account books is to be charged against officers commanding companies, the company contingent allowance being granted to meet these and other similar expenses.

Soldiers' account books are furnished to recruits in the first instance at the public expense, but the cost of renewal is charged to the soldier if lost or made away with.

Company books are to be demanded on W.O. Form 752.

List of Regimental and Company Books.

Description.	Cost of each.			Weight of each.	
	£	s.	d.	lbs.	oz.
Accoutrements, account of quartermaster's - -	0	4	0	2	0
Arms and ammunition, account of quartermaster's -	0	4	0	3	2¼
Attestations (in guard book) - - - -		—			—
Barrack cell, cash book - - - - -	0	5	6	3	4
Do. defaulter book - - - -	0	5	0	2	5
Do. journal - - - - -	0	4	6	2	7½
Do. prison register - - - -	0	6	0	4	13
Casualty book - - - - - -	0	7	0	2	15
Clothing, account of quartermaster's - - -	0	4	0	2	1
Court-martial book, officers' - - - -	0	9	0	4	6
Do. non-commissioned officers, &c. -	0	9	0	4	6
Defaulter book - - - - - -	0	11	0	5	3
Deserters, description of - - - - -	0	4	0	1	7
Fuel, forage, and provisions, account of quartermaster's	0	3	6	1	12½
Furloughs, register of - - - - -	0	6	0	2	3
Letter book, orderly room - - - -	0	6	0	0	3
Do. quartermaster's - - - -	0	6	0	3	0

BOOKS, STATIONERY, ETC.

Description.	Cost of each.			Weight of each.	
	£	s.	d.	lbs.	oz.
Letters received, guard book for - - - -	0	3	0	2	6
Libraries military, register for - - - -	0	5	6	2	15½
Marriages and baptisms, register of - - - -	0	8	0	2	12
Orders, general, in guard book - - - - -	0	3	0	3	1
Order book, regimental; Part I. Temporary -	0	2	6	1	14
Do. do. Part II. Permanent. - -	0	6	0	3	6
Returns, guard book for - - - - - -	0	3	0	2	4
Roll book, nominal and descriptive - - - -	0	11	0	5	12
Savings-bank ledger - - - - - -	0	1	6	1	3
School, attendance at, register of, adults - -	0	3	0	2	4½
Do. do. do. children - -	0	1	9	1	3½
Services, digest of - - - - - - -	0	6	0	2	14
Do. of regiment, history of - - - -	0	6	0	2	14
Do. officers, record of - - - - -	0	7	0	3	6
Services of soldiers, register of (with covers and screws) - - - - - - - - -	0	11	0	5	3
Do. do. (covers with plates and screws)	0	3	6	1	8
Do. do. (covers without do.) -	0	1	0	0	12
Do. do. (plates and screws only) - -	0	1	6	0	12
Company Books.					
Day book - - - - - - - -	0	1	9	1	1
Defaulter book - - - - - - -	0	8	0	2	6
Ledger - - - - - - - - -	0	6	0	3	4
Order book - - - - - - - -	0	1	9	1	1
Pay lists - - - - - - per quire	0	1	0	0	11
Pay-sheet and mess book - - - - -	0	7	0	4	12
Savings-bank ledger - - - - - -	0	1	6	1	4
Sheets for defaulter book - - - - quire	0	1	0	0	11
Soldiers' account book - - - - - -	0	0	3	0	2

STATIONERY.

Annual allowances for stationery, postage, &c. are granted to officers commanding according to the following scale:—

For a battalion of ten companies, 40*l.* if at home, and 30*l.* if abroad.
   ,,   ,,   six   ,,   24*l.* ,,   ,, 25*l.* ,,
   ,, the paymaster - - 15*l.* ,,   ,, 12*l.* ,,

Officers commanding companies are required to defray the expense of all stationery required for keeping the accounts of their companies, and other officers are required to provide the stationery that they require for reports, &c. at their own expense.

The following may be considered as the present average contract prices for stationery:—

	s.	d.
Envelopes, No. 1, for demy, per packet of 100 -	2	1
Official envelopes, No. 2, for foolscap, per packet of 100	1	8
,, ,, No. 5, ,, post, per packet of 100 -	0	10
India rubber, per piece - - - - -	0	3
Ink, liquid, black, quart bottle - - -	0	10
,, ,, red, half-pint bottle - - -	0	8¼
,, in powder, black, per packet (to make one pint) -	0	2
,, ,, red, ,, ,, ,, -	0	2½
Inkstand with two bottles - - -	6	7

	s.	d.
Ink glasses, square fountain	1	6
Penknife, one blade	1	0
Paper, blotting, per quire	0	6
,, cartridge ,,	2	2
,, foolscap, per ream	5	4
,, post, thin blue, 4to, per ream	6	3
Pencils, lead, per dozen	1	4
Pens, quill, per packet of 25	0	6
,, steel, box of one dozen with holder	0	9
Ruler, 18 inch	1	0
Tape, red, per piece	0	1
Wax, sealing, red, per dozen sticks, superfine	1	7
Do. do. second quality	1	3
Wafers, tin box containing two ozs.	0	4

The Queen's regulations, page 17, specify that the expense of camp colours, saluting colours, adjutant's aides, and pace sticks is to be defrayed out of the stationery allowance.

Pace sticks cost about seven shillings each, and are to last ten years, five are to be purchased and kept up at the expense of the stationery allowance, in addition to one per company, which are to be at the charge of the respective captains.

BIBLES AND PRAYER BOOKS.

Any non-commissioned officer or soldier who wishes to possess a Bible or prayer book may be supplied with either or both of them, separately or bound together in one volume. Roman Catholic prayer books and Testaments are supplied to men of that persuasion.

When any of these books are delivered to a man his name is to be written in the first page. They are expected to last ten years; any man losing or disposing of his Bible or prayer book is to be provided with another at his own expense. Should the regiment take the field, and any of these books become unavoidably lost through the casualties of the service, the owners of them may have them replaced at the public expense.

Requisitions are to be prepared in manuscript and transmitted in duplicate to the adjutant general. (*See* W. O. Circular 721, 25th October 1861).

The prices are as follows:—

	s.	d.
Bible and prayer book bound together	1	4
Bible separate	0	8½
Presbyterian Bible with psalms	0	10½
Roman Catholic prayer book and Testament	1	0

HOSPITAL EQUIPMENT.

The medicine chests, cases of instruments, and other surgical and medical appliances that are issued to regiments and battalions at home and abroad are contained in the following list. Detailed statements and explanations of their contents, with drawings of the various articles, as also the proportions of reserve equipments to accompany troops proceeding on active service, will be found in Part VII. of the Army Equipment.

	Cost.			Weight.		Number supplied to a Battalion.	
	£	s.	d.	lbs.	oz.	In Garrison.	In the Field.
Box, for books, stationery, and instruments, 32½″ long, 13½″ broad, and 15½″ deep - - - -	3	6	0	129	0	1	—
Canteens, hospital, pair, new pattern, containing plates, cutlery, cooking utensils, and various articles of hospital furniture, to be carried with pack-saddle if necessary - - - -	13	2	6	230	0	—	1
Cupping instruments in mahogany case, 8½″ long, 4½″ wide, and 4¼″ deep -	2	10	0	2	14	2	2
Fracture and dislocation apparatus in box, 42″ long, 12″ wide, and 12″ deep -	14	10	0	86	14	1	1
Medical field companion, containing a selection of medicines and appliances, calf skin case, 13″ long, 6¼″ wide, 8¼″ deep, with shoulder strap, so that it can be carried by an orderly - -	5	11	4	11	4	2	2
Water bottle, tin, holding about 2 quarts, with shoulder strap, to accompany medical field companion - - -	0	11	0	6	6	2	2
Medical comfort box for a battalion, with wine, spirits, and essence of beef, 32½″ long, 13½″ wide, 15½″ deep - -	5	10	4	128	0	—	1
Medical comfort box for a battalion, containing groceries, dimensions same as foregoing - - - -	6	9	0	127	0	—	1
Medicine chest, regimental, 38″ long, 26″ wide, 27″ deep - - -	37	3	2	319	5	1	—
Medicine chest, detachment, 34″ long, 25½″ wide, 28″ deep - - -	35	0	0	316	13	1	—
Medicine panniers, pair, wicker-work, with calf skin cover, containing medicines, instruments, and appliances; the two together forming a field operating table. Pack saddle and bridle for foregoing - - - -	*34	8	6½	241	9	—	1
Post mortem instruments, in mahogany case, 18″ long, 8¼″ wide, and 3¼″ deep	2	14	0	3	14	2	2
Stomach pump and enema apparatus, in mahogany case, 10″ long, 6½″ wide, 2″ deep - - - -	2	8	6	3	8	2	2
Surgical instruments, full set, in mahogany case and leather cover (purchased and kept up by surgeon) - - -	25	12	11	25	8	—	—

* The full set of instruments can be carried in one of the panniers in the field.

HOSPITAL EQUIPMENT.

	Cost.	Weight.	Number supplied to a Battalion.	
			In Garrison.	In the Field.
Surgical instruments, detachment case, in mahogany box and leather cover, 18" long, 8¼" wide, 3¼" deep	£ s. d. 14 19 1	lbs. oz. 11 8	1	1
Tooth instruments, extracting, in a leather roll case, 8" long, 4" diameter	5 10 6	3 6	2	2
Tooth instruments, scaling and stopping, in box, 6½" long, 4" wide, 1" deep	1 18 0	0 10	2	2

In cases where two chests or boxes are furnished, the second is intended to meet the requirements of any considerable portion of a battalion that may be detached and out of reach of head quarters. When a battalion is ordered to embark for foreign service, the pair of medicine panniers with pack saddle complete are issued.

When a battalion forms part of a moving force in the field the medicine chests and box for books and instruments will probably be left at the port of debarkation or base of operations. The other articles are to be carried in a medical store cart, which would also contain bedding and other camp equipment for 20 men, as detailed in Part VII. of Army Equipment, page 33.

An ambulance waggon is usually furnished with a small barrel of water, 14 stretchers, a light operating table, and two leather water buckets.

CAMP EQUIPMENT.

Under the head of Camp Equipment are included tents, blankets, intrenching tools, camp kettles and a variety of other articles required in addition to their regular equipment when troops are encamped, or engaged in operations in the field.

The following list shows the articles applicable to infantry as well as other services, with their prices, weights and quantities in which they are usually packed.

Name.	Price.			Weight.		Remarks.
	£	s.	d.	lbs.	ozs.	
Axe, felling, with helve -	0	4	0	6	0	A case containing 50 measures 3′ 0″ by 2′ 1″ by 1′ 6″, and weighs 353 lbs.
Axe, pick, ,, -	0	2	3	8	8	Issued loose. Length, 3′.
Bag, corn, two-bushel -	0	1	6	1	2	A bale of 100 measures 2′ 3″ by 1′ 6″ by 1′ 1″, and weighs 120 lbs.
Barrow, wheel -	0	15	3	66	0	
Blankets { field service (grey), for men.	0	5	6	3	12	Size, 7′ 2″ by 5′. A bale of 25 measures 2′ 7″ by 1′ 8″ by 1′ 5″, and weighs 104 lbs.
horse or saddle (white)	0	14	6	7	8	Size, 7′ 8″ by 6′ 4″. A bale of 25 measures 2′ 8″ by 2′ 2″ by 1′ 9″, and weighs 196 lbs.
Bucket, leather, for water (cavalry pattern).	0	7	3	3	0	Diameter at top, 10″; at bottom, 7″; depth, 10″; contents, 6 quarts. Issued by twenties, fixed one into another, and covered with matting.
Cart, water -	16	5	0	720	0	
Chain, fetlock, with double strap (latest pattern, 7/10/62 ; Circular 815).				0	15	Length of chain, 21′. Issued unpacked.
Colours, { flag (red shalloon) -	0	0	6	0	1½	
camp { poles -	0	1	3	2	12	8′ long.
{ cases (ticken)	0	0	3	0	1½	
Cord, forage -	0	0	6	0	10	Length, 21′. A bale of 250 measures 2′ 1″ by 1′ 11″ by 1′ 8″, and weighs 168 lbs.
Covers, waterproof { blanket -	0	6	4	2	2	Of vulcanized india-rubber, with six eyelet holes. Size, 6′ 6″ by 3′. A bale of 25 measures 1′ 10″ by 10″ by 10″, and weighs 60 lbs. (Approved 21/1/62.)
horse or saddle	0	7	2¼	1	12	Of blue camlet, waterproof. Size, 4′ 3″ by 3′ 5″. A bale of 25 measures 1′ 7″ by 1′ 4″ by 0′ 10″, and weighs 49 lbs. (Approved 22/10/61.)
File, for cross-cut saw, 9″ long -	0	0	6¼	0	8½	
Forage cord. *See* Cord.						
Hammer, sledge, 14 lbs. -	0	4	2	16	0	Two hammers issued for 20 wedges.
Handles, spare, for intrenching tools.	-	-	-	-	-	Tied together in bundles, and issued as required.
Hatchet, hand, American -	0	2	3	2	0	A case containing 100 measures 2′ 5″ by 1′ 6″ by 1′ 3″, and weighs 234 lbs.
Hobbles, ox hide -	-	-	-	-	-	Pattern provisionally approved 1/8/61, Cir. 724.
Hooks { bill -	0	2	0	1	12	A case containing 50 measures 1′ 8″ by 1′ 3″ by 1′ 0″, and weighs 108 lbs.
{ reaping -	0	1	3	1	0	A case containing 100 measures 2′ 2″ by 1′ 9″ by 1′ 5″, and weighs 134 lbs.
Iron, picketing, 2′ long, with a ring	0	0	7	2	8	

CAMP EQUIPMENT.

Name.	Price.			Weight.		Remarks.
	£	s.	d.	lbs.	ozs.	
Kettle, camp, Flanders, large -	0	3	9	8	8	Diameter at top, 12"; at bottom, 11"; depth, 12"; contents, 12 quarts. Issued in sets of five fixed one into another and secured by wooden "cradles." One set thus packed measures 2' 6" in length by 1' 2" in diameter, and weighs 49 lbs.
Lantern { horn -	0	2	0	2	4	
{ red -	0	11	6	2	14	
Mallets, wood { for picket posts -	0	2	6	8	0	Issued unpacked. Length with handle, 3'.
{ for tent pins	0	0	6	2	0	Issued with the pins.
Nets, forage - pair	0	2	0	2	0	A bale of 50 pairs measures 2' 4" by 1' 6" by 1' 6", and weighs 112 lbs.
Pins, tent { large - per 100	0	8	0	112	0	A proportion of pins, containing the number required for use and a few spare, is issued with each tent complete.
{ small - "	0	2	6	22	0	
Poles, tent -				various		See description of tents.
Posts, picket { long -	0	3	0	9	0	5' long, 3" in diameter } Issued unpacked.
{ short -				5	0	2½ " 3 "
Ropes, heel, cotton -	0	2	8½	1	13	A bale of 50 measures 2' 0" by 1' 6" by 1' 6", and weighs 102 lbs.
Rope, picket, 3-inch, tarred -	0	7	6	8	8	A piece 500 feet long, as issued, measures 3' in length by 1' 1" in diameter, and weighs 84 lbs.
Saddle, pack, complete -	5	2	6	64	0	Including baggage straps and leading bridles. Issued in cases containing two each, and measuring 3' 6" by 2' 9" by 2' 7"; marked with a black horse shoe.
Saw, cross-cut, 6½-feet long -	0	7	6	9	1	
Sheet, ground, waterproof. See Cover.						
Shovel with handle -	0	2	9	4	12	3¼' long. Issued unpacked.
Sickle -	0	0	10	0	10	A case containing 200 measures 2' 2" by 1' 9" by 1' 5", and weighs 157 lbs.
Spade, with handle -	0	2	9	6	0	
Stone, whet or rag -	0	0	2	1	0	
Stove -						Used in standing camps only.
Strap, buff leather, for canteen -	0	1	3	0	5	Issued as required. A ¼-ton vat will hold 500.
Tents, { hospital marquee	28	0	0	500	0	}
complete { officers' "	10	0	0	180	0	} See description below.
{ circular, single	3	15	0	70	0	}
Tools, intrenching -	-			-		The various tools are given separately.
Vases, large and small -				various		For tent poles. Issued with the tents complete.
Waterdeck. See Cover, horse.						
Wedges { 12½ inch -	0	1	5	8	8	} Wedges for field service are packed in a case, strongly battened. A case containing 20 weighs about 1 cwt.
{ 10 " -	0	1	1½	6	4	
{ 9 " -	0	1	0½	5	10	
{ 8 " -	0	0	11½	4	6	

 The *hospital marquee*, which is used also as a mess tent, consists of a double roof, a wall five feet high, a ridge pole, and three upright poles. The wall is in eight separate lengths, and each of the poles in two pieces. The width inside is 15 feet, and the extreme length is 30 feet, the ends being semi-circular. A bottom or floor of painted canvas, in four pieces is issued in addition, when the tent is used as a hospital.

 The *officers' marquee* has a double roof, of linen duck outside and ticken inside, a double wall of similar materials, a ridge pole, two upright poles and two door poles; the outside wall and each of the poles is in two pieces.

 The single *circular* or bell tent has only a roof with a curtain at the bottom a few inches wide. There is a wooden flooring, made in four quadrant shaped pieces, for use in permanent camps.

 Tents are now made of linen duck, and the cotton ones will be obsolete when the present stock is worn out. Double circular tents, with two roofs of linen, or one of cotton and one of linen, are occasionally issued. The various tents, when ready for transport, consist of the following packages:—

									Weight.
		ft.	ins.		ft.	ins.		ft. ins.	lbs.
Hospital marquee. (Pattern approved 15th June 1861, Cir. 704.)	valise, with roof and wall	4	2	by	2	2	by	1 6	356
	bag, with 4 large pins, 180 small pins, and 2 mallets.	1	9	„	1	6	„	1 6	56
	bundle of poles	7	6	„	0	10	„	0 9	121
	bottom	9	0	„	1	0	„	0 10	191
Officers' marquee	valise, with roof and wall	3	0	„	1	4	„	1 4	108
	bag, with 4 large pins, 96 small pins, and 2 mallets.	1	9	„	1	2	„	1 2	34
	bundle of poles	4	7	„	0	8	„	0 8	44
Circular single	valise, with roof, and bag containing 42 pins, and 2 mallets.	2	8	„	1	4	„	1 0	62
	pole, in two pieces	5	5	„	0	4	„	0 2	12

Picket posts.—The short picket posts have been lately introduced to replace the long ones; with the latter the rope was stretched a few feet above the ground, and the horses were secured to it by the head collar and chain used in ordinary stables. With the former the rope lies on the ground, and the horses are fastened to it by the fetlock chain issued for the purpose. Restive horses are further secured by heel ropes, which are supplied in the proportion of about 10 per cent.

Sickle and reaping hook.—The sickle is used for cutting corn, and the reaping hook for gorse or brushwood. They are generally alike in appearance, but the sickle is lighter and has a serrated edge.

PROPORTION OF CAMP EQUIPMENT ISSUED TO INFANTRY.*

Description.	Proportion when in Standing Camp.	Proportion when on Service in the Field.
Axes, helved { felling, 4½ lbs.	1 per company	5 per battalion and 1 per company.
{ pick	2 per company and 2 per battalion	5 per battalion and 1 per company.
Barrows, wheel	4 per battalion.	
Blankets, grey, field service	2 for each non-commissioned officer and man.	1 for each non-commissioned officer and man.
Brooms, heath	2 per company.	
Buckets, leather, cavalry pattern	1 per N.C. officers' and men's tent	1 for each pack saddle.
Colours, camp, with poles, &c.	6 per battalion	1 per company; 2 extra for guards.
Covers, waterproof	1 per horse	
Files, for cross-cut saw		1 per company when required.
Hammers and wedges, *sets consisting of 2 hammers and 20 wedges.*	2 per battalion	
Hatchets, hand	1 per 10 N.C. officers and men	2 for every 15 non-commissioned officers and men.
Hooks, bill	1 per 10 N.C. officers and men	1 for every 15 non-commissioned officers and men.
Kettles, camp, Flanders	1 per 8 N.C. officers and men	1 for every 5 non-commissioned officers and men.
Lanterns, horn	2 per battalion for guards	2 per battalion for guards.
Mallets, tent, spare Pins, tent } spare sets Poles, tent }		[5 per cent. on tents supplied.
Picketing Implements { fetlock chains and straps.	1 for each mounted officer.	
{ mauls	1 per battalion.	
{ posts	6 „	
{ ropes	1 „	

* W.O. Circular No. 869, 6th July 1864.

CAMP EQUIPMENT.

Description.	Proportion when in Standing Camp.	Proportion when on Service in the Field.
Saddles, pack, with straps and bridles, waterproof covers, horse blankets, surcingles, pads, stable necessaries, and picketing implements	— — — — —	1 per company. 1 for armourer's tools. 1 for paymaster. 1 for adjutant (orderly room). 1 for quartermasters' stores. 1 for entrenching tools.
Saws, cross-cut, 6½ feet	— — — — —	1 per company, but issued only when required, upon special requisition.
Shovels, with **T** handles	2 per battalion and 1 per company	5 per battalion and 1 per company.
Spades, with **T** handles	2 per battalion and 1 per company	5 per battalion and 1 per company.
Stones, whet or rag	6 per battalion	2 per battalion and 1 per company.
Stoves	1 per battalion for officers' mess 1 „ serjeants' „	—
Tents, complete, with poles, pins, mallets, pin bags, and valises. — marquees — officers' mess	1 per battalion, or 2 if more than 24 officers are present.	—
marquees — serjeants' mess	1 per battalion.	—
marquees — officers	1, or 2 circular tents, for each field officer or officer ranking as such.	—
circular	2 for each field officer or 1 officer's marquee instead.	2 for each field officer.
circular	1 for each other officer	1 for each other officer.
circular	1 per 12 N.C. officers and men	1 for every 15 non-commissioned officers and men.
circular	1 for every 2 staff serjeants	2 for staff serjeants.
circular	4 for guards	4 for guards.
circular	1 for orderly room	1 for orderly room.
circular	1 for quartermasters' stores	1 for quartermasters' stores.
circular	1 for paymaster's office	1 for paymaster's office.
circular	3 for field and staff officers' servants.	—
circular	1 per company for officers' servants	—
circular	1 for bandmaster.	—
circular	2 for tradesmen's shops, or 3 if necessary.	—
circular	2 for messman's stores and mess-servants.	—
Tubs, wood, small, for washing	1 per N.C. officers' and men's tent	—
Wedges. *See* HAMMERS.		

Canteens, haversacks, nose bags and corn sacks are supplied upon demands made through the Adjutant General, as articles of personal equipment.*

All other articles are to be demanded through the Quartermaster General. Requisitions for camp equipment must be accompanied by the following detailed statement of the strength of the corps or detachment.

	No.
Number of Companies	
Field Officers	
Other officers	
Staff serjeants	
Serjeants, rank and file, &c.,	
Officers chargers	
Public bât animals	
Private do.	

* A corn sack holds 5 bushels, costs 1s. 6d., weighs 4 lb. 12 oz. A bale of 25 measures 2 ft. 6 in. × 1 ft. 4 in. × 1 ft. 3 in., and weighs 117 lb. A canvas nose bag costs 1s. 9d., weighs 1 lb. 5 oz. A bale of 100 measures 2 ft. 1 in. × 1 ft. 7 in. × 1 ft. 5 in., and weighs 145 lbs.

General officers commanding in standing camps are empowered to authorize camp equipment to be issued in quantities not exceeding the regulated proportions; they are, however, to restrict the issues, to such articles and to such quantities as they may consider to be actually required.

When field allowance is not authorized, picketing implements, waterproof horse covers, and nose bags will be supplied free of charge for the regulated number of officers' horses. It must however be stated in the requisition, that field allowance has not been authorized.

No other articles of horse equipment will be issued for horses not the property of the public.

When any articles of camp equipment become unserviceable, or require to be replaced, a board of survey other than regimental must be assembled, consisting of three officers, one of whom where practicable, is to be an officer of the Military Store Department; the president is not to be below the rank of captain. Any articles lost otherwise than by unavoidable accident, or damaged beyond what may be considered as the effects of fair wear and tear are to be charged against the troops.

Such barrack stores as are necessary for troops when in standing camp, must be specially applied for through the Quartermaster General.

On service in the field, all articles of camp equipment may be purchased by officers with the sanction of the general commanding, provided the state of the stores admits of the sale.

Blankets, canteens, havresacks, &c. are not to be supplied to officers except upon payment. As a general rule all articles which do not form part of the personal equipment of the soldier and that are not paraded with the troops when in marching order, excepting materials for the repair of such equipment are to be demanded through the Quartermaster General.

DETAIL OF THE PERSONAL EQUIPMENT OF THE SEVERAL CLASSES OF INFANTRY.

The lists given in the following pages exhibit in detail the articles carried by the several ranks of non-commissioned officers and men of each class of infantry. It has been already stated in the introductory remarks to this work that the *cost* of the different articles must be regarded as a *comparative* rate only, as the expense of manufacture and the contract prices of materials fluctuate according to the state of the markets. The prices given have however been carefully calculated according to the latest data furnished by the department charged with the manufacture or issue of each particular store.

The entire weight carried by each man is subject to some variation according to the size of the clothing and accoutrements worn by him.

It is also important to remark that according to the Circular Memorandum dated Horse Guards 15th November 1854 the following articles are ordered to be carried in squad bags which are issued to the troops in the proportion of one to every 25 non-commissioned officers and men :—shell jacket, 1 shirt, 1 pair socks, 1 towel, 2 brushes, and such articles from the hold-all as are not immediately required. The entire diminution in the weight carried being about 5 lbs. This reduction would be to some extent modified by a variety of things that a man may be assumed to have in his possession. Among these may be enumerated water in the canteen, some portion of his rations, soap, pipeclay, rag for cleaning his rifle, money, tobacco, &c.

REGIMENT OF GUARDS.

Description.	Cost.			Weight.		Remarks.
	£	s.	d.	lbs.	oz.	
SERJEANT-MAJOR.						
Arms and Accoutrements.						
Belt, waist, buff, with sword carriages and union locket.	1	0	6	0	13¾	Rate for Coldstream Guards.
Sword and scabbard - - - -	1	12	6	2	10¾	
Havresack - - - -	0	1	0	0	10	
Canteen, wooden, with strap - -	0	2	6	1	12	On active service only.
Clothing.						
Bearskin cap, with plume and bag - -	4	4	0	1	9	No plume for Scots Fusiliers.
Boots, two pairs - - - -	0	17	0	5	10	
Gloves, white leather, pair - -	0	2	0	0	2¼	
Knot, sword, gold - - -	0	10	0	0	1½	
Leggings, leather, pair - - -	0	3	4	0	11	
Sash, silk - - - -	1	15	0	0	14½	
Trousers { black doeskin - - -	1	1	0	2	1	
{ black tartan - - -	0	19	0	1	7	
Tunic { full dress, with badges - -	10	13	3¼	3	15	Pair of 4-bar gold chevrons, with royal arms.
{ undress, no badges - -	3	0	0	3	6	
Great coat - - - -	2	12	0	6	2	
Necessaries.						
Set as detailed at page 115 - -	2	11	4	12	12	
Total - -	31	4	5¼	44	9¾	
SCHOOLMASTER.						
See page 147 - - - -	10	18	2¼	22	0¼	
QUARTERMASTER SERJEANT.						
Arms and Accoutrements.						
As for serjeant-major - - -	2	16	6	5	14½	
Clothing.						
As for serjeant-major, excepting badges on tunic	21	7	9¼	25	11¼	Pair of 4-bar gold chevrons only.
Necessaries.						
Set as detailed at page 115 - -	2	11	4	12	12	
Total - -	26	15	7¼	44	5¾	
SERJEANT INSTRUCTOR OF MUSKETRY.						
Arms and Accoutrements.						
As for serjeant-major - - -	2	16	6	5	14½	

REGIMENT OF GUARDS.

Description.	Cost.			Weight.		Remarks.
	£	s.	d.	lbs.	oz.	
Clothing.						
As for serjeant-major, excepting badges on tunic	21	10	10	25	8¼	Pair of 4-bar gold chevrons, with crossed muskets.
Necessaries.						
Set as detailed at page 115 - - -	2	11	4	12	12	
Total - -	26	17	8	44	2¾	
BAND MASTER.						
Arms and Accoutrements.						
As for serjeant-major - - -	2	16	6	5	14½	
Clothing.						
Bearskin cap, with plume and bag - -	4	4	0	1	9	
Boots, two pairs - - - -	0	17	0	5	10	
Gloves, white leather, pair - -	0	2	0	0	2¼	
Knot, sword, gold - - -	0	10	0	0	1½	
Leggings, leather, pair - - -	0	3	4	0	11	
Sash, silk - - - -	1	15	0	0	14½	
Trousers { black doeskin - -	1	1	0	2	1	
{ black tartan - -	0	19	0	1	7	
Tunic - - - - -	11	2	11½	3	9	
Shell jacket (waistcoat) - -	0	15	6	2	2½	
Great coat - - - -	2	12	0	6	2	
Necessaries.						
Set as detailed at page 115 - - -	2	11	4	12	12	
Total - -	29	9	7½	43	0¼	
DRUM MAJOR.						
Arms and Accoutrements.						
As for serjeant-major - - -	2	16	6	5	14½	
Clothing.						
Bearskin cap, with cover and plume - -	4	4	0	1	9	No plume for Scots Fusiliers.
Boots, two pairs - - - -	0	17	0	5	10	
Gloves, white leather, pair - -	0	2	0	0	2¼	
Knot, sword, gold - - -	0	10	0	0	1½	
Leggings, leather, pair - - -	0	3	4	0	11	
Sash, silk - - - -	1	15	0	0	14½	
Tassels, gold, for staff - -	0	16	6	0	2	
Trousers { black doeskin - -	0	16	0	2	1½	
{ black tartan - -	0	7	10	1	7	
Tunic, with badges - - -	9	10	10½	3	9	Wings and pair of 4-bar gold chevrons, with drum.
White shell jacket (waistcoat with sleeves) -	0	15	6	2	2½	
Great coat - - - -	1	3	6	6	2	
Necessaries.						
Set as detailed at page 115 - - -	2	11	4	12	12	
Drum major's staff - - - } for State occasions {						Provided from regimental sources.
Shoulder belt, embroidered - - }						
Cap, black velvet, jockey pattern }						
Tunic, velvet, richly laced and embroidered with royal arms. }						
Total - -	26	9	4½	43	2¾	

Description.	Cost. £	s.	d.	Weight. lbs.	oz.	Remarks.
ARMOURER SERJEANT.						
Arms and Accoutrements.						
Same as battalion drill serjeant - - -	2	4	9	6	0	
Clothing.						
As for serjeant - - - - -	11	17	8	24	0¼	
Necessaries.						
Set as detailed at page 115 - - -	2	9	3	12	11½	
Total - -	16	11	8	42	11¾	
HOSPITAL SERJEANT.						
Arms and Accoutrements.						
As for battalion drill serjeant - - -	2	4	9	6	0	
Clothing.						
As for battalion drill serjeant - - -	13	2	10½	25	4¾	
Necessaries.						
Set as detailed at page 115 - - -	2	9	3	12	11½	
Total - -	17	16	10	44	0¼	
REGIMENTAL CLERK.						
Arms and Accoutrements.						
As for serjeant-major - - - -	2	16	6	5	14½	
Clothing.						
As for serjeant-major, excepting badges - -	21	4	4	25	7¼	3-bar chevrons.
Necessaries.						
Set as detailed at page 115 - - -	2	11	4	12	12	
Total - -	26	12	2	44	1¾	
BATTALION ORDERLY-ROOM SERJEANT.						
Arms and Accoutrements.						
As for battalion drill serjeant - - -	2	4	9	6	0	
Clothing.						
As serjeant - - - - -	11	17	8	24	0¼	
Necessaries.						
Set as detailed at page 115 - - -	2	9	3	12	12	
Total - -	16	1	8	42	12¼	

REGIMENT OF GUARDS.

Description.	Cost.			Weight.		Remarks.
	£	s.	d.	lbs.	oz.	
REGIMENTAL DRILL SERJEANT.						
Arms and Accoutrements.						
As for serjeant-major (excepting union locket, see p. 103).	2	3	6	5	14½	
Clothing.						
Bearskin cap, with plume and bag	4	4	0	1	9	No plume for Scots Fusiliers.
Boots, two pairs	0	17	0	5	10	
Gloves, white leather, pair	0	2	0	0	2¼	
Knot, sword, gold	0	10	0	0	1½	
Leggings, leather, pair	0	3	4	0	11	
Sash, silk	1	15	0	0	14½	
Trousers { black doeskin	0	16	0	2	1½	
{ black tartan	0	7	10	1	7	
Tunic { full dress	3	11	8½	3	8	Pair of 3-bar gold chevrons, with lace on collar and cuffs.
{ undress	1	12	0	3	6	
Great coat	1	3	6	6	2	
Necessaries.						
Set as detailed at page 115	2	11	4	12	12	
Total	19	17	2½	44	3¼	
BATTALION DRILL SERJEANT.						
Arms and Accoutrements.						
Belt, waist, buff, with gilt union locket and sword carriages.	0	7	6	0	13¾	
Knot, sword, buff	0	1	3	0	1½	
Sword and scabbard	1	12	6	2	10¾	
Havresack	0	1	0	0	10	
Canteen, wooden, with strap	0	2	6	1	12	On active service only.
Clothing.						
Bearskin cap, with plume and bag	4	4	0	1	9	No plume for Scots Fusiliers.
Boots, two pairs	0	17	0	5	10	
Gloves, white leather, pair	0	2	0	0	2¼	
Leggings, leather, pair	0	3	4	0	11	
Sash, worsted	0	5	6	0	12	
Trousers { black doeskin	0	16	0	2	1½	
{ black tartan	0	7	10	1	7	
Tunic { full dress	3	11	8½	3	8	Pair of 3-bar gold chevrons, with lace on collar and cuffs.
{ undress	1	12	0	3	6	
Great coat	1	3	6	6	2	
Necessaries.						
Set as detailed at page 115	2	9	3	12	11¼	
Total	17	16	10	43	15¾	

EQUIPMENT OF NON-COMMISSIONED OFFICERS AND MEN.

Description.	Cost.			Weight.		Remarks.
	£	s.	d.	lbs.	oz.	
BAND SERJEANT.						
Arms and Accoutrements.						
Same as battalion drill serjeant	2	4	9	6	0	
Clothing.						
Bearskin cap, with plume and bag	4	4	0	1	9	No plume for Scots Fusiliers.
Boots, two pairs	0	17	0	5	10	
Gloves, white leather, pair	0	2	0	0	2¼	
Leggings, leather, pair	0	3	4	0	11	
Sash, silk	1	15	0	0	14½	
Trousers { black doeskin	0	16	0	2	1¼	
{ black tartan	0	7	10	1	7	
Tunic	5	6	2¾	3	7	
Waistcoat	0	15	6	2	2½	
Great coat	1	3	6	6	2	
Necessaries.						
Set as detailed at page 115	2	11	4	12	12	
Total	20	6	5¾	42	14¾	
COLOUR SERJEANT.						
As serjeant	20	12	11¼	56	6	
Badges extra	0	17	0	0	2	Special pattern for each regiment.
Total	21	9	11¼	56	8	
SERJEANT.						
Arms and Accoutrements.						
Bag, ball, buff	0	2	6	0	7	
Belts, buff { pouch	0	3	0	0	8	
{ waist, with gilding metal union locket, and frog.	0	3	8	0	12¾	
Havresack	0	1	0	0	10	
Pouch { 20 rounds, with brass ornament	0	4	6	1	4½	
{ for percussion caps, buff	0	1	0	0	2	
Sling, musket, buff	0	1	0	0	3½	
Short rifle-musket, pattern 1860, with rammer, sword bayonet and scabbard, snap cap and chain, and muzzle stopper.	5	4	9¾	10	12½	
Wrench nipple, with cramp	0	1	11½	0	6½	
Canteen, wooden, with strap	0	2	6	1	12	On active service only.
Ammunition.						
30 rounds, with 45 percussion caps	—	—	—	2	11½	
Clothing.						
Bearskin cap, with cover and plume	4	4	0	1	9	No plume for Scots Fusiliers.
Boots, two pairs	0	17	0	5	10	
Gloves, white leather, pair	0	2	0	0	2¼	
Leggings, leather, pair	0	3	4	0	11	
Sash, worsted	0	5	6	0	12	
Trousers { Oxford mixture	0	16	0	2	1½	
{ black tartan	0	7	10	1	7	

REGIMENT OF GUARDS.

Description.	Cost.			Weight.		Remarks.
	£	s.	d.	lbs.	oz.	
Tunic	3	3	0	3	7	
Waistcoat	0	15	6	2	$2\frac{1}{2}$	
Great coat	1	3	6	6	2	
Necessaries.						
Set as detailed at page 115	2	9	4	12	$11\frac{1}{2}$	
Total	20	12	$11\frac{1}{4}$	56	6	
CORPORAL.						
Arms and Accoutrements.						
As for private, excepting nipple wrench	4	4	$4\frac{1}{4}$	17	$1\frac{3}{4}$	With cramp.
Ammunition.						
60 rounds and 90 percussion caps	-	-	-	5	7	
Clothing.						
As for private	8	16	2	24	$4\frac{1}{2}$	
Badges extra	0	1	0	0	1	
Necessaries.						
As for private (*see* page 115)	1	15	9	12	$12\frac{1}{2}$	
Total	14	17	$3\frac{1}{4}$	59	$10\frac{3}{4}$	
PRIVATE.						
Arms and Accoutrements.						
Bag, ball, buff	0	2	6	0	7	
Belts, buff { pouch	0	3	0	0	8	
waist, with brass union locket and frog.	0	3	7	0	$12\frac{3}{4}$	
Havresack	0	1	0	0	10	
Pouch { 50 rounds, with brass ornament	0	6	3	2	$1\frac{1}{2}$	
for percussion caps, buff	0	1	0	0	2	
Sling, musket buff	0	1	0	0	$3\frac{1}{4}$	
Rifle-musket pattern, 1853, with rammer, bayonet, and scabbard, snap cap and chain, and muzzle stopper.	3	1	$6\frac{3}{4}$	10	$2\frac{1}{2}$	
Wrench, nipple, without cramp	0	0	$11\frac{1}{2}$	0	$4\frac{1}{2}$	
Canteen, wooden, with strap	0	2	6	1	12	On active service only.
Ammunition.						
60 rounds, with 90 percussion caps	-	-	-	5	7	
Clothing.						
Bearskin cap, with cover and plume	4	4	0	1	9	No plume for Scots Fusiliers.
Boots, two pairs	0	17	0	5	10	
Leggings, leather, pair	0	3	4	0	11	
Trousers { Oxford mixture	0	11	0	2	5	
black tartan	0	7	10	1	7	
Tunic	1	3	0	4	$9\frac{1}{2}$	
Shell jacket (waistcoat)	0	6	6	1	15	
Great coat	1	3	6	6	2	
Necessaries.						
Set as detailed at page 115	1	15	9	12	$12\frac{1}{2}$	
Total	14	15	$3\frac{1}{4}$	59	$7\frac{3}{4}$	

EQUIPMENT OF NON-COMMISSIONED OFFICERS AND MEN.

Description.	Cost.			Weight.		Remarks.
	£	s.	d.	lbs.	oz.	
DRUMMER.						
Arms, Accoutrements, and Appointments.						
Apron, buff, for side drum	0	4	0	0	10	
Belt, waist, buff, with brass union locket and frog	0	3	7	0	12¾	
Sword and scabbard	0	12	6	2	9	
Drum, with sticks and ticken cover	2	7	6	9	2	New pattern.
Havresack	0	1	0	0	10	
Canteen, wooden, with strap	0	2	6	1	12	On active service only.
Clothing.						
As for private	8	16	2	24	4½	
Distinctions on tunic extra	0	14	0	0	3	
Necessaries.						
As private (*see* page 115)	1	15	9	12	12½	
Total	17	5	0	52	11¾	
BUGLER.						
Arms, Accoutrements, and Appointments.						
Belt, waist, buff, with brass union locket, and frog	0	3	7	0	12¾	
Sword and scabbard	0	12	6	2	9	
Bugle and strings	1	3	0	1	11¼	
Flute and case (average)	0	14	0¼	0	8¾	
Havresack	0	1	0	0	10	
Canteen, wooden, with strap	0	2	6	1	12	On active service only.
Clothing.						
As drummer	9	10	2	24	7½	
Necessaries.						
As private (*see* page 115)	1	15	9	12	12½	
Total	14	2	6¼	45	3¾	
MUSICIAN.						
Arms and Accoutrements.						
Belt, waist, buff, with gilt union locket and slide and frog.	0	5	3	0	12¾	
Sword and scabbard	0	12	6	2	9	
Havresack	0	1	0	0	10	
Canteen, wooden, with strap	0	2	6	1	12	
Musical instrument						
Clothing.						
Bearskin cap, with plume and cover	4	4	0	1	9	No plume for Scots Fusiliers.
Boots, two pairs	0	17	0	5	10	
Leggings, leather, pair	0	3	4	0	11	
Trousers { Oxford mixture	0	16	0	2	1½	
{ black tartan	0	7	10	1	7	
Tunic, with gold lace laid on	5	0	0	3	7	
Shell jacket (waistcoat)	0	6	6	1	15	
Great coat	1	3	6	6	2	
Necessaries.						
As private (*see* page 115)	1	14	6½	12	12½	
Total	15	13	11½	41	8¾	

Description.	Cost.	Weight.	Remarks.
PIONEERS. TEN MEN CARRY THE FOLLOWING EQUIPMENT. *Arms, Accoutrements, and Appointments.*	£ s. d.	lbs. oz.	
Belt, waist, buff, with union locket, and frog with shifting loop.	0 3 10	0 13¾	
Havresack	0 1 0	0 10	
Sword, with sawback and scabbard	0 11 10	3 0	
Canteen, wooden, with strap	0 2 6	1 12	On active service only.
Axe, pick, with case	0 5 3	6 8	
Bill-hook ,,	0 4 9	2 4	
Shovel ,,	0 9 6	7 2	
Gun spikes, two	0 0 8	0 2½	
Clothing.			
As private	8 16 2	24 4½	
Necessaries.			
As private (see page 115)	1 15 9	12 12½	
Total	12 11 3	59 5¼	
SIX MEN CARRY THE FOLLOWING EQUIPMENT. *Arms, Accoutrements, and Appointments.*			
Sword, belt, havresack, and canteen, same as the foregoing.	0 19 2	6 3¾	
Axe, felling, with case	0 5 6	6 4	
Bill-hook ,,	0 4 9	2 4	
Spade ,,	0 9 6	6 1½	
Gun spikes, two	0 0 8	0 2½	
Clothing.			
As private	8 16 2	24 4	
Necessaries.			
As private (see page 115)	1 15 9	12 12½	
Total	12 11 6	58 0¼	
TWO MEN CARRY THE FOLLOWING EQUIPMENT. *Arms, Accoutrements, and Appointments.*			
Sword, belt, havresack, and canteen, same as the foregoing.	0 19 2	6 3¾	
Axe { felling, with case	0 5 6	6 4	
Axe { broad, and axe, hand, with case	0 10 3	6 14	
Bill-hook, with case	0 4 9	2 4	
Gun spikes, two	0 0 8	0 2½	
Clothing.			
As private	8 16 2	24 4	
Necessaries.			
As private (see page 115)	1 15 9	12 12½	
Total	12 12 3	58 12¾	

EQUIPMENT OF NON-COMMISSIONED OFFICERS AND MEN.

Description.	Cost.			Weight.		Remarks.
	£	s.	d.	lbs.	oz.	
Two Men carry the following Equipment.						
Arms, Accoutrements, and Appointments.						
Sword, belt, havresack, and canteen, same as the foregoing.	0	19	2	6	3¾	
Axe { felling, with case	0	5	6	6	4	
{ hand, and saw, with case	0	15	9	6	12	
Bill-hook, with case	0	4	9	2	4	
Gun spikes, two	0	0	8	0	2½	
Clothing.						
As private	8	16	2	24	4	
Necessaries.						
As private (see page 115)	1	15	9	12	12½	
Total	12	17	9	58	10¾	
Two Men carry the following Equipment.						
Arms, Accoutrements, and Appointments.						
Sword, belt, havresack, and canteen, same as the foregoing.	0	19	2	6	3¾	
Crowbar, with caps and strap	0	4	9	7	6½	
Case containing auger, cold and socket chisels, and hammer.	0	14	9	7	5½	
Gun spikes, two	0	0	8	0	2½	
Clothing.						
As corporal	8	17	2	24	5½	
Necessaries.						
As private (see page 115)	1	15	9	12	12½	
Total	12	12	3	58	4¼	
HOSPITAL ORDERLY.						
Arms and Accoutrements.						
Belt, buff, waist, with brass locket and frog	0	3	7	0	12¾	
Sword and scabbard (pattern for drummers)	0	12	6	2	9	
Clothing and Necessaries.						
As private	10	11	11	37	0½	
Total	11	8	0	40	6¼	
TIME-BEATER.						
As musician	15	15	2	41	6¾	
Extra for lace, &c., on tunic	2	14	0	0	6	
Total	18	9	2	41	12¾	
FOR SCOTS FUSILIER GUARDS ONLY.						
PIPE-MAJOR.						
Arms, Accoutrements, and Appointments.						
Same as pipe-major of Highland regiment (see page 117)	10	15	6	11	6	

Description.	Cost.			Weight.		Remarks.
	£	s.	d.	lbs.	oz.	
Clothing.						
Cap, Glengarry	0	3	6	0	5	
Coat, complete	4	4	9	2	14	
Kilt	1	10	6	2	2	
Leggings, leather, pair	0	3	4	0	11	
Plaid	0	12	6	2	14	
Sash, silk	1	17	6	0	14½	
Shoes, two pairs	0	16	0	5	0	
Shell jacket (waistcoat)	1	4	11½	2	3	
Necessaries.						
Same articles as pipe-major of Highland regiment (see page 126)	4	12	5¼	16	0¼	
Total	26	0	11¾	44	6¾	

PIPER.

Arms, Accoutrements, and Appointments.

Description.	Cost.			Weight.		
Same as piper of Highland regiment (see page 126)	10	11	9	11	3	
Clothing.						
Cap, Glengarry	0	3	6	0	5	
Coat, complete	1	10	0	3	7	
Kilt	0	19	4	2	11	
Leggings, leather, pair	0	3	4	0	11	
Plaid	0	4	5	2	14	
Shoes, two pairs	0	16	0	5	0	
Waistcoat	0	12	1	2	2½	
Necessaries.						
Same articles as private of Highland regiment (see page 126).	3	4	7¼	15	14¾	
Total	18	5	0¼	44	4¼	

TIME-BEATER.

Arms, Accoutrements, and Appointments.

Description.	Cost.			Weight.		
As drummer	3	11	1	15	7¾	
Clothing.						
Chaco and plume	4	18	0	1	0	
Boots, two pairs	0	17	0	5	0	
Jacket	6	14	5	2	8	
Leggings, leather, pair	0	3	4	0	11	
Trousers { red cloth (laced with gold)	2	15	4	2	0	
{ black tartan	0	7	10	1	7	
Tunic	1	7	8	3	3	
Waistcoat { red, regimental pattern	3	17	8	2	8	
{ white	0	6	6	2	0	
Necessaries.						
As private, p. 115	1	15	9	12	12½	
Total	26	14	7	48	9¼	

GENERAL LIST OF EQUIPMENTS FOR A REGIMENT OF GUARDS (COLDSTREAM), CONSISTING OF TWO BATTALIONS.

Number of Rank and File 2,000, in Twenty Companies.

Description.	Cost of each.			Weight of each.		Total No.	Total Cost.			Total Weight.	
	£	*s.*	*d.*	lbs.	oz.		£	*s.*	*d.*	lbs.	oz.
ARMS.											
Muskets, rifle, pattern 1853, complete with rammer, bayonet, bayonet scabbard, muzzle stopper, and snap cap with chain.	3	1	6¾	10	2½	1,958	6,026	19	4½	19,885	15
Short rifle, muskets, pattern 1860, complete with rammer, sword bayonet, scabbard, muzzle stopper, and snap cap with chain.	5	4	9¾	10	12½	92	482	2	9	991	14
Nipples, spare	0	0	1¾	0	0⅙	616	4	9	10	6	6¾
Wrenches, nipple, with cramps	0	1	11½	0	6½	205	20	1	5½	83	4½
Wrenches, nipple, without cramps	0	0	11½	0	4½	1,855	58	17	8½	520	9½
Swords and scabbards, staff serjeants pattern	1	12	6	2	10¾	23	37	7	6	42	12
Swords and scabbards, drummers	0	12	6	2	9	60	37	10	0	153	12
Swords and scabbards, for pioneers	0	11	10	3	0	22	13	0	4	66	0
Total	-	-	-	-	-	-	6,680	8	11½	21,750	9¾
Drummer's appointments.											
Two sets (same as line, *see* page 150)	-	-	-	-	-	-	82	10	6	227	10
ACCOUTREMENTS.											
Aprons, buff, leg, for side drum	0	4	0	0	10	20	4	0	0	12	8
Bags, ball, buff	0	2	6	0	7	2,050	256	5	0	896	14
Belts, pouch, buff	0	3	0	0	8	2,050	307	10	0	1,025	0
Belts, waist, black japanned leather, with sword carriages and snake hook, gilt furniture.	0	6	0	0	12½	2	0	12	0	1	9
Belts, waist, buff, with sword carriages, gilt furniture and slide.	0	5	6	0	9	21	5	15	6	11	13
Belts, waist, buff, with gilt slide, for	0	1	9	0	5½	20	1	15	0	6	14
band	0	1	9	0	5½	2,112	184	16	0	726	0
Canteens, wooden, with strap	0	2	6	1	12	2,153	269	2	6	3,767	12
Carriages, buff, for side drum	0	2	6	1	2½	20	2	10	0	23	2
Frogs, buff, for band	0	1	6	0	2½	20	1	10	0	3	2
Frogs, buff, for serjeants, rank and file, &c.	0	1	3	0	2½	2,090	130	12	6	326	9
Frogs, buff, with shifting loop for pioneers	0	1	6	0	3½	22	1	13	0	4	13
Havresacks	0	1	0	0	10	2,153	107	13	0	1,345	10
Knots, sword, black japanned leather	0	1	6	0	0¾	2	0	3	0	0	1½
Knots, sword, buff	0	1	3	0	1½	10	0	12	6	0	15
Lockets, union, gilt*	0	15	0	0	4¾	8	6	0	0	2	6
	0	2	0	0	4¾	33	3	6	0	9	12¾
Lockets, union, gilding metal	0	0	8	0	4¾	92	3	1	4	27	5
Lockets, union, brass	0	0	7	0	4¾	2,020	58	18	4	599	11
Ornaments for pouches	0	0	3	0	0½	2,050	25	12	6	64	1
Pouches, black leather, 20 round, with fur cap pocket.	0	4	3	1	4	92	19	11	0	115	0
Pouches, black leather, 50 " " "	0	6	0	2	1	1,958	587	8	0	4,038	6
Pouches, buff, for percussion caps	0	1	0	0	2	2,050	102	10	0	256	4
Slings, musket, buff	0	1	0	0	3½	2,050	102	10	0	448	7
Total	-	-	-	-	-	-	2,183	7	2	13,712	15¼

* Cost of union locket, gilt, for Grenadier Guards, 10*s.*, Scots Fusiliers, 7*s.* 6*d.*, Coldstreams, 15*s.*

NOTE.—Six claymores with shoulder belts are issued to each battalion of Scots Fusilier Guards.

Description.	Cost of each.	Weight of each.	Total No.	Total Cost.	Total Weight.
Pioneer's Tools, with black leather cases.	£ s. d.	lbs. oz.		£ s. d.	lbs. oz.
Two sets, (same as line, *see* page 150)	- - -	- - -	- -	23 0 8	328 8
Clothing.					
Bearskin caps, complete	4 4 0	1 9	2,153	9,042 12 0	3,864 1
Boots — pairs	0 8 6	2 13	4,306	1,830 1 0	12,110 10
Gloves, white leather	0 2 0	0 2¼	113	11 6 0	15 14¼
Leggings, leather	0 3 4	0 11	2,153	358 16 8	1,480 3
Trousers, cloth, pattern for, staff serjeants	1 1 0	2 1	8	8 8 0	16 8
Trousers, cloth, pattern for, serjeants and band	0 16 0	2 1½	125	100 0 0	261 11½
Trousers, cloth, other ranks	0 11 0	2 5	2,020	1,111 0 0	4,671 4
Trousers, black tartan, pattern for staff serjeants	0 19 0	1 7	8	7 12 0	11 8
Trousers, black tartan, other ranks	0 7 10	1 7	2,145	840 2 6	3,083 7
Tunics, dress, serjeant major	10 13 3¼	3 15	2	21 6 6½	7 14
quartermaster serjeant	6 4 5½	3 11	2	12 8 11	7 6
serjeant instructor of musketry	6 7 6	3 8	2	12 15 0	7 0
bandmaster	11 2 11½	3 9	1	11 2 11½	3 9
drum-major	9 10 10½	3 9	2	19 1 9	7 2
band serjeant	5 6 2¾	3 7	1	5 6 2¾	3 7
regimental clerk	6 1 0	3 7	1	6 1 0	3 7
orderly room serjeant	3 3 0	3 7	2	6 6 0	6 14
regimental and battalion drill serjeants	3 11 8½	3 8	5	17 18 6½	17 8
hospital serjeant	3 11 8½	3 8	1	3 11 8½	3 8
colour serjeants	4 0 0	3 9	20	80 0 0	71 4
serjeants and armourer serjeant	3 3 0	3 7	74	233 12 0	254 6
musicians	5 0 0	3 7	19	75 0 0	65 5
time beaters'	7 14 0	3 13	1	7 14 0	3 13
drummers and buglers	1 17 0	4 12½	40	74 0 0	191 4
other ranks	1 3 0	4 9½	1,980	2,277 0 0	9,095 10
Tunics, undress, pattern for, staff serjeants	3 0 0	3 6	7	21 0 0	23 10
Tunics, undress, pattern for, other ranks	1 12 0	3 6	6	9 12 0	20 4
Sashes, silk	1 15 0	0 14½	12	21 0 0	10 14
Sashes, worsted	0 5 6	0 12	101	27 15 6	75 12
Shell jackets, pattern for serjeants	0 15 6	2 2½	100	77 10 0	215 10
Shell jackets, other ranks	0 6 6	1 15	2,040	663 0 0	3,952 8
Tassels, gold lace, drum-majors — sets	0 16 6	0 2	2	1 13 0	0 4
Knots, sword, gold	0 10 0	0 1½	11	5 10 0	1 0½
Drum carriage, gold lace	0 17 6	0 6	3	2 12 6	1 2
Slings, instrument, gold lace	0 8 6	0 3	11	4 13 6	2 1
Badges, good conduct, gold for band, 1 bar	0 0 10	—	—	—	—
2 „	0 1 8	—	—	—	—
3 „	0 2 6	—	—	—	—
4 „	0 3 4	—	—	—	—
Badges, good conduct, white for privates, 1 „	0 0 2	0 0¼	—	—	—
2 „	0 0 4	0 0¼	—	—	—
3 „	0 0 6	0 0¼	—	—	—
4 „	0 0 8	0 0½	—	—	—
Badges, shooting, 1st or supplementary prize	0 6 5	0 0¼	10	3 4 2	0 5
2d	0 4 9	0 0¼	20	4 15 0	0 5
3d	0 1 0	0 0¼	180	9 0 0	2 13
Badges, colour, pair, regimental pattern	0 17 0	0 2	—	—	—
Chevrons, serjeants, gold pair	0 11 1	0 1	—	—	—
lance serjeants' worsted pair	0 1 4	0 1	—	—	—
corporals pair	0 1 0	0 1	100	5 0 0	6 4
acting corporals pair	0 1 0	0 1	—	—	—
Great coats, Staff serjeants, 1st class, drum-major, band master, and band serjeants.	2 12 0	6 2	8	20 16 0	49 2
Great coats, other ranks	1 3 6	6 2	2,143	375 0 6	13,125 14
Schoolmasters' clothing, set, *see* p. 153	8 18 2¼	18 7¼	2	17 16 4½	36 14½
Total	- - -	- - -	- -	16,443 1 4¼	52,277 0¾

Description.	Cost of each. £	s.	d.	Weight of each. lbs.	oz.	Total No.	Total Cost. £	s.	d.	Total Weight. lbs.	oz.
FOR SCOTS FUSILIER GUARDS ONLY.											
Pipers.											
Caps, Glengarry, pipe major	0	3	6	0	$6\frac{1}{2}$	1	0	3	6	0	$6\frac{1}{2}$
Caps, Glengarry, pipers	0	2	3	0	5	5	0	2	3	0	5
Coat, pipe major, green cloth	4	4	9	2	14	1	4	4	9	2	14
Coat, pipers, green cloth	1	10	0	3	7	5	7	10	0	17	3
Kilts, pipe majors	1	10	6	2	2	1	1	10	6	2	2
Kilts, pipers	0	19	4	2	11	5	4	16	8	13	7
Plaid, pipe major	0	8	7	2	14	1	0	8	7	2	14
Plaid, pipers	0	4	5	2	14	5	1	2	1	14	6
Shoes	0	8	3	5	0	12	4	16	0	60	0
Waistcoat, pipe major	1	4	$11\frac{1}{4}$	2	$2\frac{1}{2}$	1	1	4	$11\frac{1}{4}$	2	$2\frac{1}{2}$
Waistcoat, pipers	0	12	1	2	$2\frac{1}{2}$	5	3	0	5	10	$12\frac{1}{2}$
Time beaters.											
Boots, 2 pairs	0	17	0	4	10						
Chaco with plume complete	4	18	0	1	0						
Jacket	6	14	5	2	8						
Leggings, leather	0	3	4	0	11						
Trousers, red cloth, laced with gold	2	15	4	2	0	1 set	21	7	9	20	0
Trousers, black tartan	0	7	10	1	7						
Tunic	1	7	8	3	3						
Waistcoat, red regimental pattern	3	17	8	2	8						
Waistcoat, white	0	6	6	2	0						

SET OF NECESSARIES.

Description.		Numbers.	Cost. £	s.	d.	Weight. lbs.	oz.
Blacking, tin		1	0	0	2	0	8
Braces	pair	1	0	0	$10\frac{1}{2}$	0	4
Brass button		1	0	0	$1\frac{1}{2}$	0	2
Brushes, brass		1	0	0	$7\frac{1}{2}$	0	3
Brushes, clothes		1	0	0	$11\frac{1}{2}$	0	$3\frac{1}{2}$
Brushes, shaving		1	0	0	$3\frac{3}{4}$	0	1
Brushes, shoe, set of two		1	0	1	$2\frac{3}{4}$	0	$6\frac{1}{2}$
Comb		1	0	0	$2\frac{1}{2}$	0	$0\frac{1}{2}$
Hold-all		1	0	0	5	0	$2\frac{1}{2}$
Knapsack, with slings		1	0	6	$2\frac{1}{2}$	3	13
Knife, fork, and spoon	set	1	0	0	$5\frac{1}{4}$	0	$7\frac{1}{4}$
Mitts	pair	1	0	0	$11\frac{1}{2}$	0	$3\frac{3}{4}$
Razor and case		1	0	0	$4\frac{3}{4}$	0	$2\frac{3}{4}$
Shirts, cotton, or		3		—			—
Shirts, flannel		2	0	9	$5\frac{1}{2}$	1	12
Socks, worsted	pairs	3	0	3	$0\frac{3}{4}$	0	12
Sponge		1	0	0	9	0	$0\frac{3}{4}$
Stock, with clasp		1	0	0	$5\frac{3}{4}$	0	2

Description.	Numbers.	Cost.			Weight.	
		£	s.	d.	lbs.	oz.
Straps, set of, for great coat - - - - -	1	0	2	1¼	0	5
Tin, mess, with cover and strap - - - -	1	0	1	11¼	1	9
Towels - - - - - - -	2	0	1	7½	1	0
Soap - - - - - - - -	—	—			—	
Pipeclay - - - - - - -	—	—			—	
Account book, small - - - - - -	1	0	0	3	2	2
Bible and Prayer Book - - - - - -	—	—			—	
Total issued to all ranks alike - - -	1	1	12	10	12	4½
1st class staff-serjeants, regimental clerk, drill-serjeant, drum-major, and band additional :—						
Cap, forage, with gold band and peak - - -	—	0	18	6	0	7½
Total set - - - - - -	—	2	11	4	12	12
2nd class staff-serjeants and serjeants, additional :—						
Cap, forage, with gold band and strap - - -	—	0	16	6	0	7
Total set - - - - - -	—	2	9	3	12	11½
Other ranks, additional : —						
Cap, forage, with strap and badge - -	—	0	2	11½	0	8
Total set - - - - - -	—	1	15	9½	12	12½

GENERAL SUMMARY.

Description.	Cost.			Weight.		Remarks.
	£	s.	d.			
Colours, 2 pairs, with cases, complete - -	65	10	0	44	0	
Camp colours, aides, &c. - -	16	2	8	101	12	
Arms and drummers' appointments - -	6,762	19	5½	21,978	3¾	
Musical instruments - - -	158	16	8	106	1	
Accoutrements and pioneers' tools - -	2,229	8	6	14,041	7	
Ammunition, 120,240 rounds - -	240	9	8	10,896	12	
Clothing, &c. - - - -	16,443	1	4½	52,277	0¾	
Necessaries - - - -	3,944	2	4	27,510	13¼	
Two armourer's forges - -	51	13	4	788	0	
Regimental books - - -	—			—		
Regimental hospital equipment - -	847	3	1½	11,476	14½	Detailed in Part VII. of Army Equipments.
Total - - " -	30,759	7	1½	139,221	0¼	

HIGHLAND BATTALION.

Description.	Cost.			Weight.		Remarks.
	£	s.	d.	lbs.	ozs.	
SERJEANT-MAJOR.						
Arms and Accoutrements.						
Belt, shoulder, buff, with fixed frog - -	0	6	6	0	14½	
Claymore and scabbard - - - -	1	18	6	3	6½	
Havresack - - - - -	0	1	0	0	10	
Canteen, wooden, with strap - -	0	2	6	1	12	On active service only.
Clothing.						
Bonnet, with hackle, feather, and cover -	3	5	0	1	4	
Coat, with badges - - - -	3	2	0	2	14	Pair of 4-bar gold chevrons, surmounted by crowns.
Gaiters, one pair - - - -	0	2	0	0	5	
Kilt, material for - - - -	1	9	0	2	1½	
Leggings, leather, pair - - -	0	3	4	0	11	
Plaid - - - - -	0	8	7	2	14	
Sash, silk - - - - -	1	15	0	0	14½	
Shoes, two pairs - - - -	0	16	6	5	0	
Waistcoat - - - - -	1	4	11¼	2	2½	
Great coat - - - - -	2	12	0	6	2	
Necessaries.						
Set as detailed at page 126 - -	4	12	5¼	16	0¼	
Total -	21	19	3½	46	15¾	
SCHOOLMASTER.						
See page 147.	10	18	2¼	22	0¼	
QUARTERMASTER-SERJEANT.						
Same as serjeant-major, excepting badges -	21	16	3¼	46	15¾	No crowns.
SERJEANT INSTRUCTOR OF MUSKETRY.						
Same as serjeant-major, excepting badges -	21	17	3½	46	15¾	Pair of 4-bar gold chevrons, surmounted by crossed muskets.
BANDMASTER-SERJEANT.						
Same as serjeant-major, excepting distinctions on tunic.	21	12	3½	46	15¾	Gold shoulder cords, but no chevrons.
DRUM-MAJOR.						
Same as serjeant-major, excepting badges -	22	0	9½	47	1¾	Wings on shoulders, and pair of 4-bar gold chevrons, surmounted by a drum.
PIPE-MAJOR.						
Arms, Accoutrements, and Appointments.						
Belt, shoulder, black leather - -	0	5	6	0	14½	
Claymore and scabbard - - -	1	18	6	3	6½	
Havresack - - - - -	0	1	0	0	10	
Canteen, wooden, with strap - -	0	2	6	1	12	On active service only.
Pipes, Highland, set - - -	8	8	0	4	11	Provided out of band fund.

Description.	Cost.			Weight.		Remarks.
Clothing.	£	s.	d.	lbs.	oz.	
Bonnet, with hackle, feather, and cover	3	5	0	1	4	
Coat, green	2	16	0	2	10	
Gaiters, one pair	0	2	0	0	5	
Kilt, materials for	1	9	0	2	2	
Leggings, leather, pair	0	3	4	0	11	
Plaid	0	8	7	2	4	
Shoes, two pairs	0	16	6	5	0	
Shell jacket, white (waistcoat)	1	4	11¼	2	2½	
Great coat	2	12	0	6	2	
Necessaries.						
Set as detailed at page 126	4	12	5¼	16	0	
Total	28	5	3½	49	14¾	
BAND-SERJEANT.						
Same as serjeant-major, excepting badges	21	12	3½	46	15¾	Pair 4-bar chevrons.
PAYMASTER-SERJEANT, ARMOURER-SERJEANT, HOSPITAL-SERJEANT, OR ORDERLY-ROOM CLERK.						
Arms and Accoutrements.						
As for serjeant-major	2	8	6	2	11	
Clothing.						
As for serjeant	7	13	1½	24	4½	
Necessaries.						
Set as detailed at page 126	3	5	10¼	15	14¾	
Total	13	7	5¾	42	14¼	
COLOUR-SERJEANT.						
Same as serjeant	17	5	0	60	1	
Badges on tunic extra	0	9	10½	-	-	Colour badge and 3-bar gold chevrons.
Total	17	14	10½	60	1	
SERJEANT.						
Arms and Accoutrements.						
Bag, ball, buff	0	2	6	0	7	
Belts, buff { Pouch	0	3	0	0	8	
waist, with gilding metal locket, and frog.	0	3	8	0	12¾	
Havresack	0	1	0	0	10	
Pouch, 20 rounds	0	4	3	1	4	
,, for percussion caps, buff	0	1	0	0	2	
Sling, musket, buff	0	1	0	0	3½	
Short rifle, musket pattern 1860, with rammer, sword-bayonet and scabbard, snap cap and chain, and muzzle stopper.	5	4	9¾	10	12½	
Wrench, nipple, with cramp	0	1	11½	0	6½	
Canteen, wooden, with strap	0	2	6	1	12	On active service only.

Description.	Cost. £	s.	d.	Weight. lbs.	oz.	Remarks.
Ammunition.						
30 rounds, with 45 percussion caps	-		-	2	11½	Full service quantity.
Clothing.						
Bonnet, with hackle, feather, and cover	2	3	8	1	4	
Coat, with badges	1	2	4½	3	8	Pair of 3-bar white chevrons.
Gaiters, one pair	0	2	0	0	5	
Kilt, material for	0	18	4	2	11	
Leggings, leather, pair	0	3	4	0	11	
Plaid	0	5	4	2	14	
Shoes, two pairs	0	16	6	5	0	
Waistcoat	0	12	5	2	2½	
Great coat	1	3	6	6	2	
Necessaries.						
Set as detailed at page 126	3	5	10¼	15	14¾	
Total	16	19	0	60	2	
CORPORAL.						
Arms and Accoutrements.						
As for private, excepting nipple wrench	4	4	1¼	16	15¾	With cramp.
Ammunition.						
As for private	-	-	-	5	7	
Clothing.						
As for private	6	17	6	24	6½	
Badges, extra	0	0	8	0	1	Pair 2-bar white chevrons.
Necessaries.						
Set as detailed at p. 126	3	4	7¼	15	14¾	
Total	14	6	10½	62	13	
PRIVATE.						
Arms and Accoutrements.						
Bag, ball, buff	0	2	6	0	7	
Belts, buff: pouch	0	3	0	0	8	
Belts, buff: waist, with brass union locket and frog	0	3	7	0	12¾	
Havresack	0	1	0	0	10	
Pouch: 50-round	0	6	0	2	1	
Pouch: for percussion caps, buff	0	1	0	0	2	
Sling, musket, buff	0	1	0	0	3½	
Rifle musket, pattern 1853, with rammer, bayonet and scabbard, snap cap and chain, and muzzle stopper	3	1	6¾	10	2½	
Wrench, nipple, without cramp	0	0	11½	0	4½	
Canteen, wooden, with strap	0	2	6	1	11	On active service only.
Ammunition.						
60 rounds, with 90 percussion caps	-	-	-	5	7	Full service quantity.

Description.	Cost.			Weight.		Remarks.
Clothing.	£	s.	d.	lbs.	oz.	
Bonnet, with hackle, feather, and cover	2	9	8	1	4	
Coat	0	18	1	3	8½	
Gaiters, one pair	0	2	0	0	5	
Kilt, material for	0	13	9	2	11	
Leggings, leather pair	0	3	4	0	11	
Plaid	0	4	5	2	14	
Shoes, 2 pairs	0	16	6	5	0	
Waistcoat	0	6	3	1	15	
Great coat	1	3	6	6	2	
Necessaries.						
Set as detailed at page 126	3	4	7¼	15	14¾	
Total	14	5	2½	62	11½	
DRUMMER.						
Arms, Accoutrements, and Appointments.						
Apron, buff, for side drum	0	4	0	0	10	
Belt, shoulder, buff, with fixed frog	0	6	6	0	14½	
Claymore and scabbard	1	14	9	3	3½	
Drum, side, with sticks and ticken cover	2	5	6	9	2	
Havresack	0	1	0	0	10	
Canteen, wooden, with strap	0	2	6	1	12	On active service only.
Clothing.						
As for private	6	17	6	24	6½	
Distinctions on coat extra	0	5	2	0	2½	
Necessaries.						
Set as detailed at page 126	3	4	7½	15	14¾	
Total	15	1	6½	56	11¾	
BUGLER.						
Arms, Accoutrements, and Appointments.						
Belt, shoulder, buff, with fixed frog	0	6	6	0	14½	
Claymore and scabbard	1	14	9	3	3½	
Bugle and strings	1	3	0	1	11¼	
Flute and case	0	14	3	0	8¼	
Havresack	0	1	0	0	10	
Canteen, wooden, with straps	0	2	6	1	12	
Clothing.						
As drummer	7	2	8	24	9	
Necessaries.						
As private, *see* page 126	3	4	7¼	15	14¾	
Total	14	9	3¼	49	3¼	
PIPER.						
Arms, Accoutrements, and Appointments.						
Belt, shoulder, black leather, with fixed frog	0	5	6	0	14½	
Claymore and scabbard	1	14	9	3	3½	
Pipes, Highland, set	8	8	0	4	11	
Havresack	0	1	0	0	10	
Canteen, wooden, with strap	0	2	6	1	12	On active service only.

EQUIPMENT OF NON-COMMISSIONED OFFICERS AND MEN.

Description.	Cost.			Weight.		Remarks.
	£	s.	d.	lbs.	oz.	
Clothing.						
Bonnet, with hackle, feather, and cover	2	9	8	1	4	
Coat (green)	1	1	4	3	7	
Gaiters, one pair	0	2	0	0	5	
Kilt, materials for	0	18	4	2	11	
Leggings, leather, pair	0	3	4	0	11	
Plaid	0	5	4	2	14	
Shoes, 2 pairs	0	16	6	5	0	
Waistcoat	0	12	1	2	$2\frac{1}{2}$	
Great coat	1	3	6	6	2	
Necessaries.						
As private, see page 126	3	4	$7\frac{1}{4}$	15	$14\frac{3}{4}$	
Total	21	8	$5\frac{1}{4}$	51	$10\frac{1}{4}$	

MUSICIAN.

Arms, Accoutrements, and Appointments.

Description.	Cost.			Weight.		Remarks.
Belt, shoulder, buff, with fixed frog	0	6	6	0	$14\frac{1}{2}$	
Claymore and scabbard	1	14	9	3	$3\frac{1}{2}$	
Havresack	0	1	0	0	10	
Musical instrument						On active service only.
Canteen, wooden, with strap	0	2	6	1	12	
Clothing.						
Bonnet, with hackle, feather, and cover	2	9	8	1	4	
Coat	1	1	4	3	7	
Gaiters, one pair	0	2	0	0	5	
Kilt, materials for	0	18	4	2	11	
Leggings, leather, pair	0	3	4	0	11	
Plaid	0	5	4	2	14	
Shoes, 2 pairs	0	16	6	5	0	
Waistcoat	0	12	1	2	$2\frac{1}{2}$	
Great coat	1	3	6	6	2	
Necessaries.						
As private, see page 126	3	4	$7\frac{1}{4}$	15	$14\frac{3}{4}$	
Total	13	1	$5\frac{1}{4}$	47	$15\frac{1}{4}$	

PIONEERS.

FIVE MEN CARRY THE FOLLOWING EQUIPMENT.

Arms, Accoutrements, and Appointments.

Description.	Cost.			Weight.		Remarks.
Belt, waist, buff, with union locket and frog with shifting loop.	0	3	10	0	$13\frac{3}{4}$	
Havresack	0	1	0	0	10	
Sword with saw back, and scabbard	0	11	10	3	0	On active service only.
Canteen, wooden, with strap	0	2	6	1	12	
Axe, pick, with case	0	5	3	6	8	
Bill hook, ,, ,,	0	4	9	2	4	
Shovel ,, ,,	0	9	6	7	2	
Gun spikes, two	0	0	8	0	$2\frac{1}{2}$	
Clothing.						
As private	6	17	6	24	$6\frac{1}{2}$	
Necessaries.						
As private, see page 126	3	4	$7\frac{1}{4}$	15	$14\frac{3}{4}$	
Total	12	1	$5\frac{1}{4}$	62	$9\frac{1}{2}$	

Description.	Cost. £	s.	d.	Weight. lbs.	oz.	Remarks.
Three Men carry the following Equipment.						
Arms, Accoutrements, and Appointments.						
Sword, belt, havresack, and canteen, same as the foregoing.	0	19	2	6	$3\frac{3}{4}$	
Axe, felling, with case	0	5	6	6	4	
Bill-hook, " "	0	4	9	2	4	
Spade, " "	0	9	6	6	$1\frac{1}{2}$	
Gun spikes, two	0	0	8	0	$2\frac{1}{2}$	
Clothing.						
As private	6	17	6	24	$6\frac{1}{2}$	
Necessaries.						
As private, *see* page 126	3	4	$7\frac{1}{4}$	15	$14\frac{3}{4}$	
Total	12	1	$8\frac{1}{4}$	61	5	
One Man carries the following Equipment.						
Arms, Accoutrements, and Appointments.						
Sword, belt, havresack, and canteen, same as the foregoing.	0	19	2	6	$3\frac{3}{4}$	
Axe { felling, with case	0	5	6	6	4	
Axe { broad, and axe, hand, with case	0	10	3	6	14	
Bill-hook, with case	0	4	9	2	4	
Gun spikes, two	0	0	8	0	$2\frac{1}{2}$	
Clothing.						
As corporal	6	18	2	24	$7\frac{1}{2}$	
Necessaries.						
Set as detailed at page 126	3	4	$7\frac{1}{4}$	15	$14\frac{3}{4}$	
Total	12	3	$1\frac{1}{4}$	62	$2\frac{1}{2}$	
One Man carries the following Equipment.						
Arms, Accoutrements, and Appointments.						
Sword, belt, havresack, and canteen, same as the foregoing.	0	19	2	6	$3\frac{3}{4}$	
Axe { felling, with case	0	5	6	6	4	
Axe { hand, and saw, with case	0	15	9	6	12	
Bill-hook, with case	0	4	9	2	4	
Gun spikes, two	0	0	8	0	$2\frac{1}{2}$	
Clothing.						
As private	6	17	6	24	$1\frac{1}{2}$	
Necessaries.						
As private, *see* page 126	3	4	$7\frac{1}{4}$	15	$14\frac{3}{4}$	
Total	12	7	$11\frac{1}{4}$	61	$10\frac{1}{2}$	
One Man carries the following Equipment.						
Arms, Accoutrements, and Appointments.						
Sword, belt, havresack, and canteen, same as the foregoing.	0	19	2	6	$3\frac{3}{4}$	
Crowbar, with caps and strap	0	4	9	7	$6\frac{1}{4}$	

Description.	Cost.			Weight.		Remarks.
	£	s.	d.	lbs.	oz.	
Case containing auger, cold and socket chisels, and hammer.	0	14	9	7	5½	
Gun spikes, two - - - - - -	0	0	8	0	2½	
Clothing.						
As private - - - - - -	6	17	6	24	6½	
Necessaries.						
As private, *see* page 126 - - - - -	3	4	7¼	15	14¾	
Total - -	12	1	5¾	61	7½	
HOSPITAL ORDERLY.						
Arms and Accoutrememts.						
Belt, buff, waist, with brass locket and frog -	0	3	7	0	12¾	
Sword and scabbard, line pattern for drummers -	0	12	6	2	9	
Clothing.						
As private - - - - - -	6	17	6	24	6½	
Necessaries.						
As private - - - - - -	3	4	7½	15	14¾	
Total - -	10	18	2½	43	11	

GENERAL LIST OF EQUIPMENTS FOR A HIGHLAND BATTALION.

Number of Rank and File 1,000, *in Ten Companies.*

Description.	Cost of each.			Weight of each.		Total No.	Total Cost.			Total Weight.	
ARMS.	£	s.	d.	lbs.	oz.		£	s.	d.	lbs.	oz.
Rifle muskets, pattern 1853, complete with rammer, bayonet, bayonet scabbard, muzzle stopper, and snap-cap with chain.	3	1	6¾	10	2½	964	2,967	6	3	9,790	10
Short rifle muskets, pattern 1860, complete with rammer, sword bayonet, scabbard, muzzle stopper, and snap-cap with chain.	5	4	9¾	10	12½	49	256	15	9¾	528	4½
Nipples, spare - - - -	0	0	1¾	0	0⅙	304	2	4	4	3	2¾
Wrenches, nipple { with cramp - -	0	1	11½	0	6½	101	9	17	9½	41	0½
Wrenches, nipple { without cramp - -	0	0	11½	0	4½	912	43	14	0	256	8
Claymores* and scabbards { staff serjeants' pattern -	1	18	6	3	6½	11	21	3	6	87	7½
Claymores* and scabbards { drummer's „ -	1	14	9	3	3½	45	78	3	9	144	13½
Swords and scabbards { staff serjeant's pattern - -	1	12	6	2	10¾	1	1	12	6	2	10¾
Swords and scabbards { for pioneers - - -	0	11	10	3	0	11	6	10	2	33	0
Swords and scabbards { drummer's pattern (for hospital orderlies).	0	12	6	2	9	5	3	2	6	47	13
Total - -	-		-	-	-	- -	3,390	10	7¼	10,935	6½

* The claymore issued to staff-serjeants of kilted regiments is two inches shorter than that issued to regiments wearing the trews.

Description.	Cost of each.	Weight of each.	Total No.	Total Cost.	Total Weight.
Drummers' Appointments.	£ s. d.	lbs. oz.		£ s. d.	lbs. oz.
Bugles - - - - - -	1 1 0	1 6½	10	10 10 0	14 1
Strings for do. - - - - -	0 2 0	0 4¾	10	1 0 0	2 15½
Drums, side, brass, complete, with sticks and tickens.	2 7 6	9 2	10	22 15 0	91 4
Flutes { B^b, with case - - -	0 14 3	0 8¼	6	4 5 6	3 1½
Flutes { F, " - - - -	0 15 0	0 12½	2	1 10 0	1 9
Piccolo { E^b, with case - - -	0 12 3	0 7	1	0 12 3	0 7
Piccolo { F, " - - - -	0 12 6	0 7	1	0 12 6	0 7
Total - -	- -	- -	- -	41 5 3	113 13
ACCOUTREMENTS.					
Aprons, buff, leg, for side drum - -	0 4 0	0 10	10	2 0 0	6 4
Bags, ball, buff, with zinc oil bottle - -	0 2 6	0 7	1,013	126 12 6	443 3
Belts, pouch, buff - - - - -	0 3 0	0 8	1,013	151 19 6	506 8
Belts, shoulder { black japanned leather -	0 5 6	0 14½	6	1 13 0	5 7
Belts, shoulder { buff, with fixed frog, drummer's	0 5 0	1 0	40	10 0 0	40 0
Belts, waist { black japanned leather, with sword carriage and snake hook, furniture gilt.	0 6 0	0 12½	1	0 6 0	0 12½
Belts, waist { buff - - - - -	0 1 9	0 5½	1,029	90 0 9	353 11½
Canteens, wooden, with strap - -	0 2 6	1 2½	1,085	135 12 6	1,898 12
Carriages, buff { for bass drum, with swivel -	0 3 6	0 12½	1	0 3 6	0 12½
Carriages, buff { for side drum - -	0 2 6	1 2½	10	1 5 0	11 9
Frogs { buff - - - - - -	0 1 3	0 2½	1,018	63 12 6	159 1
Frogs { " with shifting loop - -	0 1 6	0 3½	11	0 16 6	2 6½
Havresacks - - - - - -	0 1 0	0 10	1,085	54 5 0	678 2
Knots, sword, black japanned leather - -	0 1 6	0 0¾	1	0 1 6	0 0¾
Lockets, union { gilding metal - -	0 0 8	0 4¾	49	1 12 8	14 4¾
Lockets, union { brass - - -	0 0 7	0 4¾	1,020	29 15 0	302 13
Pouches { 20-round, serjeant's - -	0 4 3	1 4	49	10 8 3	61 8
Pouches { 50-round - - - -	0 6 0	2 1	964	289 4 0	1,988 4
Pouches { buff, for percussion caps - -	0 1 0	0 2	1,013	50 13 0	126 10
Slings, musket, buff - - - -	0 1 0	0 3½	1,013	50 13 0	221 9½
Total - -	- -	- -	- -	1,070 14 2	6,821 11
For a kilted regiment, additional:—					
Belt, shoulder, buff, with fixed frog -	0 6 6	0 14½	10	3 5 0	9 1
Total for a kilted regiment -	- -	- -	- -	1,073 19 2	6,830 12
For a regiment wearing the trews, additional:—					
Belt, waist, buff, with sword carriages, gilt furniture, and slide.	0 5 6	0 9	10	2 15 0	5 10
Locket, union, gilt - - - -	0 2 0	0 4¾	10	1 0 0	2 15½
Total for a regiment wearing the trews -	- -	- -	- -	1,074 9 2	6,830 4½
Pioneers' Tools.					
Same as regiment of line - - -	- -	- -	- -	11 6 4	164 4

GENERAL LIST OF CLOTHING.

Description.	Cost of each.	Weight of each.	Total No.	Total Cost.	Total Weight.
Clothing.	£ s. d.	lbs. oz.		£ s. d.	lbs. oz.
Bonnets, complete, with hackle, feather, and cover — pattern for staff serjeants	3 5 0	1 4	7	22 15 0	8 12
Bonnets, complete, with hackle, feather, and cover — other ranks - -	2 9 8	1 4	1,078	2,677 0 8	1,347 8
Coats, complete — serjeant-major - - -	3 2 0	2 14	1	3 2 0	2 14
Coats, complete — quartermaster serjeant - -	2 19 0	2 14	1	2 19 0	2 14
Coats, complete — serjeant instructor of musketry (2d class).	3 0 0	2 14	1	3 0 0	2 14
Coats, complete — bandmaster serjeant - -	2 15 0	2 14	1	2 15 0	2 14
Coats, complete — drum major - - -	3 3 6	2 16	1	3 3 6	2 16
Coats, complete — pipe ,, - - -	2 16 0	2 10	1	2 16 0	2 10
Coats, complete — 2d class staff serjeants and serjeants	1 2 4½	3 8	43	48 2 1½	170 8
Coats, complete — band serjeant - - -	2 15 0	2 14	1	2 15 0	2 14
Coats, complete — colour serjeants - - -	1 12 2¾	3 8	10	16 2 3½	35 0
Coats, complete — corporals - - - -	0 18 9	3 9	49	45 18 9	174 9
Coats, complete — drummers - - -	1 3 3	3 11	20	23 5 0	73 12
Coats, complete — pipers (green) - - -	1 1 4	3 7	5	5 6 8	17 3
Coats, complete — band - - - -	1 1 4	3 7	20	21 6 8	68 12
Coats, complete — privates - - - -	0 18 1	3 8½	931	841 15 7	3,287 9
Gaiters, pairs - - - -	0 2 0	0 5	1,085	108 10 0	339 1
Kilts, material for — pattern for staff serjeants -	1 9 0	2 2	7	10 3 0	14 14
Kilts, material for — ,, serjeants, pipers, and band,	0 18 4	2 11	78	71 10 0	209 10
Kilts, material for — drummers, rank and file -	0 13 9	2 11	1,000	687 10 0	2,687 8
Leggings, leather, pairs - - -	0 3 4	0 11	1,085	180 16 4	745 15
Plaids — pattern for staff serjeants - -	0 8 7	2 14	7	3 0 1	18 4
Plaids — ,, serjeants, band, and pipers	0 5 4	2 14	78	20 16 0	224 4
Plaids — ,, for other ranks - -	0 4 5	2 14	1,000	220 16 8	2,875 0
Sashes — silk - - - - -	1 15 0	0 14½	7	12 5 0	6 5½
Sashes — worsted - - - -	0 5 6	0 12	53	14 11 6	39 12
Shoes, pairs - - - - -	0 8 3	2 8	2,170	886 1 8	5,425 0
Shell jackets (waistcoats) — pattern for staff serjeants -	1 4 11¼	2 2½	7	8 14 6¾	15 1½
Shell jackets (waistcoats) — ,, serjeants - -	0 12 5	2 2½	53	32 18 1	114 4½
Shell jackets (waistcoats) — ,, pipers and band -	0 12 1	2 2½	25	15 2 1	53 14½
Shell jackets (waistcoats) — ,, other ranks - -	0 6 3	1 15	1,000	312 10 0	1,937 8
Great coats — pattern for staff serjeants -	2 12 0	6 2	7	18 4 0	42 14
Great coats — ,, other ranks - -	1 3 6	6 2	1,078	1,266 13 0	6,602 12
Badges — good conduct (pairs) — 1 bar - - -	0 0 2½	0 0¼	—	—	—
Badges — good conduct (pairs) — 2 ,, - - -	0 0 5	0 0¼	—	—	—
Badges — good conduct (pairs) — 3 ,, - - -	0 0 7½	0 0¼	—	—	—
Badges — good conduct (pairs) — 4 ,, - - -	0 0 10	0 0½	—	—	—
Badges — shooting — 1st and supplementary prize.	0 6 3	0 0½	5	1 11 3	0 2½
Badges — shooting — 2d prize - - -	0 4 6	0 0¼	10	2 5 0	0 2¼
Badges — shooting — 3d ,, - - -	0 0 10	0 0¼	90	3 15 0	1 6½
Chevrons, pairs — lance serjeants - -	0 1 0	0 0½	—	—	—
Chevrons, pairs — lance corporals - -	0 0 4	0 0¼	—	—	—
Clothing for schoolmaster - - -	- -	- -	- -	8 18 2¼	18 7½
Total - -	- -	- -	- -	7,608 5 8	26,575 12

SET OF NECESSARIES FOR KILTED REGIMENT.

Description.		Number.	Cost. £	s.	d.	Weight. lbs.	oz.
Blacking, tin	-	1	0	0	2	0	8
Braces	pair	1	0	0	10½	0	4
Brass, button	-	1	0	0	1½	0	2
Brushes: brass	-	1	0	0	7½	0	3
Brushes: clothes	-	1	0	0	11¼	0	3½
Brushes: shaving	-	1	0	0	3¾	0	1
Brushes: shoe, set of two	-	1	0	1	2¾	0	6½
Comb	-	1	0	0	2½	0	0½
*Gaiters†	pair	1	0	2	0	0	5
*Garters	"	1	0	1	2	0	1½
Hold-all	-	1	0	0	5	0	2½
*Hose tops, tartan	pairs	2	0	3	8	0	10
Knapsack, with slings	-	1	0	6	2½	3	13
Knife, fork, and spoon	set	1	0	0	5¼	0	7¼
Mitts	pair	1	0	0	9¾	0	3¾
*Purse and belt	-	1	0	10	6	0	14½
Razor and case	-	1	0	0	4¾	0	2¾
Shirts: cotton, or	-	3	—			—	
Shirts: flannel	-	2	0	9	5½	1	12
Socks, worsted	pairs	3	0	3	0¾	0	12
Sponge	piece	1	0	0	9	0	0¾
Stock, with clasp	-	1	0	0	5¾	0	2
Straps, set of two, for great coat	-	1	0	1	0¼	0	5
Tin, mess, with cover and strap	-	1	0	1	11¾	1	9
Towels	-	2	0	1	7½	1	0
Soap	-	—	—			—	
Pipeclay	-	—	—			—	
Account book, small	-	1	0	0	3	0	2
Bible and Prayer Book	-	—	—			—	
Total issued to all ranks alike	-	—	2	8	8¾	14	2¾
1st class staff-serjeants, drum and pipe-majors, band-serjeants, additional :—							
Cap, forage, cloth, with band	-	—	1	0	0	0	6½
*Trews, staff	-	—	1	3	8½	1	7
Total set	-	—	4	12	5¼	16	0¼
2nd class staff-serjeants and serjeants, additional :—							
Cap, forage, Glengarry	-	—	0	3	6	0	5
*Trews	-	—	0	13	7½	1	7
Total set	-	—	3	5	10¼	15	14¾
Other ranks, additional :—							
Cap, forage, Glengarry	-	—	0	2	3	0	5
*Trews	-	—	0	13	7½	1	7
Total set	-	—	3	4	7¼	15	14¾

* Highland regiments wearing the trews are not supplied with gaiters, garters, hose, purses, or trews as articles of necessaries. The cost and weight of a set of necessaries is therefore—

2*l.* 11*s.* 4¾*d.* and 12 lb. 10¼ oz. for staff-serjeants.
1*l.* 14*s.* 10¼*d.* „ 12 lb. 8¾ oz. for serjeants.
1*l.* 13*s.* 7¼*d.* „ 12 lb. 8¾ oz. for other ranks.

† A second pair of gaiters is issued as part of clothing.

GENERAL SUMMARY.

(Kilted Battalion).

Description.	Cost.	Weight.	Remarks.
	£ s. d.	lbs. oz.	
Colours, pair, with cases, complete - -	32 15 0	22 0	
Camp colours, aides, &c. - - -	8 11 4	50 14	
Arms and drummers' appointments - -	3,431 15 10¼	11,049 3½	
Musical instruments - - - -	194 15 0	134 3	
Accoutrements - - - -	1,085 5 6	6,995 9	
Ammunition, 59,310 rounds - -	118 12 5	5,375 0	
Clothing - - - -	7,608 5 8	26,575 12	
Necessaries - - - -	3,517 18 7¼	17,275 14	
Armourer's forge - - -	25 16 8	394 0	
Regimental books - - - -	- - -	- -	
Regimental hospital equipment - -	423 11 6¾	5,738 7¼	Detailed in Part VII. of Army Equipments.
Total - - -	16,447 6 7¼	73,610 14¾	

BATTALION OF RIFLES.

Description.	Cost.			Weight.		Remarks.
	£	s.	d.	lbs.	oz.	
SERJEANT-MAJOR.						
Arms and Accoutrements.						
Belt, black, leather, with sword carriages and snake hook.	0	6	0	0	12½	
Knot, sword, black leather	0	1	6	0	0¾	
Sword, with leather scabbard (hilt and mountings steel).	1	12	0	2	10	
Havresack	0	2	6	0	3	
Canteen, wooden, with strap	0	2	6	1	12	On active service only.
Clothing.						
Boots, two pairs	0	17	0	5	10	
Chaco and cover	0	12	8¾	0	10½	
Leggings, leather, pair	0	3	4	0	11	
Trousers { green doeskin	1	0	0	2	0	
{ green tartan	0	17	6	1	7	
Tunic, green cloth, with badges	2	11	6	2	11½	Four chevrons and crowns on both arms.
Great coat	2	12	0	6	2	
Necessaries.						
Set, as detailed at page 141	3	16	5¼	13	13	
Total	14	15	0	38	7¼	
SCHOOLMASTER.						
Same equipment as in other services.	10	18	2¼	22	0¼	
QUARTERMASTER-SERJEANT.						
Same as serjeant-major, excepting badges on tunic and on fatigue jacket.	14	9	0	38	7¼	No crowns.
SERJEANT-INSTRUCTOR OF MUSKETRY.						
Same as serjeant-major, excepting badges on tunic and on fatigue jacket.	14	16	0	38	7¼	Four chevrons, surmounted by crossed muskets.
BANDMASTER-SERJEANT.						
Same as serjeant-major, excepting distinctions on tunic and on fatigue jacket.	14	16	6	38	11¾	Shoulder cords, but no chevron or other badges.
BUGLE-MAJOR.						
Same as serjeant-major, excepting badges on tunic and on fatigue jacket.	14	16	0	38	15¾	Four chevrons, surmounted by a bugle.

Description.	Cost.			Weight.		Remarks.
PAYMASTER SERJEANT, HOSPITAL-SERJEANT, ARMOURER-SERJEANT, OR ORDERLY-ROOM CLERK.	£	s.	d.	lbs.	oz.	
Arms and Accoutrements.						
Same as serjeant-major	2	4	6	5	6	
Clothing.						
Boots, two pairs	0	17	0	5	10	
Chaco and cover	0	4	7½	0	10½	
Leggings, leather, pair	0	3	4	0	11	
Trousers { green kersey	0	13	0	2	3	
Trousers { green tartan	0	6	9¾	1	7	
Tunic	0	19	8	3	2	
Great coat	1	3	6	6	2	
Necessaries.						
Set detailed at page 135	2	7	2½	13	14	
Total	8	19	7¾	39	1¾	
BAND-SERJEANT.						
Same as bandmaster-serjeant, excepting badges	14	6	6	38	11¾	Four chevrons.
Musical instrument		—			—	
Total	14	6	6	38	11¾	
COLOUR-SERJEANT.						
Equipment as for serjeant	13	3	5¼	56	9¼	
Colour badge and bar extra (4*s.* 6*d.* and 2½*d.*)	0	4	8½	0	3	
Total	13	8	1¾	56	12¼	
SERJEANT.						
Arms and Accoutrements.						
Bag, ball, black leather	0	2	3	0	8	
Belts, black leather { pouch	0	1	9	0	9	
Belts, black leather { waist, snake hook, and sliding frog	0	3	0	0	8¾	
Havresack	0	2	6	0	3	
Pouch, 50 round	0	6	0	2	1	
Plate { for pouch belt		—			—	Rifle Brigade only.
Plate { for percussion caps, black leather	0	0	9	0	2	
Sling, rifle, black leather	0	1	0	0	4½	
Short rifle musket, pattern 1860, with rammer, sword bayonet, and scabbard, snap, cap, and chain, and muzzle stopper.	5	4	9¾	10	12½	
Whistle and chain	0	2	6	0	3½	Rate for 60th Rifles.
Wrench, nipple, with cramp	0	1	11½	0	6½	
Canteen, wooden, with strap	0	2	6	1	12	On active service only.
Ammunition.						
60 rounds, with 90 percussion caps	-	-	-	5	7	Full service quantity.

BATTALION OF RIFLES.

Description.	Cost. £ s. d.	Weight. lbs. oz.	Remarks.
Clothing.			
Boots, two pairs	0 17 0	5 10	
Chaco and cover	0 4 7½	0 10½	
Leggings, leather, pair	0 3 4	0 11	
Trousers { green kersey	0 13 0	2 3	
{ green tartan	0 6 9¾	1 7	
Tunic	0 19 8	3 2	
Great coat	1 3 6	6 2	
Necessaries.			
Set as detailed at page 135	2 7 2½	13 14	
Regulations for field exercise, *see* page 91	—	—	
Total	13 4 2	56 9¼	

CORPORAL.

Arms and Accoutrements.

As for serjeant, excepting whistle and chain	6 6 6¼	17 9¼	
Ammunition.			
60 rounds, with 90 caps	—	5 7	Full service allowance.
Clothing.			
As for private	4 2 7½	19 11½	
Badges extra	0 0 8	0 0½	
Necessaries.			
As for private, *see* page 135	2 3 2½	14 0	
Total	12 13 0	56 12¼	

PRIVATE.

Arms and Accoutrements.

Bag, ball, black leather	0 2 3	0 8	
Belts, black leather { pouch	0 1 9	0 9	
{ waist, with snake hook and sliding frog	0 3 0	0 8¾	
Havresack	0 2 6	0 3	
Pouch { 50 rounds	0 6 0	2 1	
{ for percussion caps, black leather	0 0 9	0 2	
Sling, musket, black leather	0 1 0	0 4½	
Short rifle-musket, pattern 1860, with rammer, sword bayonet and scabbard, snap cap and chain, and muzzle-stopper.	5 4 9¾	10 12½	
Wrench, nipple, without cramp	0 0 11½	0 4½	
Canteen, wooden, with strap	0 2 6	1 12	On active service only.
Ammunition.			
60 rounds, with 90 percussion caps	—	5 7	
Clothing.			
Boots, two pairs	0 17 0	5 10	
Chaco and cover	0 4 7½	0 10½	
Leggings, leather, pair	0 3 4	0 11	

EQUIPMENT OF NON-COMMISSIONED OFFICERS AND MEN.

Description.	Cost.			Weight.		Remarks.
	£	s.	d.	lbs.	oz.	
Trousers { green kersey	0	9	0	2	2	
{ green tartan	0	6	9¾	1	7	
Tunic	0	18	4	3	1	
Great coat	1	3	6	6	2	
Necessaries.						
Set as detailed at page 135	2	3	2½	14	0	
Total	12	11	4	56	3¾	

BUGLER.

Arms, Accoutrements, and Appointments.

Description.	Cost.			Weight.		Remarks.
Belt, waist, black leather, with snake hook and frog.	0	3	0	0	8¾	
Haversack	0	2	6	0	3	
Sword and scabbard	0	9	3	2	9	
Bugle and strings	1	3	0	1	11¼	
Canteen, wooden with strap	0	2	6	1	12	On active service only.
Clothing.						
Boots, 2 pairs	0	17	0	5	10	
Chaco and cover	0	4	7½	0	10½	
Leggings, leather, pair	0	3	4	0	11	
Trousers, { green jersey	0	13	0	2	3	
{ green tartan, serjeants' cloth	0	6	9¾	1	7	
Tunic	1	0	5	3	6	
Great coat	1	3	6	6	2	
Necessaries.						
As private, see p. 135	2	3	2¼	14	0	
Total	8	12	1½	40	13½	

MUSICIAN.

Arms, Accoutrements, and Appointments.

Description.	Cost.			Weight.		Remarks.
Belt, waist, black leather, with snake hook and frog.	0	3	0	0	8¾	
Haversack	0	2	6	0	3	
Sword and scabbard (same as bugler)	0	9	3	2	9	
Canteen, wooden, with strap	0	2	6	1	12	On active service only.
Musical instrument, see p. 45	—			—		
Clothing.						
As for bugler, except distinctions on tunic	4	7	9¼	19	15½	
Necessaries.						
As for private, see p. 135	2	3	2½	14	0	
Total	7	8	2¾	39	0¼	

BATTALION OF RIFLES.

Description.	Cost.			Weight.		Remarks.
	£	s.	d.	lbs.	oz.	
PIONEERS.						
FIVE MEN CARRY THE FOLLOWING EQUIPMENT.						
Arms, Accoutrements, and Appointments.						
Belt, waist, black leather, with snake hook, sliding frog with shifting loop.	0	3	3	0	9	
Havresack	0	2	6	0	3	
Sword with sawback and scabbard	0	11	10	3	0	
Canteen, wooden, with strap	0	2	6	1	12	On active service only.
Axe, pick, with case	0	5	3	6	8	
Bill hook with case	0	4	9	2	4	
Shovel with case	0	9	6	7	2	
Spikes, gun, 2	0	0	8	0	$2\frac{1}{2}$	
Clothing.						
As private	4	2	$7\frac{1}{4}$	19	$11\frac{1}{2}$	
Necessaries.						
As private, *see* p. 135	2	3	$2\frac{1}{2}$	14	0	
Total	8	6	$0\frac{3}{4}$	55	4	
THREE MEN CARRY THE FOLLOWING EQUIPMENT.						
Arms, Accoutrements, and Appointments.						
Sword, belt, havresack and canteen, same as the foregoing.	1	0	1	5	8	
Axe, felling, with case	0	5	6	6	4	
Bill hook, with case	0	4	9	2	4	
Spade, with case	0	9	6	6	$1\frac{1}{4}$	
Spikes, gun, 2	0	0	8	0	$2\frac{1}{2}$	
Clothing.						
As private	4	2	$7\frac{1}{4}$	19	$11\frac{1}{2}$	
Necessaries.						
As private, *see* p. 135	2	3	$2\frac{1}{2}$	14	0	
Total	8	6	$3\frac{3}{4}$	54	$0\frac{1}{2}$	
ONE MAN CARRIES THE FOLLOWING EQUIPMENT.						
Arms, Accoutrements, and Appointments.						
Sword, belt, havresack and canteen, same as the foregoing.	1	0	1	5	8	
Axe, felling, with case	0	5	6	6	4	
Axe, broad, and axe hand, with case, &c.	0	10	3	6	14	
Bill hook, with case	0	4	9	2	4	
Spikes, gun, 2	0	0	8	0	$2\frac{1}{2}$	
Clothing.						
As private	4	2	$7\frac{1}{4}$	19	$11\frac{1}{2}$	
Necessaries.						
As private, *see* p. 135	2	3	$2\frac{1}{2}$	14	0	
Total	8	7	$0\frac{3}{4}$	54	12	

EQUIPMENT OF NON-COMMISSIONED OFFICERS AND MEN.

Description.	Cost.			Weight.		Remarks.
	£	s.	d.	lbs.	oz.	
ONE MAN CARRIES THE FOLLOWING EQUIPMENT.						
Arms, Accoutrements, and Appointments.						
Sword, belt, havresack and canteen, same as foregoing.	1	0	1	5	8	
Axe, { felling, with case	0	5	6	6	4	
{ hand, and saw, with case, &c.	0	15	9	6	12	
Bill hook, with case	0	4	9	2	4	
Gun, spikes, 2	0	0	8	0	$2\frac{1}{2}$	
Clothing.						
As private	4	2	$7\frac{1}{4}$	19	$11\frac{1}{2}$	
Necessaries.						
As private, see p. 135	2	3	$2\frac{1}{2}$	14	0	
Total	8	12	$6\frac{3}{4}$	54	10	
ONE MAN CARRIES THE FOLLOWING EQUIPMENT.						
Arms, Accoutrements, and Appointments.						
Sword, belt, havresack, and canteen, same as foregoing.	1	0	1	5	8	
Crow bar, with caps and strap	0	4	9	7	$6\frac{1}{2}$	
Case containing auger, cold chisel, socket do. and hammer.	0	14	9	7	$5\frac{1}{2}$	
Spikes, gun, 2	0	0	8	0	$2\frac{1}{2}$	
Clothing.						
As corporal	4	3	$3\frac{1}{4}$	19	12	
Necessaries.						
As private, see p. 135	2	3	$2\frac{1}{2}$	14	0	
Total	8	6	$8\frac{3}{4}$	54	$2\frac{1}{2}$	
HOSPITAL ORDERLY.						
Arms and Accoutrements.						
Belt, waist, with snake hook and sliding frog	0	3	0	0	$8\frac{3}{4}$	
Sword and scabbard, bugler's	0	9	3	2	9	
Havresack	0	2	6	0	3	
Canteen, wooden, with strap	0	2	6	1	12	On active service only.
Clothing.						
As private	4	2	$7\frac{1}{4}$	19	$11\frac{1}{2}$	
Necessaries.						
As private, see p. 135	2	3	$2\frac{1}{2}$	14	0	
Total	7	3	$0\frac{3}{4}$	38	$12\frac{1}{4}$	

GENERAL LIST OF EQUIPMENTS FOR A BATTALION OF RIFLES.

Number of Rank and File 1,000, *in Ten Companies.*

Description.	Cost of each.			Weight of each.		Total No.	Total Cost.			Total Weight.	
ARMS.	£	s.	d.	lbs.	oz.		£	s.	d.	lbs.	oz.
Short rifle muskets, pattern 1860, complete with rammer, sword bayonet, bayonet scabbard, muzzle stopper and snap cap with chain.	5	4	9¾	10	2½	1,013	5,308	15	0¾	10,921	6½
Nipples, spare - - - - -	0	0	1¾	0	0⅙	304	2	4	4	3	2⅔
Wrenches, nipple { with cramp - -	0	7	11½	0	6½	101	9	17	9½	41	0½
Wrenches, nipple { without cramp - -	0	0	11½	0	4½	912	43	14	0	256	8
Swords and scabbards { staff serjeants, line pattern -	1	12	6	2	10¾	1	1	12	6	2	10¾
Swords and scabbards { " rifle " -	1	12	0	2	10	10	16	0	0	26	4
Swords and scabbards { drummer's pattern - -	0	9	3	2	9	45	20	16	3	115	5
Swords and scabbards { for pioneers - - -	0	11	10	3	0	11	6	10	2	33	0
Buglers' Appointments.											
Bugles - - - - - -	1	1	0	1	6½	20	21	1	0	28	2
Strings for ditto - - - -	0	2	0	0	4¾	20	2	0	0	5	15
Total - - -	-	-	-	-	-	- -	5,432	11	1¼	11,432	6¼
ACCOUTREMENTS.											
Bags, ball, black leather, with zinc oil bottle -	0	2	3	0	8	1,013	113	19	3	406	8
Belts { pouch, black leather - - -	0	1	9	0	9	1,013	88	12	9	469	13
Belts { waist black leather, with sword carriage and snake hook, furniture gilt.	0	6	0	0	12½	1	0	6	0	0	12½
Belts { do., but furniture silver plated -	0	6	0	0	12½	10	3	0	0	7	13
Belts { black leather, with snake hook -	0	2	0	0	5½	1,069	106	18	0	367	7½
Canteens, wooden, with strap - -	0	2	6	1	12	1,079	134	17	6	1,738	4
Frogs { black leather - - - -	0	1	0	0	3¼	1,058	52	18	0	214	14½
Frogs { " with shifting loop -	0	1	3	0	3½	11	0	13	9	2	6½
Havresacks, waterproof, with strap - -	0	2	6	0	3	1,079	134	17	6	202	5
Knots, sword, black leather - - -	0	1	6	0	0¾	11	0	16	6	0	8¼
Plates, bronzed, for pouch belt (issued to Rifle brigade only).	0	2	0	—		—	—			—	
Pouches { 50 round, with fur cap pocket attached	0	6	0	2	1	1,013	303	18	0	2,089	5
Pouches { black leather, for percussion caps -	0	0	9	0	2	1,013	37	19	9	126	10
Slings, rifle, black leather - - -	0	1	0	0	4½	1,013	50	13	0	284	14½
Whistles and chains { rate for 60th Rifles -	0	2	6	0	3½	49	6	2	6	10	11½
Whistles and chains { " Rifle brigade -	—			—		—	—			—	
Pioneer's Tools and Black Leather Cases.											
Same as line, p. 150 - - - -	-	-	-	-	-	- -	11	6	4	164	4
Total - - -	-	-	-	-	-	- -	1,046	19	0	6,075	5¼
CLOTHING.											
Boots, pairs - - - - -	0	8	6	2	13	2,158	917	3	0	6,069	6
Chacos and covers { pattern for staff serjeants -	0	12	8¾	0	10½	6	3	16	4½	3	15
Chacos and covers { " other ranks -	0	4	7¼	0	10½	1,073	248	2	7½	704	2½
Leggings, leather, pairs - - -	0	3	4	0	11	1,079	179	16	8	741	13
Trousers, cloth { doeskin, pattern, for staff serjeants	1	0	0	2	0	6	6	0	0	12	0
Trousers, cloth { Kersey " serjeants, buglers, and musicians.	0	13	0	2	3	93	60	9	0	203	7
Trousers, cloth { Kersey, for other ranks - -	0	9	0	2	2	980	941	0	0	2,082	8
Trousers, green tartan { pattern for staff serjeants -	0	17	6	1	7	6	5	5	0	8	10
Trousers, green tartan { for other ranks - -	0	6	9¾	1	7	1,073	365	9	9¼	1,542	7

Description.	Cost of each.	Weight of each.	Total No.	Total Cost.	Total Weight.
	£ s. d.	lbs. oz.		£ s. d.	lbs. oz.
Tunics — serjeant major	2 11 6	2 11½	1	2 11 6	2 11½
Tunics — quartermaster serjeant	2 8 6	2 11½	1	2 8 6	2 11½
Tunics — serjeant instructor of musketry	2 12 0	2 11½	1	2 12 0	2 11½
Tunics — bandmaster serjeant	2 6 0	3 0	1	2 6 0	3 0
Tunics — bugle major	2 12 0	3 4	1	2 12 0	3 4
Tunics — 2nd class staff serjeants, and serjeants	0 19 8	3 2	43	42 5 8	134 6
Tunics — colour serjeants	1 4 4½	3 5	10	12 7 9	33 2
Tunics — band serjeant	2 6 0	3 0	1	2 6 0	3 0
Tunics — band	0 19 6	3 4	20	19 10 0	65 0
Tunics — buglers	1 0 5	3 6	20	25 0 0	67 8
Tunics — corporals	0 19 0	3 1½	49	46 11 0	151 9½
Tunics — privates	0 18 4	3 1	931	853 8 4	2,851 3
Great coats — pattern for staff serjeants	2 12 0	6 2	6	15 12 0	36 12
Great coats — " other ranks	1 3 6	6 2	1,073	1,260 15 6	6,572 2
Badges — good conduct, 1 bar	0 0 1¼	0 0¼	—	—	—
Badges — " 2 "	0 0 2½	0 0¼	—	—	—
Badges — " 3 "	0 0 3¾	0 0¼	—	—	—
Badges — " 4 "	0 0 5	0 0½	—	—	—
Badges — shooting — 1st or supplementary prize	0 4 6	0 0½	5	1 2 6	0 2½
Badges — shooting — 2nd prize	0 2 9	0 0¼	10	1 7 6	0 2½
Badges — shooting — 3rd prize	0 0 4	0 0¼	90	18 0 0	1 6½
Chevrons, pair — lance serjeants	0 1 0	0 0½	—	—	—
Chevrons, pair — " corporals	0 0 4	0 0¼	—	—	—
Schoolmaster, *see* page 153	- - -	- -	- -	8 18 2¼	18 7¼
Total	- - -	- -	- -	5,046 16 11	21,217 8½

SET OF NECESSARIES.

Description.	Number.	Cost.	Weight.
		£ s. d.	lbs. oz.
Blacking, tin	1	0 0 2	0 8
Braces, pair	1	0 0 10½	0 4
Brushes — clothes	1	0 0 11½	0 3½
Brushes — shaving	1	0 0 3¾	0 1
Brushes — shoe, set of two	1	0 1 2¾	0 6½
Comb	1	0 0 2½	0 0½
Holdall	1	0 0 5	0 2½
Knapsack, with slings and great coat straps	1	0 6 11¼	4 2
Knife, fork and spoon, set	1	0 0 5¼	0 7¼
Mitts, pair	1	0 0 11¾	0 3¾
Razor and case	1	0 0 4¾	0 2¾
Shirts — cotton or	3	- -	—
Shirts — flannel	2	0 9 5½	1 12
Socks, worsted	3	0 3 0¾	0 12
Sponge	1	0 0 9	0 0¾
Stock and clasp	1	0 0 5¾	0 2
Tin, mess, with cover and strap	1	0 1 10¾	1 9
Towels	2	0 1 7½	1 0
Soap	—	—	—
Pipeclay	—	—	—
Account book, small	1	0 0 3	0 2
Bible and Prayer-book	—	—	—
Total issued to all ranks alike	- -	1 10 5¼	11 15½

Description.	Number.	Cost.	Weight.
		£ s. d.	lbs. oz.
Serjeant-major additional :—			
Cap, forage, green cloth (average) - - -	1	0 17 6	0 6½
Jacket, fatigue - - - - - -	1	1 8 6	1 7
Total set, serjeant-major's - -	- -	3 16 5¼	13 13
Quartermaster-serjeant, bandmaster and band-serjeant, additional :—			
Cap, forage, green cloth (average)* - - -	1	0 17 6	0 6½
Jacket, fatigue - - - - - -	1	1 5 6	1 7
Total set - - - - - -	- -	3 13 5¼	13 13
Bugle-major and instructor of musketry, additional :—			
Cap, forage, green cloth (average)* - - -	1	0 17 6	0 6½
Jacket, fatigue - - - - - -	1	1 9 0	1 7
Total set - - - - - -	- -	3 16 11¼	13 13
2nd class staff serjeants and serjeants, additional :—			
Cap, forage, green Kilmarnock, with strap - -	1	0 3 3¼	0 6½
Jacket, fatigue - - - - - -	1	0 13 6	1 8
Total set - - - - - -	- -	2 7 2½	13 14
Other ranks, additional :—			
Cap, forage, green Kilmarnock, with strap - -	1	0 1 9¼	0 6½
Jacket, fatigue - - - - - -	1	0 11 0	1 10
Total set - - - - - -	- -	2 3 2½	14 0

GENERAL SUMMARY.

Description.	Cost.	Weight.	——
	£ s. d.	lbs. ozs.	
Camp colours, aides, &c. - - -	8 11 4	50 14	
Arms and buglers' appointments - -	5,432 11 1¼	11,432 6¼	
Musical instruments - - - -	158 16 8	106 1	
Accoutrements and pioneers' tools - -	1,046 19 0	6,075 5¼	
Ammunition, 60,780 rounds - - -	121 11 3	5,508 3	Full supply carried on service.
Clothing - - - - -	5,046 16 11	21,217 8	
Necessaries - - - - -	2,351 5 2	15,098 4	
Armourer's forge - - - -	25 16 8	394 0	
Regimental books - - - -	—	—	
Regimental hospital equipment - -	423 11 6¾	5,738 7¼	Detailed in Part VII. of Army Equipment.
Total - - -	14,615 19 8	65,621 0¾	

* The pattern of the forage cap for staff serjeants varies in the different corps.

EQUIPMENT OF NON-COMMISSIONED OFFICERS AND MEN.

BATTALION OF THE LINE.

Description.	Cost.	Weight.	Remarks.
SERJEANT-MAJOR.			
Arms and Accoutrements.	£ s. d.	lbs. oz.	
Belt, waist, buff, with gilt union locket and sword carriages.	0 7 6	0 10¾	
Knot, sword	0 1 3	0 1½	
Sword and scabbard	1 12 6	2 10¾	
Havresack	0 1 0	0 10	
Canteen	0 2 6	1 12	On active service only.
Clothing.			
Boots, two pairs	0 17 0	5 10	
Chaco	0 10 5	0 10½	
Leggings, leather pair	0 3 4	0 11	
Sash, silk	1 15 0	0 14½	
Trousers { cloth	0 18 3	2 1	
{ blue tartan	0 15 7½	1 7	
Tunic with badges	2 8 4	2 9	4-bar gold chevron with crown.
Great coat	2 12 0	6 2	
Necessaries.			
Set as detailed at p. 145	3 14 3	14 2	
Total	15 18 11½	40 0	
SCHOOLMASTER.			
See p. 147	10 18 2¼	22 0¼	
QUARTERMASTER-SERJEANT.			
Arms and Accoutrements.			
As for serjeant-major	2 4 9	6 0	
Clothing.			
As for serjeant-major, excepting badges on tunic	9 16 11½	20 1	4-bar gold chevron.
Necessaries.			
Set, see p. 147	3 11 3	14 2	
Total	15 12 11½	40 3	

BATTALION OF THE LINE.

Description.	Cost.			Weight.		Remarks.
	£	s.	d.	lbs.	oz.	
SERJEANT-INSTRUCTOR OF MUSKETRY.						
Arms and Accoutrements.						
As for serjeant-major	2	4	9	6	0	
Clothing.						
As for serjeant-major, excepting badges on tunic	9	17	8½	20	1	4-bar gold chevron and crossed muskets.
Necessaries.						
Set, see p. 145	3	13	9	14	2	
Total	15	16	2½	40	3	
BANDMASTER-SERJEANT.						
Arms and Accoutrements.						
As for serjeant-major	2	4	9	6	0	
Clothing.						
As for serjeant-major, excepting distinctions on tunic.	9	11	7½	20	5	Gold shoulder cords, no chevrons.
Necessaries.						
Set, see p. 145	3	11	1	14	2	
Total	15	7	5½	40	7	
DRUM-MAJOR.						
Arms and Accoutrements.						
As for serjeant-major	2	4	9	6	0	
Clothing.						
As for serjeant-major, excepting distinctions on tunic.	10	0	7½	20	8	4-bar gold chevron with drum.
Necessaries.						
Set, see p. 145	3	14	9	14	2	
Drum-major's staff	-	-	-	-	-	} Provided from regimental funds.
Shoulder belt, embroidered	-	-	-	-	-	
Total	16	0	1½	40	10	
PAYMASTER-SERJEANT, ARMOURER-SERJEANT, HOSPITAL-SERJEANT, OR ORDERLY ROOM CLERK.						
Arms and Accoutrements.						
As for serjeant-major	2	4	9	6	0	
Clothing.						
Same as serjeant	4	11	0½	20	9	
Necessaries.						
As for serjeant, see p. 145	2	6	9½	14	3	
Total	9	2	7	40	12	

EQUIPMENT OF NON-COMMISSIONED OFFICERS AND MEN.

Description.	Cost.			Weight.		Remarks.
	£	s.	d.	lbs.	oz.	
BAND-SERJEANT.						
Same as bandmaster-serjeant	15	7	5½	40	7	4-bar gold chevron.
COLOUR-SERJEANT.						
Arms, Accoutrements, and Appointments.						
Same as serjeant	6	5	8¼	16	14¼	
Ammunition.						
Same as serjeant	—	—	—	2	11½	
Clothing.						
Same as serjeant	4	11	0½	20	9	
Badges on tunic extra	0	4	10¾	0	1½	Gold chevron and colour badge.
Necessaries.						
As serjeant, see p. 145	2	6	9½	14	3	
Total	13	8	5	54	7¼	
SERJEANT.						
Arms, Accoutrements, and Appointments.						
Bag, ball, buff	0	2	6	0	7	
Belts { pouch	0	3	0	0	8	
Belts { waist, with gilding metal union locket, and frog.	0	3	8	0	12¾	
Havresack	0	1	0	0	10	
Pouch, 20 round	0	4	3	1	4	
„ for percussion caps, buff	0	1	0	0	2	
Sling, musket, buff	0	1	0	0	3½	
Short rifle musket, pattern 1860, with rammer, sword bayonet and scabbard, snap cap and chain, and muzzle stopper.	5	4	9¾	10	12½	
Wrench, nipple, with cramp	0	1	11½	0	6½	
Canteen, wooden, with strap	0	2	6	1	12	On active service only.
Ammunition.						
30 rounds with 45 percussion caps	—	—	—	2	11½	Full service quantity.
Clothing.						
Boots, two pairs	0	17	0	5	10	
Chaco	0	4	7¼	0	10½	
Leggings, leather	0	3	4	0	11	
Sash, worsted	0	5	6	0	12	
Trousers { cloth	0	11	1	2	1½	
Trousers { blue serge	0	7	2¾	1	7	
Tunic	0	18	9½	3	3	
Great coat	1	3	6	6	2	
Necessaries.						
Set detailed at p. 145	2	6	9½	14	3	
Total	13	3	6¼	54	5¾	

3976.

Description.	Cost.			Weight.		Remarks.
	£	s.	d.	lbs.	oz.	
CORPORAL.						
Arms and Accoutrements.						
As for private, but nipple wrench *with* cramp	4	4	$1\frac{1}{4}$	17	$1\frac{1}{4}$	
Ammunition	-	-	-	5	7	
Clothing.						
As for private	4	0	$10\frac{1}{2}$	20	1	
Badges extra	0	0	4	0	$0\frac{1}{2}$	
Necessaries.						
As for private	2	2	$10\frac{3}{4}$	14	5	
Total	10	8	$2\frac{1}{2}$	56	$14\frac{3}{4}$	
PRIVATE.						
Arms and Accoutrements.						
Bag, ball, buff	0	2	6	0	7	
Belts, buff { pouch	0	3	0	0	8	
waist, with brass union locket and frog.	0	3	7	0	$12\frac{3}{4}$	
Havresack	0	1	0	0	10	
Pouch, 50 round	0	6	0	2	1	
„ for percussion caps, buff	0	1	0	0	2	
Sling, musket, buff	0	1	0	0	$3\frac{1}{2}$	
Rifle musket, pattern 1853, with rammer, bayonet and scabbard, snap-cap and chain, and muzzle stopper.	3	1	$6\frac{3}{4}$	10	$2\frac{1}{2}$	
Wrench, nipple, without cramp	0	0	$11\frac{1}{2}$	0	$4\frac{1}{2}$	
Canteen, wooden, with strap	0	2	6	1	12	On active service only.
Ammunition.						
60 rounds with 90 percussion caps	-	-	-	5	7	Full service quantity.
Clothing.						
Boots, 2 pairs	0	17	0	5	10	
Chaco	0	4	$7\frac{1}{4}$	0	$10\frac{1}{2}$	
Leggings, leather	0	3	4	0	11	
Trousers { cloth	0	8	$9\frac{1}{2}$	2	5	
blue tartan	0	7	$2\frac{3}{4}$	1	7	
Tunic	0	16	5	3	$3\frac{1}{2}$	
Great coat	1	3	6	6	2	
Necessaries.						
Set as detailed at p. 145	2	2	$10\frac{3}{4}$	14	5	
Total	10	6	$10\frac{1}{2}$	56	$12\frac{1}{4}$	
DRUMMER.						
Arms, Accoutrements, and Appointments.						
Apron, buff, side drum	0	4	0	0	10	
Belt, waist, buff. with brass union locket and frog	0	3	7	0	$12\frac{3}{4}$	
Sword and scabbard	0	12	6	2	9	
Drum with sticks and ticken cover	2	7	6	9	2	
Havresack	0	1	0	0	10	
Canteen, wooden, with strap	0	2	6	1	12	On active service only.

Description.	Cost.			Weight.		Remarks.
Clothing.	£	*s.*	*d.*	lbs.	oz.	
As for private - - - - -	4	0	$10\frac{1}{2}$	20	1	
Distinctions on tunic extra - - -	0	4	$5\frac{1}{2}$	0	3	
Necessaries.						
As private - - - - -	2	2	$10\frac{3}{4}$	14	5	
Total - -	9	19	$3\frac{3}{4}$	50	$1\frac{3}{4}$	
BUGLER.						
Arms, Accoutrements, and Appointments.						
Belt, waist, buff, with brass union locket and frog	0	3	7	0	$12\frac{3}{4}$	
Sword and scabbard - - - -	0	12	6	2	9	
Bugle and strings - - - -	1	3	0	1	$11\frac{1}{4}$	
Flute and case (average cost and weight) -	0	14	$0\frac{1}{4}$	0	$8\frac{3}{4}$	
Havresack - - - - -	0	1	0	0	10	
Canteen, wooden, with strap - - -	0	2	6	1	12	On active service only.
Clothing.						
As drummer - - - - -	4	5	4	20	4	
Necessaries.						
As private, *see* p. 145 - - - -	2	2	$10\frac{3}{4}$	14	5	
Total - -	9	4	10	42	$8\frac{3}{4}$	
MUSICIAN.						
Arms and Accoutrements.						
Belt, sword, and scabbard, havresack and canteen same as for drummer - - - -	0	19	7	5	$11\frac{3}{4}$	
Musical instrument - - - -		—			—	
Clothing.						
Boots, two pairs - - - - -	0	17	0	5	10	
Chaco - - - - - -	0	4	$7\frac{1}{4}$	0	$10\frac{1}{2}$	
Leggings, leather - - - -	0	3	4	0	11	
Trousers { cloth - - - - -	0	11	1	2	$1\frac{1}{2}$	
Trousers { blue tartan - - - -	0	7	$2\frac{3}{4}$	1	7	
Tunic - - - - - -	0	17	6	2	11	
Great coat - - - - -	1	3	6	6	2	
Necessaries.						
Set as detailed at p. 145 - - - -	2	3	$2\frac{1}{4}$	14	4	
Total - -	7	7	$0\frac{1}{4}$	39	$4\frac{3}{4}$	
PIONEERS.						
Five Men carry the following Equipment.						
Arms, Accoutrements, and Appointments.						
Belt, waist, buff, with union locket, and frog with shifting loop - - - - -	0	3	10	0	$13\frac{3}{4}$	
Havresack - - - - - -	0	1	0	0	10	
Sword, with saw-back and scabbard - -	0	11	10	3	0	
Canteen, wooden, with strap - -	0	2	6	1	12	On active service only.

Description.	Cost.			Weight.		Remarks.
	£	s.	d.	lbs.	oz.	
Axe, pick, with case - - - -	0	5	3	6	8	
Bill hook, with case - - - -	0	4	9	2	4	
Shovel, with case - - - -	0	9	6	7	2	
Gun spikes, two - - - - -	0	0	8	0	2½	
Clothing.						
As private - - - - -	4	0	10½	20	1	
Necessaries.						
As private, *see* p. 145 - - - -	2	2	10¾	14	5½	
Total - -	8	3	1¼	56	10¾	

THREE MEN CARRY THE FOLLOWING EQUIPMENT.

Arms, Accoutrements, and Appointments.

Description.	£	s.	d.	lbs.	oz.
Sword, belt, havresack, and canteen, same as the foregoing - - - - -	0	19	2	6	1¾
Axe, felling, with case - - - -	0	5	6	6	4
Bill hook, with case - - - -	0	4	9	2	4
Spade, with case - - - -	0	9	6	6	1½
Gun spikes, two - - - - -	0	0	8	0	2½
Clothing.					
As private - - - - -	4	0	10½	20	1
Necessaries.					
As private, *see* p. 145 - - - -	2	2	10¾	14	5
Total - -	8	3	4¼	55	4¾

ONE MAN CARRIES THE FOLLOWING EQUIPMENT.

Arms, Accoutrements, and Appointments.

Description.	£	s.	d.	lbs.	oz.
Sword, belt, havresack and canteen, same as foregoing - - - - -	0	19	2	6	1¾
Axe, felling, with case - - - -	0	5	6	6	4
Axe, broad, and axe, hand, with case - -	0	10	3	6	14
Bill hook, with case - - - -	0	4	9	2	4
Gun spikes, two - - - - -	0	0	8	0	2½
Clothing.					
As private - - - - -	4	0	10½	20	1
Necessaries.					
As private, *see* p. 145 - - - -	2	2	10¾	14	5
Total - -	8	4	1¼	56	0¼

ONE MAN CARRIES THE FOLLOWING EQUIPMENT.

Arms, Accoutrements, and Appointments.

Description.	£	s.	d.	lbs.	oz.
Sword, belt, havresack, and canteen, same as foregoing - - - - -	0	19	2	6	1¾
Axe, felling, with case - - - -	0	5	6	6	4
Axe, hand, and saw, with case, &c. -	0	15	9	6	12
Bill hook, with case - - - -	0	4	9	2	4
Gun spikes, two - - - - -	0	0	8	0	2½

Description.	Cost.			Weight.		Remarks.
Clothing.	£	*s.*	*d.*	lbs.	oz.	
As private - - - - -	4	0	10½	20	1	
Necessaries.						
As private, *see* p. 145 - - - -	2	2	10¾	14	5	
Total - -	8	9	7¼	55	14¼	
ONE MAN CARRIES THE FOLLOWING EQUIPMENT. *Arms, Accoutrements, and Appointments.*						
Sword, belt, havresack, and canteen, same as foregoing - - - - - - -	0	19	2	6	1¾	
Crowbar, with caps and strap - - -	0	4	9	7	6½	
Case containing auger, cold chisel, socket chisel, and hammer - - - - -	0	14	9	7	5½	
Gun spikes, two - - - - - -	0	0	8	0	2½	
Clothing.						
As corporal - - - - - -	4	1	2½	20	1½	
Necessaries.						
As private, *see* p. 145 - - - -	2	2	10¾	14	5	
Total - -	8	3	5¼	55	6¾	
HOSPITAL ORDERLY. *Arms and Accoutrements.*						
Same as musician - - - -	0	19	7	5	11¾	
Clothing and Necessaries.						
As private - - - - -	6	3	9¼	34	6	
Total - -	7	3	4¼	40	1¾	

GENERAL LIST OF EQUIPMENTS FOR A BATTALION OF THE LINE.

Number of Rank and File 1,000, *in Ten Companies.*

Description.	Cost of each.			Weight of each.		Total No.	Total Cost			Total Weight.	
ARMS.											
Rifle muskets, pattern 1853, complete with rammer, bayonet, bayonet scabbard, muzzle stopper, and snap cap with chain.	3	1	6¾	10	2½	964	2,967	6	3	9,790	0
Short Rifle muskets, pattern 1860, complete with rammer, sword-bayonet, scabbard, muzzle stopper, and snap cap with chain.	5	4	9¾	10	12½	49	256	15	9¾	528	4½
Nipples, spare - - - -	0	0	1¾	0	0⅙	304	2	4	4	3	2¾
Wrenches, nipple { with cramp - -	0	1	11½	0	6½	101	9	17	9½	41	0½
Wrenches, nipple { without cramp - -	0	0	11½	0	4½	912	43	14	0	256	8
Swords and scabbards { staff-serjeant's pattern	1	12	6	2	10¾	11	17	17	6	29	6¼
Swords and scabbards { drummers' pattern -	0	12	6	2	9	45	28	2	6	115	5
Swords and scabbards { for pioneers - -	0	11	10	3	0	11	6	10	2	33	0
Total - -	-		-	-	-	-	3,332	8	4½	10,796	11

Description.	Cost. of each.			Weight of each.		Total No.	Total Cost.			Total Weight.	
*Drummer's Appointments.**	£	s.	d.	lbs.	oz.		£	s.	d.	lbs.	oz.
Bugles - - - - -	1	1	0	1	6½	10	10	10	0	14	1
Strings for ditto - - - - -	0	2	0	0	4¾	10	1	0	0	2	15½
Drums, side, brass, complete with sticks and tickens.	2	7	6	9	2	10	22	15	0	91	4
Flutes { in B♭, with case - - -	0	14	3	0	8¼	6	4	5	6	3	1½
Flutes { in F ,, ,, - - -	0	15	0	0	12½	2	1	10	0	1	9
Piccolo { in E♭ ,, ,, - - -	0	12	3	0	7	1	0	12	3	0	7
Piccolo { in F ,, ,, - - -	0	12	6	0	7	1	0	12	6	0	7
Total set of appointments -	-		-	-	-	- -	41	5	3	113	13
Accoutrements.											
Aprons, buff, leg, for side drum† - -	0	4	0	0	10	10	2	0	0	6	4
Bags, ball, buff, with zinc oil bottle - -	0	2	6	0	7	1,013	126	12	6	443	3
Belts { pouch, buff - -	0	3	0	0	3	1,013	151	19	6	506	8
Belts { waist { black leather, with sword carriages and snake hook.	0	6	0	0	12½	1	0	6	0	0	12½
Belts { waist { buff, with sword carriages, staff-serjeant's pattern.	0	5	6	0	9	10	2	19	0	5	10
Belts { waist { buff - - -	0	1	9	0	5½	1,069	93	10	9	367	7½
Canteens, wooden, with strap - -	0	2	6	1	12	1,079	134	17	6	1,888	4
Carriages, buff { side drum, new pattern† -	0	2	6	1	2½	10	1	5	0	11	9
Carriages, buff { for bass drum, with swivel -	0	3	6	0	12½	1	0	3	6	0	12½
Frogs { buff - - - - -	0	1	3	0	2½	1,058	66	2	6	165	5
Frogs { ,, with shifting loop (pioneer's) -	0	1	6	0	3½	11.	0	16	6	2	6½
Havresacks - - - - - -	0	1	0	0	10	1,079	53	19	0	674	6
Knots, sword { black japanned leather -	0	1	6	0	0¾	1	0	1	6	0	0¾
Knots, sword { buff - - - -	0	1	3	0	1½	10	0	12	6	0	15
Lockets, union { gilt, for staff-serjeants -	0	2	0	0	4¾	10	1	0	0	2	15½
Lockets, union { gilding metal, for serjeants -	0	0	8	0	4¾	49	1	12	8	14	4¾
Lockets, union { brass - - -	0	0	7	0	4¾	1,020	29	15	0	302	13
Pouches { 20 round, serjeants' - -	0	4	3	1	4	49	10	8	3	61	8
Pouches { 50 ,, rank and file - -	0	6	0	2	1	964	289	4	0	1,988	4
Pouches { buff, for percussion caps - -	0	1	0	0	2	1,013	50	13	0	126	10
Slings, musket, buff - - - -	0	1	0	0	3½	1,013	50	13	0	221	9½
Whistles and chains, for light infantry only -	0	2	6	0	3½	49	—			—	
Total - -	-		-	-	-	- -	1,068	11	8	6,791	9½
Pioneer's Tools and Black Leather Cases.											
Bill hook, case and loop - - -	0	4	9	2	4	10	2	7	6	22	8
Crowbar, set of caps and strap - -	0	4	9	7	6½	1	0	4	9	7	6½
Felling axe, and case tipped with brass -	0	5	6	6	4	5	1	7	6	25	4
Hand axe and broad axe, case and shoulder belt.	0	10	3	6	14	1	0	10	3	6	14
Pick axe and case - - - -	0	5	3	6	8	5	1	6	3	32	8
Saw and hand axe, case and cap with shoulder belt and straps.	0	15	9	6	12	1	0	15	9	6	12
Shovel, case, shoulder belt and straps -	0	8	9	7	2	5	2	3	9	35	10
Spade, case, shoulder belt and straps - -	0	9	6	6	1½	3	1	8	6	18	4½
Small tools, case with shoulder belt - set	0	14	9	7	5½	1	0	14	9	7	5½
Spikes, gun, common - - -	0	0	4	0	1¼	22	0	7	4	1	11½
Total set - -	-		-	-	-	- -	11	6	4	164	4

* Side drums, flutes, and piccolos are not issued to regiments of light infantry. They are supplied in lieu, with ten additional bugles.

† Leg aprons and side drum carriages are not issued to battalions of light infantry.

Description.	Cost of each.			Weight of each.		Total No.	Total Cost.			Total Weight.	
CLOTHING.	£	s.	d.	lbs.	oz.		£	s.	d	lbs.	oz.
Boots, pairs	0	8	6	2	13	2,158	917	3	0	6,069	6
Chacos, with covers: pattern for staff serjeants	0	10	5	0	10½	6	3	2	6	3	15
Chacos, with covers: other ranks	0	4	7¼	0	10½	1,073	214	12	0	703	15½
Leggings, leather, pairs	0	3	4	0	11	1,079	179	16	8	741	13
Sashes: silk	1	15	0	0	14½	6	10	10	0	5	7
Sashes: worsted	0	5	6	0	12	53	14	11	6	39	12
Trowsers: cloth: pattern for staff serjeants	0	18	3	2	1	6	5	9	6	12	6
Trowsers: cloth: „ serjeants and band	0	11	1	2	1½	73	40	9	1	152	13½
Trowsers: cloth: „ other ranks	0	8	9½	2	5	1,000	439	11	8	2,312	8
Trowsers: blue tartan: „ staff serjeants	0	15	7½	1	7	6	4	13	9	8	10
Trowsers: blue tartan: „ other ranks	0	7	2¾	1	7	1,073	387	16	10¾	1,542	7
Tunics: serjeant-major	2	8	4	2	9	1	2	8	4	2	9
Tunics: quartermaster-serjeant	2	5	4	2	9	1	2	5	4	2	9
Tunics: serjeant instructor of musketry	2	6	1	2	9	1	2	6	1	2	9
Tunics: bandmaster-serjeant	2	0	0	2	13	1	2	0	0	2	13
Tunics: drum-major	2	9	0	3	0	1	2	9	0	3	0
Tunics: band-serjeant	2	0	0	2	13	1	2	0	0	2	13
Tunics: colour-serjeants	1	3	8¼	3	4½	10	11	16	10½	32	13
Tunics: staff serjeants 2nd class, and serjeants	0	18	9½	3	3	43	40	8	0½	137	1
Tunics: corporals	0	16	9	3	4	49	41	0	3	159	4
Tunics: drummers	1	0	10½	3	6½	20	20	17	6	68	2
Tunics: band	0	17	6	2	11	20	17	10	0	53	12
Tunics: privates	0	16	5	3	3½	931	764	3	11	2,996	10½
Great coats: pattern for staff-serjeants	2	12	0	6	2	6	15	12	0	36	12
Great coats: „ other ranks	1	3	6	6	2	1,073	1,260	15	6	6,572	2
Badges: good conduct: 1 bar	0	0	1¼	0	0¼	—	—			—	
Badges: good conduct: 2 „	0	0	2½	0	0¼	—	—			—	
Badges: good conduct: 3 „	0	0	3¾	0	0¼	—	—			—	
Badges: good conduct: 4 „	0	0	5	0	0½	—	—			—	
Badges: shooting: 1st supplementary prize	0	4	6	0	0½	5	1	2	6	0	2½
Badges: shooting: 2nd prize	0	2	9	0	0¼	10	1	7	6	0	2½
Badges: shooting: 3rd „	0	0	4	0	0¼	90	1	10	0	1	6½
Chevrons: lance-serjeants	0	0	6	0	0½	—	—			—	
Chevrons: lance-corporals	0	0	2	0	0¼	—	—			—	
Clothing, for schoolmaster	-	-	-	-	-	- -	8	18	2¼	18	7½
Total	-	-	-	-	-	- -	4,446	7	7	21,686	2

SET OF NECESSARIES.

Description.		Number.	Cost.			Weight.	
			£	s.	d.	lbs.	oz.
Blacking	tin	1	0	0	2	0	8
Braces	pair	1	0	0	10½	0	4
Brass button	-	1	0	0	1½	0	2
Brushes: brass	-	1	0	0	7½	0	3
Brushes: clothes	-	1	0	0	11½	0	3½
Brushes: shaving	-	1	0	0	3¾	0	1
Brushes: shoe, set of two, for blacking and polishing	-	1	0	1	2¾	0	6½
Comb	-	1	0	0	2½	0	0½
Holdall	-	1	0	0	5	0	2½
Knapsack, with slings	-	1	0	6	2½	3	13
Knife, fork, and spoon	set	1	0	0	5¼	0	7¼
Mitts	pair	1	0	0	11½	0	3¾
Razor and case	..	1	0	0	4¾	0	2¾

Description.		Number.	Cost. £	s.	d.	Weight. lbs.	oz.
Shirts { cotton, or		3		—		—	
Shirts { flannel		2	0	9	5½	1	12
Socks, worsted	pairs	3	0	2	9¾	0	12
Sponge		1	0	0	9	0	0¾
Stock and clasp		1	0	0	5¾	0	2
Straps, set of two, for great coat		1	0	1	0¼	0	5
Tin, mess, with cover and strap		1	0	1	11¼	1	9
Towels		2	0	1	7½	1	0
Soap		—		—		—	
Pipe-clay		—		—		—	
Account book, small		1	0	0	3	0	2
Bible and prayer book		—		—		—	
Total issued to all ranks alike		- -	1	11	3	12	4½
Serjeant-major additional :—							
Cap, forage, blue cloth (average)		- -	0	10	6	0	6½
Jacket, fatigue		- -	1	12	6	1	7
Total set		- -	3	14	3	14	2
Quartermaster-serjeant additional :—							
Cap, forage, blue cloth (average)		- -	0	10	6	0	6½
Jacket, fatigue		- -	1	9	6	1	7
Total set		- -	3	11	3	14	2
Serjeant instructor of musketry additional :—							
Cap, forage, blue cloth (average)		- -	0	10	6	0	6½
Jacket, fatigue		- -	1	12	0	1	7
Total set		- -	3	13	9	14	2
Bandmaster, or band-serjeant additional :—							
Cap, forage, blue cloth (average)		- -	0	10	6	0	6½
Jacket, fatigue		- -	1	9	4	1	7
Total set		- -	3	11	1	14	2
Drum-major :—							
Cap, forage, blue cloth (average)		- -	0	10	6	0	6½
Jacket, fatigue		- -	1	13	0	1	7
Total set		- -	3	14	9	14	2
2nd class staff-serjeants and serjeants additional :—							
Cap, forage, blue Kilmarnock, with strap and numeral		- -	0	3	9¾	0	6½
Jacket, fatigue		- -	0	11	8¾	1	8
Total set		- -	2	6	9½	14	3
Band additional :—							
Cap, forage, blue Kilmarnock, with strap and numeral		- -	0	1	9¾	0	6½
Jacket, fatigue, white		- -	0	10	1½	1	9
Total set		- -	2	3	2¼	14	4
Others additional :—							
Cap, forage, blue Kilmarnock, with strap and numeral		- -	0	1	9¾	0	6½
Jacket, fatigue		- -	0	9	10	1	10
Total set		- -	2	2	10¾	14	5

GENERAL LIST OF EQUIPMENTS.

GENERAL SUMMARY.

Description.	Cost.			Weight.		Remarks.
	£	s.	d.	lbs.	oz.	
Colours, pair, with cases complete - -	32	15	0	22	0	
Camp colours, aides, &c. - -	8	11	4	50	14	
Arms and drummers' appointments - -	3,373	13	7¼	10,796	11	
Musical instruments - - - -	158	16	8	106	1	
Accoutrements and pioneers' tools - -	1,079	18	0	6,955	14	
Ammunition, 59,310 rounds - - -	118	12	5	5,375	0	Full supply carried on service.
Clothing - - - - -	4,446	7	7	21,686	2	
Necessaries - - - - -	2,328	11	5	15,440	4	
Armourers' forge - - - -	25	16	8	394	0	
Regimental books - - - -	-	-	-	-	-	
Regimental hospital equipment - -	423	11	6¾	5,538	7¼	Detailed in Part VII. of Army Equipment.
Total - - - -	11,996	14	3	66,565	5¼	

SCHOOLMASTERS.

	£	s.	d.	lbs.	oz.	
Arms and Appointments.						
Belt, waist, black leather, with sword carriages and snake hook.	0	6	0	0	12½	The uniform and appointments for schoolmasters are identical for all branches of the service (*see* W. O. Circulars 840 and 756).
Knot, sword, black leather - - -	0	1	6	0	1½	
Sword and scabbard - - - -	1	12	6	2	10¾	
Clothing.						
Boots, allowance in lieu of annual - -	1	0	0	5	10	
Cap and cover - - - - -	0	7	4	0	7	
Frock coat, with Shoulder knots { 1st class	3	3	7¼	3	0	
2nd „	3	1	1¼			
3rd „	2	18	7¼			
4th „	2	16	1¼			
Sash silk - - - - -	1	15	0	0	14½	
Trousers, black doeskin - - -	0	18	3	2	0	
Cloak - - - - - -	1	17	9	6	8	
Necessaries and other Articles.						
According to requirement.	—			—		
Total (average) - - -	10	18	2¼	22	0¼	

TABLE OF THE COMPARATIVE ANNUAL COST OF PERSONAL EQUIPMENT FOR THE SEVERAL CLASSES OF INFANTRY.

Description.	Guards.	Line.		
		Highland.	Rifles.	Others.
	£ s. d.	£ s. d.	£ s. d.	£ s. d.
STAFF-SERJEANT.				
Arms and accoutrements, viz.:—				
Sword or claymore	0 2 8½	0 3 2½	0 2 8	0 2 8½
Sword belt	—	0 0 6½	0 0 6	0 0 7½
Sword knot	—	—	0 0 1½	0 0 1¼
Havresack	0 0 1	0 0 1	0 0 1	0 0 1
Clothing, viz.:—				
Head dress	0 14 0	0 8 6	0 6 4½	—
Gloves	0 2 0	—	—	—
Tunic or coat for full dress	7 10 0	2 18 8	2 9 4	2 4 9
Tunic for undress, or waistcoat	0 3 0	0 19 6	—	—
Cloth trousers	1 1 0	—	1 0 0	0 18 3
Tartan or summer do.	0 9 6	—	0 8 9	0 7 10
Plaid	—	0 4 2	—	—
Kilt	—	1 16 0	—	—
Sash	0 8 9	0 8 9	—	0 8 9
Sword knot	0 10 0	—	—	—
Leather leggings	0 1 1	0 1 1	0 1 1	0 1 1
Boots or shoes	0 17 0	0 16 6	0 17 0	0 17 0
Great coat	0 10 5	0 10 5	0 10 5	0 10 5
Total	12 9 6½	8 7 5	5 16 4	5 11 7¼
SERJEANT.				
Arms and accoutrements, viz.;—				
Rifle musket, complete with bayonet, &c.	0 8 8¾	0 8 8¾	0 8 8¾	0 8 8¾
Ball bag	0 0 2¼	0 0 2¼	0 0 2¼	0 0 2¼
Pouch belt	0 0 3	0 0 3	0 0 1¾	0 0 3
Waist belt, complete	0 0 3½	0 0 3½	0 0 3	0 0 3½
Havresack	0 0 1	0 0 1	0 0 1	0 0 1
Pouch	0 0 3	0 0 3	0 0 6	0 0 3
Pouch for percussion caps	0 0 1	0 0 1	0 0 0¾	0 0 1
Musket sling	0 0 1	0 0 1	0 0 1	0 0 1
Nipple wrench	0 0 2	0 0 2	0 0 2	0 0 2
Whistle and chain	—	—	0 0 2½	—
Clothing, viz.:—				
Head dress	0 14 0	0 6 0	0 2 3¾	0 2 4
Tunic or coat	3 3 0	1 4 6	0 19 8	0 18 9½
Waistcoat	0 15 6	0 13 6	—	—
Cloth trousers	0 16 0	—	0 13 0	0 11 1
Tartan or summer do.	0 3 5	—	0 3 5	0 3 7½
Plaid	—	0 1 5	—	—
Kilt	—	0 16 9	—	—
Sash	0 1 4½	0 1 4½	—	0 1 4½
Leather leggings	0 1 1	0 1 1	0 1 1	0 1 1
Boots or shoes	0 17 0	0 16 6	0 17 0	0 17 0
Great coat	0 5 10½	0 5 10½	0 5 10½	0 5 10½
Total	7 7 4¾	4 17 1¾	3 12 9¼	3 11 3¾

Description.	Guards.	Line.		
		Highland.	Rifles.	Others.
	£ s. d.	£ s. d.	£ s. d.	£ s. d.
PRIVATE.				
Arms and accoutrements, viz. :—				
Rifle musket, complete, with bayonet, &c.	0 5 1½	0 5 1½	0 8 8¾	0 5 1½
Ball bag	0 0 2½	0 0 2½	0 0 2¼	0 0 2½
Pouch belt	0 0 3	0 0 3	0 0 1¾	0 0 3
Waist belt, complete	- - -	- - -	0 0 3	- - -
Havresack	0 0 1	0 0 1	0 0 1	0 0 1
Pouch	0 0 6	0 0 6	0 0 6	0 0 6
Pouch for percussion cap	0 0 1	0 0 1	0 0 0¾	0 0 1
Musket sling	0 0 1	0 0 1	0 0 1	0 0 1
Nipple wrench	0 0 1	0 0 1	0 0 1	0 0 1
Clothing, viz. :—				
Head dress	0 14 0	0 6 0	0 2 3¾	0 2 4
Tunic or coat	1 3 0	1 1 2	0 18 4	0 16 5
Waistcoat	0 6 6	0 6 8	—	—
Cloth trousers	0 11 0	- - -	0 9 0	0 8 9½
Tartan or summer do.	0 3 5	- - -	0 3 5	0 3 7½
Plaid	- - -	0 0 11	—	—
Kilt	- - -	0 11 3	—	—
Leather leggings	0 1 1	0 1 1	0 1 1	0 1 1
Boots or shoes	0 17 0	0 16 6	0 17 0	0 17 0
Great coat	0 5 10½	0 5 10½	0 5 10½	0 5 10½
Total	4 8 3½	3 15 10½	3 5 1¾	3 1 4½

Necessaries are omitted in the above table, as they are only issued once to each man at the public expense, and are afterwards replaced at the soldier's expense as they become unserviceable, and thus the exact *annual* cost is not susceptible of calculation.

MARKS FOR PACKAGES AND STORES.

The following method of marking stores and packages sent to an army in the field, in order to facilitate their collection, arrangement, and delivery, was approved in 1861, and notified in Circular 732, 21/12/61; most of the articles for which the different marks are adopted are included in the general equipment of an army.

Mark.	Class of Stores.
Balls { one blue ball	Ordnance, carriages, shot of all kinds, empty shells, and general stores *for field service*.*
two ,,	Similar articles *for siege service*.
one red ball	Small arms, accoutrements, and the implements or materials for their repair.
Crosses { one red cross	Medicines and medical instruments.
one black cross	Medical comforts.
two ,,	Hospital and barrack stores.
Diamonds* (two red diamonds)	Ammunition for artillery or small arms, including live shells and combustible stores.
Heart (one black heart)	Clothing and necessaries.
Horse shoes { one black horse shoe	Harness and saddlery; pack-saddles included.
two ,,	Wagons and carts for transport of stores.
Squares { one black square	Intrenching tools, nails, &c.
two ,,	Materials for hutting or building (except nails).
Triangles { one red triangle	Miscellaneous stores.
two black ,,	Camp equipage, (except intrenching tools and pack saddles).
Trefoil (one green trefoil or club)	Food, forage, fuel, and light.

* Ordnance carriages and stores for *naval* service are marked with a blue ball and a red diamond.

LIST OF PLATES.

   I. Officers' Swords.
  II. Officers' Sword Belts.
 III. Officers' Belts.
  IV. Arms. Rifle Muskets.
   V. Arms. Rifle Musket, Pattern 1853. Furniture of Stock.
  VI. Arms. Rifle Muskets. Details of Barrel, Nipple, Wrenches, &c.
 VII. Arms. Rifle Muskets. Details of Lock.
VIII. Arms. Swords and Claymores.
  IX. Arms. Flutes, Bugles, and Highland Pipes.
   X. Arms. Drums.
  XI. Pioneers' Tools and Appointments.
 XII. Pioneers' Tools and Appointments.
XIII. Pioneers' Tools and Appointments.
 XIV. Accoutrements.
  XV. Accoutrements.
 XVI. Accoutrements.
XVII. Armourer's Forge.
XVIII. Armourer's Tools.
 XIX. Armourer's Tools.
  XX. Armourer's Tools.
 XXI. Articles for Musketry Instruction.
XXII. Articles for Musketry Instruction.

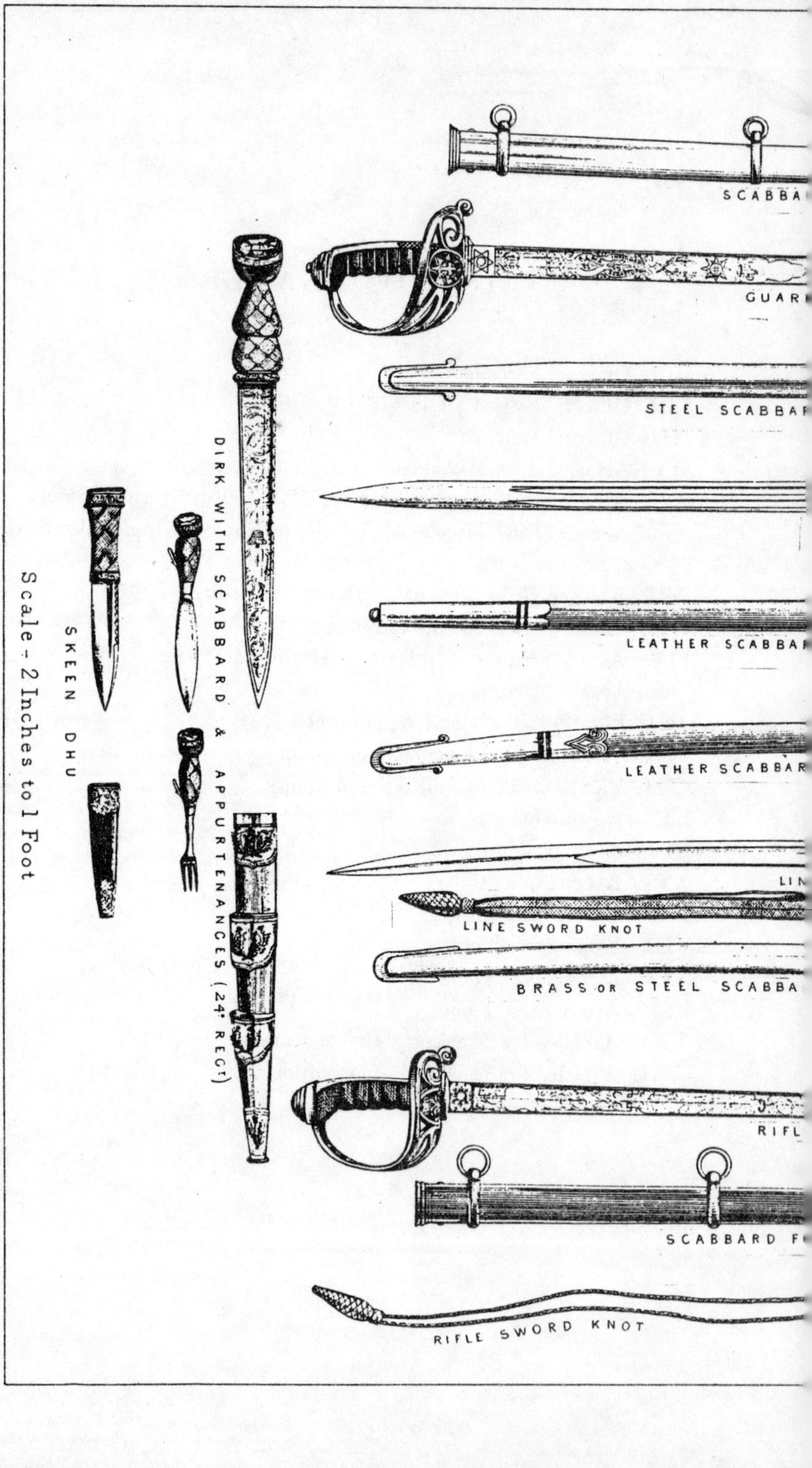
SCABBA
GUAR
STEEL SCABBAR
LEATHER SCABBAR
LEATHER SCABBAR
LIN
LINE SWORD KNOT
BRASS OR STEEL SCABBA
RIFL
SCABBARD F
RIFLE SWORD KNOT
DIRK WITH SCABBARD & APPURTENANCES (24th REGt)
SKEEN DHU
Scale - 2 Inches to 1 Foot

Engd & printed at the Topl Depot War Office, under the direction of Capt. M. Petrie, 14th Regt, Topogl Staff. Col. Sir H. James, R.E. F.R.S. M.R.I.A. &c. Director

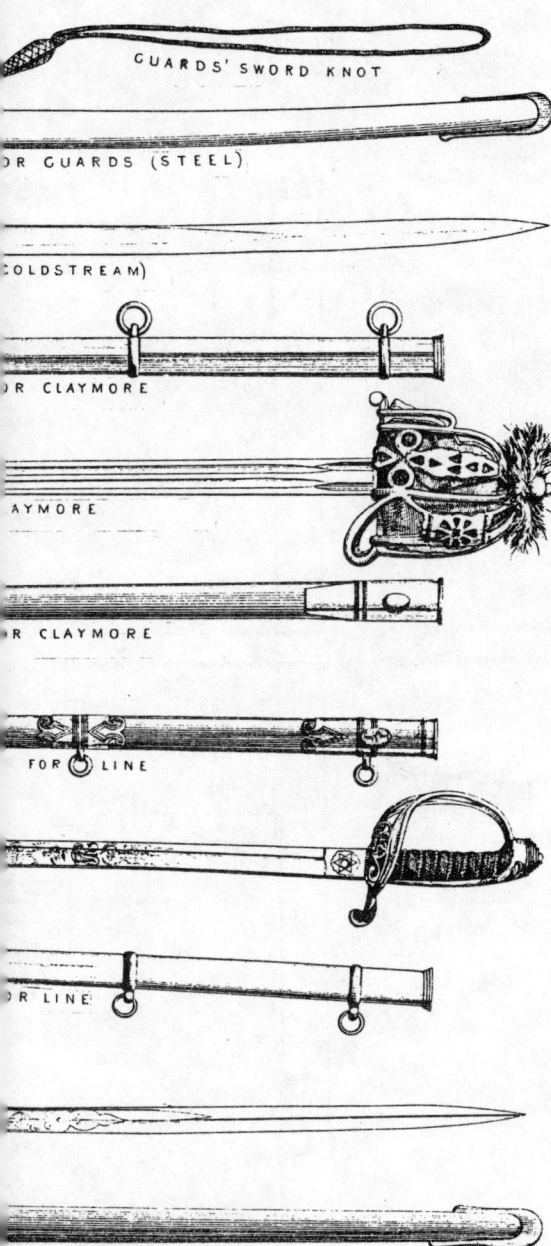

OFFICERS' SWORDS.

PLATE I

PLATE II

OFFICERS' SWORD BELTS.

GOLD LACE
BELT FOR GUARDS
WHITE
LEATHER BELT

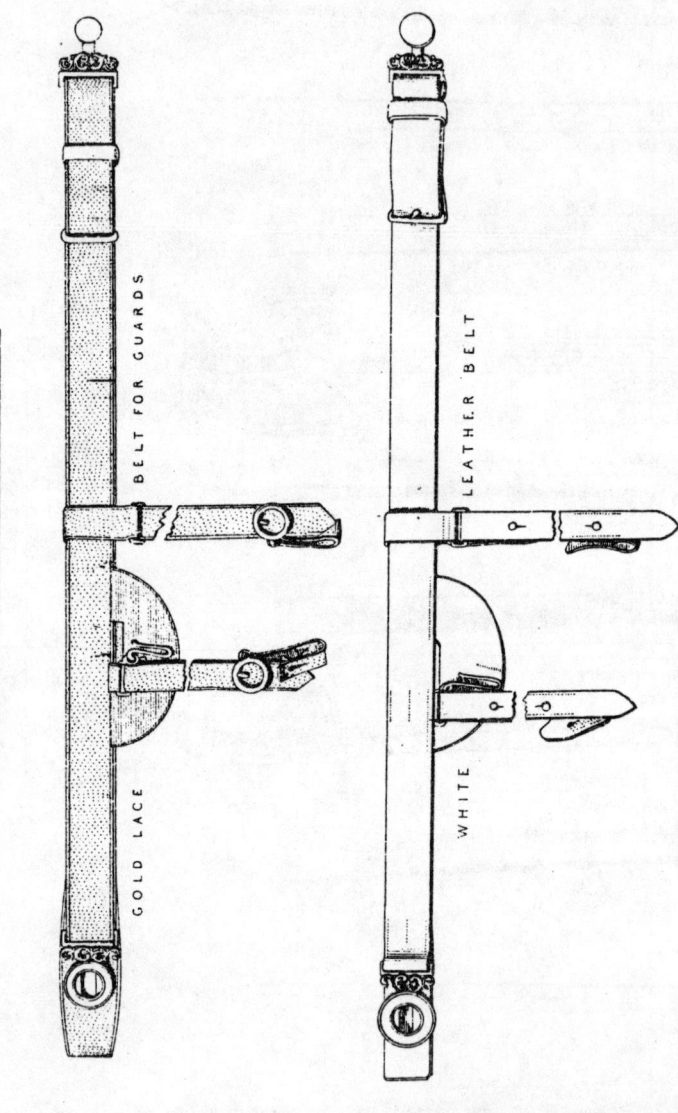

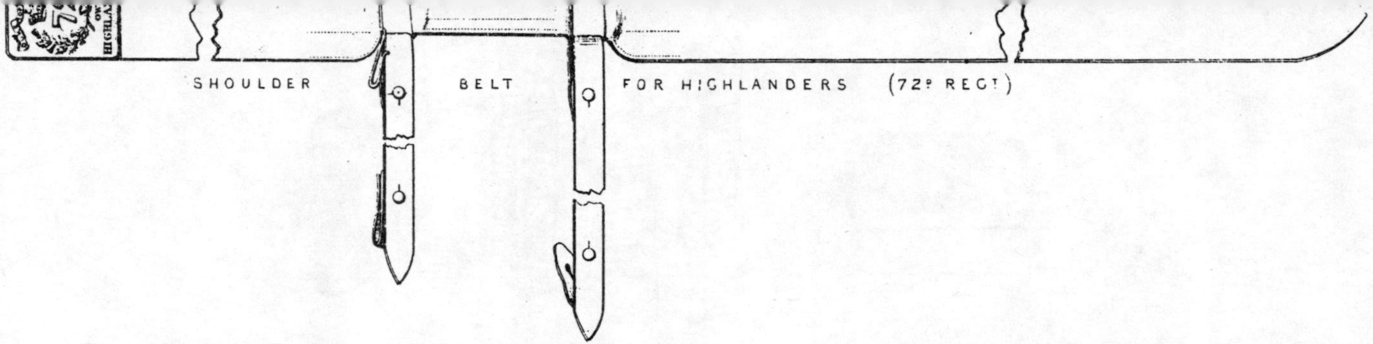

SHOULDER BELT FOR HIGHLANDERS (72ᴰ REGᵀ)

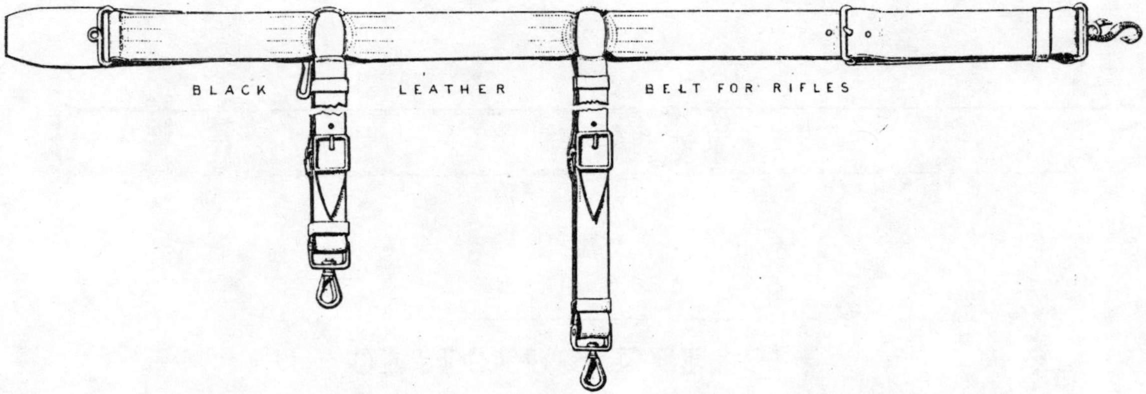

BLACK LEATHER BELT FOR RIFLES

Scale-2 Inches to 1 Foot

Engᵈ & printed at the Topˡ Depᵗ War Office, under the direction of Capt. N. Farie. 14ᵗʰ Regᵗ Topˡ Staff
Colˡ Sir H James. R.E. F.R.S. M.R.I.A. &c. Director

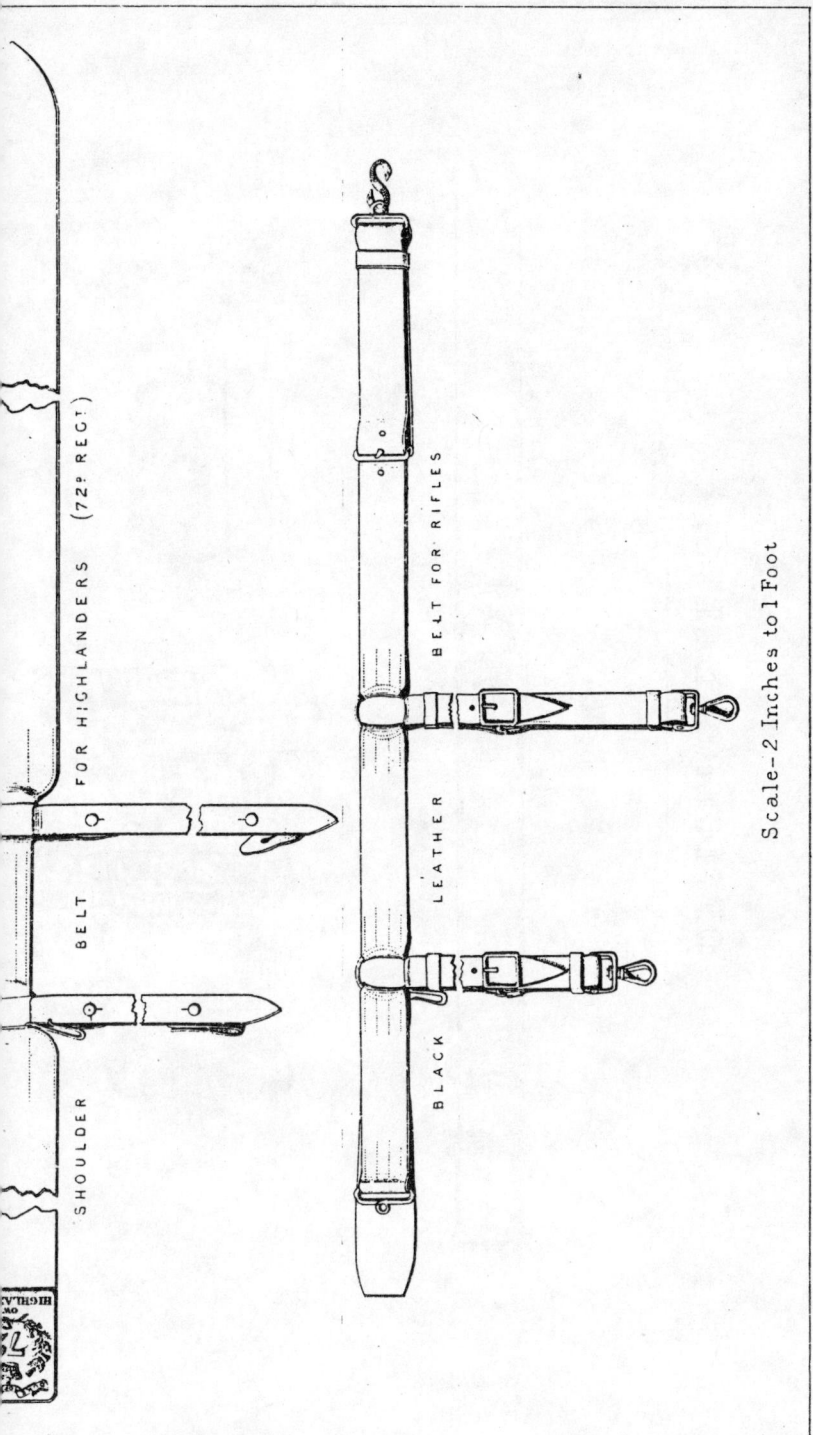

PLATE III

OFFICERS' BELTS.

SHOULDER BELT FOR MEDICAL STAFF

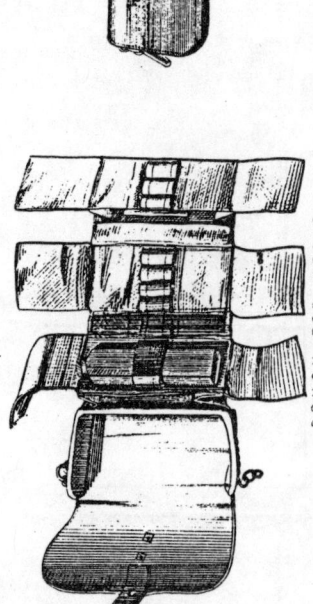

POUCH FOR MEDICAL STAFF

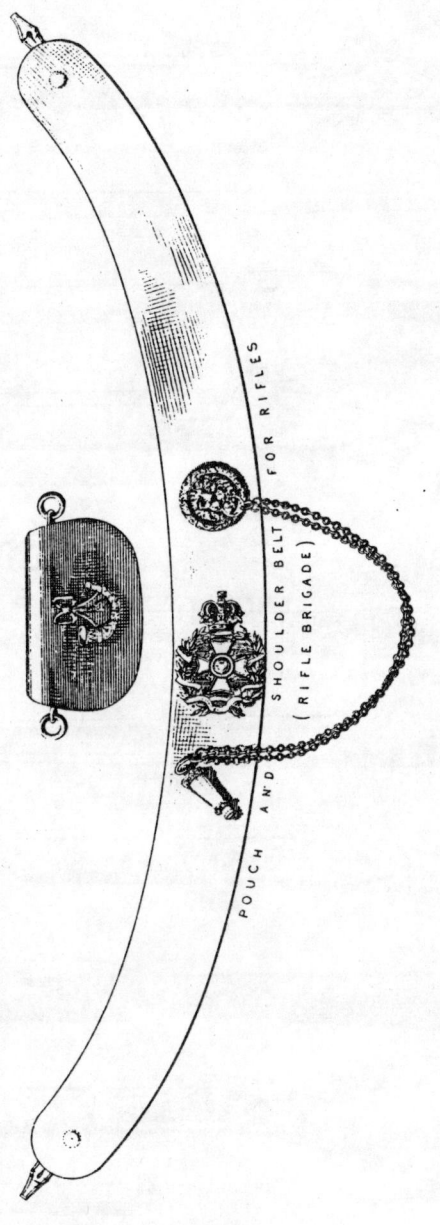

POUCH AND SHOULDER BELT
(RIFLE BRIGADE)

WAIST BELT FOR DIRK (71ST HIGHLANDERS)

Scale - 2 Inches to 1 Foot.

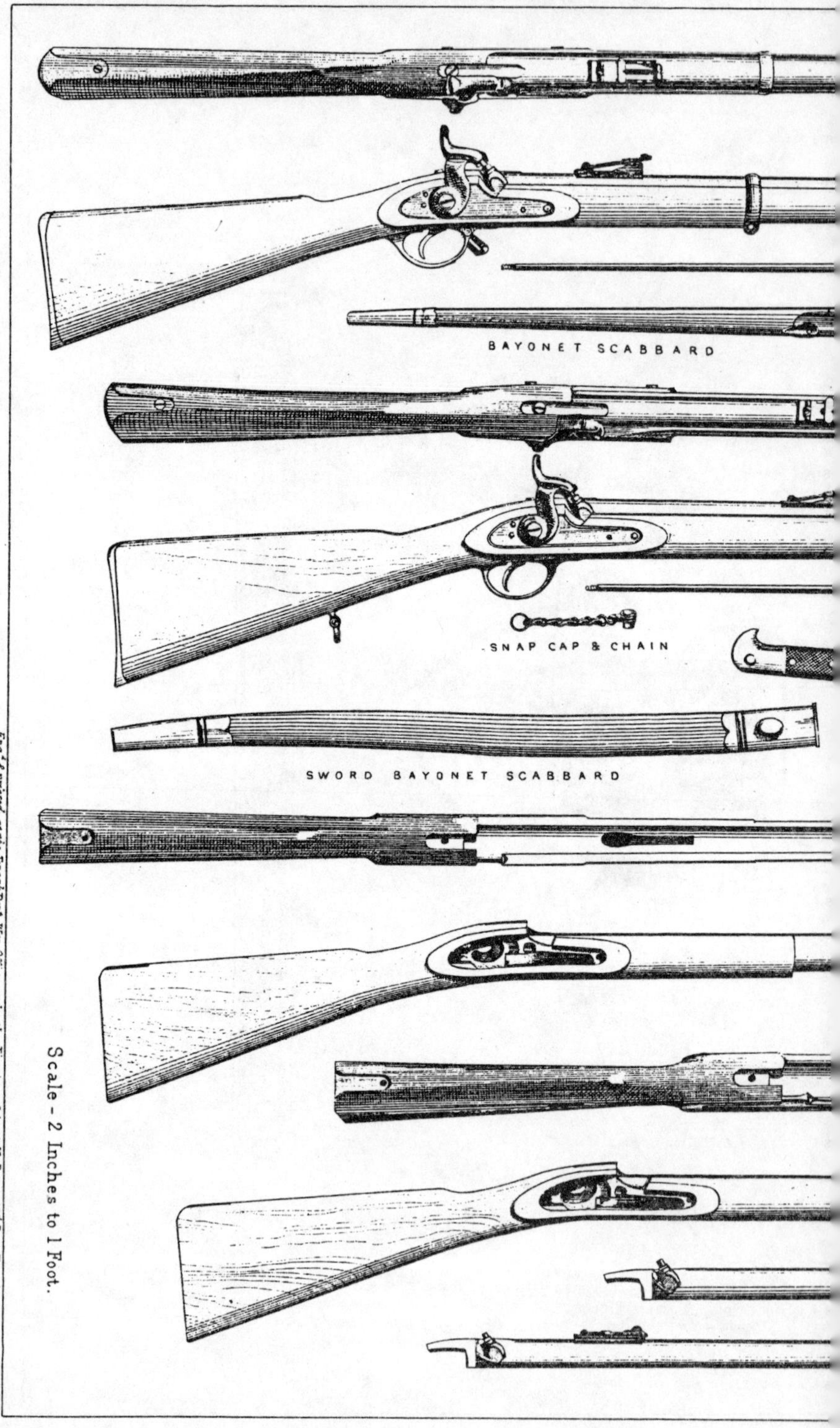
BAYONET SCABBARD
SNAP CAP & CHAIN
SWORD BAYONET SCABBARD
Scale - 2 Inches to 1 Foot.

Eng.d & printed at the Topog.l Dep.t, War Office, under the direction of Capt. ... Pierce, 14th Reg.t Top.l Staff, Col.l Sir H. James, R.E. F.R.S. M.R.I.A. ...

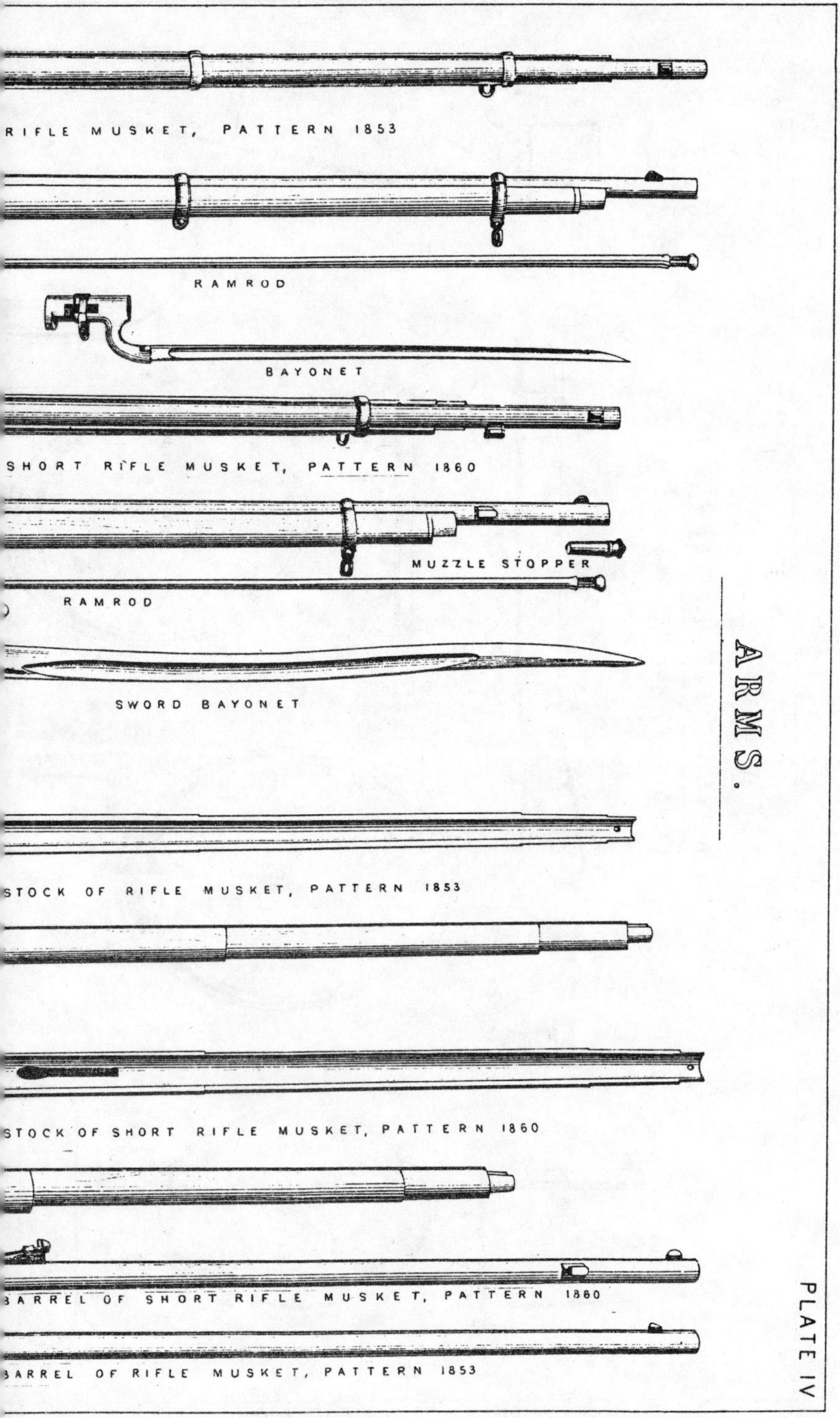
ARMS.
RIFLE MUSKET, PATTERN 1853
RAMROD
BAYONET
SHORT RIFLE MUSKET, PATTERN 1860
MUZZLE STOPPER
RAMROD
SWORD BAYONET
STOCK OF RIFLE MUSKET, PATTERN 1853
STOCK OF SHORT RIFLE MUSKET, PATTERN 1860
BARREL OF SHORT RIFLE MUSKET, PATTERN 1860
BARREL OF RIFLE MUSKET, PATTERN 1853
PLATE IV

PLATE V

ARMS.

ENFIELD RIFLE MUSKET._PATTERN 1853.

FURNITURE FOR STOCK.

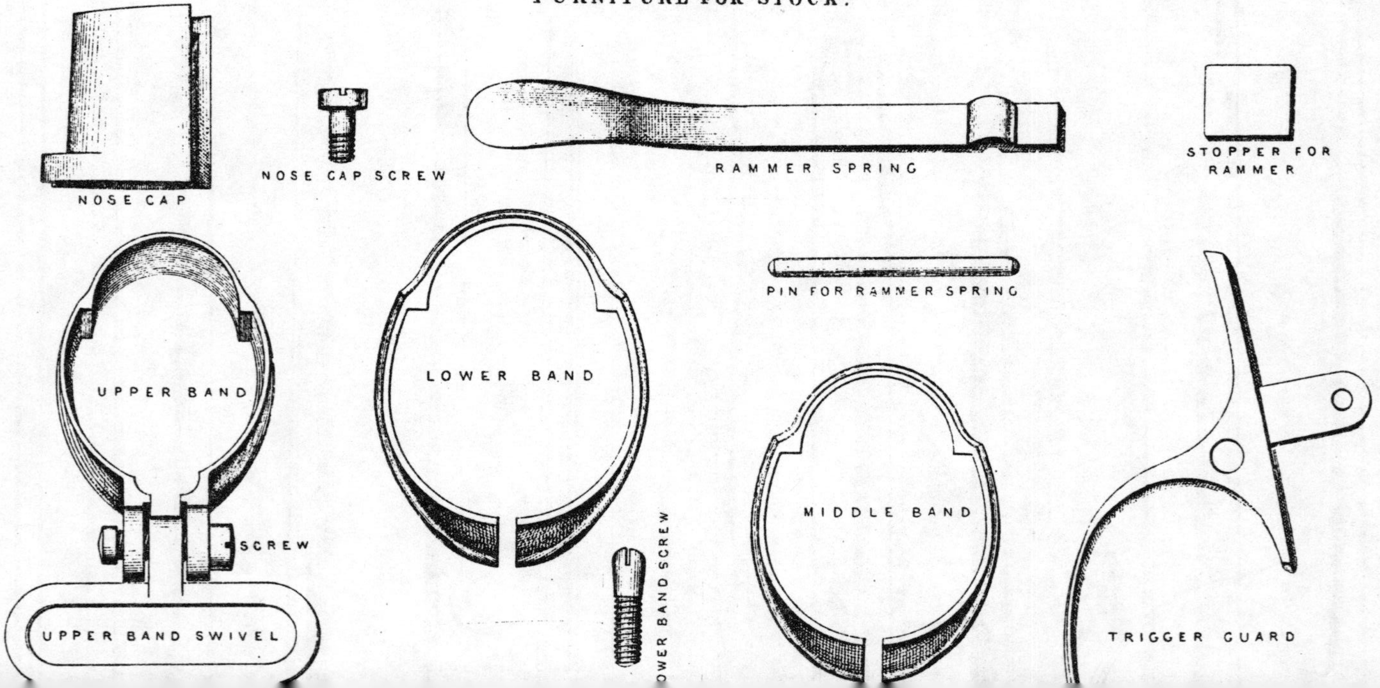

NOSE CAP
NOSE CAP SCREW
RAMMER SPRING
STOPPER FOR RAMMER
UPPER BAND
SCREW
UPPER BAND SWIVEL
LOWER BAND
OWER BAND SCREW
PIN FOR RAMMER SPRING
MIDDLE BAND
TRIGGER GUARD

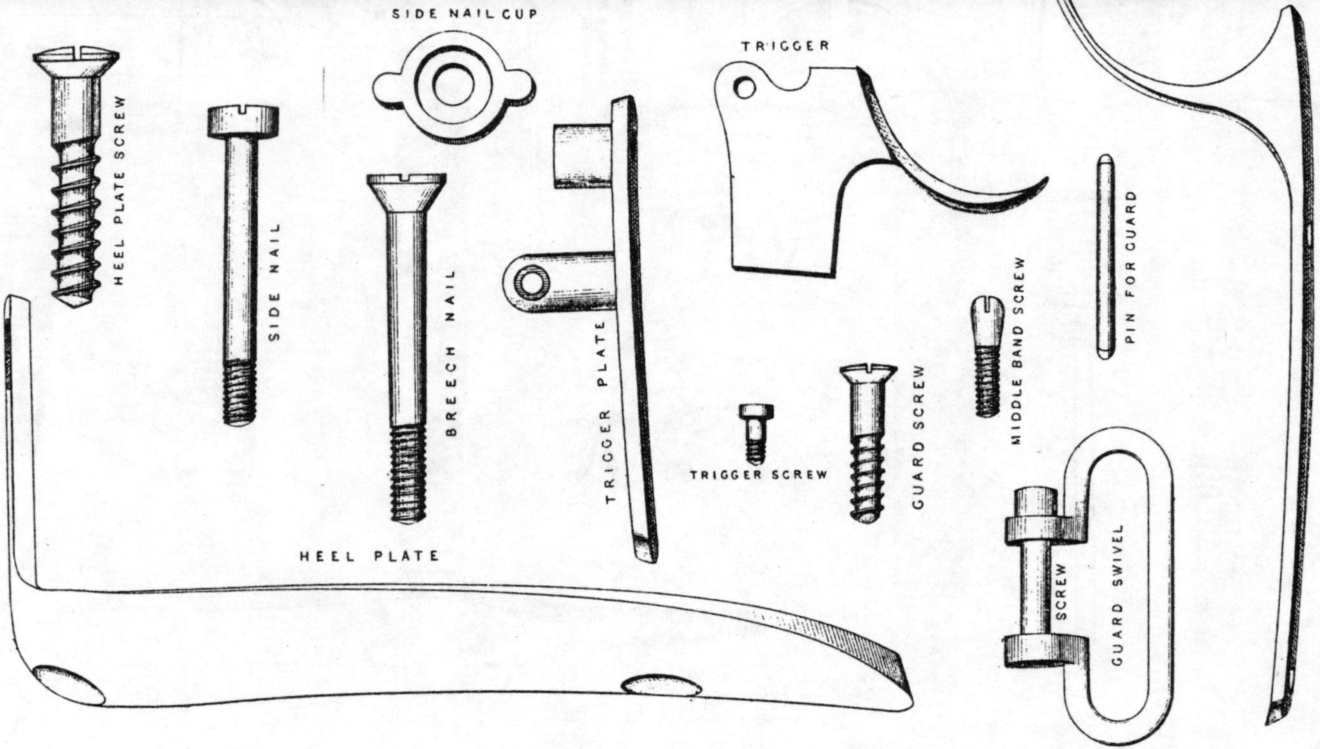
SIDE NAIL CUP
TRIGGER
HEEL PLATE SCREW
SIDE NAIL
BREECH NAIL
TRIGGER PLATE
PIN FOR GUARD
MIDDLE BAND SCREW
TRIGGER SCREW
GUARD SCREW
HEEL PLATE
SCREW
GUARD SWIVEL

(FULL SIZE)

*Eng.d & printed at the Top.l Dep.t War Office, under the direction of Capt. M. Petrie, 14th Reg.t Top.l Staff.
Col.l Sir H. James, R.E. F.R.S. M.R.I.A. &c. Director.*

ARMS.

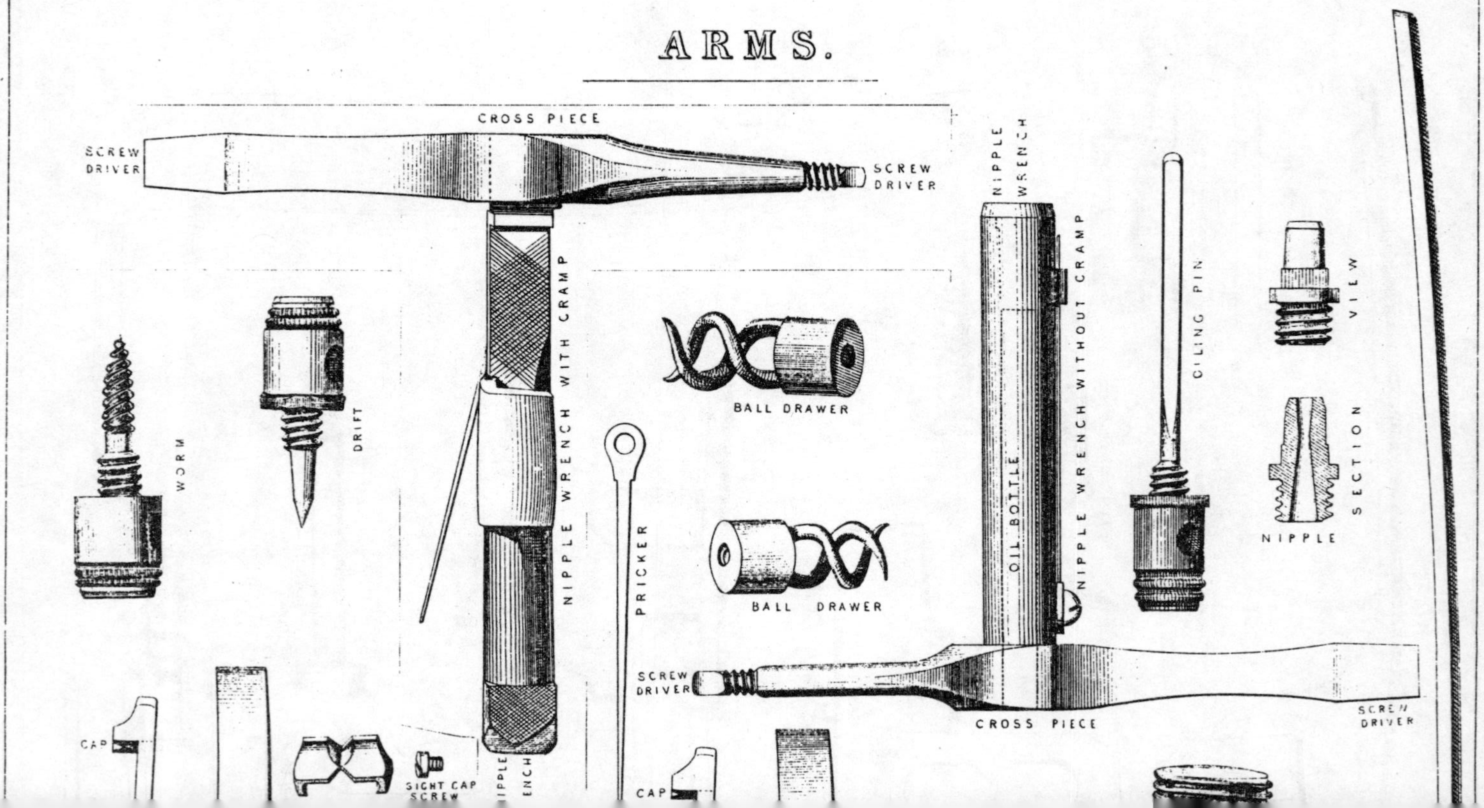
CROSS PIECE
SCREW DRIVER
SCREW DRIVER
NIPPLE WRENCH WITH CRAMP
WORM
DRIFT
PRICKER
BALL DRAWER
BALL DRAWER
NIPPLE WRENCH
OIL BOTTLE
NIPPLE WRENCH WITHOUT CRAMP
OILING PIN
VIEW
SECTION
NIPPLE
SCREW DRIVER
CROSS PIECE
SCREW DRIVER
CAP
SIGHT CAP SCREW
IPPLE
ENCH
CAP

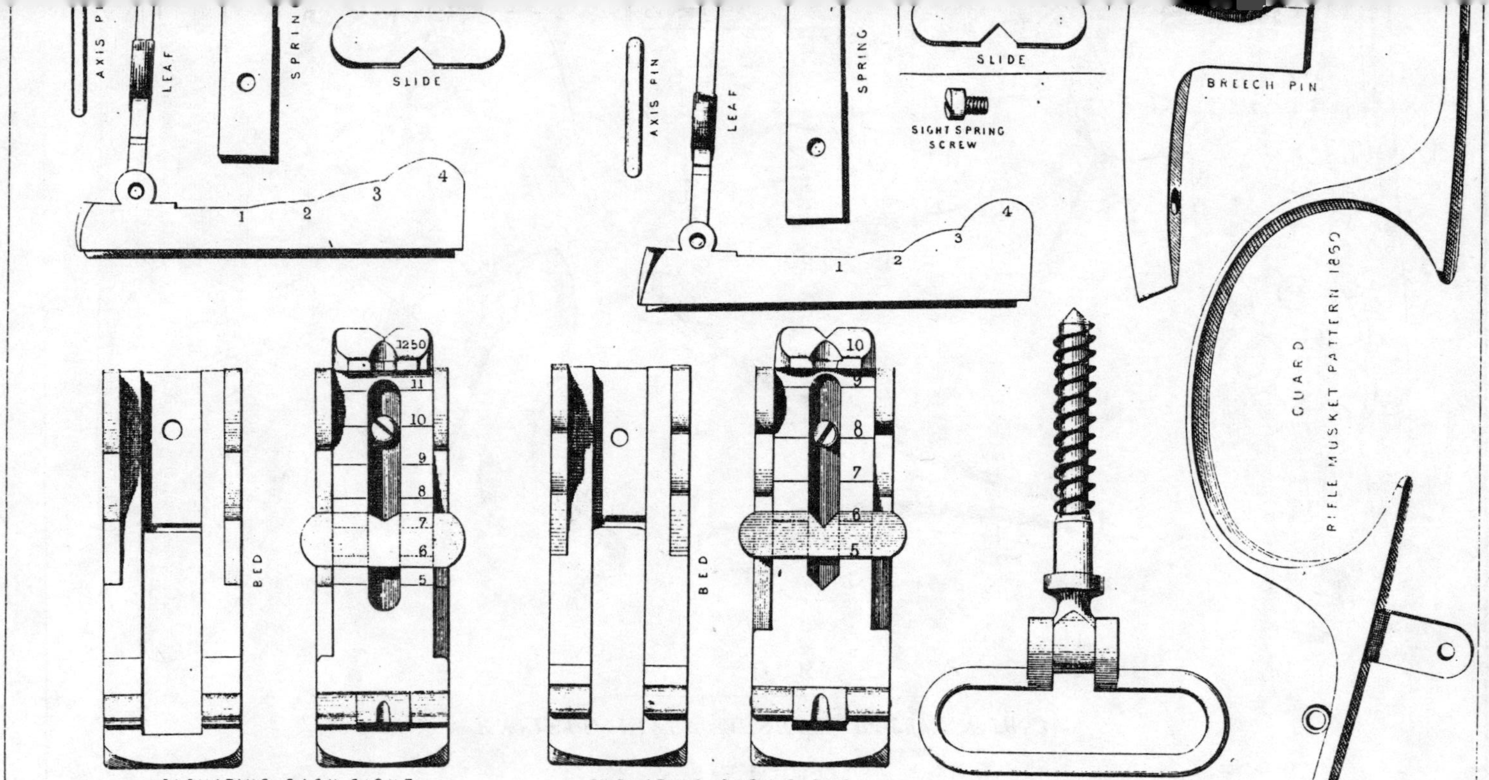
AXIS PIN
LEAF
SPRING
SLIDE
SIGHT SPRING SCREW
BREECH PIN
GUARD
RIFLE MUSKET PATTERN 1850
BED
1
2
3
4
5
6
7
8
9
10
11
1250
BUTT SWIVEL

ELEVATING BACK SIGHT
SHORT RIFLE MUSKET (PATTERN 1860)

ELEVATING BACK SIGHT
RIFLE MUSKET (PATTERN 1853)

BUTT SWIVEL
SHORT RIFLE MUSKET (PATTERN 1860)

(FULL SIZE)

*Engd. & printed at the Topl. Depl. War Office under the direction of Capt. M. Petrie 14th Regt. Topl. Staff
Col. Sir H. James R.E. F.R.S. M.R.I.A. &c. Director.*

PLATE VII

ARMS.

ENFIELD RIFLE MUSKET.—PATTERN 1853.

LOCK.

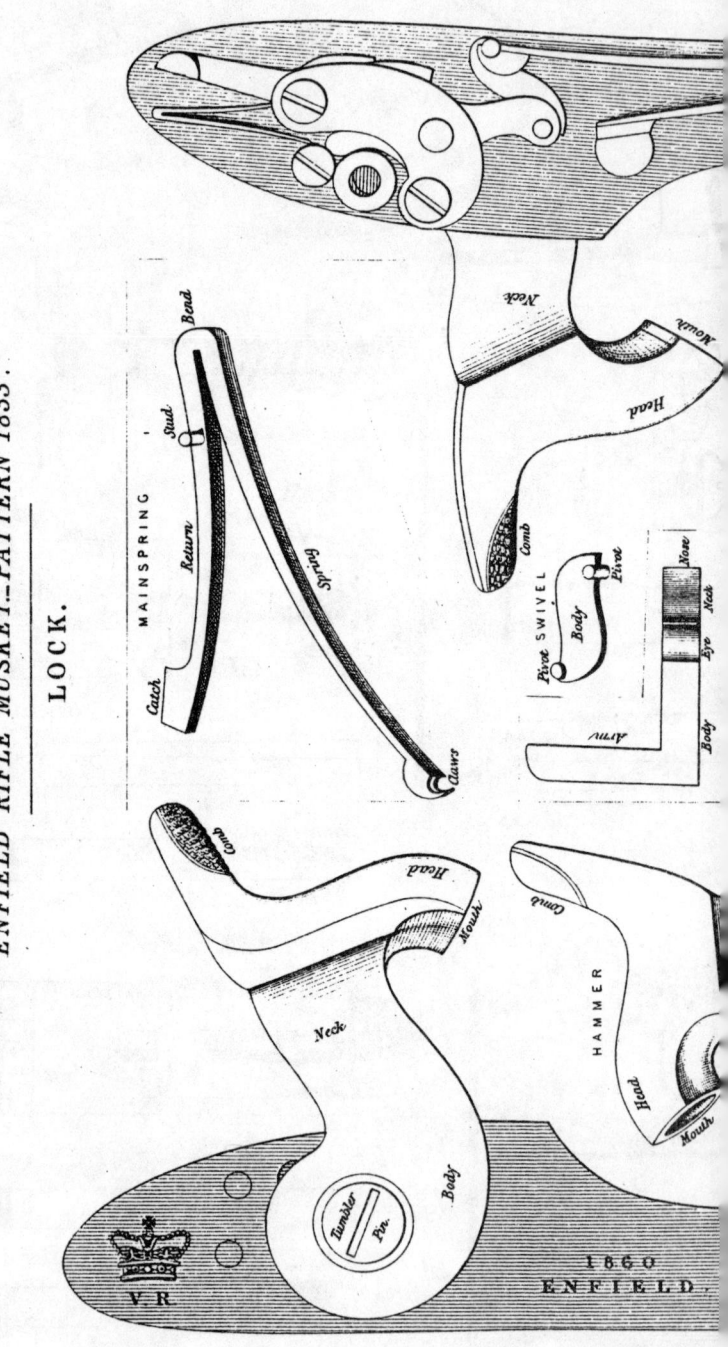

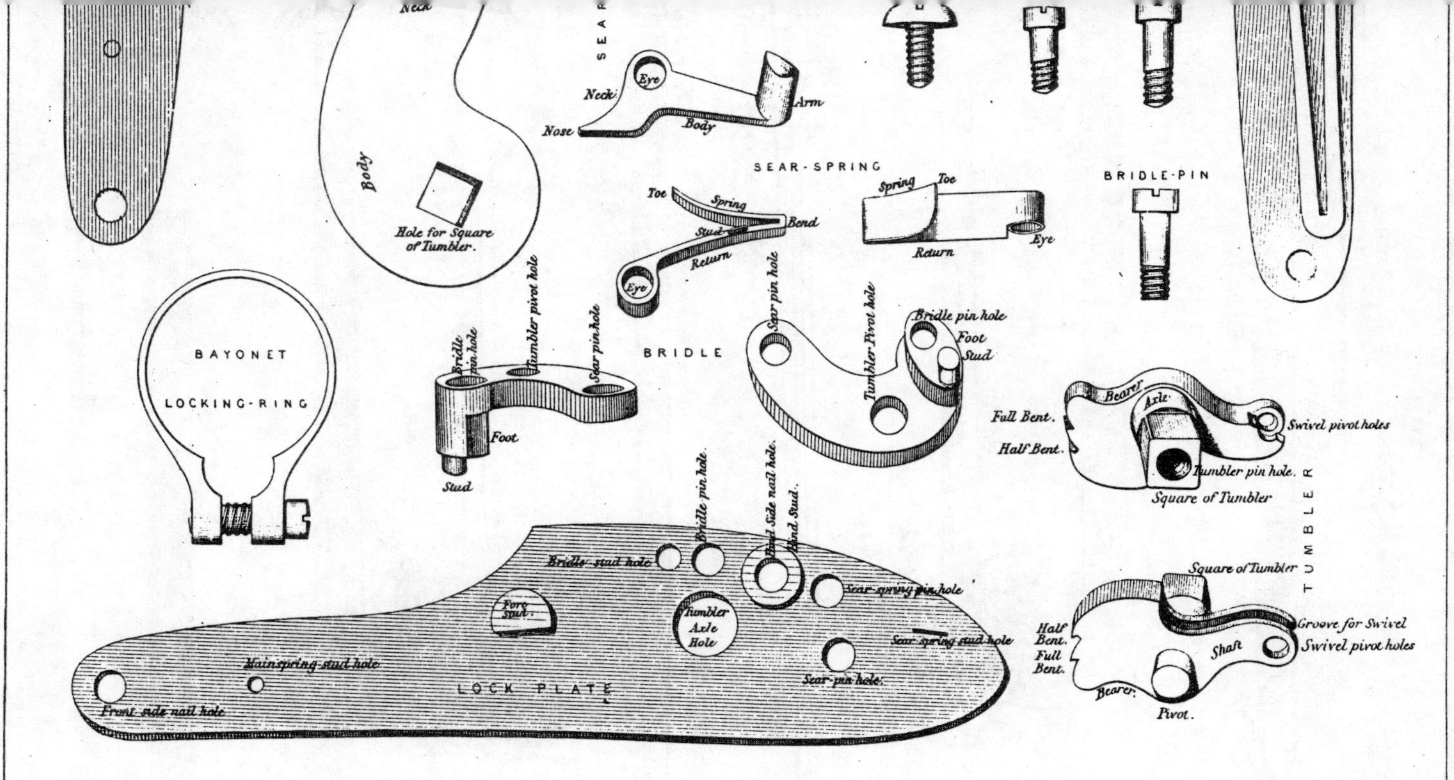
SEAR
Neck
Eye
Arm
Nose
Body
Hole for Square of Tumbler.
SEAR-SPRING
Toe
Spring
Bend
Stud
Return
Eye
BRIDLE-PIN
BAYONET
LOCKING-RING
Bridle pin hole
Tumbler pivot hole
Sear pin hole
Foot
Stud
BRIDLE
Tumbler-Pivot hole
Bridle pin hole
Full Bent.
Half Bent.
Bearer
Axle
Swivel pivot holes
Tumbler pin hole.
Square of Tumbler
TUMBLER
Bridle-pin hole.
Hind Side nail hole.
Hind Stud.
Bridle-stud hole
Sear-spring pin hole
Fore Stud.
Tumbler Axle Hole
Sear-spring stud hole
Mainspring stud hole
Sear-pin hole.
LOCK PLATE
Front side nail hole
Square of Tumbler
Groove for Swivel
Swivel pivot holes
Half Bent.
Full Bent.
Shaft
Bearer.
Pivot.

(FULL SIZE)

Engd. & printed at the Topl. Depr. War Office, under the direction of Capt. M. Petrie, 14th. Regt. Topl. Staff.
Col. Sir H. James. R.E. F.R.S. M.R.I.A. &c. Director

DRUMMERS' SWORD (LINE PATTERN)

STAFF SERJEANTS' CLAYMORE

STAFF SERJEANTS' CLAYMORE, REG^{TS} WEARING TREWS

CLAYMORE FOR DRUMMERS, PIPERS, &c

BUGLERS' SWORD, FOR RIFLES

Scale—2 Inches to 1 Foot

Eng^d & printed at the Top^l Dep^t, War Office, under the direction of Capt. M. Eyre, 14th Reg^t, Top^l Staff
Col. Sir H. James, R.E. F.R.S. M.R.I.A. &c. Director

PLATE VIII

ARMS.

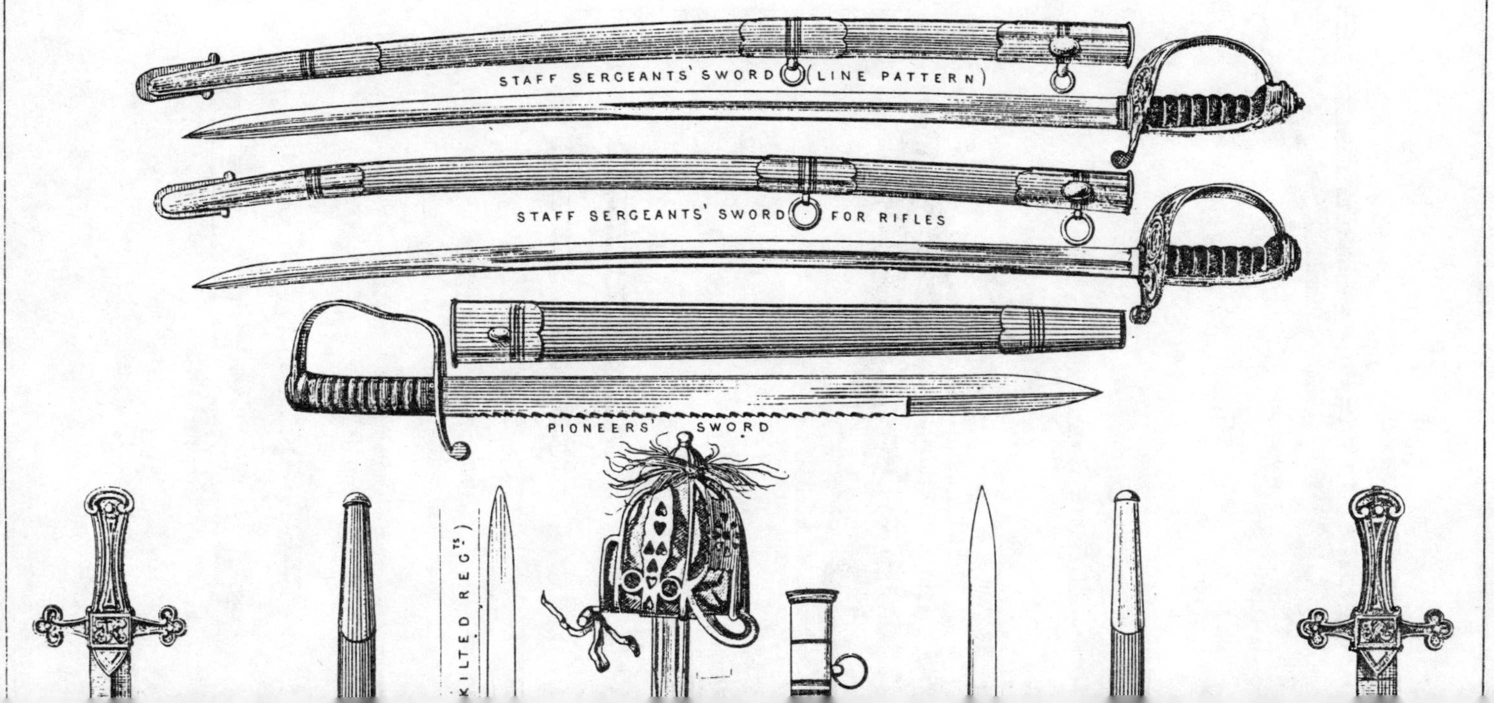

STAFF SERGEANTS' SWORD (LINE PATTERN)
STAFF SERGEANTS' SWORD FOR RIFLES
PIONEERS' SWORD
KILTED REGTS.)

PLATE IX

ARMS.

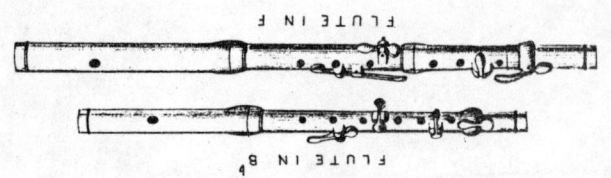

FLUTE IN F

FLUTE IN B♭

PICCOLO IN F

PICCOLO IN E♭

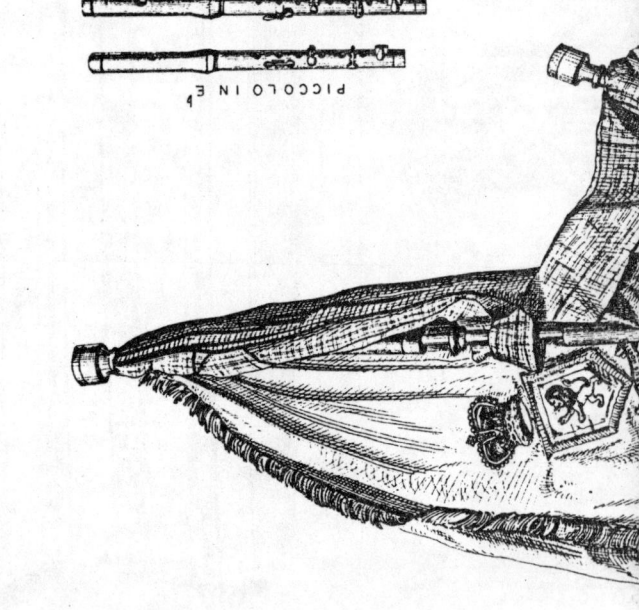

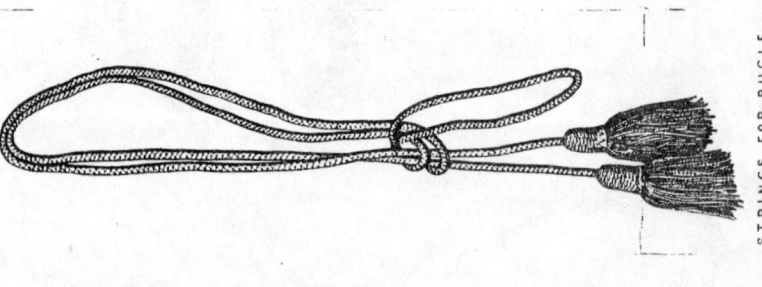

STRINGS FOR BUGLE

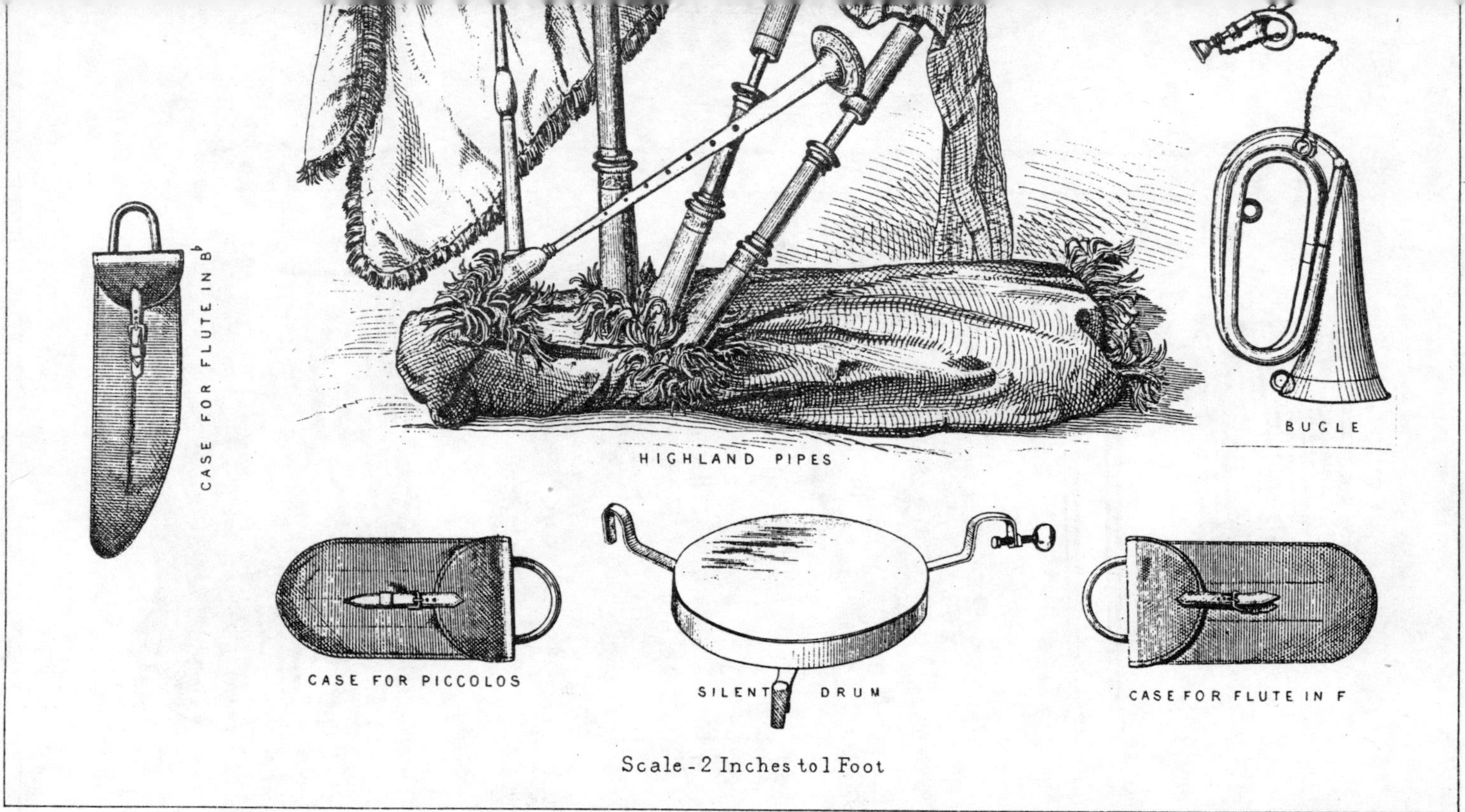
CASE FOR FLUTE IN B♭
HIGHLAND PIPES
BUGLE
CASE FOR PICCOLOS
SILENT DRUM
CASE FOR FLUTE IN F
Scale - 2 Inches to 1 Foot

Eng^d. & printed at the Top^l. Dep^t. War Office, under the direction of Capt. M. Petrie, 14th. Reg^t. Top^l. Staff. Col^l. Sir H. James, R.E. F.R.S. M.R.I.A. &c. Director.

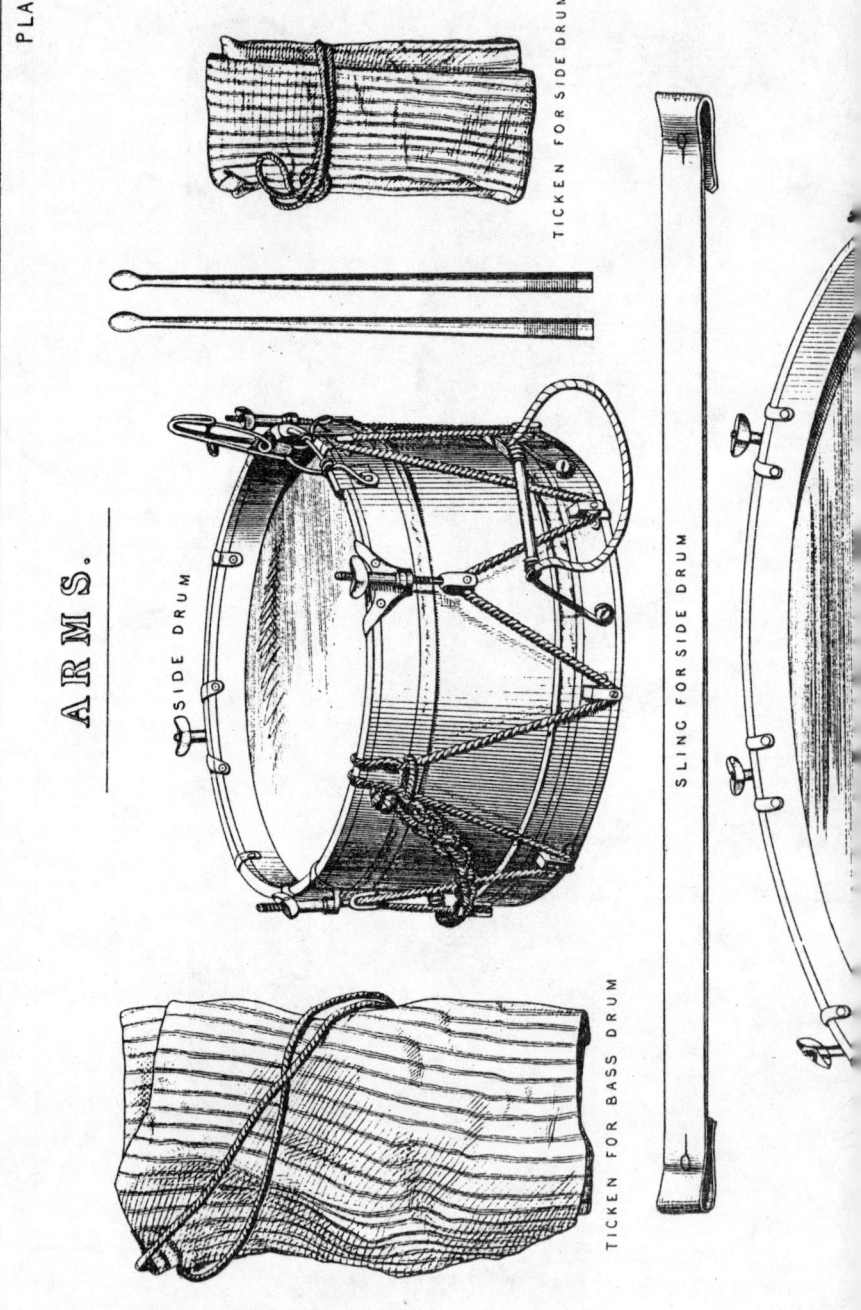

PLATE X

ARMS.

TICKEN FOR SIDE DRUM

SIDE DRUM

TICKEN FOR BASS DRUM

SLING FOR SIDE DRUM

BASS DRUM

Scale – 2 Inches to 1 Foot.

PIONEERS' TOOLS AND APPOINTMENTS.

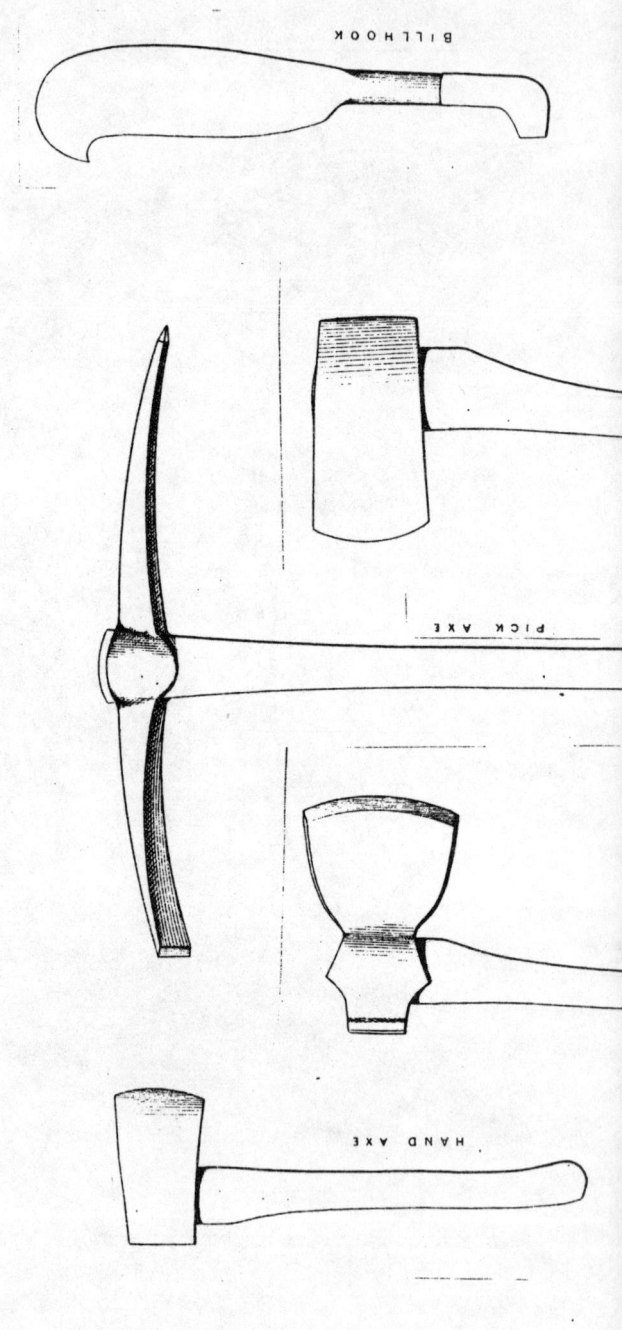

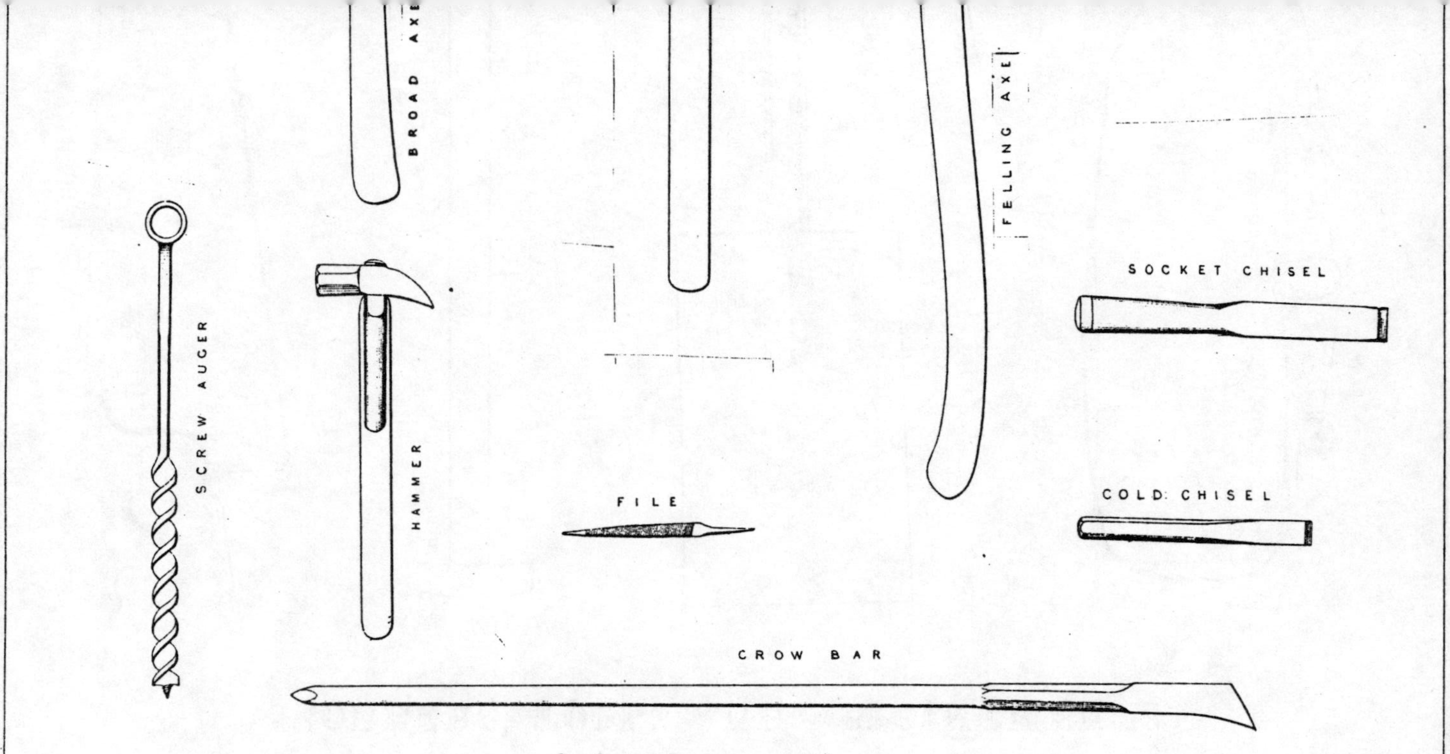
BROAD AXE
FELLING AXE
SOCKET CHISEL
SCREW AUGER
HAMMER
FILE
COLD CHISEL
CROW BAR

Scale - 2 Inches to 1 Foot

Eng. & printed at the Top^l Dep^t War Office, under the direction of Capt. M Petrie, 14th Reg^t Top^l Staff.
Col^l Sir H James, R.E. F.R.S. M.R.I.A. &c. Director.

PLATE XII

PIONEERS' TOOLS AND APPOINTMENTS.

SAW
SPADE
CASE FOR
HAND & BROAD
AXES

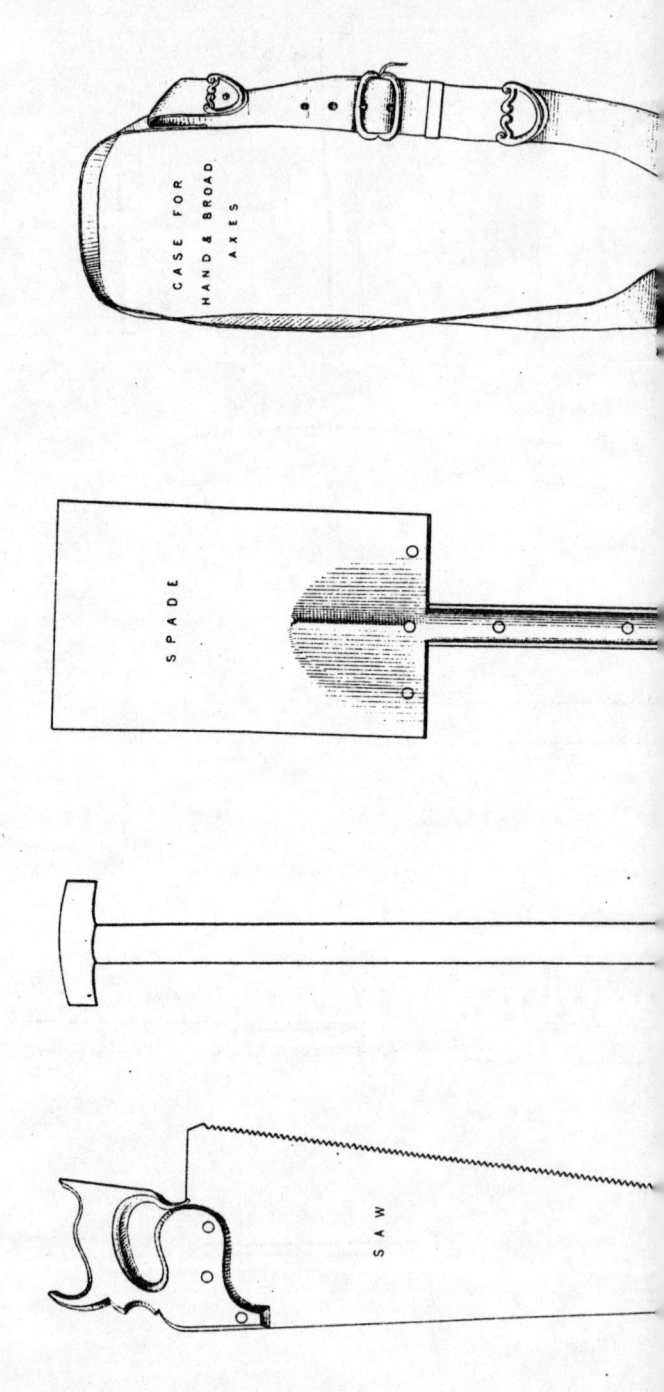

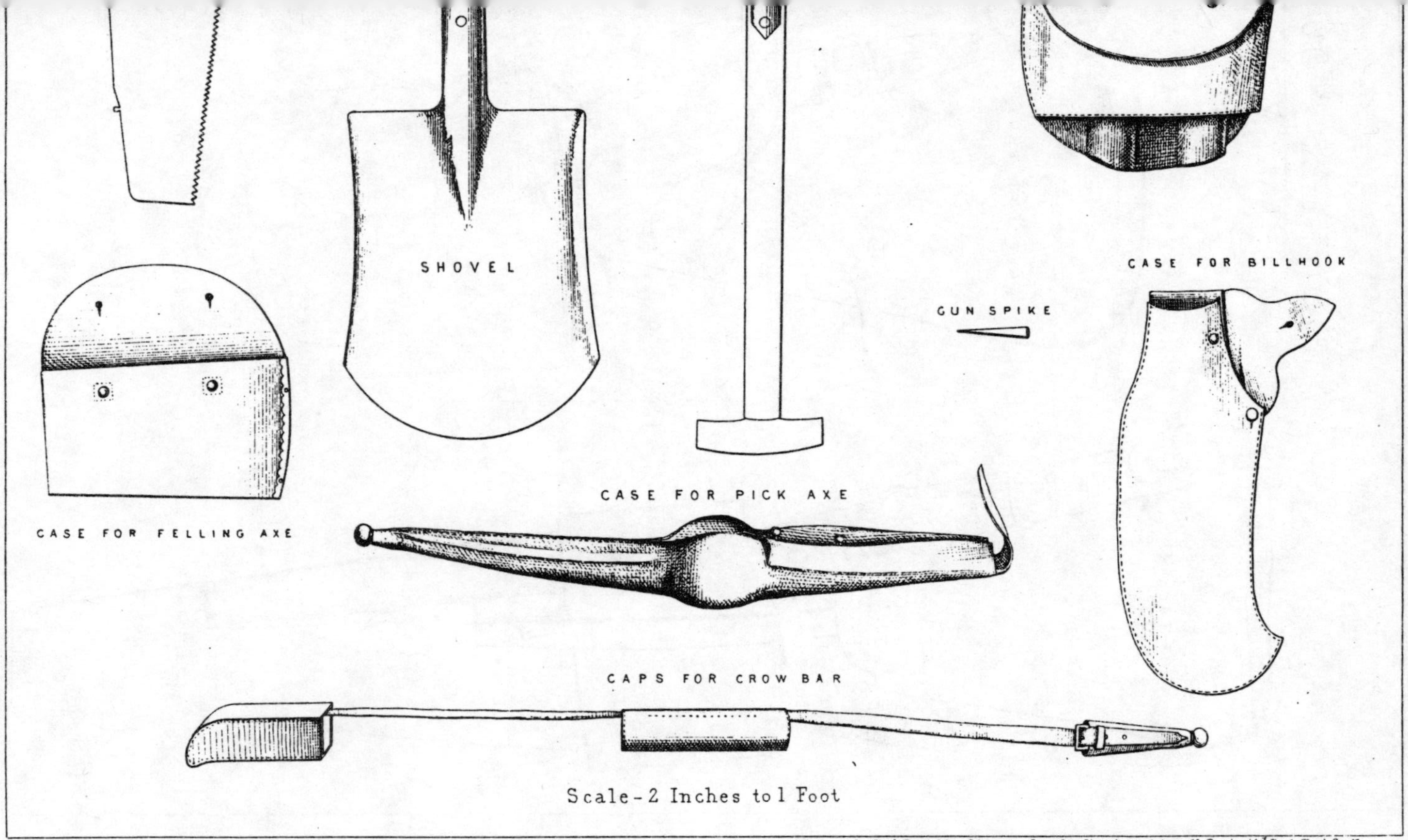
SHOVEL
CASE FOR BILLHOOK
GUN SPIKE
CASE FOR FELLING AXE
CASE FOR PICK AXE
CAPS FOR CROW BAR
Scale-2 Inches to 1 Foot

Eng. & printed at the Topl. Depl. War Office, under the direction of Capt. M. Petrie, 14th Regt. Topl. Staff.
Coll. Sir H. James. R.E. F.R.S. M.R.I.A. &c. Director.

PIONEERS' TOO[LS]

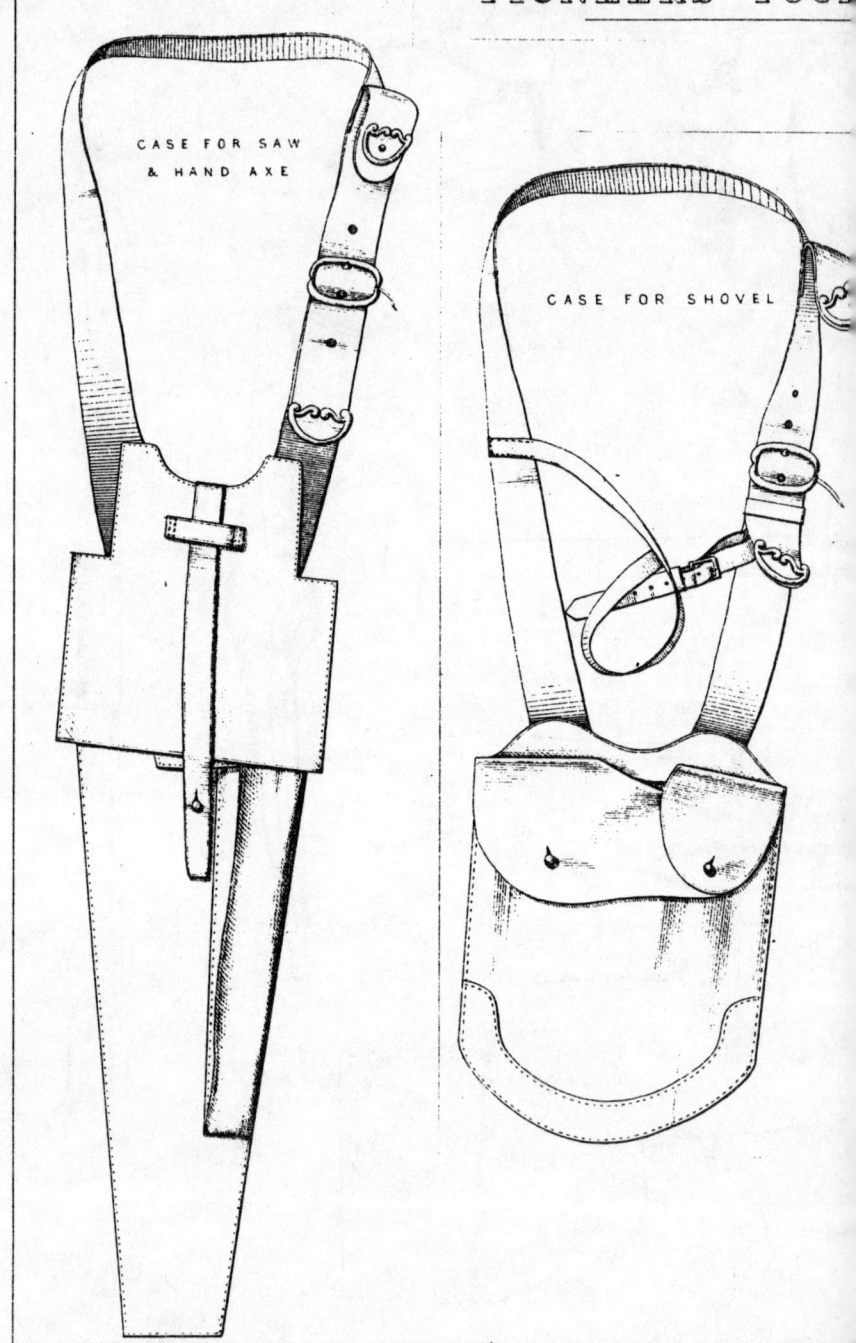

CASE FOR SAW & HAND AXE

CASE FOR SHOVEL

AND APPOINTMENTS.

PLATE XIII

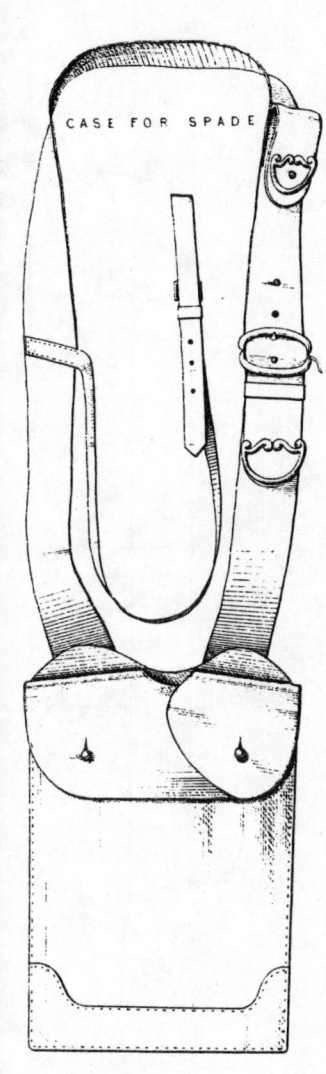
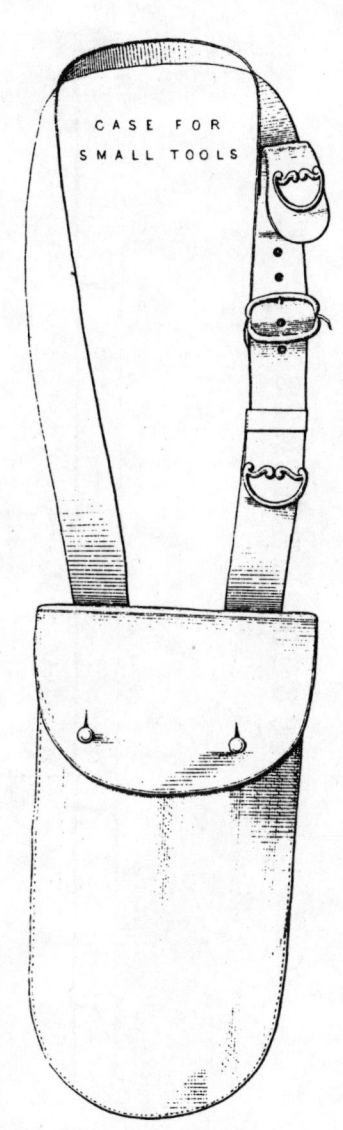

Scale - 2 Inch to 1 Foot.

PLATE XIV

ACCOUTREMENTS.

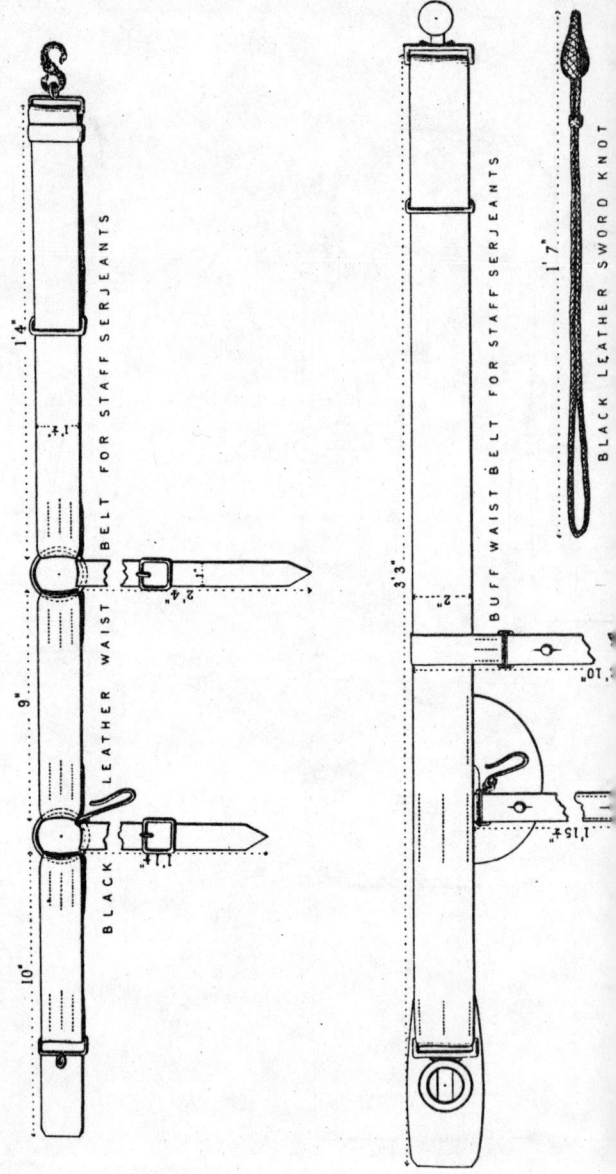

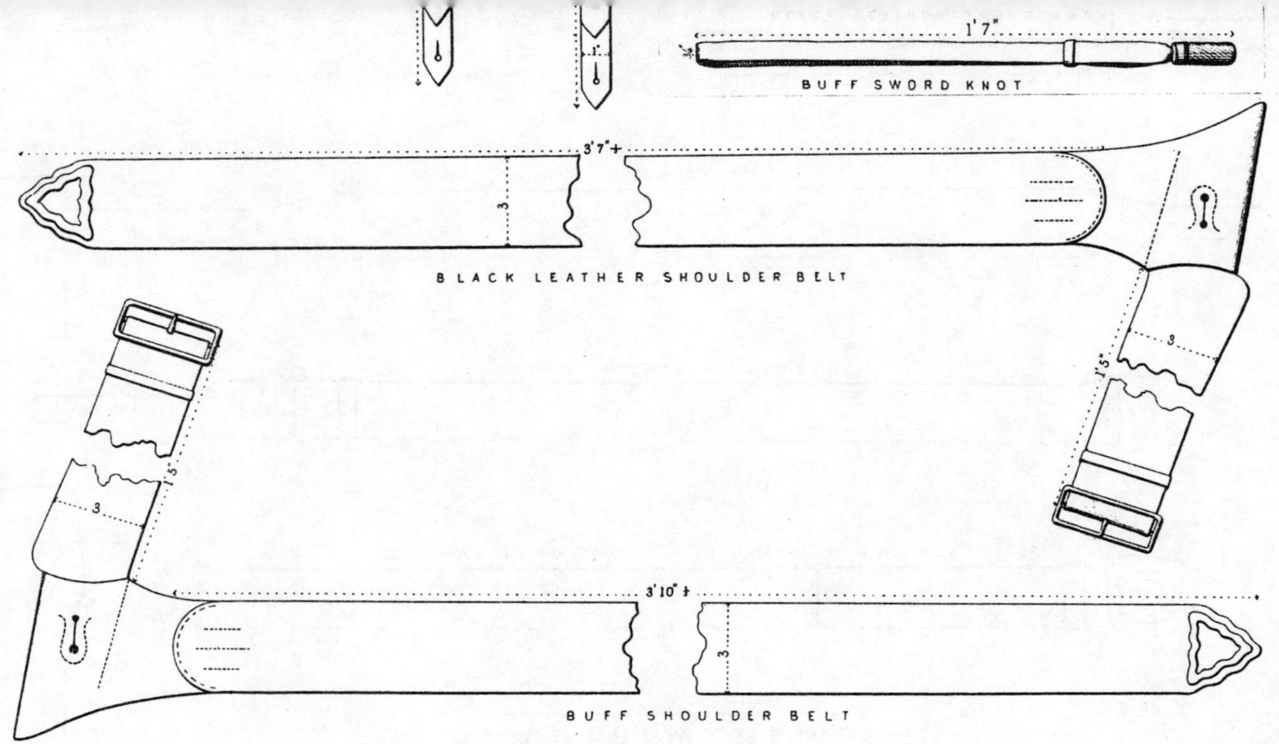
1' 7"
BUFF SWORD KNOT
3' 7" +
3
1.5"
BLACK LEATHER SHOULDER BELT
3' 10" +
3
1.5
BUFF SHOULDER BELT

Scale - 2 In. to 1 Foot.

Engd. & printed at the Topl. Dept. War Office, under the Direction of Capt. M Petrie 14th Regt. Topl. Staff.
Col. Sir H. James. R.E. F.R.S. M.R.I.A. Director

PLATE XV.

ACCOUTREMENTS.

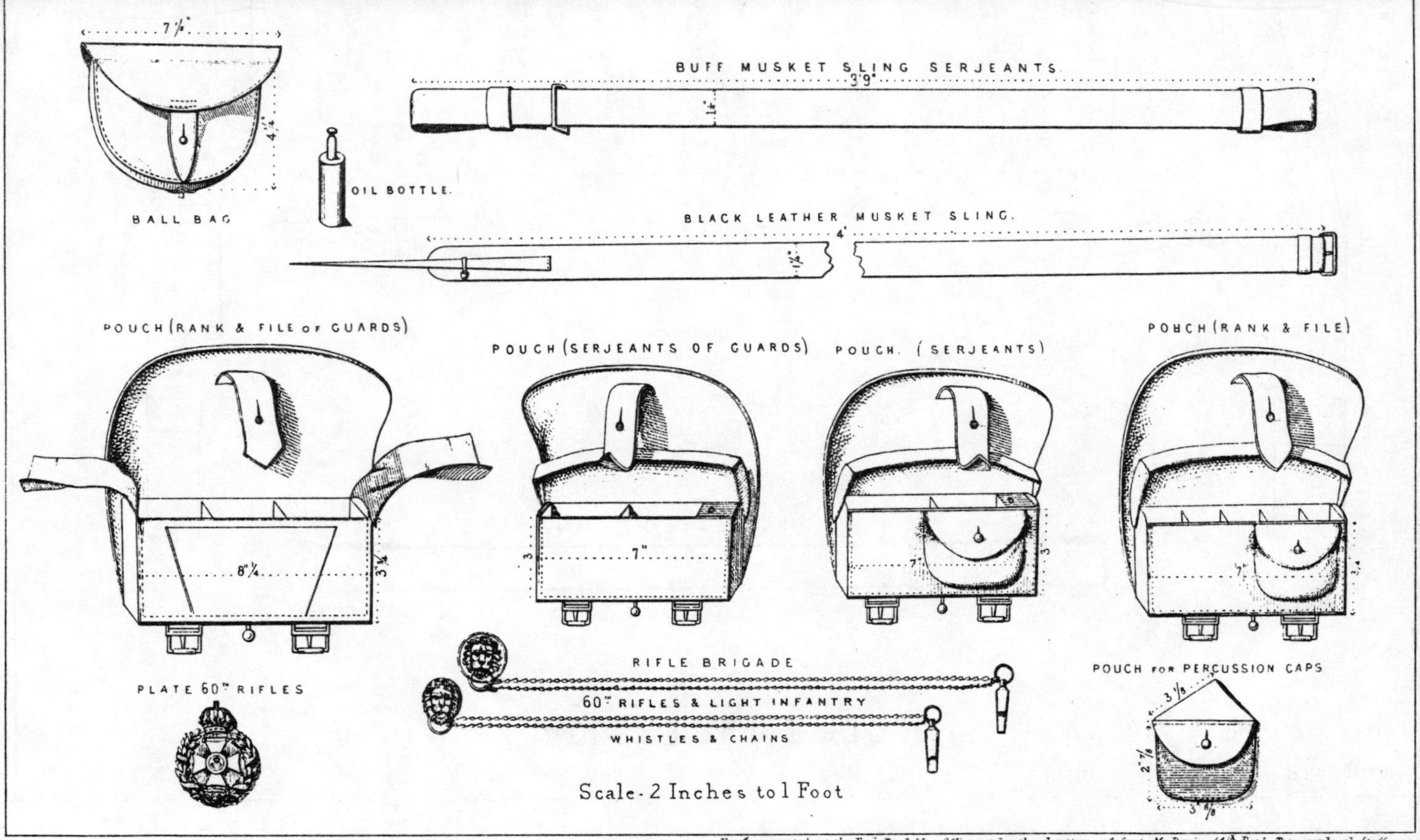

7 1/2"
4 1/4
BALL BAG
OIL BOTTLE.
BUFF MUSKET SLING SERJEANTS.
3'9"
1 1/4"
BLACK LEATHER MUSKET SLING.
4'
1 1/4"
POUCH (RANK & FILE OF GUARDS)
8" 1/4
3 1/4
POUCH (SERJEANTS OF GUARDS)
3
7"
POUCH. (SERJEANTS)
7"
3
POUCH (RANK & FILE)
7"
3 1/4
PLATE 60TH RIFLES
RIFLE BRIGADE
60TH RIFLES & LIGHT INFANTRY
WHISTLES & CHAINS
POUCH FOR PERCUSSION CAPS
3 1/8
2 7/8
3 1/8
Scale-2 Inches to 1 Foot

Engd & printed at the Topl Depl War Office, under the direction of Capt. M. Petrie 14th Regt Topographical Staff. Coll Sir H. James, R.E. F.R.S. M.R.I.A. &c. Director

PLATE XVI

ACCOUTREMENTS.

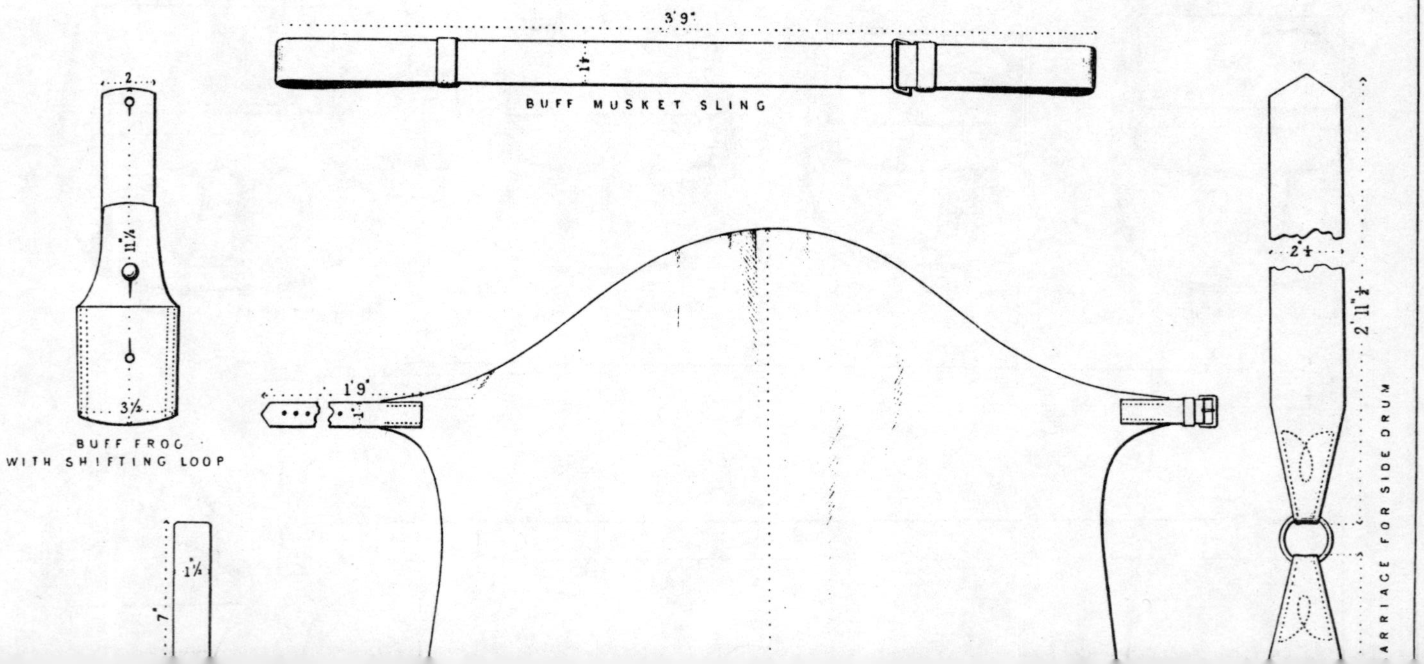
3' 9"
1¼
BUFF MUSKET SLING
2
11¼
3½
BUFF FROG
WITH SHIFTING LOOP
1' 9"
1
1½
7"
2¼
2' 11"¼
ARRIACE FOR SIDE DRUM

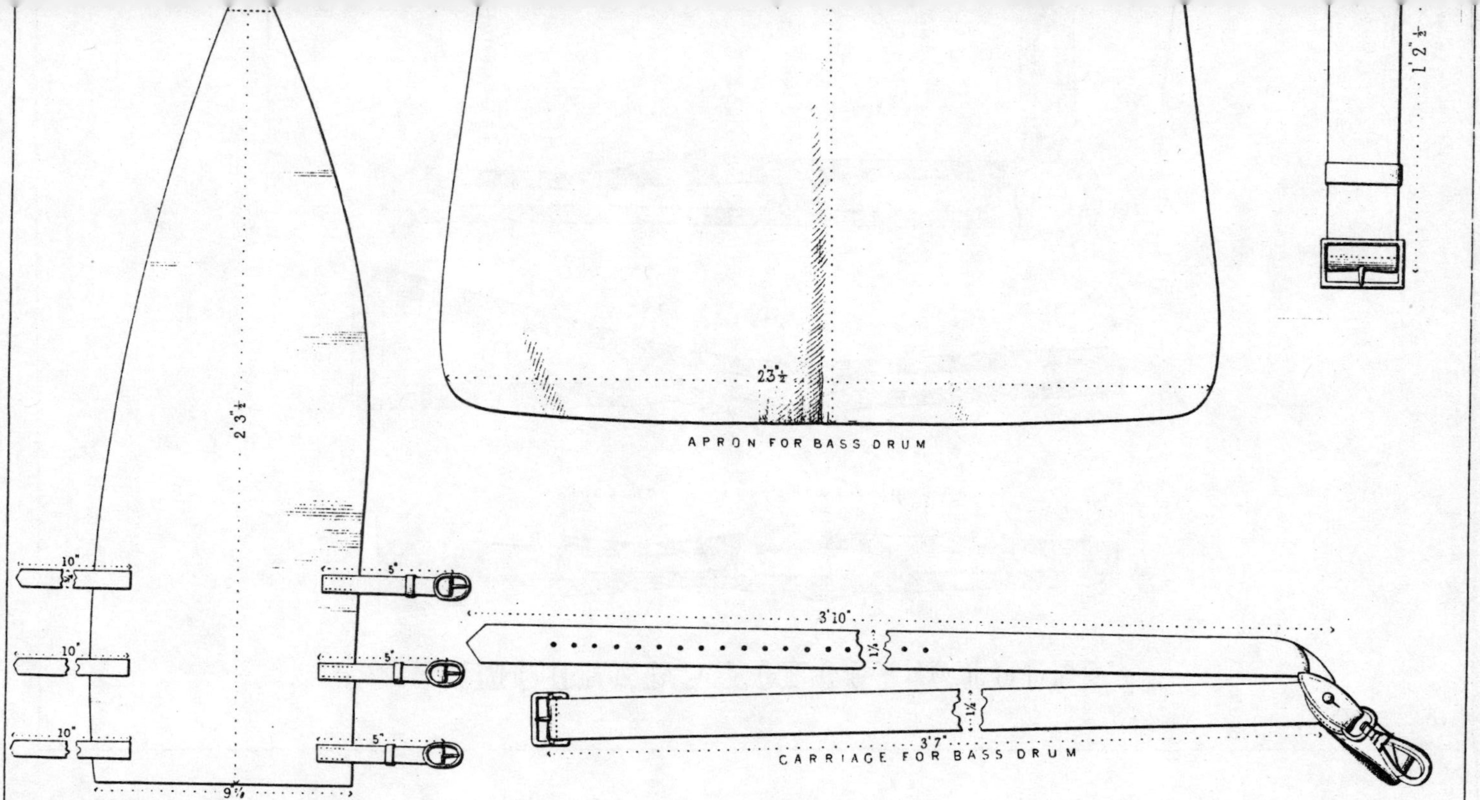
1' 2½"
23½"
APRON FOR BASS DRUM
2' 3½"
10"
10"
10"
5"
5"
5"
9½
LEG APRON FOR SIDE DRUM
3' 10"
1½
1¼
3' 7"
CARRIAGE FOR BASS DRUM

Scale - 2 Inches to 1 Foot

Eng.d & printed at the Top.l Dep.t, War Office, under the direction of Capt. M. Petrie 14th Reg.t Topog.l Staff. Col. Sir H. James. R.E. F.R.S. M.R.I.A. Director.

PLATE XVII

ARMOURER'S FORGE AND TOOLS.

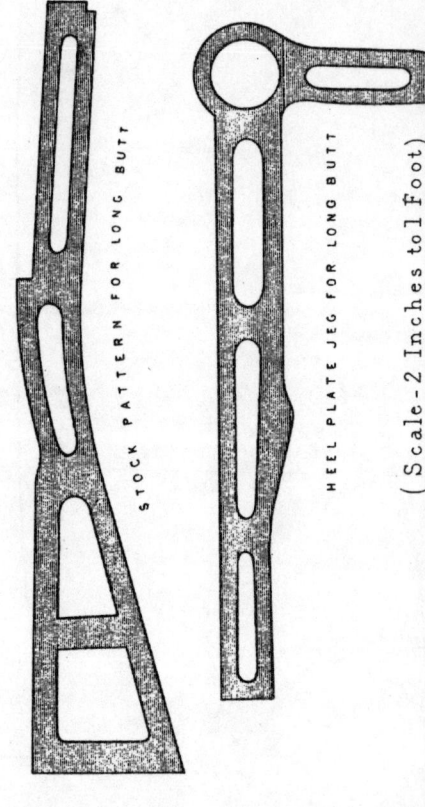

STOCKING JEG FOR SHORT & LONG BUTT

STOCK PATTERN FOR LONG BUTT

HEEL PLATE JEG FOR LONG BUTT

(Scale – 2 Inches to 1 Foot)

FORGE COMPLETE

(Scale - 1 Inch to 1 Foot)

Engd. & Printed at the Topl. Depot. War Office under the direction of Capt. M. Ferne 14th Topl. Staff
Col. Sr. H. James R.E. F.R.S. M.R.I.A Director

PLATE XVIII

ARMOURER'S TOOLS.

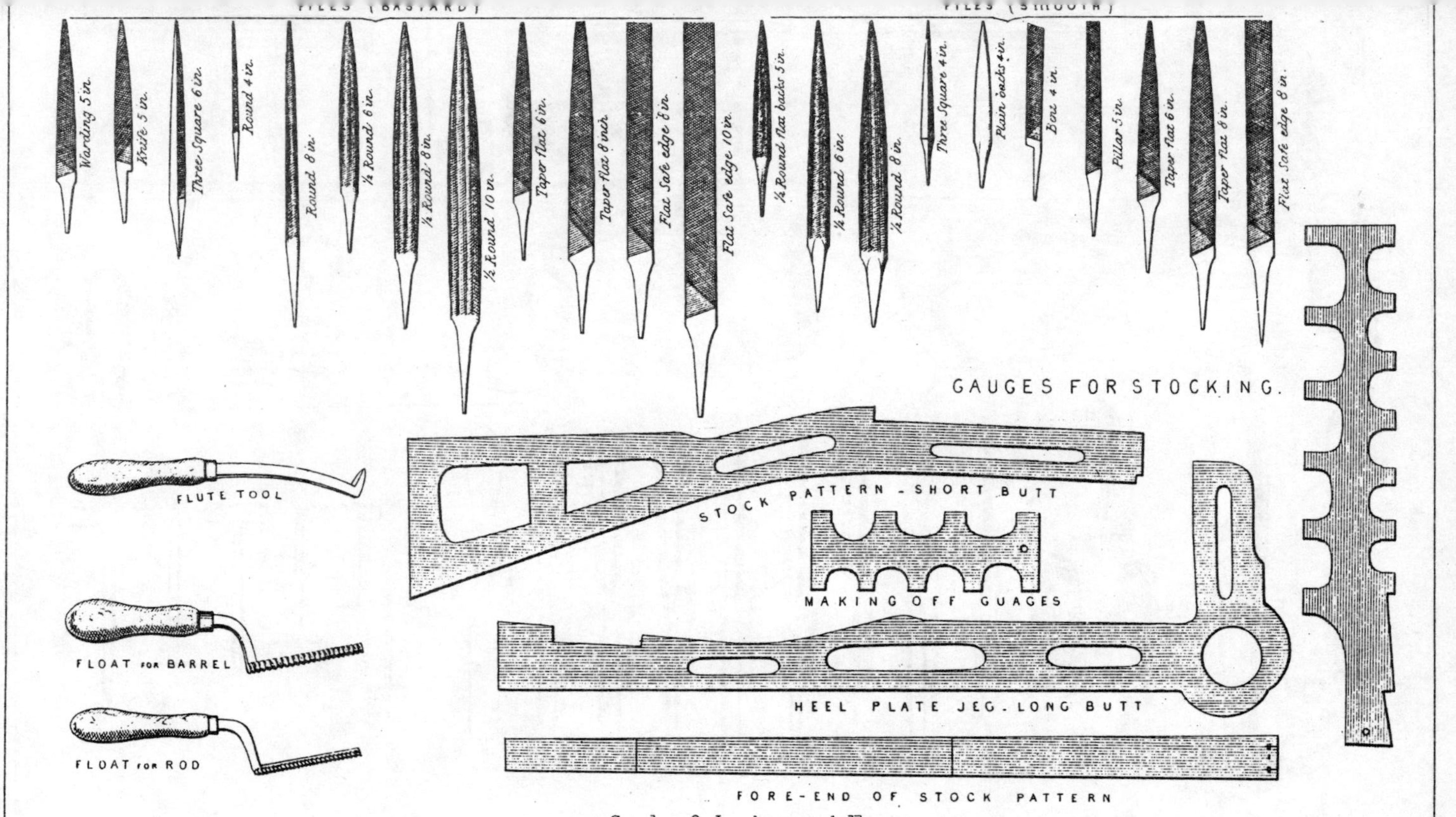
FILES (BASTARD)
Warding 5 in.
Knife 5 in.
Three Square 6 in.
Round 4 in.
Round 8 in.
½ Round 6 in.
½ Round 8 in.
½ Round 10 in.
Taper flat 6 in.
Taper flat 8 inch
Flat Safe edge 8 in.
Flat Safe edge 10 in.
FILES (SMOOTH)
½ Round flat backs 5 in.
½ Round 6 in.
½ Round 8 in.
Three Square 4 in.
Plain backs 4 in.
Bow 4 in.
Pillar 5 in.
Taper flat 6 in.
Taper flat 8 in.
Flat Safe edge 8 in.
GAUGES FOR STOCKING.
FLUTE TOOL
STOCK PATTERN - SHORT BUTT
MAKING OFF GUAGES
FLOAT FOR BARREL
HEEL PLATE JEG. LONG BUTT
FLOAT FOR ROD
FORE-END OF STOCK PATTERN

Scale - 2 Inches to 1 Foot

Engd. & printed at the Topl. & Statl. Dept. War Office, under the direction of Capt. M. Petrie 14th Regt. Topl. Staff
Col. Sir H. James R.E. F.R.S. M.R.I.A. director

PLATE XIX

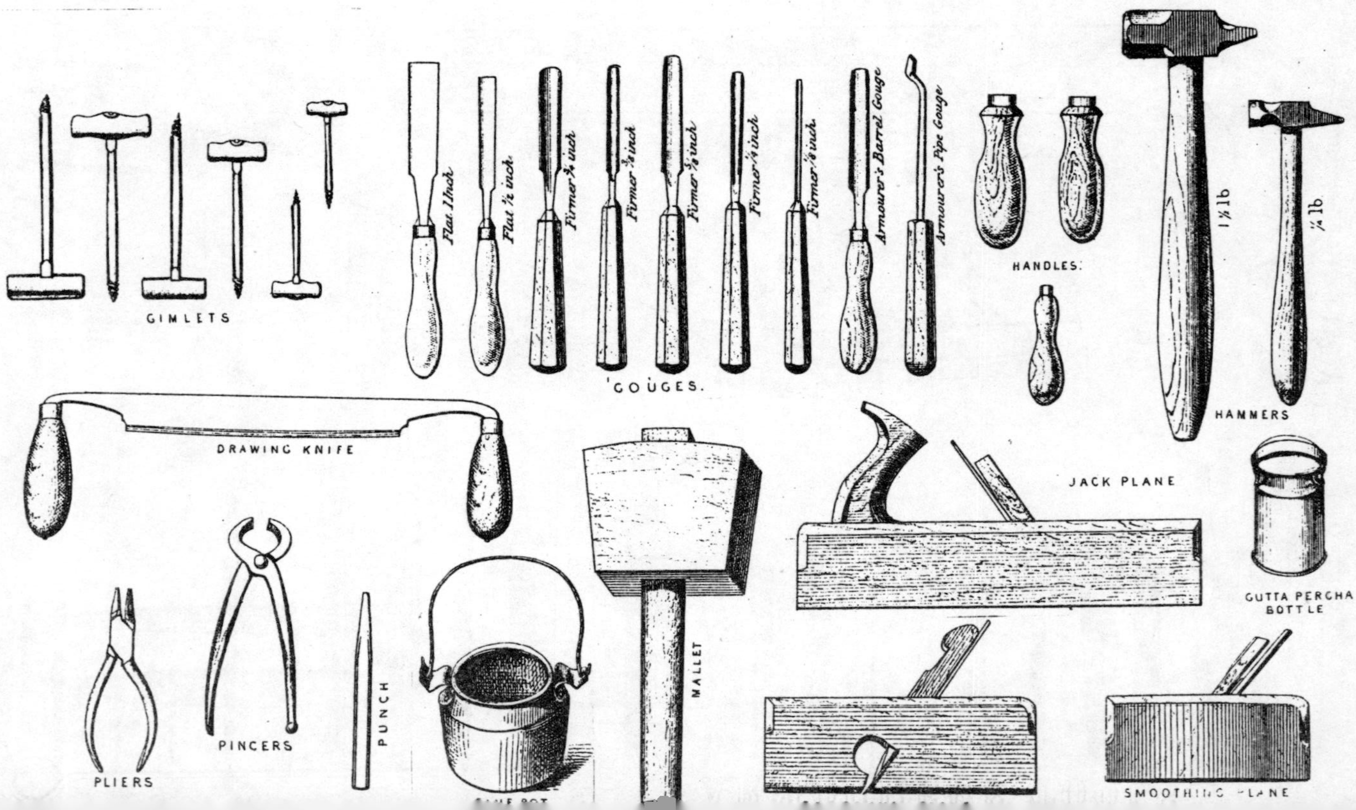

GIMLETS
Flat 1 Inch
Flat ½ inch
Firmer ¾ inch
Firmer ⅜ inch
Firmer ⅝ inch
Firmer ¼ inch
Firmer ⅛ inch
Armourer's Barrel Gouge
Armourer's Pipe Gouge
GOUGES.
HANDLES.
1¼ lb
¼ lb
HAMMERS
DRAWING KNIFE
JACK PLANE
GUTTA PERCHA BOTTLE
PLIERS
PINCERS
PUNCH
MALLET
SMOOTHING PLANE

ARMOURERS' TOOLS.

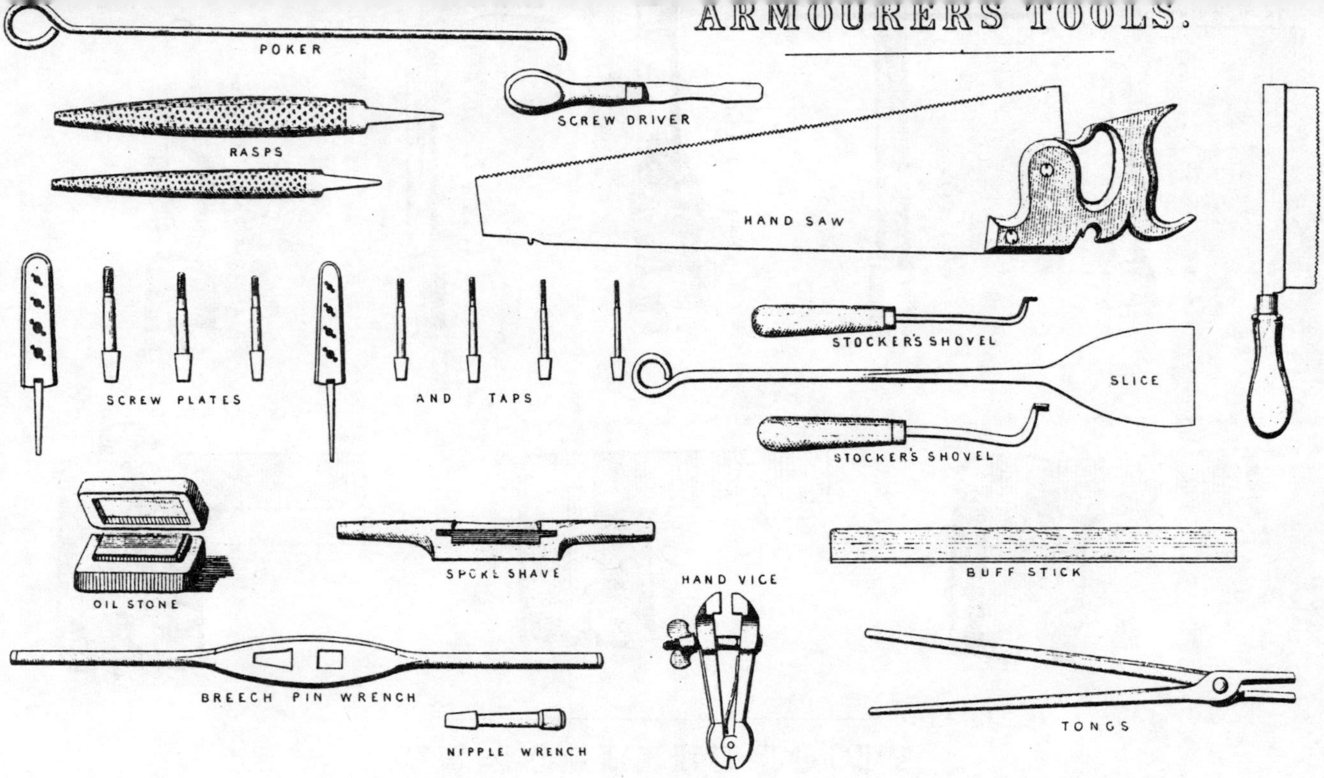
POKER
SCREW DRIVER
RASPS
HAND SAW
SLITTING SAW
SCREW PLATES
AND TAPS
STOCKER'S SHOVEL
SLICE
STOCKER'S SHOVEL
OIL STONE
SPOKE SHAVE
BUFF STICK
HAND VICE
BREECH PIN WRENCH
NIPPLE WRENCH
TONGS

Scale - 2 Inches to 1 Foot

Engᵈ & printed at the Topˡ Depᵗ War Office, under the direction of Capt. M. Petrie. 14ᵗʰ Regᵗ Topˡ Staff. Colˡ Sir H. James. R.E. F.R.S. M.R.I.A. &c. Director.

ARMOURER'S TOOLS.

PLATE XX

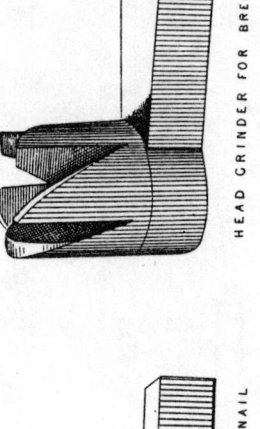

HEAD GRINDER FOR BREECH NAIL

PLUG GRINDER FOR LOCK PIN

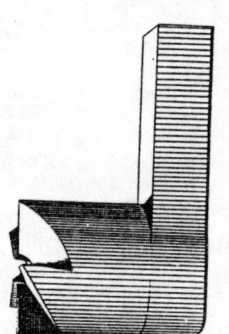

SHANK GRINDER FOR SIDE NAIL

DRILL FOR PIVOT OVAL

PLUG GRINDER FOR BREECH NAIL

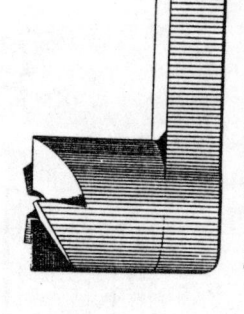

DRILL FOR SEAR OVAL

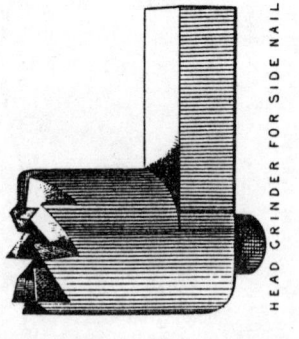

HEAD GRINDER FOR SIDE NAIL

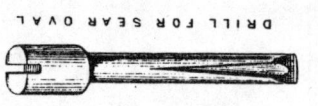

PLUG GRINDER FOR SIDE NAIL

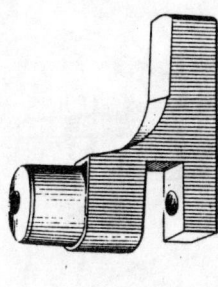

HEAD GRINDER FOR LOCK PIN

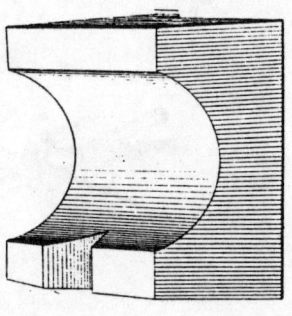

SHANK GRINDER FOR LOCK PIN

SEAR OVAL

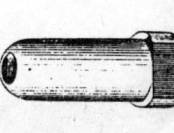

PIVOT OVAL

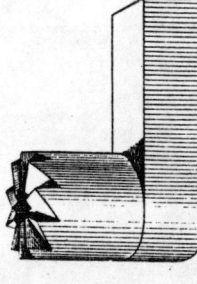

BRASS CLAM (PATTERN 1853)

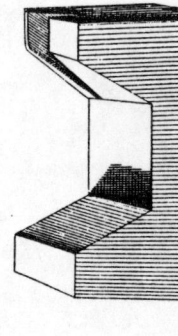

BRASS CLAM (PATTERN 1853)

(FULL SIZE)

Eng.d & printed at the Topog.l Dep.t War Office under the direction of Capt. H. Petrie R.E. Esq.r
Col.l Sir H. James R.E. F.R.S. M.R.I.A. &c Director

PLATE XXI

ARTICLES FOR MUSKETRY INSTRUCTION.

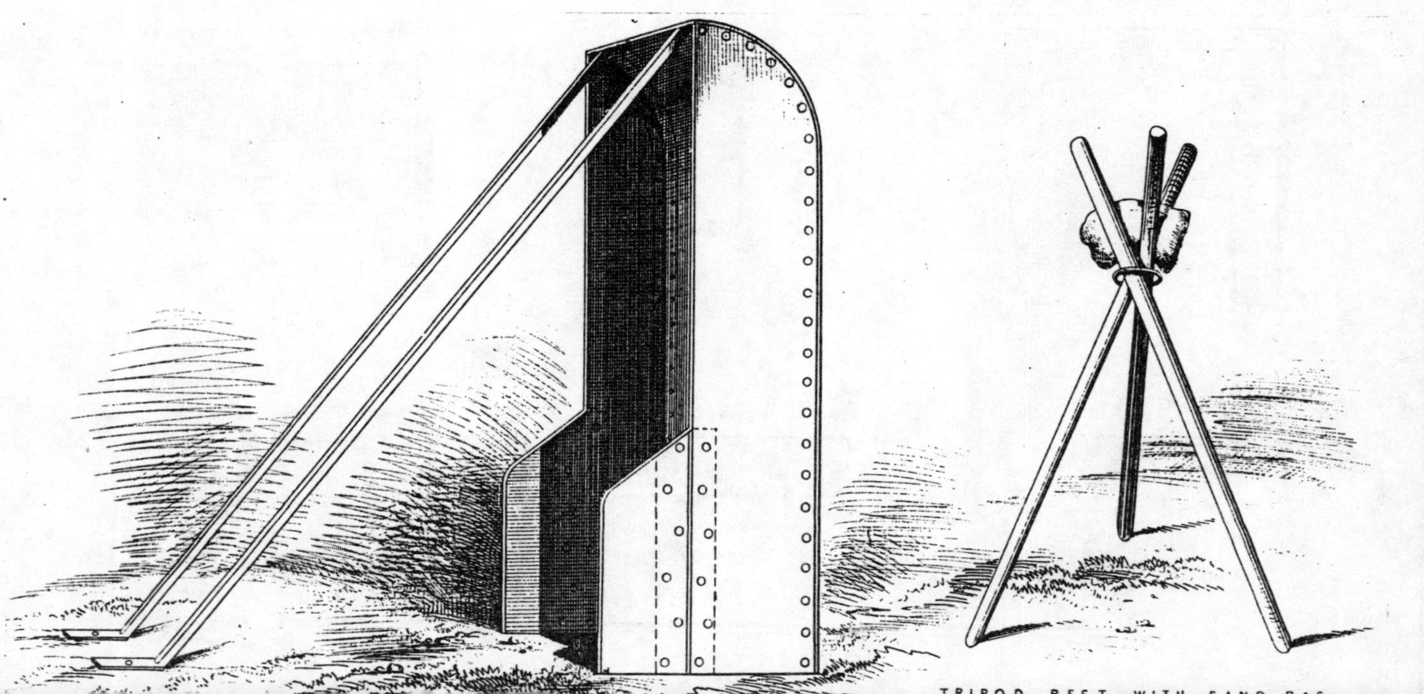

TRIPOD REST WITH SAND BAG

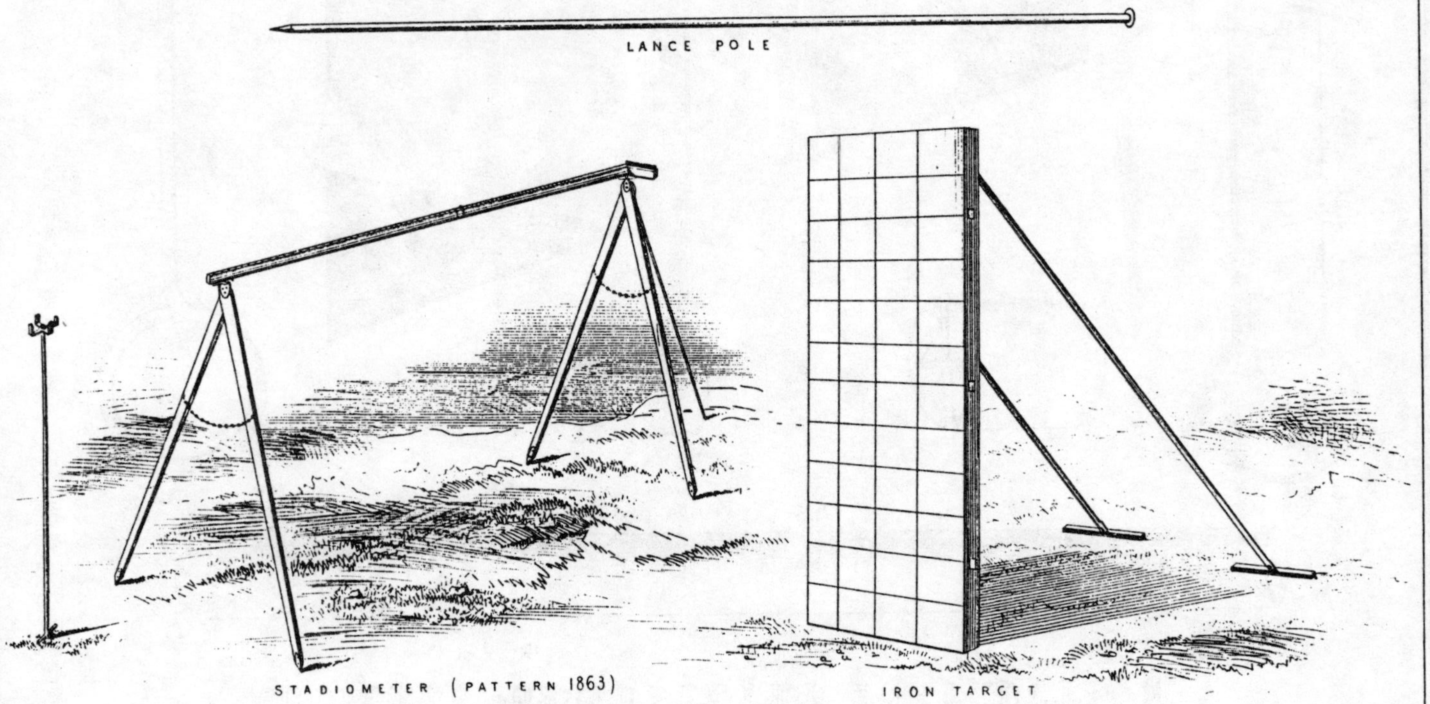
LANCE POLE
STADIOMETER (PATTERN 1863)
IRON TARGET

(Scale ½ Inch to 1 Foot)

Engd & Printed at the Topl Dept War Office under the direction of Capt. M. Petrie 14th Regt Topographl Staff
Coll Sir H James R.E. F.R.S. M.R.I.A. & Director.

PLATE XXII

ARTICLES FOR MUSKETRY INSTRUCTION.

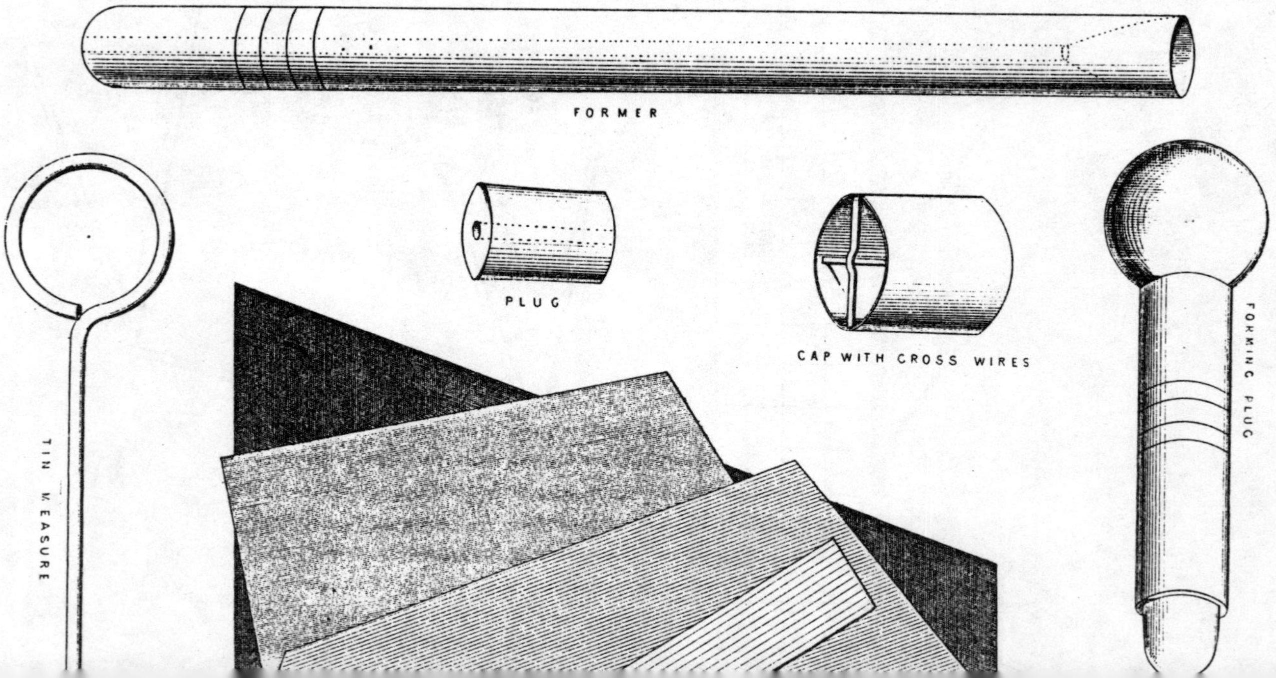
FORMER
TIN MEASURE
PLUG
CAP WITH CROSS WIRES
FORMING PLUG

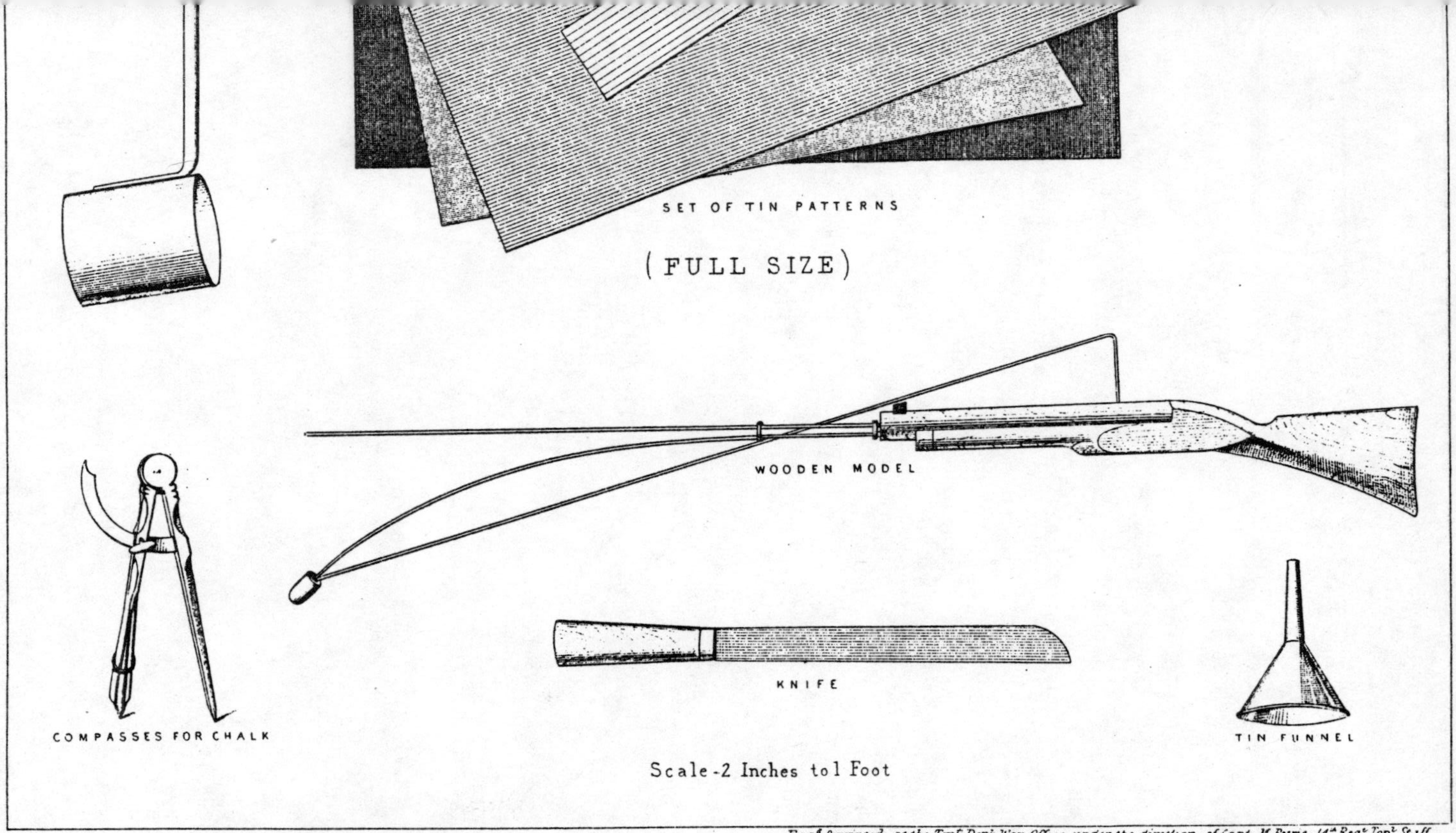
SET OF TIN PATTERNS
(FULL SIZE)
WOODEN MODEL
KNIFE
COMPASSES FOR CHALK
TIN FUNNEL
Scale-2 Inches to 1 Foot

Engd. & printed at the Topl. Depl. War Office under the direction of Capt. M. Petrie 14th Regt. Topl. Staff
Col. Sir H James R.E. F.R.S. M.R.I.A. &c. Director.

FIELD EXERCISE

AND

EVOLUTIONS

OF

INFANTRY,

AS REVISED

By Her Majesty's Command,

1867.

LONDON:

Printed under the Superintendence of Her Majesty's Stationery Office,

AND SOLD BY

W. CLOWES AND SONS, 14, Charing Cross; HARRISON AND SONS, 59, Pall Mall;
W. H. ALLEN & Co., 13, Waterloo Place; W. MITCHELL, 39, Charing Cross; and LONGMAN AND Co., Paternoster Row.

ALSO BY

A. AND C. BLACK, Edinburgh;
ALEX. THOM, Abbey Street, and E. PONSONBY, Grafton Street, Dublin.

RIFLE EXERCISES.

GENERAL DIRECTIONS.

I.

Names of Parts of the Rifle.—Recruits, before they commence to learn the Manual and Platoon exercises, must be taught the names of the different parts of the rifle, as shown in Plate X.

II.

Formation of Squad.—Soldiers will be formed in squads of single rank to learn the Manual and Platoon exercises by Numbers and in Quick Time; after which they will practise in two ranks what they have learned in one rank, as directed in Part I., Section 40.*

III.

Instructor to have Rifle.—The instructor should always be provided with a rifle when at drill, in order that he may be able to show the recruit the required positions and movements.

IV.

The Rifle to be used with care.—The rifle must be carefully handled, as any rough usage will injure it.

V.

How to carry the Rifle.—Rifles when unloaded are to be carried with the hammer down on the nipple; when loaded, they are to be carried at half-cock.

---

* Not reproduced in this edition

PLATE X.

NAMES OF PARTS OF THE RIFLE.

LONG RIFLE.

A A.	Barrel.
a.	Muzzle.
b.	Fore sight.
c.	Back sight. { *d.* Flap. *e.* Slide.
f.	Nipple-lump.
g.	Breech-block.
B B.	Stock.
a'.	Nose cap.
b'.	Upper band.
c'.	Middle band.
d'.	Lower band.
e'.	Projection.
f'.	Butt { *g'.* Small. *h'.* Heel. *k'.* Toe.
C C.	Lock.
a a.	Hammer.
b b.	Comb of hammer.
D.	Trigger.
E.	Trigger-guard or guard.
F.	Snap cap.
G G.	Sling.
H.	Stopper.
K K.	Rod. { *a.* Head or jag. *b.* Point.
L L.	Bayonet.
a.	Blade.
b.	Bend.
c.	Socket.
d.	Locking ring.
M.	Scabbard.

SHORT RIFLE.

A A.	Barrel.
a.	Muzzle.
b.	Fore sight.
c.	Catch.
d.	Back sight. { *e.* Flap. *f.* Slide.
g.	Nipple-lump.
h.	Breech-block.
B B.	Stock.
a'.	Nose cap.
b'.	Upper band.
c'.	Lower band.
d'.	Projection.
e'.	Butt. { *f'.* Small. *g'.* Heel. *h'.* Toe.
C C.	Lock.
a a.	Hammer.
b b.	Comb of hammer.
D.	Trigger.
E.	Trigger-guard or guard.
F.	Snap cap.
G G.	Sling.
H.	Stopper.
K K.	Rod. { *a.* Head or jag. *b.* Point.
L L.	Sword.
a.	Blade.
b.	Hilt.
c.	Guard and ring.
d.	Spring.
M.	Scabbard.

The side of the rifle on which the lock is placed is called the lock side.

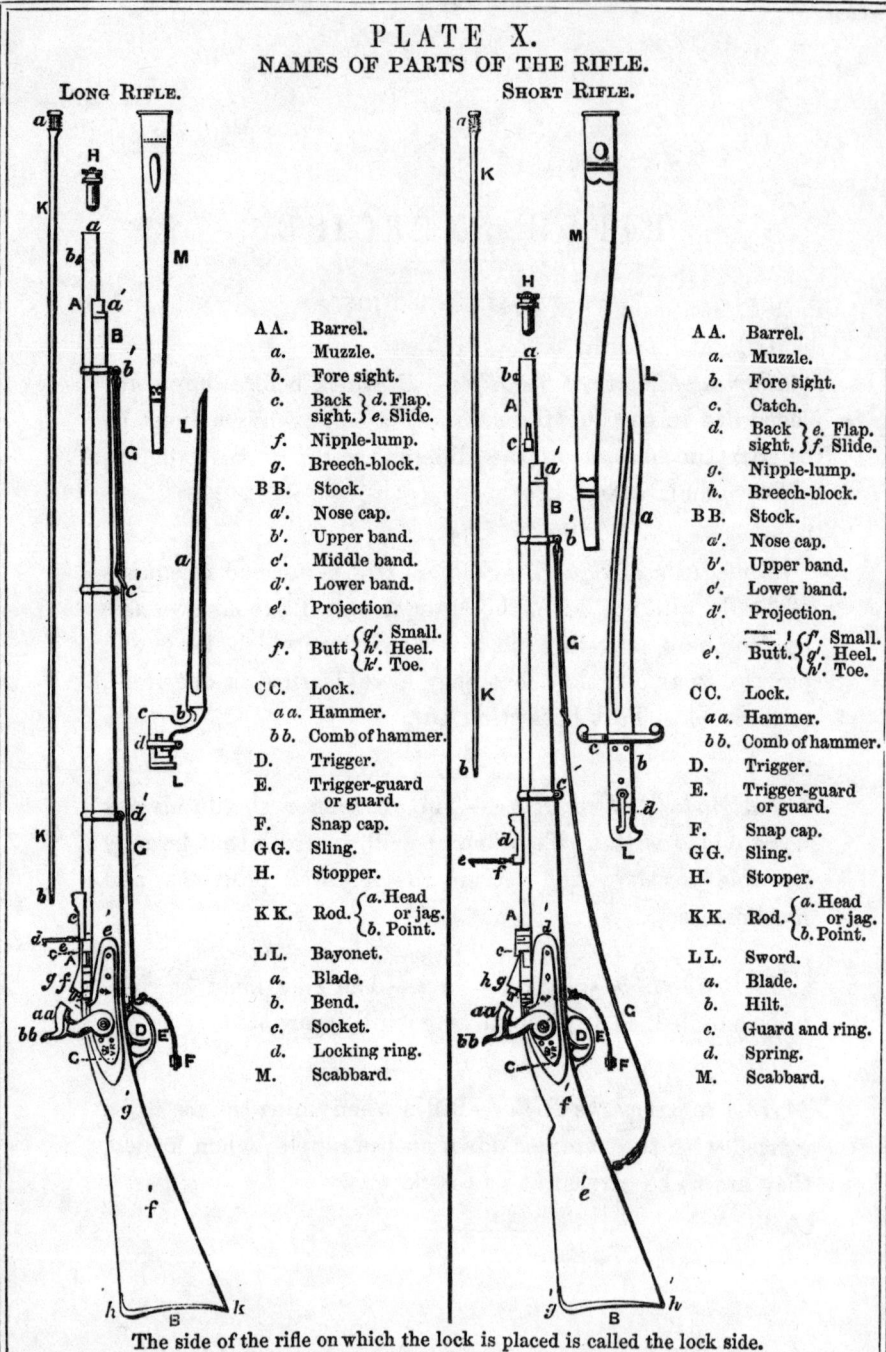

Manual Exercises.

S. 1. *Manual Exercise with the Long Rifle.*

1. *By Numbers.*

I.

The Order.—The recruit will first fall in as directed in Part I., Section 24*; the rifle will then be placed perpendicularly at his right side, the butt on the ground, its toe in line with the toe of the right foot ; the right hand to be placed flat on the outside of the stock, thumb on the sling, the barrel to be pressed to the hollow of the shoulder.

When the rifle has been properly placed at "The Order," the recruit will be instructed always to fall in on parade, or for drill, with it in that position.

II.

Fix—

Bayonets.

Fixing Bayonets.—On the word *Fix*, by a sharp turn of the wrist bring the thumb of the right hand round the rear of the barrel and grasp the rifle, thumb between the stock and the thigh ; at the same time seize the socket of the bayonet with the left hand, knuckles to the front, thumb to the rear, fingers pointing to the ground, left elbow to the rear.

On the word *Bayonets*, push the muzzle of the rifle a little forward ; at the same time draw the bayonet ; and as soon as the point clears the scabbard turn it up, keeping the elbow down and the upper part of the arm close to the body. Place the socket of the bayonet on the

---

* Not reproduced in this edition

muzzle (the flat part of the blade to the front), and when it falls on the block of the foresight turn it with the thumb from left to right, and press it home; then, with the thumb, turn the locking ring in the same direction under the block of the foresight. Lastly, drop the left hand to the side, and bring the rifle to "The Order" (No. I.).

III.

Shoulder—

The Shoulder from the Order.—On the word *Shoulder*, grasp the rifle as in the first motion of "Fixing Bayonets" (No. II.)

Arms.

On the word *Arms*, give the rifle a cant upwards with the right hand, and seize it below the lower band, keeping the barrel close to the shoulder.

Two.

Bring the rifle with the right hand to the left side, and seize it with the left hand, which will grasp the inside of the butt with the first two joints of the fingers; the forefinger to be half an inch from, the thumb in front of, the heel, the wrist slightly turned out, the fingers to rest lightly against the thigh. The rifle will rest against the hollow of the left shoulder, the fore part of the butt nearly even with the front of the thigh. As the left hand seizes the rifle, the right will be dropped to the side.

IV.

Present—Arms.

The Present Arms.—Turn the lock to the front, and seize the rifle with the right hand under the guard without moving it from the shoulder; thumb and fingers to be round the stock, arm close to the body.

Two. Without moving the head, raise the rifle with the right hand perpendicularly in front of the centre of the body, and place the left hand smartly on the sling, the wrist on the trigger-guard, the fingers pointing upwards, the thumb close to the fore finger (its point in line with the mouth), the left elbow to be close to the butt, the right elbow and butt close to the body.

Three. Bring the rifle down close in front of the centre of the body, sling to the front, as low as the right hand will admit without constraint, and grasp it with the left hand, the little finger touching the projection above the lock plate, thumb between stock and barrel, the right hand lightly holding the small of the butt, fingers slanting downwards; at the same time place the hollow of the right foot against the left heel, both knees straight. The weight of the rifle to be supported by the left hand.

V.

Shoulder-Arms. *The Shoulder from the Present Arms.*—By a turn of the right wrist, bring the rifle to the left side, and seize it with the left hand as directed in the second motion of "The Shoulder from the Order" (No. III.); fingers of the right

PART III.—RIFLE EXERCISES.

Two. hand to remain under the hammer (first two joints round the stock), thumb between the stock and barrel, arm close to the body; at the same time bring the right foot to its original position.

Two. Drop the right hand to the side.

VI.

Port–Arms. *The Port.*—Seize the small of the butt with the right hand, arm close to the body.

Two. Bring the rifle to a slanting position in front of the body, lock to the front, the barrel crossing opposite the point of the left shoulder; and meet it at the same time with the left hand immediately below the lower band, thumb and fingers round the rifle; the left wrist to be opposite the left breast, both elbows close to the body.

VII.

As a front rank, Charge–Bayonets. *The Charge.*—Turning on the heels, point the right foot to the right, the left full to the front, and bring the rifle down to nearly a horizontal position at the right side, with the muzzle inclining a little upward; the right wrist to rest against the hollow of the thigh below the hip, the right hand to grasp the small of the butt, the thumb and fingers of the left hand to be round the rifle.

As a rear rank, Charge–Bayonets. Remain steady at "The Port."

VIII.

Shoulder-Arms. — **The Shoulder from the Charge, as a Front Rank.**—Bring the rifle to the left side, and seize it with the left hand, as directed in the second motion of "The Shoulder from the Order" (No. III.), facing at the same time to the front; the right hand remaining as described in the first motion of "The Shoulder from the Present Arms" (No. V.).

Two. Drop the right hand to the side.

Shoulder-Arms. — **The Shoulder from the Port, as a Rear Rank.**—Bring the rifle with the right hand to the left side, and seize it with the left hand, as directed in the second motion of "The Shoulder from the Order" (No. III.), the right hand remaining as described in the first motion of "The Shoulder from the Present Arms" (No. V.).

Two. Drop the right hand to the side.

IX.

Advance-Arms. — **The Advance Arms.**—Turn the lock to the front and seize the rifle as in the first motion of "The Present Arms" (No. IV.).

Two. Carry the rifle, close into the body, to the right side with the right hand, and seize it with the left hand close above the lower band; at the same time seize the guard with the thumb and forefinger of the right hand at the full extent of the arm, remaining fingers under the hammer.

Three. Drop the left hand to the side.

X.

Order-Arms.
> *The Order from the Advance Arms.—* Seize the rifle with the left hand, little finger in line with the point of the right shoulder, arm close to the body.

Two.
> Extend the fingers and thumb of the right hand, and lower the rifle with the left hand until the butt touches the ground; the left arm and rifle to be kept close to the body.

Three.
> Drop the left hand to the side.

XI.

Advance-
> *The Advance Arms from the Order.—* On the word *Advance*, grasp the rifle as in the first motion of "Fixing Bayonets" (No. II.).

Arms.
> On the word *Arms*, raise the rifle by a cant with the right hand, and lay hold of it as in the second motion of "The Advance Arms" (No. IX.).

Two.
> Drop the left hand to the side.

XII.

Shoulder-Arms.
> *The Shoulder from the Advance Arms.* —Seize the rifle with the left hand, little finger in line with the right elbow, and raise it about one inch, without moving the barrel from the shoulder; at the same time slip the thumb of the right hand

MANUAL EXERCISE FOR THE LONG RIFLE. 207

Two.

under the hammer, bringing the fingers under the guard, both arms to be close to the body.

By a turn of the right wrist, bring the rifle up to the left side, seizing it with the left hand as in the second motion of "The Shoulder from the Order" (No. III.), the right hand remaining as described in the first motion of "The Shoulder from the Present Arms" (No. V.).

Three. Drop the right hand to the side.

XIII.

Support-Arms.

The Support.—Raise the rifle about one inch, and seize the small of the butt with the right hand, fingers and thumb round the stock, arm close to the body.

Two.

Bring the left arm under the hammer, fingers of the left hand extended, with the thumb close to the forefinger; the hammer to rest on the arm midway between the wrist and elbow, the elbow to be kept close to the body.

Three. Drop the right hand to the side.

XIV.

Shoulder-Arms.

The Shoulder from the Support.—Seize the small of the butt as directed in the first motion of "The Support" (No. XIII.).

Two. Drop the left hand and grasp the butt, as in the second motion of "The Shoulder from the Order" (No. III.), but with the elbow a little bent.

Three. Drop the right hand smartly to the side, at the same time allowing the left arm to sink to its full extent.

XV.

Slope-Arms. *The Slope.*—Without moving the upper part of the arm, raise the rifle until the guard is pressed gently against the hollow of the shoulder, and the lower part of the arm becomes horizontal, the toe of the butt to point to the centre of the left thigh.

XVI.

Shoulder-Arms. *The Shoulder from the Slope.*—Drop the left arm gently to its full extent.

XVII.

Order-Arms. *The Order from the Shoulder.*—Seize the rifle with the right hand close above the lower band, keeping the elbow as close to the body as possible.

Two. Bring the rifle down to the right side, allowing the little finger to slip behind the barrel as it descends, and place the butt quietly on the ground at "The Order" (No. I.).

Three. Place the right hand on the stock &c., as directed in No. I.

XVIII.

Unfix–

Bayonets.

Unfixing Bayonets.—On the word *Unfix*, grasp the rifle, as in the first motion of " Fixing Bayonets " (No. II.).

On the word *Bayonet*, push the muzzle a little forward, and lay hold of the rifle with the left hand immediately above the upper band, thumb and fingers round the stock and barrel, arm close to the body. Raise the right hand and seize the socket of the bayonet between the forefinger and thumb, fingers closed in the hand, knuckles to the front, arm close to the body. With the second joint of the forefinger of the right hand, turn the locking ring to the left, then extend the fingers under the bend, raise the bayonet, turn it to the left, and remove it from the muzzle. Drop the point of the bayonet towards the scabbard, inclining the palm of the hand to the front as it falls, and place the little finger on the top of the socket; at the same time, force the muzzle of the rifle back to the hollow of the right shoulder with the left hand, which is immediately to be removed and placed on the top of the scabbard to guide the bayonet in, the elbow to the rear and as close to the body as possible. Lastly, drop the arms to their position at " The Order " (No. I.).

Of the foregoing motions, Nos. IV.–XVIII. are performed in the " Review Exercise." *See* Section 10 of this Part.

XIX.

Slope— { *The Slope from the Order.*—On the word *Slope*, grasp the rifle as in the first motion of "Fixing Bayonets" (No. II.).

Arms. { On the word *Arms*, carry the rifle to the left side and seize it with the left hand as directed in the second motion of "The Shoulder from the Order" (No. III.). at the same time dropping the right hand to the side.

Two. { Raise the rifle to "The Slope" (No. XV.).

XX.

Order–Arms. { *The Order from the Slope.*—Drop the left arm to its full extent, and seize the rifle with the right hand as directed in the first motion of "The Order from the Shoulder" (No. XVII.).

Two. *Three.* } As detailed in No. XVII.

XXI.

Trail— { *The Trail.*— On the word *Trail*, grasp the rifle as in the first motion of "Fixing Bayonets" (No. II.).

Arms. { On the word *Arms*, give the rifle a cant upwards with the right hand, seizing it below the lower band, and bring it to a horizontal position at the full extent of the arm, fingers and thumb round the rifle.

XXII.

Order–Arms. — **The Order from the Trail.**—Bring the rifle to a perpendicular position at the right side, allowing it to slip through the fingers to the ground at the position described in "The Order" (No. I.).

Arms must never be trailed with fixed bayonets, except by the front rank before charging.

In the foregoing exercises great care must be taken to preserve the squareness of the body and to avoid raising or sinking either shoulder.

XXIII.

Advance–Arms.
Two. — As detailed in No. XI.

XXIV.

Trail–Arms. — **The Trail from the Advance Arms.**—Seize the rifle with the left hand, little finger in line with the right elbow, arm close to the body.

Two. — Raise the right hand, and seize the rifle below the lower band; then bring it to the position described in "The Trail" (No. XXI.), at the same time dropping the left arm to the side.

XXV.

Advance–Arms. — **The Advance Arms from the Trail.**—Bring the rifle to a perpendicular position, and seize it with the left hand close above the lower band, at the same time raising it slightly and seizing it with the right hand, as in the second motion of "The Advance Arms" (No. IX.).

Two. — Drop the left hand to the side.

XXVI.

Order–Arms.
Two.
Three.
} As detailed in No. X.

XXVII.

Ground–

Arms.

Ground Arms.—On the word *Ground*, grasp the rifle as directed in the first motion of "Fixing Bayonets" (No. II.).

On the word *Arms*, turn the rifle on the heel, lock to the rear, raise it off the ground, and give the butt a cant to the rear; sink the body, bending both knees, and place the rifle flat on the ground, the lock upwards, muzzle inclined to the right front, hammer in line with the heels; rise at once, and return to the position of attention.

XXVIII.

Take up–
Arms.
{ Sink the body as in grounding arms, take up the rifle, and come to "The Order" (No. I.).

XXIX.

The Short Trail.—Grasp the rifle with the right hand, and raise it from the ground, keeping the barrel to the shoulder.

XXX.

Stand at–
Ease.
} As detailed in Part I., Section 2.

The Secure.—For the protection of the rifle in wet weather, the soldier will be allowed to carry it as follows:—

The rifle to be under the left arm, butt to the rear, the hammer to be close up under the armpit, the barrel slanting

MANUAL EXERCISE FOR THE LONG RIFLE. 213

downwards, and inclining to the right front; the rifle to be firmly grasped with the left hand, which is to be rather lower than the hip; left elbow a little to the rear. On the word *Change Arms*, the rifle to be carried under the right arm in like manner.

2. *In Quick Time.*

The recruit having been thoroughly instructed in the Manual Exercise by Numbers will be taught to perform it in Quick Time; the foregoing words of command being given without the numbers, and executed as above detailed, resting a pause of quick time between each motion. A pause of the slow time should be made between the first and last part of each command, except in fixing bayonets, when longer time should be given.

3. *Motions of the Rifle performed on the March.*

The recruit will learn to perform the following motions of the rifle while marching; they may be taught at first while he is marking time; each motion should be done as the left foot comes to the ground, both in the slow and quick march; to this end the word of command should be completed as the right foot is coming to the ground.

When soldiers standing in line with ordered arms and unfixed bayonets step off from "The Order," they will come to "The Trail" as they take the first step;—when standing in line with bayonets fixed, or in file, they will come to "The Advance Arms" as they move off; returning in each case to "The Order" as they halt, or halt and front;—when marching in line or in fours with trailed arms, and ordered to turn into file, or form two deep, they will come to "The Advance Arms" as they turn, or form, and will trail again on turning into line or forming four deep.

Soldiers will not, as a general rule, be marched off from "The Order" in field movements; but will be brought to

"The Slope" before stepping off, except when required to move at "The Shoulder."

Soldiers marching with sloped arms, when halted, will remain at "The Slope:" except after forming or wheeling into line, in which case they will come to "The Shoulder" as they halt, returning to "The Slope" on receiving the word "*Eyes front;*" or on halting after a charge in line, when they will come to "The Shoulder."

When soldiers are marched off from "The Shoulder," they will step off, remaining at "The Shoulder;"—when marching in slow time with shouldered arms, and ordered to break into quick time, they will slope arms as they take the first pace in that time;—when marching in quick time with sloped arms, and ordered to take up the slow time, they will remain at "The Slope."

When a soldier with sloped arms is required to turn to the right (or left) about, he will come to "The Shoulder" on the first pace of the turn, and having completed his turn in three paces will slope again on the fourth, the pace on which he steps off in his new direction;—when with trailed arms, he will bring his rifle to a perpendicular position by a turn of the wrist on the first pace of the turn, and trail again on the fourth pace.

When soldiers standing with sloped arms are required to face about, they will come to "The Shoulder" as the foot is drawn back, returning to "The Slope" when they have completed the face.

When ordered to mark time from the halt the foregoing rules will apply.

When men standing with ordered arms are directed to form fours, to close to the right or left, to step back, or to take any named number of paces to the front, they will come to "The Short Trail."

Arms are never to be carried at "The Trail" when loaded.

MOTIONS OF THE LONG RIFLE ON THE MARCH. 215

For directions for pivot men, see **Part II., General Principles, No. XIX.**; for skirmishers and supports, see **Part V., General Principles, No. X.***

Quick–March or Mark Time–Quick.
  From the Halt at Ordered Arms.—On the word *Quick* (or *Mark time*) grasp the rifle as in the first motion of "Fixing Bayonets" (No. II.). On the word *March* (or *Quick*) step off (or commence marking time) and bring the rifle to "The Trail" on the first pace.

Advance–Arms.
  The Advance Arms from the Trail.—As on the halt.

Trail–Arms.
  The Trail from the Advance Arms.—As on the halt.

Change–Arms.
  Changing Arms at the Trail.—Raise the rifle to a perpendicular position at the right side; carry it to the left side, and pass it into the left hand, then lower it to "The Trail," at the same time dropping the right hand to the side.

Change–Arms.
  Change the rifle back to the right side in a similar manner.

Squad–Halt.
  Halt and come at once to "The Order."

Shoulder–Arms.—As already described.

Slow–March, or Mark Time–Slow.
  Step off (or commence marking time), remaining at "The Shoulder."

Break into Quick Time–Quick.
  Break into Quick Time and come to "The Slope."

* Not reproduced in this edition

PART III.—RIFLE EXERCISES.

Fix–Bayonets. — *Fixing Bayonets.* — Bring the rifle down as in trailing arms, but with the barrel slanting upwards in front of the right breast, fix bayonets as at the halt, then return at once to "The Slope."

Shoulder–Arms. — *The Shoulder from the Slope.* —As on the halt.

Support–Arms. — *The Support.*—As on the halt.

Shoulder–Arms. — *The Shoulder from the Support.*—As on the halt.

Slope–Arms. — As on the halt.

Change–Arms. — *Changing Arms at the Slope.*—Pass the left hand up quickly and seize the small of the butt, fingers and thumb round the stock ; at the same time seize the butt with the right hand, two first joints of the fingers round the stock, thumb in front of the heel; raise the rifle to a perpendicular position, carry it across the body and place it on the right shoulder, then drop the left hand to the side.

Change–Arms. — Carry the rifle back to the left shoulder in a similar manner.

Charging.—Soldiers marching in quick time will be taught to charge as follows :—

As a Front Rank, Prepare to Charge. — Bring the rifle to "The Trail," without losing the square position of the body or the regularity of the step.

Charge. — Bring the rifle to the position of "The Charge," and increase the pace to the double march.

MANUAL EXERCISE FOR THE SHORT RIFLE.

As a Rear Rank, Prepare to Charge. } Continue to move at "The Slope."

Charge. { Break into double time, continuing at "The Slope."

Squad–Halt. { Halt, and come to "The Shoulder," both as a front and rear rank.

S. 2. *The Manual Exercise with the Short Rifle.*
1. *By Numbers.*

I.

The Order.—The recruit will first fall in as directed in Part I., Section 24.* The rifle will then be placed perpendicularly at his right side, the butt on the ground, its toe in line with the toe of the right foot. The right arm to be slightly bent; the right hand to seize the rifle between the bands, thumb pressed against the thigh, fingers slanting towards the ground.

When the rifle has been properly placed at "The Order," the recruit will be instructed always to fall in on parade, or for drill, with it in that position.

II.

Shoulder-Arms. { *The Shoulder from the Order.*—Give the rifle a cant upwards with the right hand, catching it with the left hand in line with the elbow; at the same time seize the guard with the forefinger and thumb of the right hand, at the full extent of the arm, the remaining fingers under the hammer; the upper part of the barrel to rest in the hollow of the shoulder.

Two. { Drop the left hand to the side.

* Not reproduced in this edition

III.

Present-Arms.

The Present Arms.—Seize the rifle with the left hand at the lower band, raising it a few inches by slightly bending the right arm, without moving the barrel from the shoulder; then slip the thumb of the right hand under the hammer, and the fingers under the guard slanting downwards; both arms close to the body.

Two. Without moving the head, raise the rifle with the right hand perpendicularly in front of the centre of the body, lock to the front; at the same time place the left hand smartly on the stock, the wrist on the trigger-guard, fingers pointing upwards, thumb close to the forefinger (its point in line with the mouth); the left elbow to be close to the butt, the right elbow and butt close to the body.

Three. Bring the rifle down close in front of the centre of the body, guard to the front, as low as the right hand will admit without constraint, and grasp it with the left hand, the little finger touching the projection above the lock-plate, thumb between stock and barrel, the right hand lightly holding the small of the butt, fingers slanting downwards; at the same time place the hollow of the right foot against the left heel, both knees straight. The weight of the rifle to be supported by the left hand.

MANUAL EXERCISE FOR THE SHORT RIFLE. 219

IV.

Shoulder-Arms. — *The Shoulder from the Present Arms.*—Bring the rifle to the right side, and seize it with the right hand, as directed in the first motion of "The Shoulder from the Order" (No. II.), the left hand remaining to steady it to its place, arm close to the body; at the same time bring the right foot to its original position.

Two. — Drop the left hand to the side.

V.

Support-Arms. — *The Support.*—Bring the butt across, till the lock is in front of the centre of the body, back of the hand to the front, the barrel resting on the right arm; and place the left hand on the right.

VI.

Shoulder-Arms. — *The Shoulder from the Support.*—Bring the rifle to "The Shoulder" (No. II.), and at the same time drop the left hand to the side.

VII.

Order-Arms. — *The Order.*—Seize the rifle with the left hand, little finger in line with the point of the right shoulder; arm close the body.

Two. — Bring the rifle down in the left hand nearly to the ground, keeping the arm and rifle close to the body; then seize it with the right hand between the bands as described in "The Order" (No. I.), and place the butt quietly on the ground, dropping the left hand at the same time to the side.

L 2

VIII.

Fix–Swords.

Fixing Swords.—Place the rifle with the right hand between the knees, guard to the front, and seize the scabbard with the left hand, turning the handle of the sword towards the right front; then seize the handle with the right hand, knuckles downwards, and draw the sword to the front; turn the point upwards when it is well clear of the body, and seize the rifle with the left hand above the upper band. Place the back part of the handle against the lock side of barrel, knuckles to the right, arm close to the body, and slide the spring on to the catch, and the ring on to the muzzle; lastly, seize the rifle with the right hand between the bands, drop the left hand to the side, and return to "The Order" (No. I.).

IX.

Shoulder–Arms.
Two.

As detailed in No. II.

X.

Port–Arms.

Two.

The Port.—Seize the rifle as in the first motion of "The Present Arms" (No. III.).

Bring the rifle to a slanting position in front of the body, lock to the front, the barrel crossing opposite the point of the left shoulder; seize it at the same time with the thumb and fingers of the right hand round the small of the butt, the thumb and fingers of the left hand

MANUAL EXERCISE FOR THE SHORT RIFLE. 221

remaining round the rifle; the left wrist to be opposite the left breast, both elbows close to the body.

XI.

As a Front Rank, Charge-Swords.

The Charge.—Turning on the heels, point the right foot to the right, the left full to the front, and bring the rifle to nearly a horizontal position at the right side, with the muzzle inclining a little upwards; the right wrist to rest against the hollow of the thigh below the hip, the right hand to grasp the small of the butt, the thumb and fingers of the left hand to be round the rifle.

As a Rear Rank, Charge-Swords.

emain steady at "The Port."

XII.

Shoulder-Arms.

The Shoulder from the Charge as a Front Rank.—Raise the rifle to a perpendicular position at the right side, and seize it with the right hand as directed in the first motion of "The Shoulder from the Order" (No. II.); at the same time face to the front, the left hand remaining in its place, arm close to the body.

Two. Drop the left hand to the side.

Shoulder-Arms.

The Shoulder from the Port as a Rear Rank.—Bring the rifle with the left hand to the right side, seize it with the right hand, as directed in the first motion of "The Shoulder from the Order" (No. II.), the left hand remaining in its place, arm close to the body.

Two. Drop the left hand to the side.

XIII.

Slope-Arms. — *The Slope.*—Seize the rifle as in the first motion of "The Present Arms" (No. III.).

Two. — Bring the rifle on to the left shoulder, and seize it with the left hand, the first two joints of the fingers grasping the inside of the butt, the forefinger half-an-inch from the heel, the thumb in front of the heel, the muzzle slanting to the rear, and the guard pressed gently against the hollow of the shoulder. The upper part of the left arm to be close to the side, the lower part of the arm to be horizontal, the toe of the butt to point to the centre of the left thigh; the right hand holding the small of the butt, thumb and fingers round the stock, arm close in to the body.

Three. — Drop the right hand to the side.

XIV.

Shoulder-Arms. — *The Shoulder from the Slope.*—Seize the small of the butt with the right hand, fingers and thumb round the stock, arm close in to the body.

Two. — Bring the rifle to the right side, and seize it as directed in the first motion of "The Shoulder from the Order" (No. II.); the left hand to seize the rifle close above the lower band to steady it to the shoulder.

Three. — Drop the left hand to the side.

XV.

Order-Arms. *Two.* } As detailed in No. VII

XVI.

Unfix-Swords.

Unfixing Swords.—Bring the rifle with the right hand between the knees, guard to the front. Place the left hand on the guard of the sword, knuckles to the front, and seize the handle with the right hand, knuckles to the front, fingers pointing downwards, forefinger on the spring. Tighten the knees on the rifle, press the spring, and gently raise the sword upwards; when clear of the muzzle drop the point, with the edge to the front, towards the scabbard, raising the right elbow as it falls; at the same time seize the scabbard with the left hand and guide the sword into it. Lastly, seize the rifle with the right hand, between the bands, and come to "The Order" (No. I.), taking the time from the right.

Of the foregoing motions, Nos. III.–XVI. are performed in the "Review Exercise." *See* Section 10 of this Part.

XVII.

Slope-Arms.

The Slope from the Order.—Carry the rifle to the left side and seize the butt with the left hand, the first two joints of the fingers grasping the inside of the butt, the forefinger half-an-inch from, the thumb in front of, the heel: at the same time drop the right hand to the side.

Two. Raise the rifle until the guard presses gently against the hollow of the shoulder, muzzle to point to the rear.

XVIII.

Order–Arms. — *The Order from the Slope.*—Drop the left arm to its full extent, and seize the rifle with the right hand between the bands.

Two. — Carry the rifle to the right side and come to " The Order " (No. I.).

XIX.

Trail–Arms. — *The Trail.*—Give the rifle a cant upwards with the right hand, seizing it close behind the back-sight, and bring it to a horizontal position at the full extent of the arm, fingers and thumb round the rifle.

XX.

Shoulder–Arms. — *The Shoulder from the Trail.*—Bring the rifle to a perpendicular position, and seize it with the left hand close above the lower band, at the same time raising it slightly, and holding it as directed in the first motion of " The Shoulder from the Order " (No. II.).

Two. — Drop the left hand to the side.

XXI.

Trail–Arms. — *The Trail from the Shoulder.*—Seize the rifle with the left hand, little finger in line with the right elbow, arm close to the body.

Two. — Seize the rifle with the right hand close behind the back-sight; then bring it down to "The Trail," at the same time dropping the left hand to the side.

XXII.

Order–Arms.
The Order from the Trail.—Bring the rifle to a perpendicular position at the right side, allowing it to slip through the fingers to the ground at "The Order" (No. I.).

Arms must never be trailed with fixed swords, except by the front rank before charging.

XXIII.

Shoulder–Arms.
Two. } As detailed in No. II.

XXIV.

Sling–Arms.
The Sling.—Seize the rifle as in the first motion of "The Present Arms" (No. III.).

Two.
Bring the rifle across the body, turning the barrel to the front, so that the sling may pass over the left shoulder; then seize the sling with the right hand close over the left shoulder.

Three.
Bring the rifle down under the left arm, left hand close to the upper band, and resting against the thigh, forefinger slanting downwards between the stock and barrel; at the same time drop the right hand to the side.

XXV.

Shoulder–Arms.
The Shoulder from the Sling.—Raise the muzzle and bring the rifle to the right side with the left hand, seizing it with the right hand at "The Shoulder."

Two.
Drop the left hand to the side.

XXVI.

Order–Arms.
Two. } As detailed in No. XI.

Great care must be taken to preserve the squareness of the body and to avoid raising or sinking the shoulder in the foregoing exercises.

XXVII.

Ground–Arms. { *Ground Arms.*—Turn the rifle on the heel, lock to the rear, sink the body, bending both knees; and place the rifle flat on the ground, the lock up, muzzle inclining to the right front, hammer in line with the heels; rise at once, and return to the position of attention.

XXVIII.

Take-up-Arms. { Sink the body as in grounding arms, take up the rifle, and come to "The Order" (No. I.)

XXIX.

The Short Trail.—Raise the rifle from the ground, keeping the barrel close to the shoulder.

XXX.

Stand at–Ease. { Push the muzzle of the rifle to the front with the right hand, arm close to the side; at the same time carry back the right foot as described in Part I., Section 2.*

The Secure.—For the protection of the rifle in wet weather, the soldier will be allowed to carry it as follows:—

* Not reproduced in this edition

MANUAL EXERCISE FOR THE SHORT RIFLE. 227

The rifle to be under the right arm, butt to the rear, the hammer to be close up under the armpit, the barrel slanting downwards and inclining to the left front; the rifle to be firmly grasped with the right hand, which is to be rather lower than the hip; right elbow a little to the rear. On the word *Change Arms*, the rifle to be carried under the left arm in like manner.

2. *In Quick Time.*

As described in No. 2 of the preceding Section.

3. *Motions of the Rifle performed on the March.*

The recruit will learn to perform the following motions of the rifle while marching; they may be taught at first while he is marking time; each motion to be done on the left foot, as described in No. 3 of the preceding Section.

When soldiers standing in line with unfixed swords step off from "The Order," they will come to "The Trail" as they take the first step;—when standing in line with swords fixed, or in files, they will come to "The Shoulder"; returning, in each case, to "The Order," when they halt or halt and front;—when marching in line or to a flank in fours with trailed arms, and ordered to turn into file, or form two deep, they will come to "The Shoulder" as they turn or form, and will trail again on turning from file into line, or forming fours;—when they halt and front from file they will order.

When soldiers standing with shouldered arms receive the command *Slow* (or *Quick*) *March*, they will step off, remaining at "The Shoulder;" when the word is *Double March*, they will come to "The Slope."

When soldiers marching with sloped arms and unfixed

swords are halted, they will come to "The Order;" when swords are fixed, to "The Shoulder."

When a soldier with trailed arms is required to turn to the right (or left) about, he will bring his rifle to a perpendicular position by a turn of the wrist on the first pace of the turn, and having completed his turn in three paces, will trail again on the fourth, the pace on which he steps off in his new direction;—if at "The Slope," he will bring the rifle to a perpendicular position on the first pace of the turn, and slope again on the fourth pace.

The above rules will equally apply when the soldier is ordered to mark time from the halt.

When men standing with ordered arms are directed to form fours, to close to the right or left, to step back, or to take any named number of paces to the front, they will come to "The Short Trail."

Soldiers will never be marched off from "The Order" when their arms are loaded, but will be directed to slope, except when required to move at "The Shoulder."

For directions for skirmishers and supports, *see* Part V. General Principles, No. X.*

Quick-March or *Mark Time-Quick.*	*From the Halt with ordered Arms.*—Step off (or commence marking time), bringing the rifle to "The Trail" as the first step is taken.
Shoulder-Arms.	*The Shoulder from the Trail.*—As on the halt.
Trail-Arms.	*The Trail from the Shoulder.*—As on the halt.

* Not reproduced in this edition

MOTIONS OF THE SHORT RIFLE ON THE MARCH.

Change-Arms. — **Changing Arms at the Trail.**—Raise the rifle to a perpendicular position at the right side; carry it to the left side, and pass it into the left hand, then lower it to "The Trail," at the same time dropping the right hand to the side.

Change-Arms. — Change the rifle back to the right side in a similar manner.

Shoulder-Arms. — As already taught.

Slope-Arms. — As on the halt.

Change-Arms. — **Changing Arms at the Slope.**—Pass the left hand up quickly and seize the small of the butt, fingers and thumb round the stock; at the same time seize the butt with the right hand, two first joints of the fingers round the stock, thumb in front of the heel; raise the rifle to a perpendicular position, carry it across the body and place it on the right shoulder, then drop the left hand to the side.

Change-Arms. — Carry the rifle back to the left shoulder in a similar manner.

Squad-Halt. — Halt and come at once to "The Order."

Charging.—Soldiers will be taught to charge as follows:

Fix-Swords. — As already taught.

Shoulder-Arms. — As already taught.

Quick-March. — Step off at the shoulder.

As a Front Rank, Prepare to Charge.	Bring the rifle to "The Trail" without losing the square position of the body or the regularity of the step.
Charge.	Bring the rifle to the position of "The Charge" (No. XI.,) and increase the pace to the double march.
As a Rear Rank, Prepare to Charge.	Bring the rifle to "The Slope" as on the halt.
Charge.	Break into the double march, continuing at "The Slope."
Squad— Halt.	Halt and come to "The Shoulder," both as a front and rear rank.

Fixing Swords on the March.—When soldiers are required to fix swords while marching with trailed arms, they will change the rifle into the left hand, then draw the sword with the right hand, bringing it out of the scabbard between the left arm and the body, inclining the barrel of the rifle upwards, muzzle opposite the left breast, and fix the sword as on the halt; this done, they will carry the rifle with the left hand to the right side, seize it at "The Shoulder," and drop the left hand to the side, continuing to move on with shouldered arms.

S. 3. *The Manual Exercise for the Long and Short Rifle in Two Ranks, and Piling Arms.*

1. *Manual Exercise in Two Ranks.*—When recruits have been taught all the motions of the manual exercise, either singly or in squads in single rank, they will be practised in squads of two ranks.

2. *Movements performed at Open and Close Order.*—The manual exercise is performed with the ranks at open order. Before troops formed in line are required to salute by presenting arms, the rear rank will be ordered to take open order; but when they salute in quarter distance column, they will present in close order.

3. *Distance between Ranks with trailed Arms.*—For the instructions on this head, see Part I., Section 38.*

4. *Motions of both Ranks the same.*—The motions of the rifle in the manual exercise are performed in the same manner by both ranks, excepting in "The Charge."

5. *Piling Arms.*—In addition to the motions of the rifle taught in single rank, the squad in two ranks will be taught to pile arms as follows; ranks standing at close order.

Pile—

On the word *Pile*, the rear rank will take a pace of nine inches to the rear, and the front-rank men will draw back the right foot ready to face to the right about.

Arms.

On the word *Arms*, the front rank will face about, bringing their rifles with them at the short trail; the whole will then place the butts of their rifles between their feet, locks from them; after which the right file rear rank and the left file front rank will incline their rifles

---

* Not reproduced in this edition

towards each other, and cross rods. This done, the front-rank man of the right file will with his left hand seize the rifle of the front-rank man of his left file by the muzzle, bearing it from him, and with his right hand lock rods by passing his own by the left of the rods and to the right of the muzzles of the other rifles; lastly, the left file rear rank will lodge his rifle between the muzzles of the rifles of the front rank, sling uppermost. When there is an odd file, each man of the file will lodge his rifle against the pile nearest his right hand.

Stand–clear. Ranks take a pace of nine inches backwards and face towards the pivot flank.

Stand–to. Ranks facing towards the pivot flank will face inwards and close on their arms by taking a pace of nine inches forward.

Unpile– On the word *Unpile,* seize the rifle with the right hand under the top band, the front-rank men at the same time drawing back their right feet ready to face to the right about.

Arms. On the word *Arms,* unlock the rods without hurry, by inclining the butts inwards, and come to "The Order." The front rank will then *front,* and the rear rank close on it by taking a pace of nine inches forward.

It is necessary to be careful in piling and unpiling arms to prevent damage being done to the rods and sights.

S. 4. *The Platoon Exercise for the Long and Short Snider Breech-loading Rifle.*

The recruit, having acquired a thorough knowledge of the several motions of the rifle as detailed in the MANUAL EXERCISE, will next be taught the PLATOON EXERCISE. The squad to fall in at "The Order."

The recruit will be instructed:—
1stly. To load and fire standing.
2ndly. To fire and load kneeling.

Each of these exercises will be taught:—
1stly. By Numbers.
2ndly. In Quick Time.

The motions of the long and of the short rifle, and as a front and rear rank being, with few exceptions, alike, it has only been considered necessary to describe separately the parts where any difference exists.

Squads are not to be instructed in the Platoon Exercise by Numbers, either standing or kneeling, otherwise than in single rank.

1. *To Load and Fire standing, by Numbers, from " The Order."*

Caution,—*Platoon Exercise by Numbers, as a Front* (or *Rear*) *Rank standing.*

Load.
⎧ Turn on both heels to the right-half face, carrying the rifle round with the body; and, with the long rifle, place the thumb of the right hand behind the barrel to seize it. The right foot to point to the right, the left to the front, eyes to look to the front.

Two.
Advance the left foot, moving the body with it, ten inches to the left front (viz., six to the front and eight to the left), toes to point to the front; at the

same time, bring the rifle to a horizontal position at the right side, with the small of the butt just in front of the right hip, grasping the stock with the left hand between the lower band and the projection in front of the lock plate, thumb between stock and barrel, and half-cock with the thumb of the right hand, fingers behind the trigger-guard. The left elbow to be kept close to the body as a support for the rifle,—the right hand to hold the small of the butt lightly, with the elbow to the rear, thumb resting on the comb of the hammer. As a rear rank, the left foot to be advanced six inches, the body moving with it, and the butt to be four inches above the hip.

Three.

Open the breech by a sharp turn of the right hand from left to right, then carry the hand to the pouch and take hold of a cartridge at the rim with the forefinger and thumb.

To open the breech, place the thumb on the thumb-piece of the breech-block, and the forefinger along the nipple-lump, the remaining fingers to be closed in the hand.

Four.

Put the cartridge into the barrel, pressing it well home with the thumb, and close the breech firmly by canting the breech-block to the left with the fingers; then carry the hand to the small of the butt, and hold it lightly with the fingers behind the trigger-guard, thumb pointing to the muzzle.

PLATOON EXERCISE. 235

When the feet are at right angles, as detailed in the 2nd motion, care must be taken not to increase the angle by turning the toes of the right foot to the rear, which would tend to alter the proper position of the right shoulder in firing.

At — yards.
Ready.
{ Adjust the back-sight—full-cock with the thumb of the right hand, fingers behind the trigger-guard—and fix the eyes steadfastly on some object in front. Thumb to point to the muzzle after cocking.

The back-sight will be adjusted as follows:—With the forefinger and thumb of the right hand, move the sliding bar until the top is even with the line, or at the place on the flanges showing the distance named; then, if necessary, raise the flap carefully, preventing it from springing up with a jerk, and afterwards carry the hand back to the small of the butt.

Present.
{ Bring the rifle smartly to the shoulder, pointing the muzzle a few inches below the object on which the right eye is fixed, and place the forefinger round the trigger like a hook, but without pressing it, that part between the first and second joint to rest on it.

The centre of the butt to be pressed firmly to the shoulder with the left hand,—the top of the butt to be even with the top of the shoulder,—the left elbow to be under the rifle as a support—the right elbow to be raised nearly square with, (but not too high), and well in front of, the right shoulder; to form a bed for the butt,—the right hand to hold the small of the butt lightly, thumb pointing to the muzzle—the left eye to be closed. This

PART III.—RIFLE EXERCISES.

Two. motion is to be performed without moving the left hand from its grasp, or bending the body, or raising the heels.

Raise the muzzle steadily, until the top of the fore-sight is brought in a line with the object through the notch of the back-sight, pressing the trigger at the same time without the least motion of the hand, eye, or arm, until the hammer falls, still keeping the eye fixed on the object.

Three. Bring the rifle to a horizontal position at the right side,—shut down the flap of the back-sight, if raised, without moving the sliding bar,—half-cock,—open the breech,—and, holding the breech-block firmly with the forefinger and thumb, by means of the thumb-piece and nipple-lump, draw it back as far as possible by a jerk, raising the muzzle of the rifle slightly in doing so, to remove the empty cartridge-case,—let the breech-block go back, and at the same time cant the rifle sharply over to the right by a turn of the wrist, to allow the case to fall out, bringing the rifle again to the horizontal position,—then carry the right hand to the pouch, and take hold of a cartridge at the rim with the forefinger and thumb.

Four. Proceed with the 4th motion of the "*Load*" (No. 1) as before detailed.

As the first motion of the "*Present*" will not be learned without practice and much care, the instructor will frequently give the command *As you were*, when the recruit

PLATOON EXERCISE.

will bring the rifle to the right side without moving any part of his body but his arms, or his eyes from the object to be aimed at. The instructor will then point out the defects observed. By this means the recruit will soon be accustomed to get into the position readily, and will acquire a full command of his rifle with the left hand.

The squad will also be brought back to the "*Ready*" by the command *As you were* after the 1st and 2nd motions of the "*Present*," for the instructor to explain that which follows next in order; the recruits maintaining the erect position of the body, and keeping the eyes fixed on the object they are to aim at.

Particular attention is to be given to the following points in the "*Present*." The body is to be firm and upright,—the butt to be pressed firmly into the hollow of the shoulder, so as to avoid the kick which will otherwise take place from the recoil on the explosion of the powder,—the rifle to rest solidly on the left hand, and to be firmly grasped, but without rigidity of muscle,—the back-sight to be upright. In aiming, and pressing the trigger, the breathing to be restrained. The right eye to continue fixed on the object after snapping, to ascertain if the aim has been deranged by the movement of the trigger or body. The position of the head with reference to the butt, when taking aim, must depend entirely on the elevation used. With small elevation, the butt must be brought to the head by raising the shoulder, or the cheek must be so placed on the butt, by bending the head a little forward (not sideways), as to get the eye fixed on the object through the notch of the back-sight; as the distances increase, the head must be raised or the shoulder lowered.

When giving the command *Ready*, some distance should always be named; if, however, the distance be omitted the soldier must judge it for himself, and adjust his sight accordingly.

Too much pains cannot be taken to ensure that the soldier takes a deliberate aim at some object whenever he brings the rifle to the "*Present:*" for this purpose, small bulls-eyes are to be marked on the barrack wall.

2. *To Shoulder, Slope, or Order Arms by Numbers, from the position of "Load" standing.*

	To Shoulder or Slope with the Long Rifle.	To Shoulder with the Short Rifle.
By Numbers, Shoulder (or *Slope*) *Arms.*	On the word *Arms*, turn on the right heel to the front; at the same time bring the left foot back to the right, and the rifle with the right hand to "The Shoulder," the fingers of the right hand to be under the hammer, and close to the lockside of the stock, thumb between stock and barrel;—or to "The Slope," the right hand still holding the small of the butt.	On the word *Arms*, turn on the right heel to the front; at the same time bring the left foot back to the right, and raise the rifle to a perpendicular position at the right side with the left hand, seizing it with the forefinger and thumb of the right hand round the trigger-guard, the remaining fingers under the hammer; the left hand to hold the rifle under the lower band.
Two.	Drop the right hand smartly to the side.	Drop the left hand smartly to the side.

To Order.

Order—Arms. On the word *Arms*, turn on the right heel to the front; at the same time bring the left foot back to the right, and with the right hand, which is to seize the rifle close in front of the left, place the butt quietly on the ground at the right side, as detailed in the Manual Exercise.

PLATOON EXERCISE.

3. *To come to the "Ready" standing by Numbers, from "The Shoulder," "The Slope," or "The Order."*

	From "The Shoulder" or "The Slope" with the Long Rifle.	From "The Shoulder," with the Short Rifle.
By Numbers, As a Front, (or *Rear*) *Rank. At — yards. Ready.*	Turn on both heels to the right-half face, and at the same time seize the rifle with the right hand at the small of the butt.	Turn on both heels to the right-half face, and at the same time seize the rifle with the left hand under the lower band, bending the right arm slightly to do so.

Two. { Advance the left foot, moving the body with it; at the same time bring the rifle to a horizontal position at the right side, as detailed in the 2nd motion of the "*Load*" (No. 1),—adjust the back-sight,—full-cock—and fix the eyes on some object in front.

From "The Order."

By Numbers, As a Front, (or *Rear*) *Rank. At — yards. Ready.* } Proceed as directed in the first motion of the "*Load*" (No. 1).

Two. { Proceed as above directed in the 2nd motion of the "*Ready*" from "The Shoulder."

4. *To Fire a Volley and Shoulder (Slope, or Order) standing, by Numbers, from the position of "Load," when it is not intended to re-load.*

Caution,—*By Numbers, Fire a Volley and Shoulder (Slope, or Order).*

At — yards. Ready. } As before detailed.

240 PART III.—RIFLE EXERCISES.

Present.
Two. } As before detailed.

Three. { As before detailed: and after throwing out the empty cartridge-case, shut the breech,—ease springs,—then rest a pause of the slow time, and, taking the time from the right, turn on the right heel to the front, and shoulder (slope, or order) at the same time; waiting a pause of quick time before quitting the hand, in coming to "The Shoulder" or "The Slope."

5. *To Load standing by Numbers, from "The Shoulder" or "The Slope."*

Caution,—*Platoon Exercise by Numbers, as a Front (or Rear) Rank standing.*

Load. { Proceed as directed for the 1st motion of the "*Ready*" from "The Shoulder" (No. 3).

Two.
Three.
Four. { Proceed as directed in the 2nd, 3rd, and 4th motions of the "*Load*" from "The Order" (No. 1).

6. *To Half-cock Arms if at the "Ready."*

Half-cock—
Arms. { Place the thumb of the right hand on the comb of the hammer, and the forefinger on the trigger, and draw both back until the sear is disengaged from the full bent of the tumbler,—then let the hammer gently down until it passes the half bent, and (removing the forefinger from the trigger) draw it back to the half bent again,—shut down the flap of the back-sight if raised,—and carry the right

PLATOON EXERCISE.

hand to the small of the butt, fingers behind the trigger-guard, thumb pointing to the muzzle.

7. To Ease-springs when at the Half-cock.

Ease-springs. — Place the thumb of the right hand on the comb of the hammer, and the forefinger on the trigger, and draw both back until the sear is disengaged from the half bent of the tumbler,—then let the hammer gently down (removing the forefinger from the trigger) on the nipple,—and carry the right hand to the small of the butt, fingers behind the trigger-guard, thumb pointing to the muzzle.

8. To unload when it is not required to fire off the charge.

Unload—Rifles. — When at the position of "*Load*," open the breech,—draw the breech-block back as far as possible by a jerk, raising the muzzle of the rifle slightly in doing so to withdraw the cartridge; let the breech-block go back, and at the same time cant the rifle sharply over to the right to allow the cartridge to fall into the hand: —then shut the breech with the fingers, bringing the rifle again to the horizontal position,—return the cartridge to the pouch,—and ease springs.

9. To Load and Fire standing, in Quick Time.

The recruit having been thoroughly instructed in the Platoon Exercise by Numbers, standing, will next be taught to perform it in Quick Time by the following words of command, which are to be executed as before detailed, resting a pause of quick time between each motion.

PART III.—RIFLE EXERCISES.

Caution,—*Platoon Exercise as a Front* (or *Rear*) *Rank standing.*

Load.	In four motions.
At — yards. }	
Ready. }	In one motion.
Present.	In four motions.
Shoulder (Slope, or Order)—Arms. }	In two motions;—one motion for " The Order."
Fire a Volley, and Shoulder (Slope, or Order). At — yards. Ready. }	In two motions.
Present. {	In three motions, and having closed the breech, eased springs, &c., turn to the front and shoulder (slope or order).

10. *To Fire and Load kneeling, by Numbers.*

The squad having loaded standing, and being at " The Order," " The Shoulder," or " The Slope," will be instructed as follows.

Caution,—*By Numbers, as a Front* (or *Rear*) *Rank kneeling, fire a Volley.*

At — yards.
Ready.

Proceed as detailed for the 1st motion of the "*Ready*" from "The Shoulder" or "The Order" (No. 3).

Two.

Bring the rifle to a horizontal position at the right side as in the 2nd motion of the "*Load*" from "The Order" (No. 1); at the same time, sink on the right knee twelve inches to the rear and six to the right of the left heel, and square with the right foot, bringing the weight of the body at once on the right heel, and place the left forearm six inches behind, and nearly square with, the left knee, the butt to rest against the right side;—then adjust the back-sight—full-cock,—and fix the eyes on some object in front.

The right knee of the rear rank to be twelve inches to the right when on the ground; the left forearm on, and nearly square with, the left knee.

As the length of the leg in very tall men is greater than the breadth of the body, it will be impossible, in close order, to get the knee square with the foot; in such cases, therefore, the knee is to be inclined to the front, but not beyond the inside of the right foot of the man on the right.

Present. As detailed when firing standing, placing the left elbow at once over the left knee as a support. The body is not to be raised off the heel in bringing the rifle to the shoulder.

Two. As detailed when firing standing.

Three. As detailed when firing standing, bringing the left forearm on the left leg as directed in the 2nd motion of the "*Ready*" kneeling (No. 10).

Four. As detailed when firing standing.

The instructions which follow the "*Present*" standing are applicable to this position when on the knee.

When required to come to the "*Ready*" kneeling from the position of "*Load*" standing, the left foot will be brought back to the right before sinking on the knee.

11. *To Shoulder, Slope, or Order Arms by Numbers, from the position of " Load " kneeling.*

By Numbers, Shoulder (or *Slope*)—*Arms.* On the word *Arms*, spring to *attention*, turning on the left heel to the front, and shoulder (or slope) at the same time as before detailed.

Two. Drop the hand smartly to the side.

Order—Arms. { On the word *Arms,* spring to *attention,* turning on the left heel to the front, and order at the same time as before detailed.

12. *To Fire a Volley and Shoulder (Slope, or Order), by Numbers, from the position of "Load" kneeling, when it is not intended to re-load.*

Caution.—*By Numbers, Fire a Volley and Shoulder (Slope or Order).*

At — yards.
Ready. { Adjust the back-sight—full-cock,— and fix the eyes on some object in front.

Present.
Two. } As before detailed.

Three. { As before detailed: and after throwing out the empty cartridge-case, shut the breech,—ease springs,—then rest a pause of slow time, and, taking the time from the right, spring to *attention,* turning on the left heel to the front, and shoulder (slope, or order) at the same time; waiting a pause of quick time before quitting the hand, in coming to " The Shoulder " or " The Slope."

13. *To Fire and Re-load kneeling, in Quick Time.*

The recruit having been thoroughly instructed in the motions of firing and loading on the knee by Numbers, will next be taught to perform them in Quick Time by the following words of command, which are to be executed as before detailed, resting a pause of quick time between each motion.

Caution.—*As a Front,* (or *Rear*) *Rank kneeling, Fire a Volley.*

At — yards.
Ready. } In two motions.

Present. In four motions.

Shoulder (Slope, or Order)—Arms. In two motions.

As a Front (or *Rear*) *Rank kneeling, Fire a Volley and Shoulder (Slope or Order).*
At — yards.
Ready.
} In two motions; one motion for "The Order."

Present. { In three motions, and having closed the breech, eased springs, &c., spring to *attention* to the front, and shoulder (slope, or order) at the same time.

14. Loading and Firing in two Ranks.

When the recruit has learned all the motions of the Platoon Exercise, standing and kneeling, in single rank, he will practise them in two ranks; also the following modes of firing:—

1. Volleys, both ranks standing } with the long rifle,
2. Volleys, both ranks kneeling } only.
3. Volleys, front rank kneeling.
4. Independent firing, both ranks standing.
5. Independent firing, both ranks kneeling.
6. Independent firing, front rank kneeling.

With the long rifle, except in square, when it is required to fire volleys otherwise than with both ranks standing, the caution *Fire a volley* will be preceded by the words "*Front rank* (or *Both ranks*) *kneeling.*"

With the short rifle, except in square, Volley firing will invariably take place front rank kneeling, without any previous caution to that effect.

In Independent firing, if required to kneel, the caution will be preceded by the words "*Both ranks* (or *Front rank*) *kneeling.*"

In both Volley and Independent firing, the rank (or ranks) required to kneel will sink on the knee on the word "*Ready.*"

PART III.—RIFLE EXERCISES.

Upon the following *cautions* for loading and firing, the rear rank will take a pace of nine inches to the front; resuming its distance on returning to "The Shoulder," "The Slope," or "The Order."

For Loading.

Platoon Exercise.
As with Cartridge.
With Blank (or *Ball*) *Cartridge.*
} With the long rifle, only.

For Firing.

Fire a Volley. (With the long rifle, only.)
Independent firing.
Prepare for Cavalry.

15. *Independent firing standing or kneeling.*

Caution,—*Independent firing.*

At — yards.
Ready.
} As before detailed.

Commence— firing.
{ Each man of the front rank will come to the "*Present*" independently of his right or left hand man, and, when he returns to the position of "*Load*," his rear rank man will come to the "*Present*," and so continue alternately until the " Cease firing" is ordered. The flap or the back-sight, if raised, is not to be put down until after the last round is fired.

It is to be observed that, when firing both ranks standing or both kneeling, the two men of a file are not to be at the "*Present*" at the same time. When the front rank man is at the position of "*Load*," the rear rank man is to come to the "*Present*," and *vice versâ*, to keep up a continuous fire.

PLATOON EXERCISE. 247

Cease—firing. { Each file, when it completes its loading, will slope arms if armed with the long rifle, order if armed with the short rifle. Files that may have made ready when this command is given will half-cock their rifles before they slope or order arms.

When firing independently, as above detailed, the commands *Commence firing*, and *Cease firing*, are to be given on the drum or bugle.

The Platoon Review Exercise is detailed in S. 10.

In all firings, except in the case of a battalion volley, and in firing by wings, the officer commanding the company will fall to the rear of its centre on the caution; returning to his post when the men come to "The Slope" or "The Order."

S. 5. *Preparing for Cavalry.*

The recruits, having a thorough knowledge of the different modes of firing in the ranks, will now be formed into four ranks, and practised to receive cavalry, as in square, four deep.

This practice will be commenced on the march with sloped (or trailed) arms; on the command *Halt;* or *Halt, right-about-face,* the men will order arms and fix bayonets (or swords). When the movement is performed from the halt, the front company will order and fix bayonets (or swords) when the remainder get the command *Quick-march.* The men who halt without word of command will in either case order and fix as they halt.

Prepare for— Cavalry. { The second and fourth ranks will take a pace of nine inches to the front.

Ready. { The first and second ranks will sink at once upon the right knee, as a front and rear rank, and, at the same time, place the butts of their rifles (which are not to be full-cocked) on the ground against the inside of their right knees, locks uppermost, with the muzzles slanting upwards so that the point of the bayonet or sword may be about the height of a horse's nose; the left hand to grasp the rifle firmly immediately above the lower band, the right hand to hold the small of the butt, the left arm to rest upon the leg about six inches from the knee. The third and fourth ranks will come to the "*Ready*" (the muzzles of their rifles slightly inclined upwards), adjust the back-sight, full-cock, and fix their eyes on some object in front.

Independent firing— or, *Front* (or *Rear*) *face*, or *Right* (or *Left*) *face*, or *Front and Rear* (or *Right and Left*) *faces, Independent firing— Commence.*   Proceed with the independent firing as before detailed.

Cease—firing.   As before detailed.

Kneeling Ranks (or *Kneeling Ranks of the— face.*)—*Fire a Volley.*   This caution to be given, should it be deemed necessary to fire a volley.

MODES OF FIRING.

At — yards.
Ready.
{ Come to the loading position, bringing the weight of the body on the right heel, and proceed as before detailed.

Present.
{ As before detailed, and after loading, should there be time, bring the rifle at once to resist Cavalry; if there is not time to load before coming down, the loading is to take place on the knee, by word of command.

Order — Arms.
{ This command will apply also to the standing ranks, if at "The Slope."

The above detail applies equally to squares formed two or three deep, with the exception that the front rank only will kneel to resist Cavalry.

S. 6. *To fire a Feu-de-Joie.*

For this mode of firing the line will be drawn up at open order, as described in Part IV., S. 4*; except that the commanding officer will take post in the rear.

With Blank Cartridge, Load. } Muzzles of rifles to slant upwards when loading.

Ready.   Full-cock the rifle.

Present.   Rifles to be elevated at an angle of 45°.

The right-hand man of the front rank commences the fire, which will run down the front and up the rear, as quickly as possible. When the right-hand man of the rear rank has fired, the whole will glance their eyes to the right to bring the rifle to the loading position and load, and remain steady, waiting for the word.

Ready,
Present.
} As before directed.

The same to be repeated a third time.

After the third fire, having removed the empty cartridge-

---
* Not reproduced in this edition

case, &c., the whole will remain steady at the loading position.

Shoulder—Arms.

The commanding officer will then move to the front and give the following commands:—

Present—Arms.
Shoulder—Arms.
Order—Arms.
Three cheers.

When artillery are present and are ordered to fire 21 guns, seven will be fired before each round of the feu-de-joie.

S. 7. *Street Firing.*

A column at open, half, or quarter distance, formed in a street or in narrow ground where deployment is impracticable, may be required to fire either when advancing or retiring. It will be performed in the following manner:—

1. *Street firing advancing.*—Three companies will be ordered to advance from the column, leaving sufficient room between them and the remainder of the column for a gun or body of cavalry to form. The second and third companies will close on the first. When required to fire, on the word THIRD COMPANY, BOTH RANKS STANDING, FIRE A VOLLEY, FIRST AND SECOND COMPANIES KNEELING. AT — YARDS, READY, the two front companies will kneel down, and on the word PRESENT the third will fire over their heads; the second company will then receive the word SECOND COMPANY, BOTH RANKS STANDING, FIRE A VOLLEY. AT — YARDS, READY, on which it will spring up, and on the word PRESENT will deliver its fire; lastly, the front company will fire kneeling: each company will as usual load as soon as it has fired. The front company may then be ordered to rise and charge, or the first and second companies may be ordered to open out to half distance from the rear, and all three then be wheeled back by sub-

MODES OF FIRING. 251

divisions to each side of the street to allow the gun to fire between them, or the cavalry to charge; it may occasionally be of use to extend files along each side of the street to fire up into the windows.

2. *Street firing and retiring.*— In retiring, the front company, after firing ten rounds, or less if ordered, will face outwards by sub-divisions, file to the rear, re-form company, load, and remain halted until its front is again clear, or the whole column is put in motion. The moment the front of the second company is clear it will give its fire in like manner, face outwards by sub-divisions, and file to the rear as above directed; and so on by companies in succession: when the front of the column occupies the whole breadth of the street, the outward files of companies will double in the rear, to give the companies, which have fired, room to pass.

It must never be forgotten, in entering towns or villages occupied by the enemy, that the first thing to be done, on gaining a footing in the place, is to clear the houses on both flanks, and the column should on no account proceed through the streets without previously occupying the houses on either hand: the troops employed for that purpose breaking through partition walls, or pushing on from house to house, so as to accompany the march of the main body and protect its flanks.

S. 8. *Application of the Modes of Firing.*

No definite rules can be laid down with respect to the application, on service, of the various modes of firing; the commanding officer must use his discretion on this point, being guided in his decision by the nature of the country, the description of troops with whom he is engaged, and the quality of the arms with which they are equipped. It is, however, very important that the men should be required to fire individually or by platoon in that position which will present the smallest object to the enemy, and at the same time give the greatest facility for moving forward or backward as may be ordered.

The following remarks are intended more as suggestions for parade purposes than as definite rules.

All movements should be covered by skirmishers firing independently. In all formations of line firing should commence after formation, as soon as the front is clear of the skirmishers; companies forming in succession should frequently be made to fire as soon as they are formed, which will accustom the remaining companies to move steadily during the noise of firing. The standing ranks of squares should be ordered to fire the moment the square has prepared for cavalry.

In firing by companies, when the first company comes to the loading position the next company will receive the words *At—yards—ready*. When firing from centre to flanks, the right centre company will commence, then the left centre company will take up the fire, then the company on the right of the right centre company, and so on alternately to the flanks.

S. 9. Rifle Exercises for Serjeants.

The serjeants of all infantry regiments will be taught the manual and platoon exercises for the short rifle.

Serjeants; when moving with their companies or with the battalion will remain with unfixed swords, except while they are escorting the colours, and when they are in a square, in which cases they will have their swords fixed.

Serjeants will stand at ease and come to attention with the men, they will also shoulder arms, slope or trail arms, and order arms with them, but will perform no other motions of the rifle with the men. The serjeants, during the performance of the manual and platoon exercises by the rank and file, will remain steady at the shoulder.

REVIEW EXERCISE. 253

Recover–Arms. ⎧ *The Recover.*—Serjeants will recover arms as follows :—Seize the rifle as directed in the first motion of "The Present Arms," then raise it perpendicularly in front of the face, right hand grasping the small of the butt, thumb as high as the mouth, barrel to the front; at the same time place the left hand under the butt, thumb in front of the heel, first two joints of the fingers round the side of the butt.

While a serjeant marking a point is extending an arm, as directed in Part IV., General Principle V.*, he will hold his rifle by the small of the butt with the other hand, resting the toe against his chest.

Serjeants marking points on which men are to dress when forming line will stand with recovered arms; when they mark the points for their companies to form upon simultaneously in column, as in forming on parade, they will take their distances and covering with recovered arms, and when they are correctly covered they will shoulder arms on the word *Steady* from the adjutant or other person dressing them; but when they mark the ground for their companies to form upon in succession, as in forming column from line, they will take up their covering with recovered arms, but will come to "The Shoulder" without word of command when correctly dressed. The serjeant giving a base point in front or rear of a flank company of formation, when forming column from line, and in closing on, or opening out from, a front or rear company in column, will remain at "The Recover" until the word *Steady* is given.

REVIEW EXERCISE.
S. 10. *Review Exercise.*

At inspections or reviews the manual and platoon exercise will be performed by the men judging their own time, as

* Not reproduced in this edition

PART III.—RIFLE EXERCISES.

directed in ss. 1 and 2, (No. 2.) and s. 4, of this Part. The men standing at ease at "The Order," with fixed bayonets, will be called to attention, and ordered to shoulder and take open order, as described in Part VII., Section 1; after which the words of command will be as follows:—

For the Long Rifle.

Caution. MANUAL—EXERCISE.
I. PRESENT—ARMS.
II. SHOULDER—ARMS.
III. PORT—ARMS.
IV. CHARGE—BAYONETS.
V. SHOULDER—ARMS.
VI. ADVANCE—ARMS.
VII. ORDER—ARMS.
VIII. ADVANCE—ARMS.
IX. SHOULDER—ARMS.
X. SUPPORT—ARMS.
XI. SHOULDER—ARMS.
XII. SLOPE—ARMS.
XIII. SHOULDER—ARMS.
XIV. ORDER—ARMS.
XV. UNFIX—BAYONETS.
REAR RANK TAKE CLOSE—ORDER. MARCH.

Caution. PLATOON—EXERCISE.
LOAD.
FIRE A VOLLEY AT 300 YARDS.
READY. PRESENT.
BOTH RANKS KNEELING.
FIRE A VOLLEY.
AT 300 YARDS.
READY. PRESENT.
FIRE A VOLLEY AND SHOULDER.
AT 300 YARDS.
READY. PRESENT.
ORDER—ARMS.
STAND AT—EASE.

For the Short Rifle.

Caution. MANUAL—EXERCISE.
I. PRESENT—ARMS.
II. SHOULDER—ARMS.
III. SUPPORT—ARMS.
IV. SHOULDER—ARMS.
V. ORDER—ARMS.
VI. FIX—SWORDS.
VII. SHOULDER—ARMS.
VIII. PORT—ARMS.
IX. CHARGE—SWORDS.
X. SHOULDER—ARMS.
XI. SLOPE—ARMS.
XII. SHOULDER—ARMS.
XIII. ORDER—ARMS.
XIV. UNFIX—SWORDS.
REAR RANK TAKE CLOSE—ORDER. MARCH.

Caution. PLATOON—EXERCISE.
LOAD.
FIRE A VOLLEY AT 300 YARDS.
READY. PRESENT.
FIRE A VOLLEY AND SHOULDER.
AT 300 YARDS.
READY. PRESENT.
ORDER—ARMS.
STAND AT—EASE.

INSPECTING A COMPANY.

S. 11. *Manner of Inspecting a Company on Parade.*
The Company to fall in at " The Order."
Fix—Bayonets (or *Swords*).
Rear rank take Open order—March.

The inspecting officer will now pass down the ranks to ascertain that the appointments, clothing, &c., are clean, and in good order.

Unfix—Bayonets (or *Swords*).
Shoulder—Arms.

For Inspection, { When at "The Port," half-cock the
Port—Arms. rifle, and open the breech, holding the block between the forefinger and thumb of the right hand by means of the thumb-piece and nipple-lump.

The officer will again go down the ranks to see that the breech-shoe and breech-block are free from rust, and otherwise clean, also to see that the breech-block is free in its action. Each soldier, as the officer approaches within one file of him, will turn the barrel of his rifle full to the front with his left hand, lock downwards, and draw back the breech-block with his right hand.

Rear rank take Close order—March.

Examine— { Both ranks will come to the position
Arms. of "The Charge," with the muzzle of the rifle so inclined as to enable the officer to look through the barrel. The rear-rank men, in turning to the right, will raise their rifles perpendicularly, so as to clear the front-rank men when coming down to the charge.

The officer will now proceed to look through each barrel to see that it is clean and free from rust. The soldier, when the officer passes the file nearest to him, will close the breech,—ease springs,—order arms,—and stand at ease.

PART III.—RIFLE EXERCISES.

BAYONET EXERCISE.

S. 11. *Bayonet or Sword Bayonet Exercise.*
1. *General Directions.*

Formation of Squad.—When recruits have been thoroughly instructed in the manual and platoon exercises and modes of firing, they will be taught the bayonet exrcise; for this purpose they will, in the first instance, be formed in squads of not more than sixteen men in single rank.

Method of Teaching.—The recruits will first be taught the exercises in slow and quick time by numbers, after which they will be taught to perform them judging their own time in the review exercise, and with such variation from the regular order of the drill as the instructor may require, frequently changing quickly from one movement to another.

Position.—In attaining a good and firm position, care must be taken not to allow the limbs to be rigid, as any stiffness will prevent the promptness of action requisite to give effect to the bayonet.

Giving Points at Marks.—In order to teach the recruit to deliver the thrust in a proper direction, a cross bar upon poles may be erected, from which balls can be suspended, and a squad being drawn up in front, should be practised in giving point at them.

2. *Preliminary Drill.*

The squad, having fallen in in single rank as above directed, will be formed into two deep, as follows:—

Shoulder–Arms.

Prepare for Bayonet-Exercise. } Odd numbers stand fast, even numbers face to the right about.

Quick–March. { Even numbers move four paces to the rear, halt and front.

Port–Arms. As usual.

Charge-Bayonets. { As usual. In the Bayonet Exercise, this is called the " First Position."

Preliminary Drill in Slow (or Quick) Time. } Caution.

BAYONET OR SWORD BAYONET EXERCISE.

The feet will be kept at right angles to each other throughout the following exercises.

Second-Position. — Draw back the right foot twenty-four inches, the body resting upon it, the heels in line with each other, both knees bent, and kept well apart, the right directly over the foot, the left easy and flexible, pointing to the front.

Third-Position. — Advance the body by extending the right leg and bending forward the left leg without moving or raising the feet.

Second-Position. — As before.

Advance. — Move forward the left foot six inches, and follow with the right the same length of step.

Retire. — Step back with the right foot six inches, and follow with the left the same length of step.

Double-Advance. — Bring up the right foot to the left, and step out again with the left to the "Second Position."

Double-Retire. — Bring the left foot back to the right, and step back again with the right to the "Second Position."

First-Position. — Bring up the right heel to the left, straightening the knees.

Shoulder-Arms. As usual, resuming the proper front.
Order-Arms.
Stand at-Ease.

In this and the following drills each movement will be repeated as often as may be necessary, but the recruit must not be kept too long in the same position; and when it is necessary for an awkward man to repeat any particular portion of the drill, the rest should be allowed to stand at ease.

258   PART III.—RIFLE EXERCISES.

3. *Guards and Points, by Numbers.*

Attention.
Shoulder–Arms.
Port–Arms.
Charge–Bayonets.
} As usual.

Guards and Points by Numbers; in Slow (or Quick) Time. } Caution.

Guard. — Fall back to the "Second Position," with the knees well apart, the back and neck bent and chest drawn in, the rifle retaining the position of "Charge Bayonet," except that the right wrist will be upon the upper part of the hip, the left elbow close to and in front of the body, the point of the bayonet directed towards the height of a man's breast. Plate XVII., Fig. 1.

Point. — Without quitting the hold or losing the balance of the rifle advance it gradually to the full extent of the arms; at the same time incline forwards to the "Third Position," the right elbow rather under and close to the stock, and lower the head, as in taking aim. Plate XVII., Fig. 2.

Two. — Resume slowly the position of "Guard."

Low-Guard. — Bring the rifle to the "Low Guard" by turning the sling uppermost, and raising the butt and right elbow as high as the head, the back of the hand towards the right ear, and the bayonet pointing downwards to the front. Plate XVIII., Fig. 1.

Point. — As before, but downwards; and as the rifle gradually descends, turn the barrel upwards. Plate XVIII., Fig. 2.

Two.	{ Resume the position of the "Low Guard."
High–Guard.	{ Bring the rifle to the "High Guard" by lowering the right wrist to the hip; the left hand to be opposite the breast. Plate XIX., Fig. 1.
Point.	As before, but upwards. Pl. XIX., Fig. 2.
Two.	{ Resume the position of the "High Guard."
Head–Parry.	{ Raise the rifle, turning the sling upwards till the left wrist is as high as, and opposite to, the forehead; the butt slanting downwards. Plate XX.
Two.	Return to the "High Guard."
Shorten–Arms.	{ Throw back the rifle to the full extent of the right arm, lowering the point of the bayonet direct to the front, the barrel resting upon the left arm, just above the elbow; and carry back the body by extending the left leg. Plate XXI.
Point.	{ As before, direct to the front, as in Plate XVII., Fig. 2.
Two.	Return to the "Shorten Arms."
Guard.	As before.
Shoulder–Arms.	As from the position of "*Load*" standing.
Order–Arms. *Stand at–Ease.*	} As usual.

When it is necessary to repeat a thrust in the above practice, the command "*As you were*" will be given instead of "*Two.*"

The first guard and point are intended to be used against a man on foot, on level ground; the low guard and point when standing on a height, such as a parapet, against a man below; the high guard and point against a man standing on a height, or against a mounted man. The thrust of a bayonet or lance can be parried by a slight movement of the rifle to the right or left when at either of the three guards. In order to protect the head from a sabre cut, the rifle will be raised to "The Head Parry."

4. *Guards and Points in an Oblique Direction by Numbers.*

Attention. *Shoulder—Arms.* *Port—Arms.* *Charge-Bayonets.*	As usual.
Variations of Guard and Point by Numbers, in Slow (or Quick) Time.	Caution.
Guard.	As before.
Right.	Keeping the feet steady, and retaining the position of "Guard," turn the body to the right front, so as to present the bayonet in that direction.
Point.	As before, to the right front.
Two.	Return to "Guard" to the right front.
Left.	Turn the body as before, but to the left front.
Point.	As before, to the left front.
Two.	Return to "Guard" to the left front.
Low—Guard. *Point.* *Two.*	As before, to the left front.
High—Guard. *Point.* *Two.*	As before, to the left front.
Right.	Retaining the position of the "High Guard," turn the body to the right front.
Point.	As before, to the right front.
Two.	Return to the "High Guard" to the right front.
Low—Guard. *Point.* *Two.*	As before, to the right front.

BAYONET OR SWORD BAYONET EXERCISE.

Guard.	As before.
Shoulder–Arms. ⎫ *Order–Arms.* ⎬ *Stand at–Ease.* ⎭	As before.

5. *Points to the Rear by Numbers.*

In order to bring the body and limbs into equal action on both sides, the preceding practices should be performed with the right shoulder and foot foremost, the squad being faced about, as follows:—

Attention. ⎫ *Shoulder–Arms.* ⎪ *Port–Arms.* ⎬ *Charge–* ⎪ *Bayonets.* ⎭	As usual.

The caution will be given as before, according to the exercise which is to be performed.

Guard.	As before.
About.	Straighten the knees and raise the rifle perpendicularly in front of the centre of the body; at the same time turn to the right about upon the heels, the right foot pointing to the proper rear, the left foot to its left, and smartly changing the hold of the rifle with the right hand at the balance, and grasping the small of the stock with the left hand, sink down again to the position of "Guard," by bending the knees, and bringing the weight of the body on the left leg.

6. *Exercises in Quick Time.*

The movements detailed in the preceding numbers having been taught in slow time, they will next be practised in quick time; that is, the movements explained in No. 2 will be made more rapidly, and in Nos. 3 and 4 the thrust will be delivered quicker, especially at the latter part, and in withdrawing the rifle on the word *Two*, the motion will also be quicker, especially at the commencement.

PART III.—RIFLE EXERCISES.

7. *Bayonet Exercise in Single Rank.*

The guards and points will also be practised in single rank without intervals, the squad being re-formed in single rank for that purpose.

The whole of the practices detailed in Nos. 2, 3, and 4 will then be performed, after which the squad will be brought to its proper front from the position of "Guard," as follows:—

About.   As before directed.

Shoulder–Arms.
Order–Arms.   } As usual.
Stand at–Ease.

8. *Review Exercise.*

In the review exercise the soldiers will perform the second motion, judging their own time without the word *Two*, the point being given, and the rifle drawn back to the position from which it was delivered in quick, but marked, time.

For this exercise the squad, company, or battalion will be drawn up in line.

Prepare for Bayonet Exercise. { The odd numbers of the front rank stand fast; the remainder, including the colour party, the captains, coverers, and supernumerary rank, go to the right about.

Quick–March. { Those who have faced about will move direct to the rear; the even numbers of the front rank, four paces; the odd numbers of the rear rank, seven paces; the even numbers of the rear rank, eleven paces; the colour party, captains, and coverers eighteen paces, and the supernumerary ranks fourteen paces; each man halting and fronting at his proper distance, and the ranks dressing by the right: after the captains have moved back as above directed, they will move to the rear of the centre of their companies.

Review Exercise.   Caution.

BAYONET OR SWORD BAYONET EXERCISE. 263

Guard. { Seize the small of the butt with the right hand, and come down at once to the position of " Guard."

Point. { Deliver the point to the front, rest a pause of slow time, and return to " Guard," each movement being swiftly and smartly executed.

The remaining points will be performed in like manner by the following commands, viz. : *Low–Guard, Point. High–Guard, Point. Head–Parry. Shorten–Arms, Point. Guard. Right, Point. Left, Point. Low–Guard, Point. High–Guard, Point. Right, Point. Low–Guard, Point. Guard. About.*

The above exercise will then be performed with the right shoulder and leg foremost, and when it is completed, line will be formed as follows :—

Shoulder–Arms, Form Line, Quick–March.—The ranks in rear will move up to their proper places in two deep.

Order–Arms. As usual.

Stand at–Ease. As usual.

9. *Review Exercise in two Ranks.*

The exercise should also be practised in two ranks without intervals, thus:—the men standing in the formation with intervals described in the preceding Section, will receive the command *Form Ranks, Quick–March ;* on which the even numbers of each rank will move up between the odd numbers; the odd (or even) numbers will then be faced about, so that the movements may be performed, by alternate men, to the front and rear at the same time.

10. *Review Exercise in Quick Time.*

When the men are perfect in the exercise, it may be performed without any further words of command than *Review Exercise in Quick Time—Guard,* upon which they will go regularly through the movements, executing them smartly, but resting a pause of slow time between each motion.

PLATE XI.

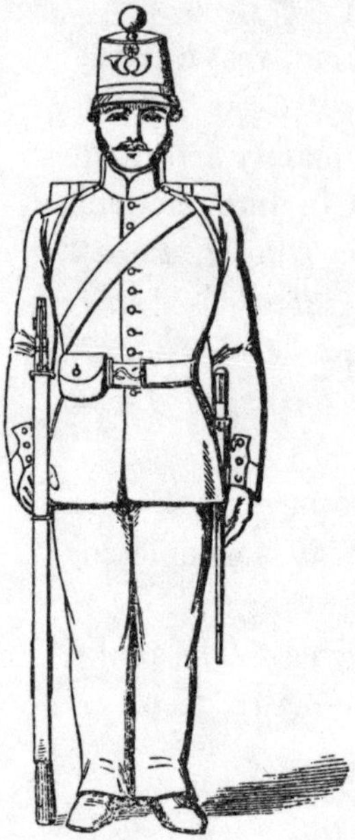

THE ORDER.

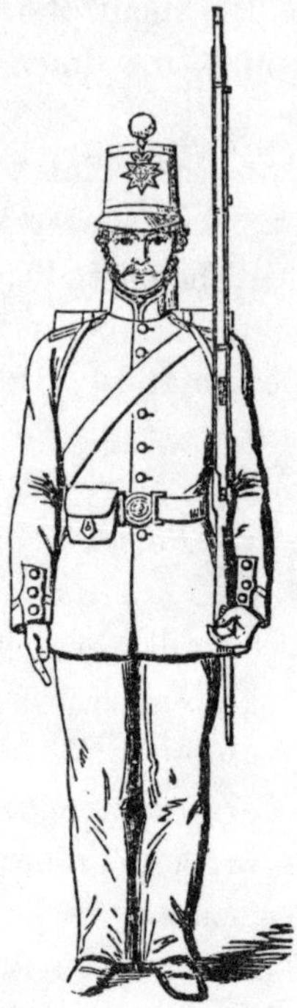

THE SHOULDER.

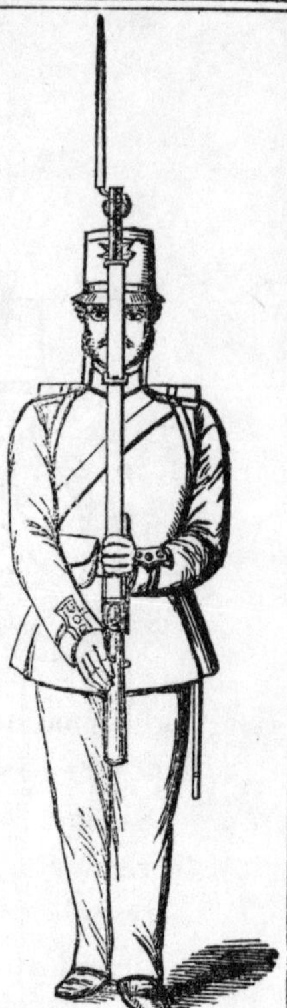

THE PRESENT.

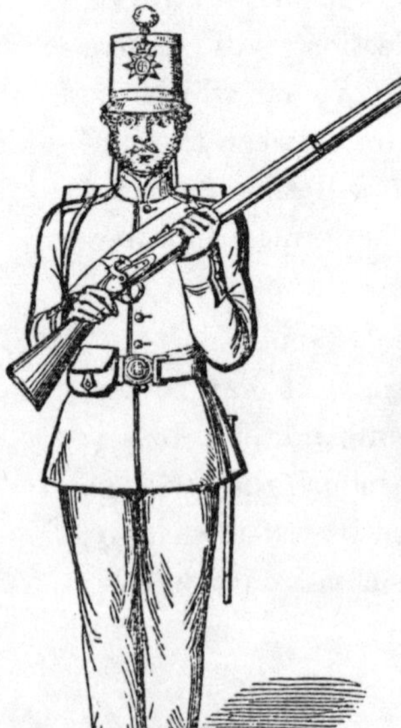

THE PORT.

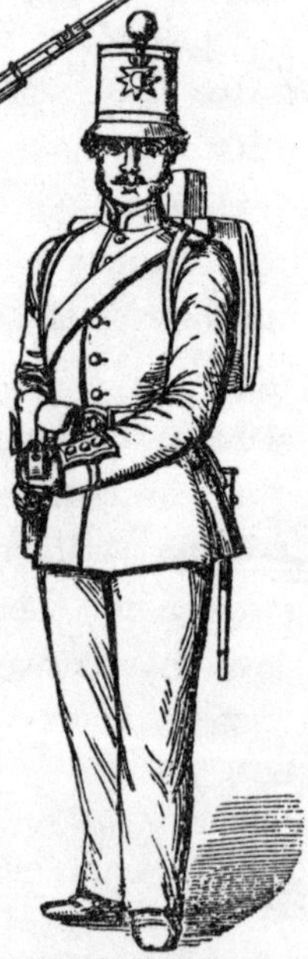

THE CHARGE.

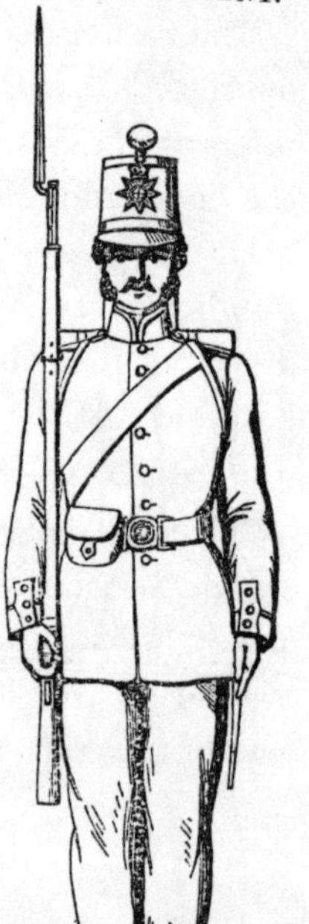

THE ADVANCE.

PLATE XII.

THE SUPPORT.

THE SLOPE.

THE TRAIL.

STAND AT EASE.

THE SECURE.

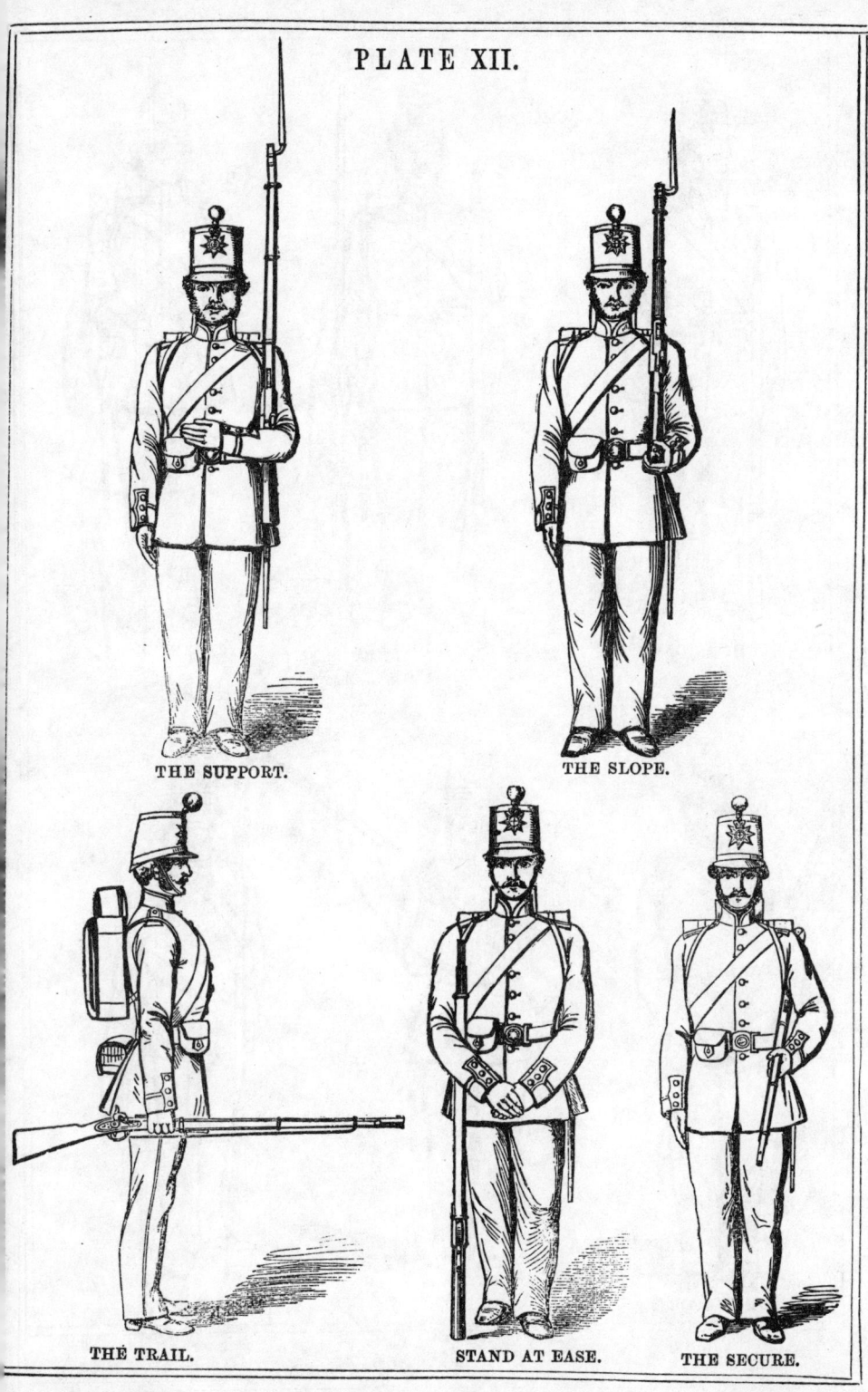

PLATE XIII.

THE ORDER.

THE SHOULDER.

THE PRESENT.

THE SUPPORT.

THE PORT.

THE CHARGE.

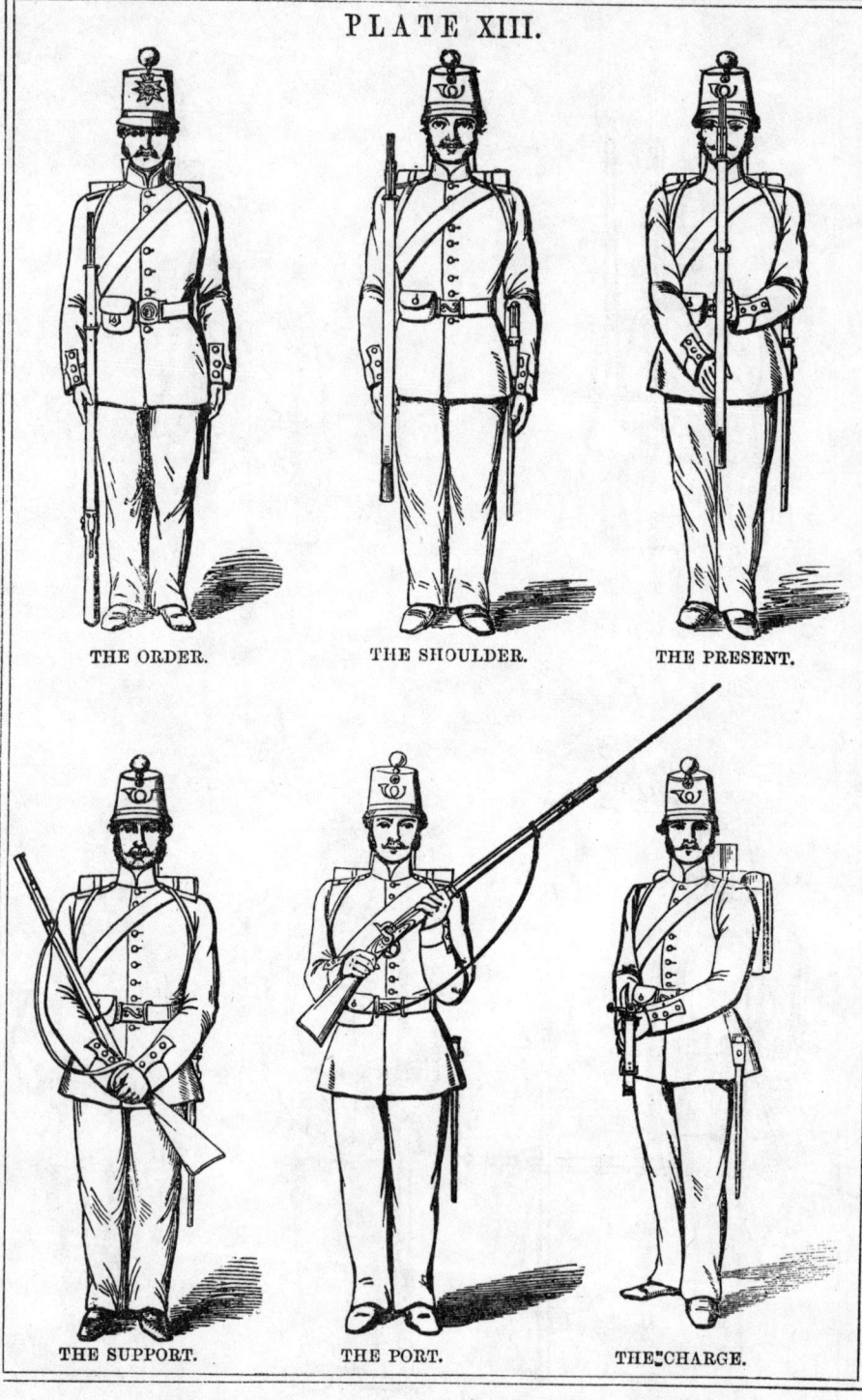

PLATE XIV.

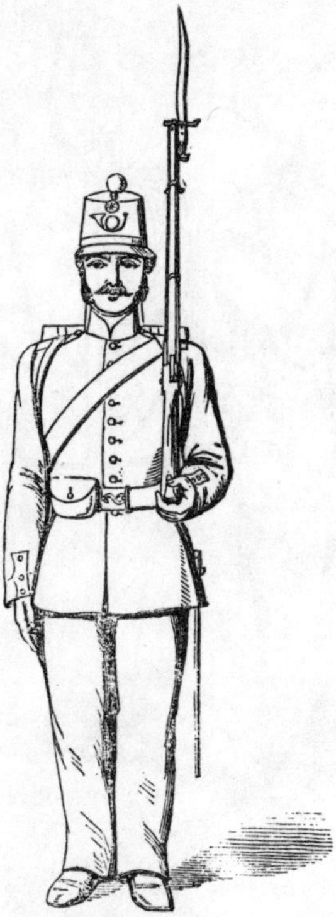

THE SLOPE.

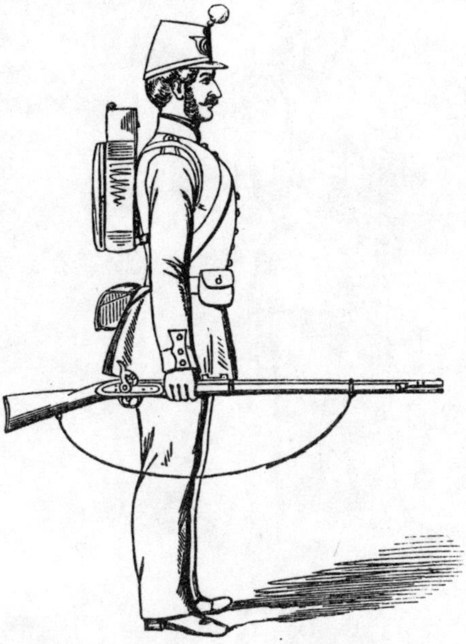

THE TRAIL.

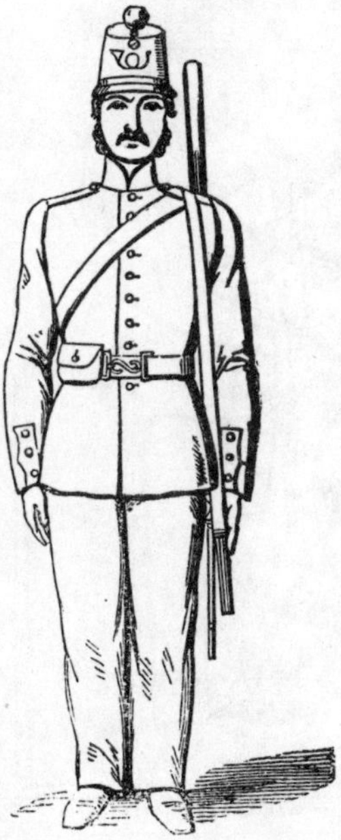

THE SLING.

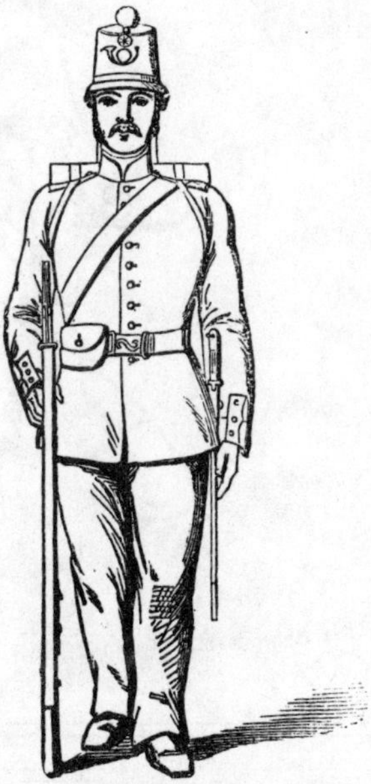

STAND AT EASE.

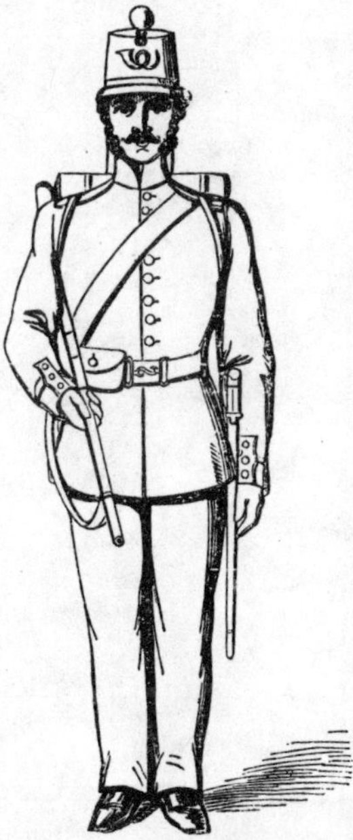

THE SECURE.

PLATE XV.

AS A FRONT RANK
STANDING, READY.

AS A REAR RANK STANDING,
PRESENT (1st Motion).

AS A FRONT RANK KNEELING,
READY.

AS A REAR RANK, KNEELING,
PRESENT (1st Motion).

PART III.—RIFLE EXERCISES.

PLATE XVI.

PREPARE FOR CAVALRY. READY.

PLATE XVII.

Fig. 1.

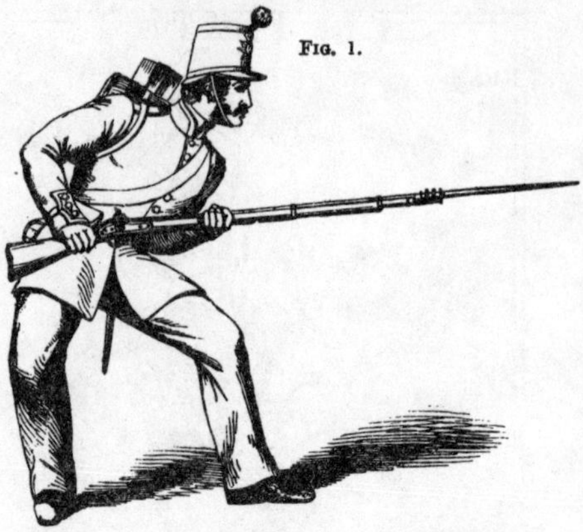

GUARD.

Fig. 2.

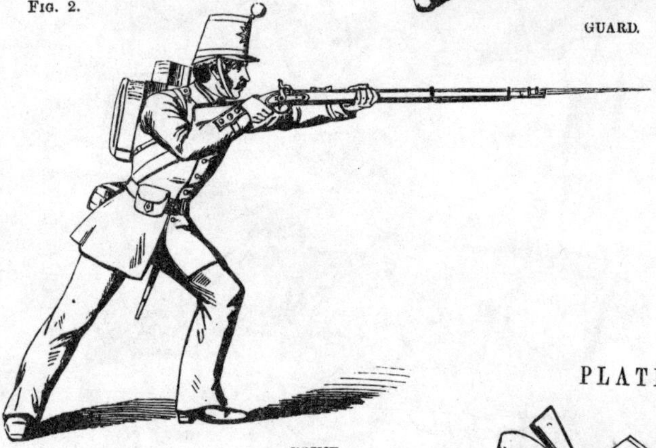

POINT.

PLATE XVIII.

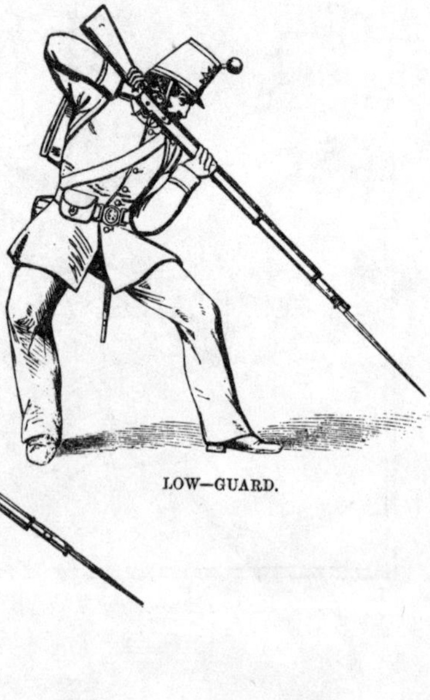

LOW—GUARD.

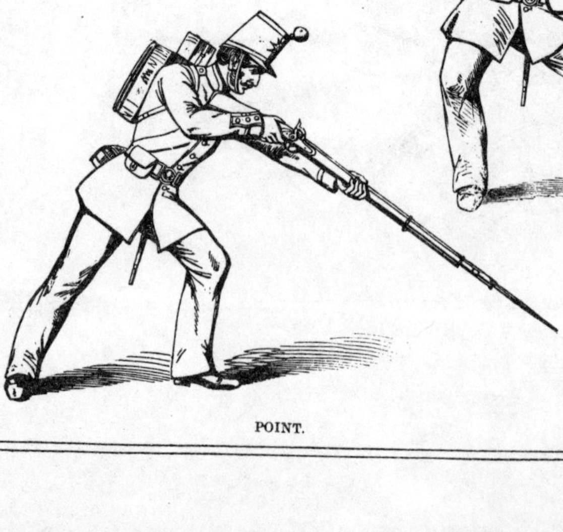

POINT.

PLATE XIX.

FIG. 1.

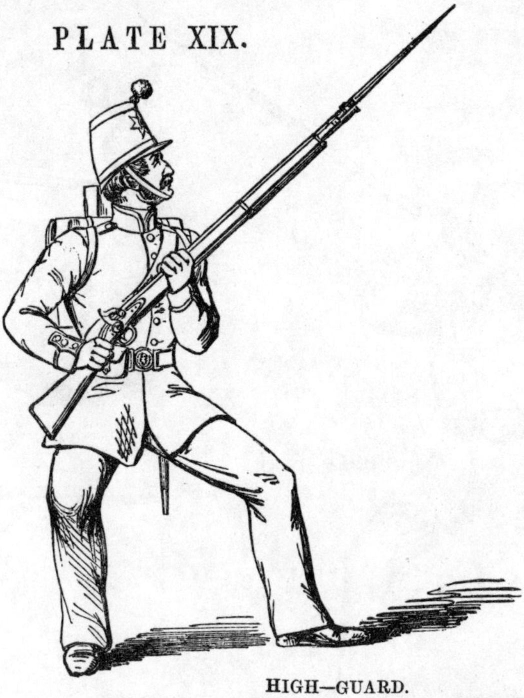

HIGH—GUARD.

FIG. 2.

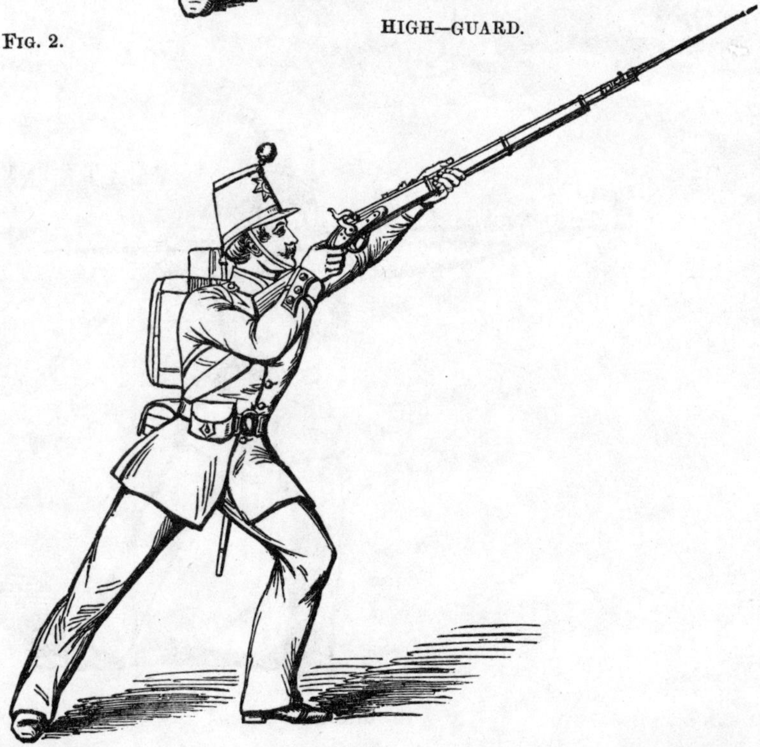

POINT.

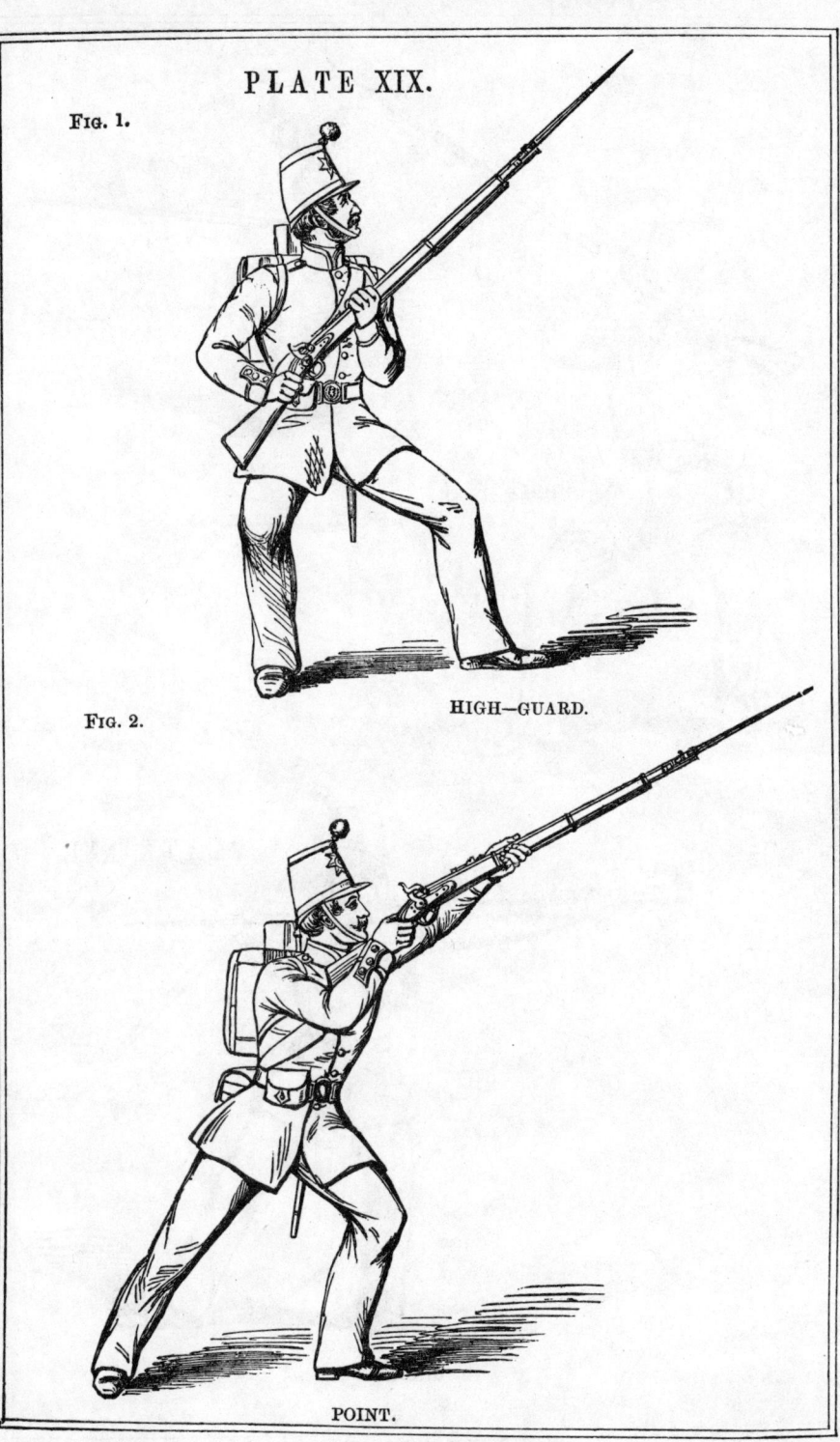

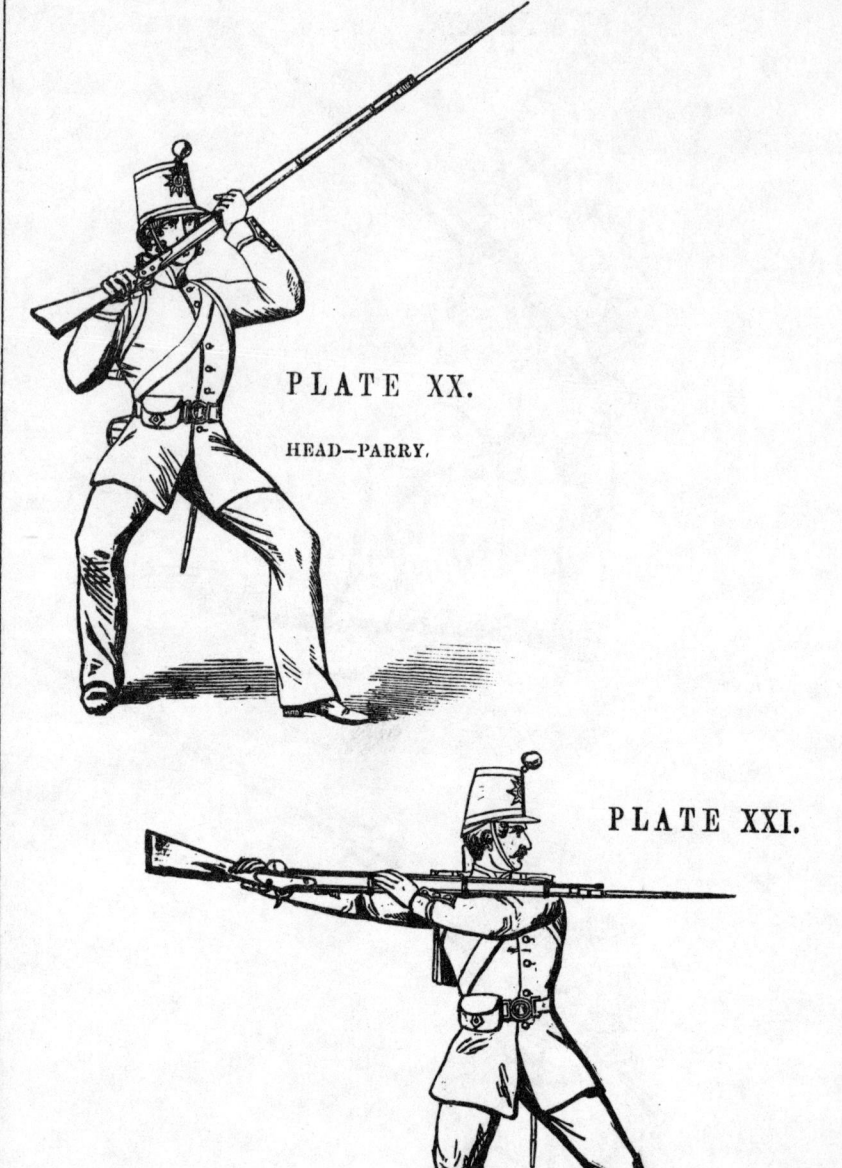

PLATE XX.

HEAD—PARRY.

PLATE XXI.

SHORTEN ARMS.